CELTIC SONGS

PREFACE

Gathering with friends and family to play music together is an important aspect of cultures all over the globe. It provides a way to celebrate and pass on the history and legends of a society. Celtic music remains a popular and vital example of this tradition. These songs from Ireland, Scotland, Wales and the Hebrides Islands are a living example of a musical heritage that reaches back centuries to its roots. There are songs that lament loss, celebrate triumph and laugh at the absurdities of life.

Round up a group of friends and enjoy the experience of playing this music for the simple joy it can provide. The music for each song displays the chord diagrams for five instruments: ukulele, baritone ukulele, guitar, mandolin and banjo. The chord diagrams indicate basic, commonly used finger positions. More advanced players can substitute alternate chord formations. The melody is notated for singing but it would be well within the style of Celtic music to play that line on violin, flute or penny whistle.

There are lots of great recordings of Celtic music that are easily available to you. In order to understand the style and traditions connected to these songs listen to some classic recordings of groups like: The Chieftains, The Dubliners, The High Kings, The Irish Rovers, The Clancy Brothers and Gaelic Storm. You can also hear some of these same songs performed in more contemporary styles by Irish bands like: The Pogues, Flogging Molly and Dropkick Murphys.

– Marty Gross

Arranged by Marty Gross

ISBN 978-1-4950-8799-8

HAL•LEONARD®
7777 W. BLUEMOUND RD. P.O. BOX 13819 MILWAUKEE, WI 53213

In Australia Contact:
Hal Leonard Australia Pty. Ltd.
4 Lentara Court
Cheltenham, Victoria, 3192 Australia
Email: ausadmin@halleonard.com.au

Standard Ukulele

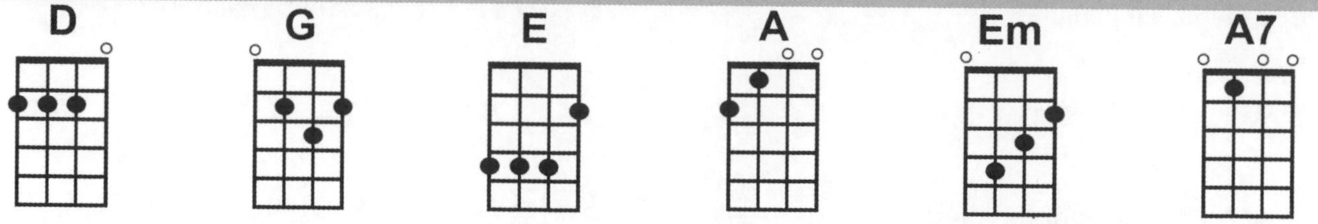

Baritone Ukulele

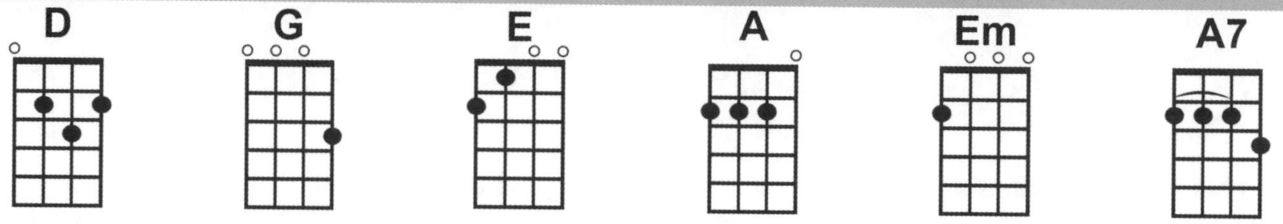

Guitar

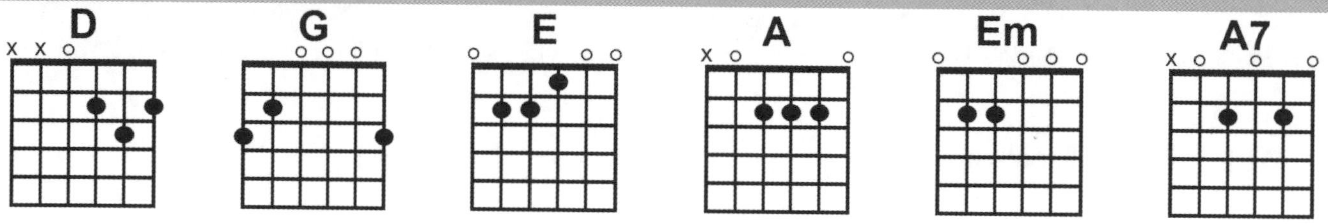

Mandolin

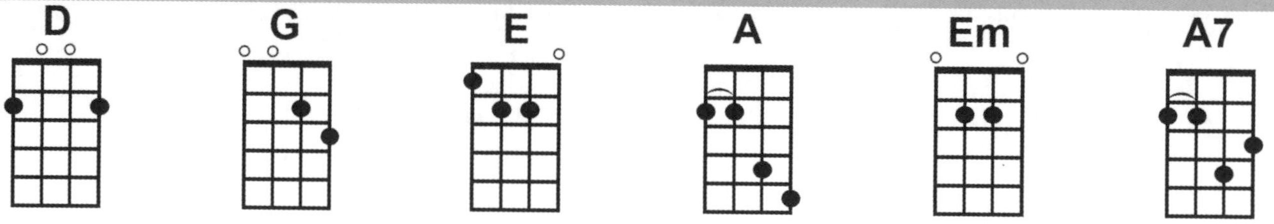

Banjo

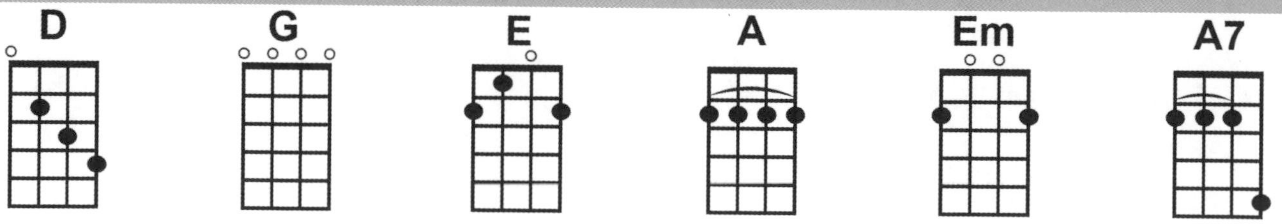

All Through the Night

Welsh Folksong

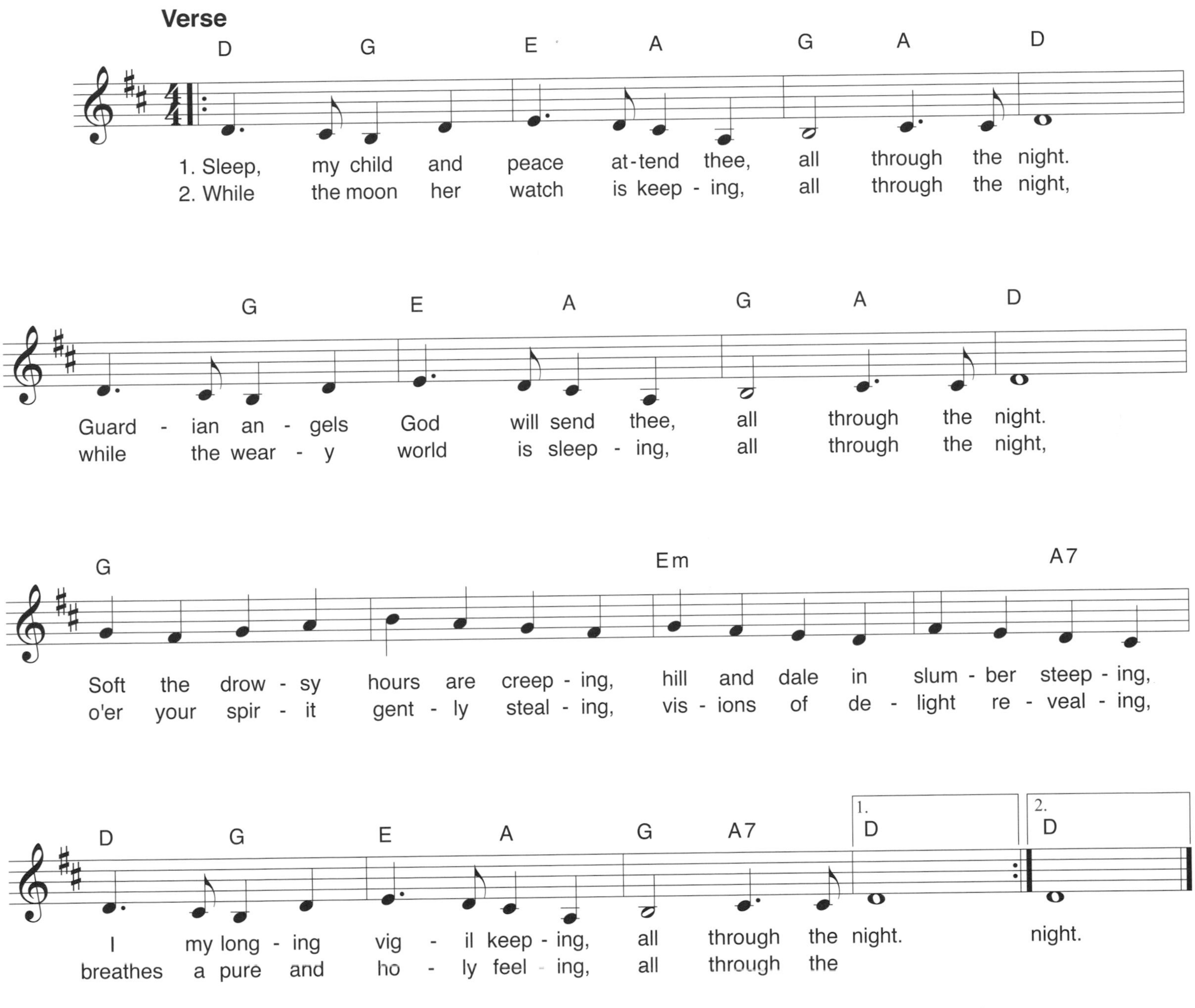
Verse
D G E A G A D
1. Sleep, my child and peace at-tend thee, all through the night.
2. While the moon her watch is keep - ing, all through the night,
G E A G A D
Guard - ian an - gels God will send thee, all through the night.
while the wear - y world is sleep - ing, all through the night,
G Em A7
Soft the drow - sy hours are creep - ing, hill and dale in slum - ber steep - ing,
o'er your spir - it gent - ly steal - ing, vis - ions of de - light re - veal - ing,
D G E A G A7 1. D 2. D
I my long - ing vig - il keep - ing, all through the night. night.
breathes a pure and ho - ly feel - ing, all through the

Standard Ukulele

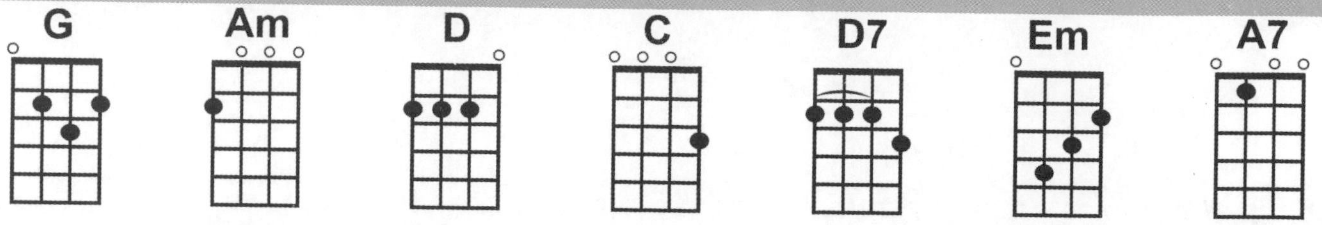
G
Am
D
C
D7
Em
A7

Baritone Ukulele

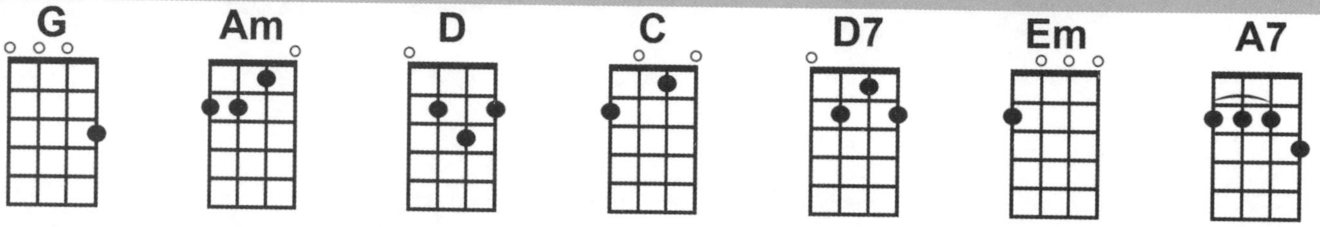
G
Am
D
C
D7
Em
A7

Guitar

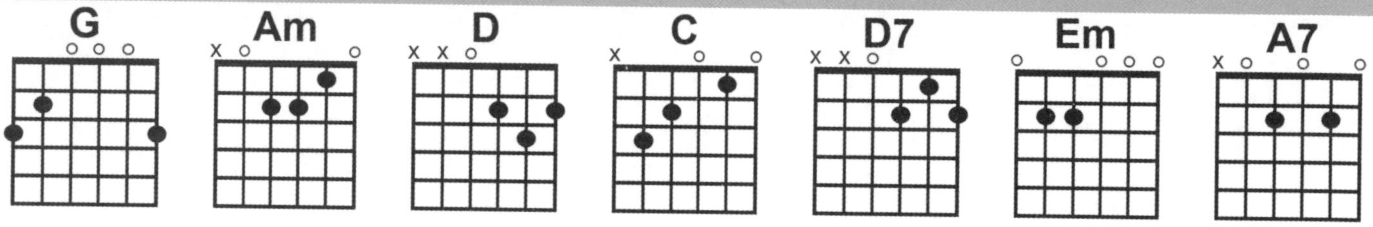
G
Am
D
C
D7
Em
A7

Mandolin

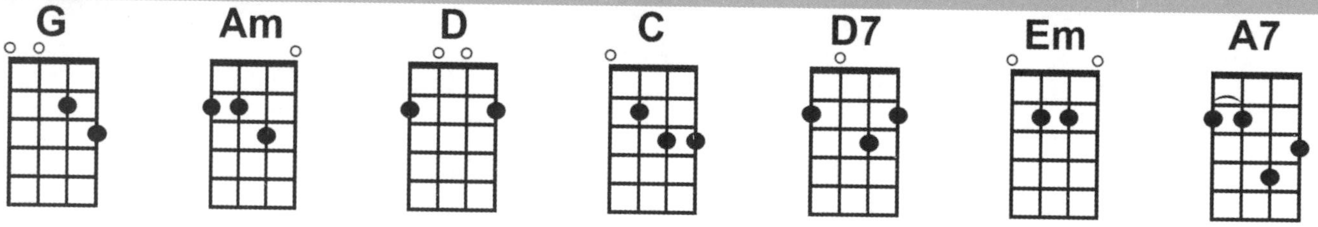
G
Am
D
C
D7
Em
A7

Banjo

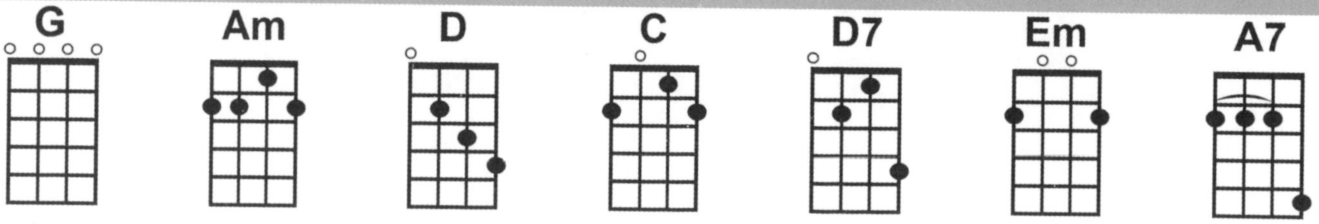
G
Am
D
C
D7
Em
A7

The Ash Grove

Old Welsh Air

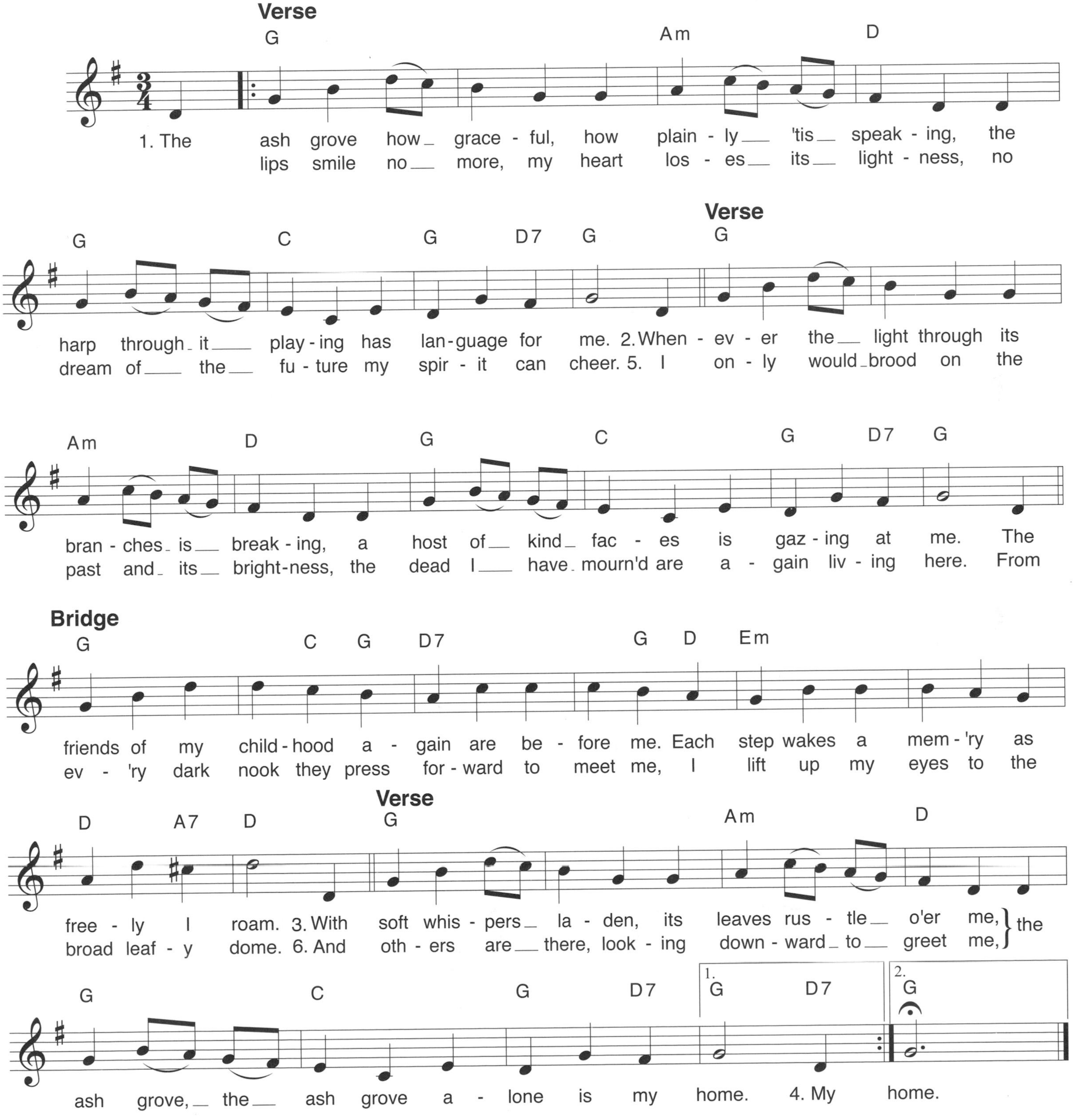
Verse
G Am D
1. The ash grove how grace - ful, how plain - ly 'tis speak - ing, the
lips smile no more, my heart los - es its light - ness, no
G C G D7 G
harp through it play - ing has lan - guage for me.
dream of the fu - ture my spir - it can cheer.
Verse
G
2. When - ev - er the light through its
5. I on - ly would brood on the
Am D G C G D7 G
bran - ches is break - ing, a host of kind fac - es is gaz - ing at me. The
past and its bright - ness, the dead I have mourn'd are a - gain liv - ing here. From
Bridge
G C G D7 G D Em
friends of my child - hood a - gain are be - fore me. Each step wakes a mem - 'ry as
ev - 'ry dark nook they press for - ward to meet me, I lift up my eyes to the
D A7 D
free - ly I roam.
broad leaf - y dome.
Verse
G Am D
3. With soft whis - pers la - den, its leaves rus - tle o'er me, the
6. And oth - ers are there, look - ing down - ward to greet me,
G C G D7
ash grove, the ash grove a - lone is my
1. G D7
home. 4. My
2. G
home.

Standard Ukulele

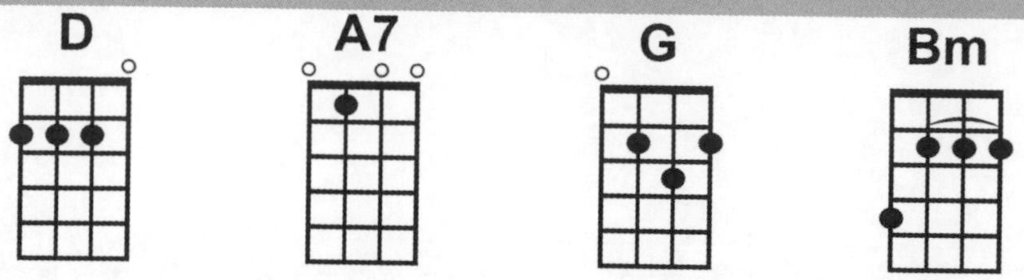
D
A7
G
Bm

Baritone Ukulele

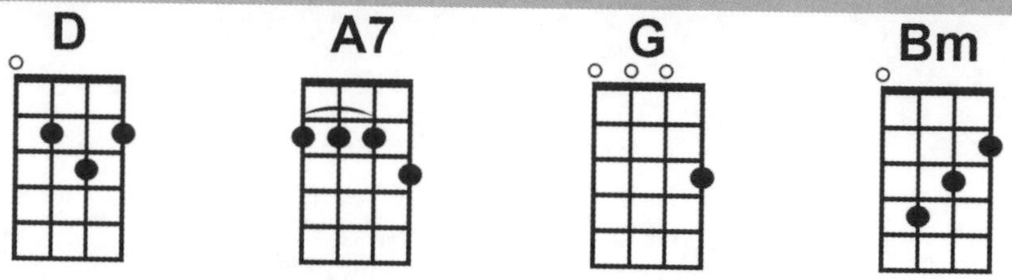
D
A7
G
Bm

Guitar

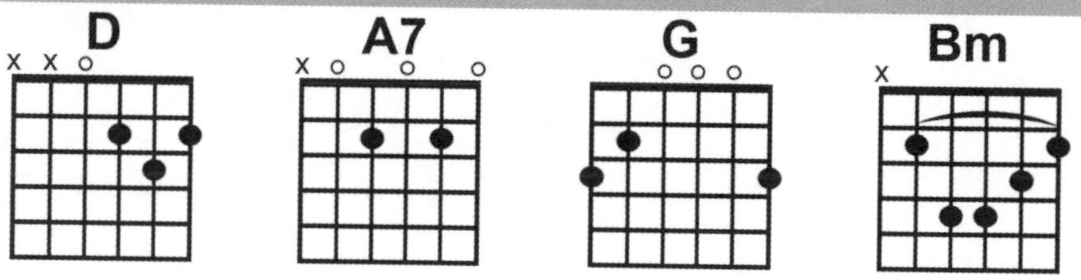
D
A7
G
Bm

Mandolin

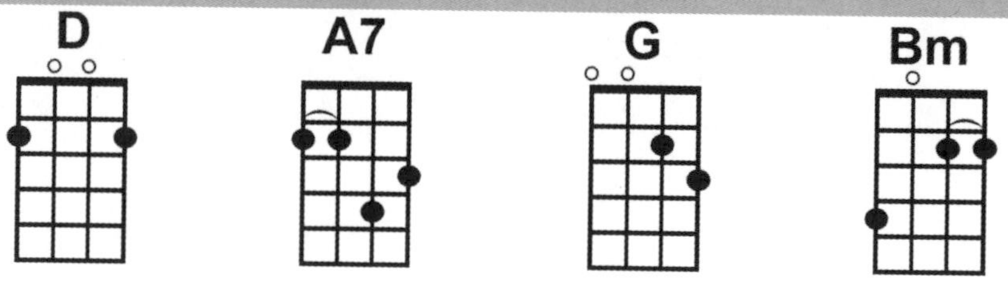
D
A7
G
Bm

Banjo

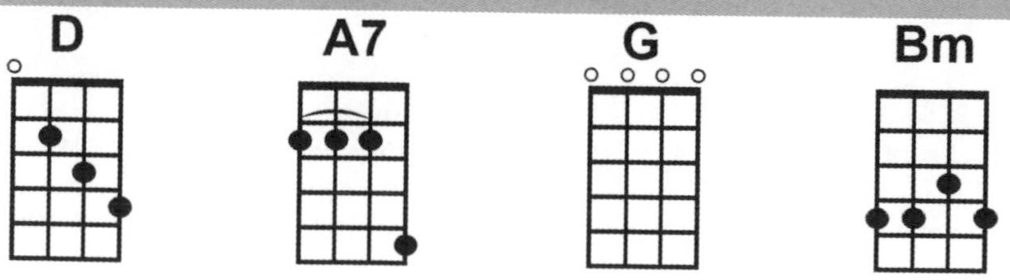
D
A7
G
Bm

Auld Lang Syne

Words by Robert Burns
Traditional Scottish Melody

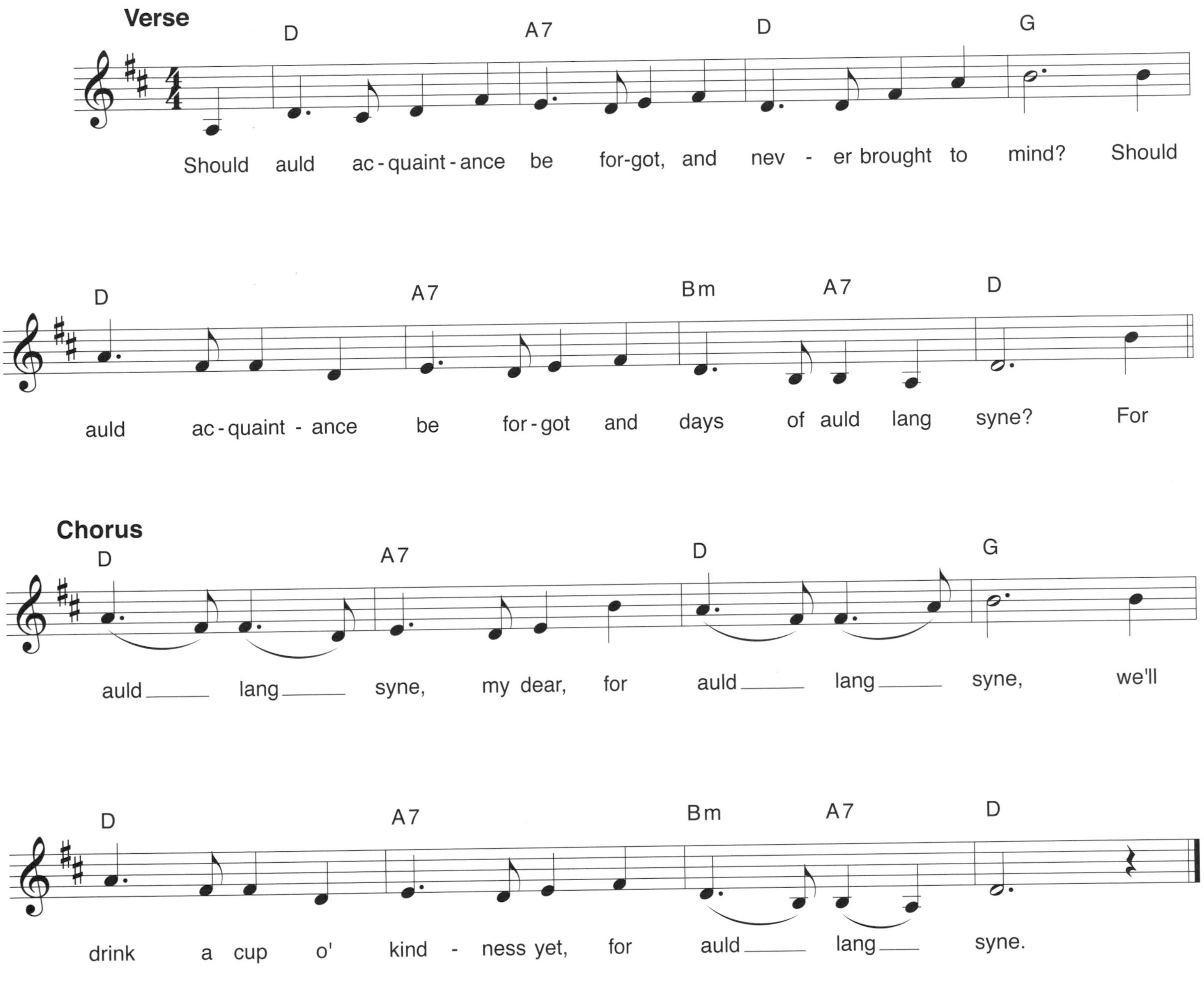
Verse
D A7 D G
Should auld ac-quaint-ance be for-got, and nev - er brought to mind? Should
D A7 Bm A7 D
auld ac-quaint - ance be for-got and days of auld lang syne? For
Chorus
D A7 D G
auld lang syne, my dear, for auld lang syne, we'll
D A7 Bm A7 D
drink a cup o' kind - ness yet, for auld lang syne.

Standard Ukulele

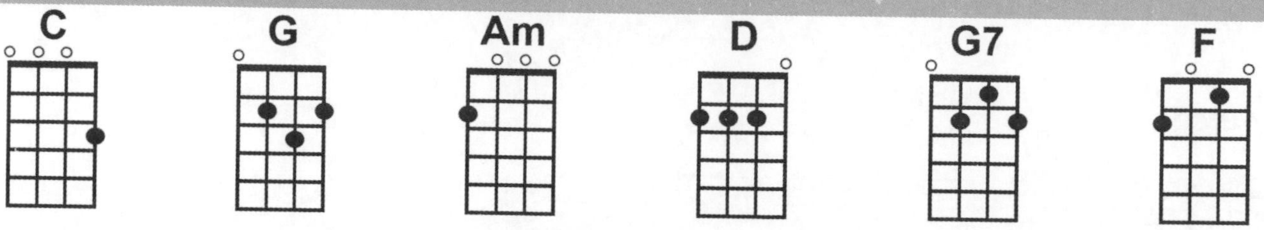
C
G
Am
D
G7
F

Baritone Ukulele

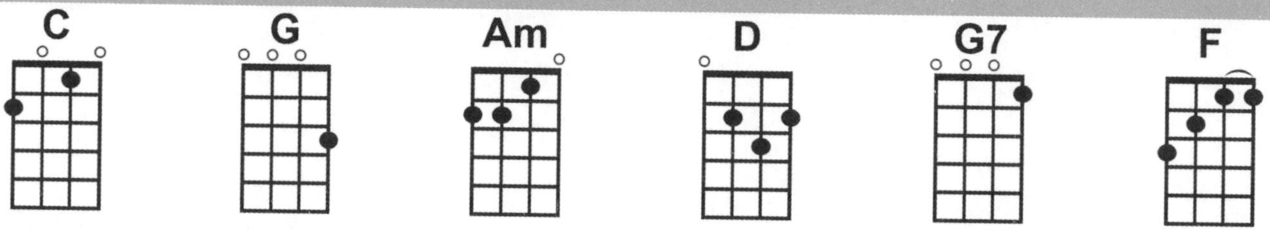
C
G
Am
D
G7
F

Guitar

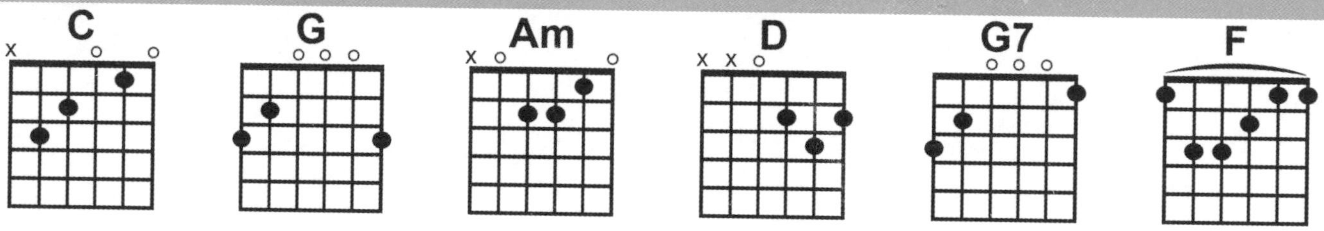
C
G
Am
D
G7
F

Mandolin

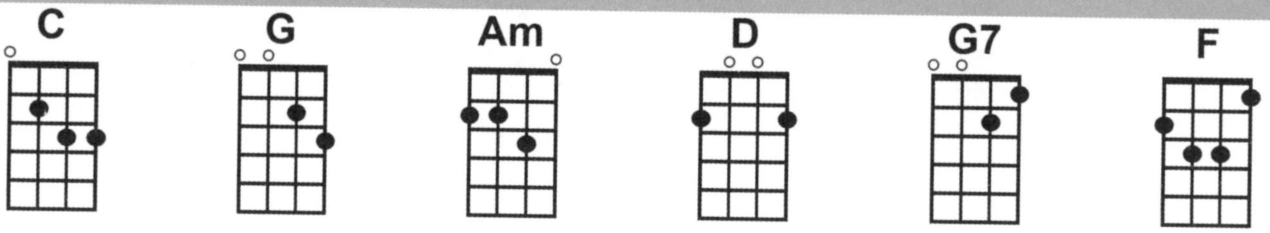
C
G
Am
D
G7
F

Banjo

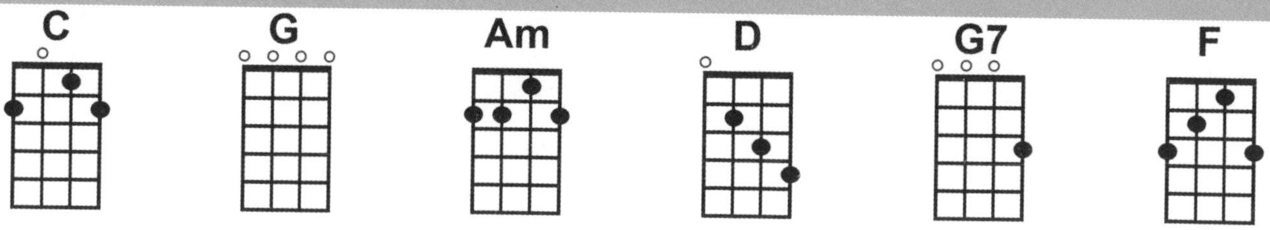
C
G
Am
D
G7
F

Barbara Allen

Traditional

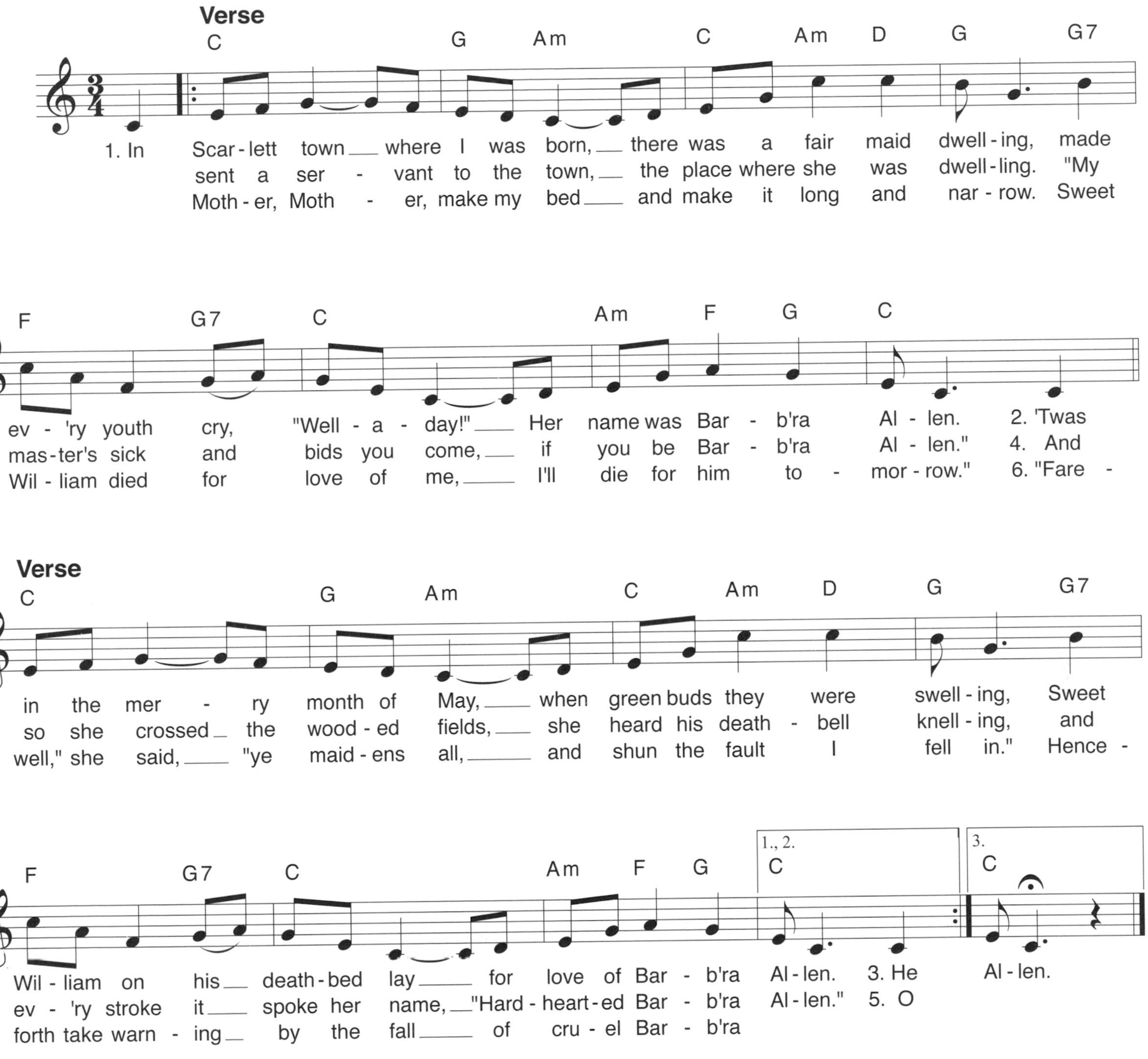
Verse
C G Am C Am D G G7
1. In Scar-lett town where I was born, there was a fair maid dwell-ing, made
sent a ser - vant to the town, the place where she was dwell-ling. "My
Moth-er, Moth - er, make my bed and make it long and nar-row. Sweet
F G7 C Am F G C
ev - 'ry youth cry, "Well - a - day!" Her name was Bar - b'ra Al - len. 2. 'Twas
mas-ter's sick and bids you come, if you be Bar - b'ra Al - len." 4. And
Wil - liam died for love of me, I'll die for him to - mor-row." 6. "Fare -
Verse
C G Am C Am D G G7
in the mer - ry month of May, when green buds they were swell-ing, Sweet
so she crossed the wood-ed fields, she heard his death - bell knell-ing, and
well," she said, "ye maid-ens all, and shun the fault I fell in." Hence -
F G7 C Am F G
Wil - liam on his death-bed lay for love of Bar - b'ra
ev - 'ry stroke it spoke her name, "Hard-heart-ed Bar - b'ra
forth take warn - ing by the fall of cru - el Bar - b'ra
1., 2.
C
Al - len. 3. He
Al - len." 5. O
3.
C
Al - len.

Standard Ukulele

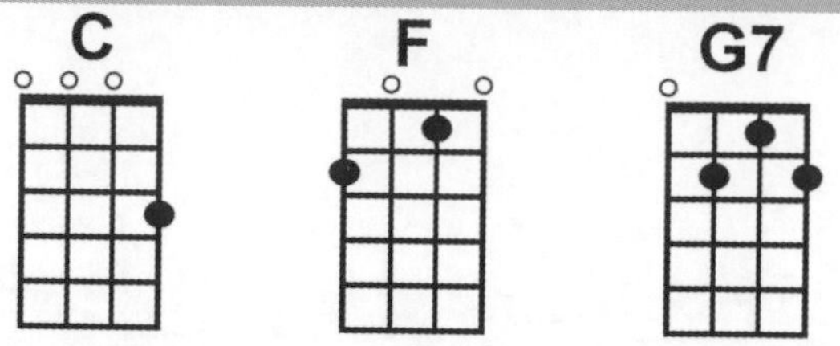

Baritone Ukulele

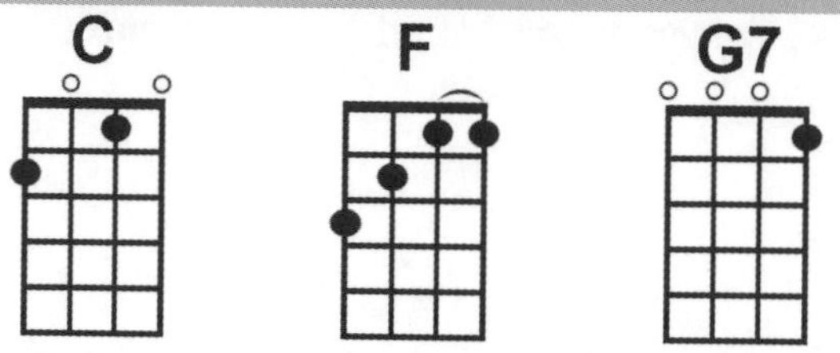

Guitar

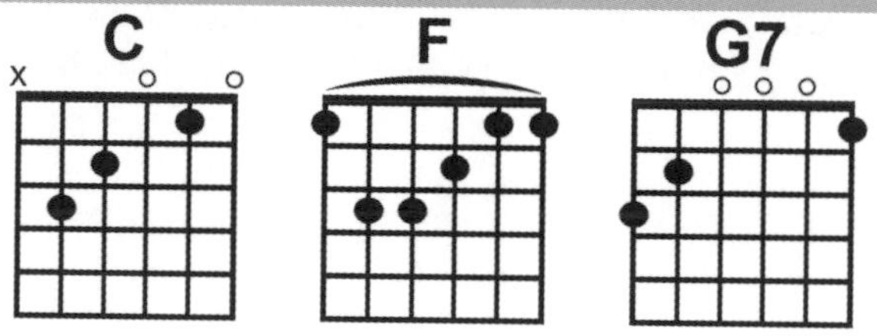

Mandolin

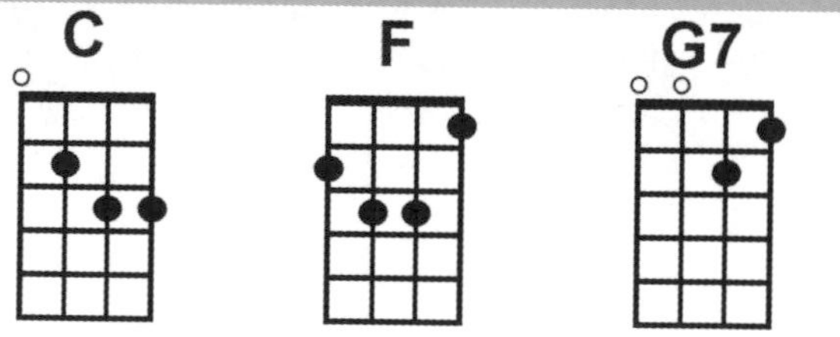

Banjo

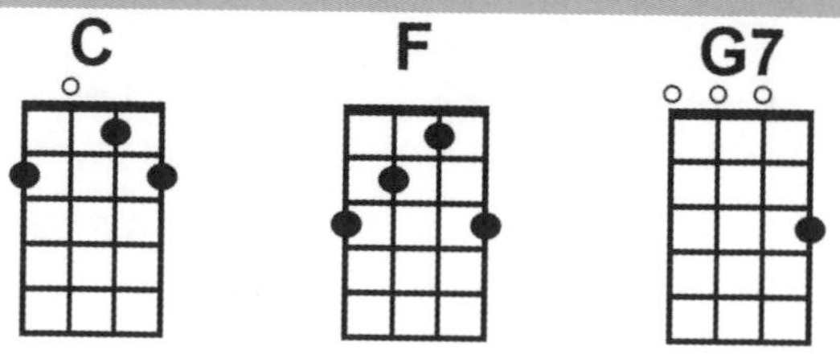

Believe Me, If All Those Endearing Young Charms

Words and Music by Thomas Moore

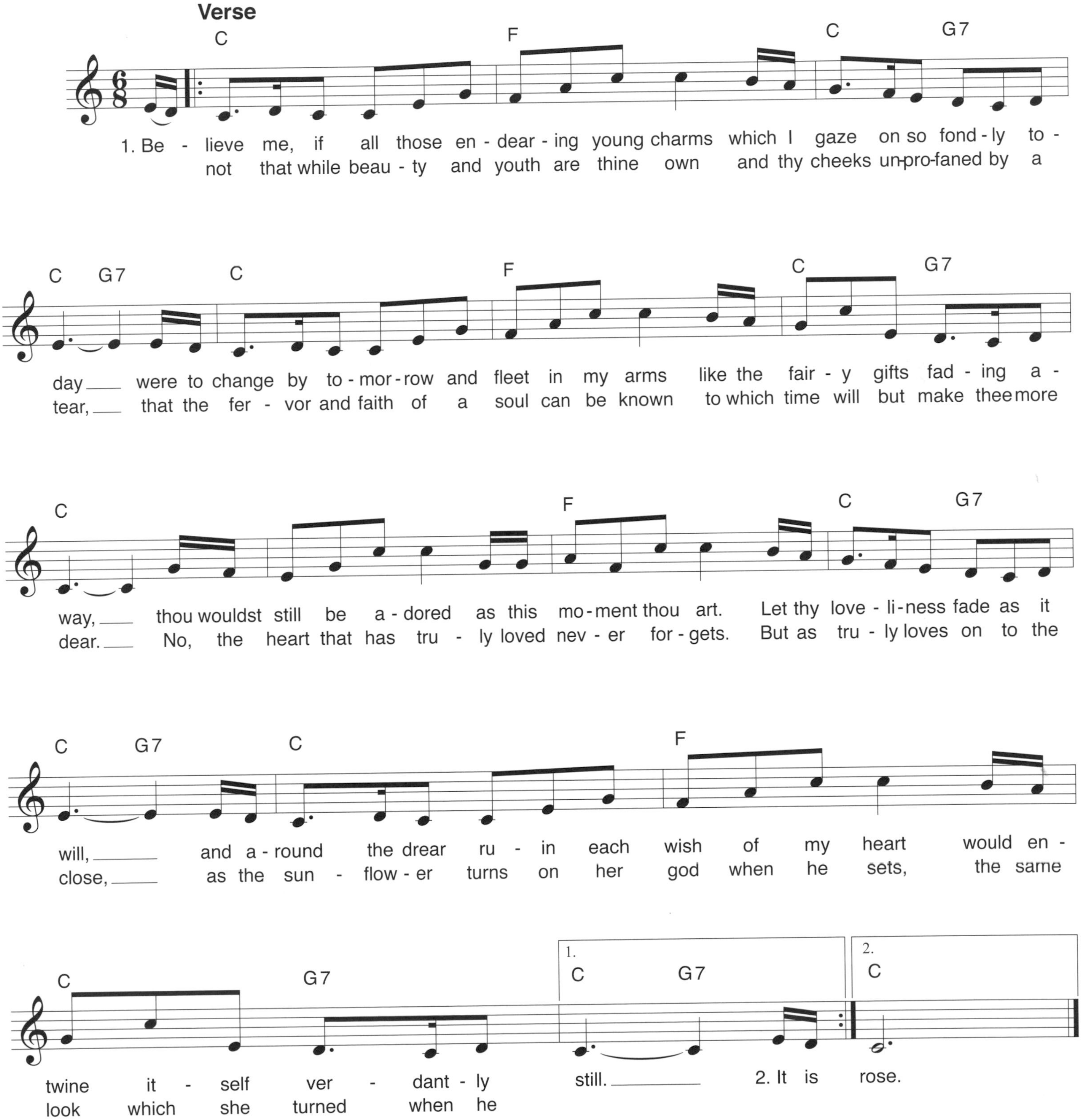
Verse
C F C G7
1. Be - lieve me, if all those en - dear - ing young charms which I gaze on so fond - ly to -
not that while beau - ty and youth are thine own and thy cheeks un-pro-faned by a
C G7 C F C G7
day were to change by to - mor - row and fleet in my arms like the fair - y gifts fad - ing a -
tear, that the fer - vor and faith of a soul can be known to which time will but make thee more
C F C G7
way, thou wouldst still be a - dored as this mo - ment thou art. Let thy love - li - ness fade as it
dear. No, the heart that has tru - ly loved nev - er for - gets. But as tru - ly loves on to the
C G7 C F
will, and a - round the drear ru - in each wish of my heart would en -
close, as the sun - flow - er turns on her god when he sets, the same
C G7 1. C G7 2. C
twine it - self ver - dant - ly still. 2. It is rose.
look which she turned when he

Standard Ukulele

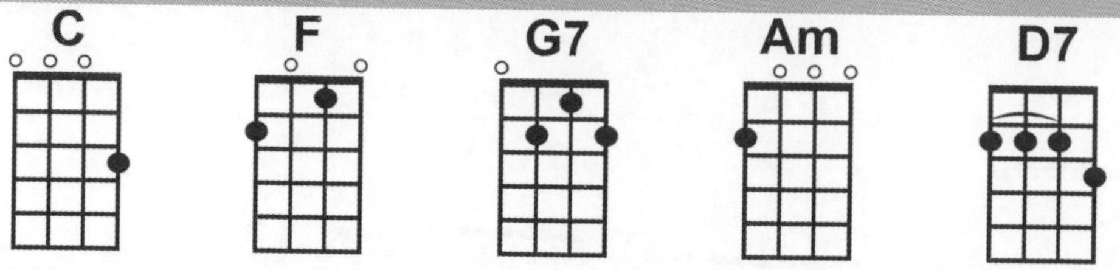
C
F
G7
Am
D7

Baritone Ukulele

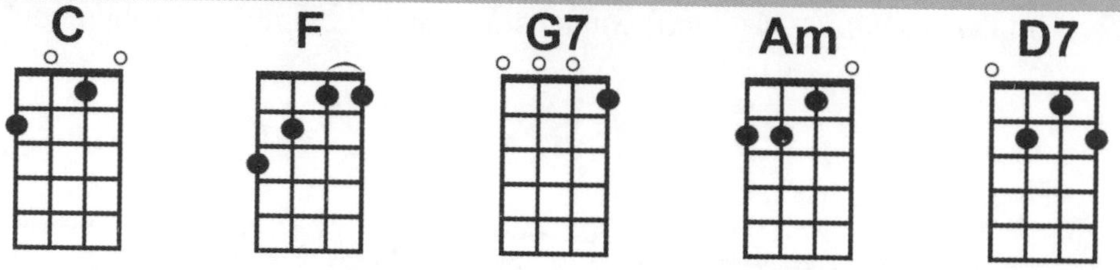
C
F
G7
Am
D7

Guitar

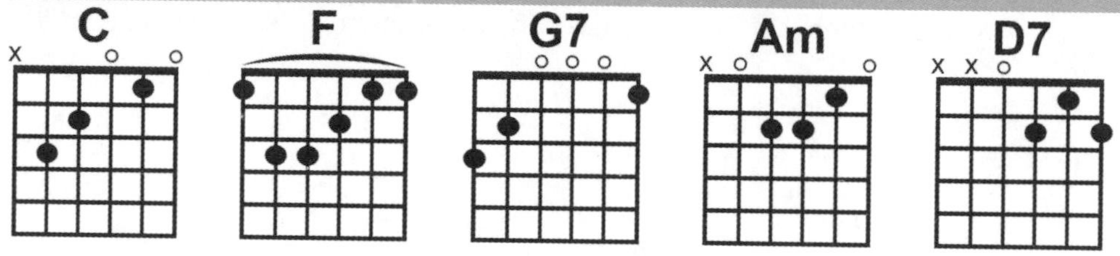
C
F
G7
Am
D7

Mandolin

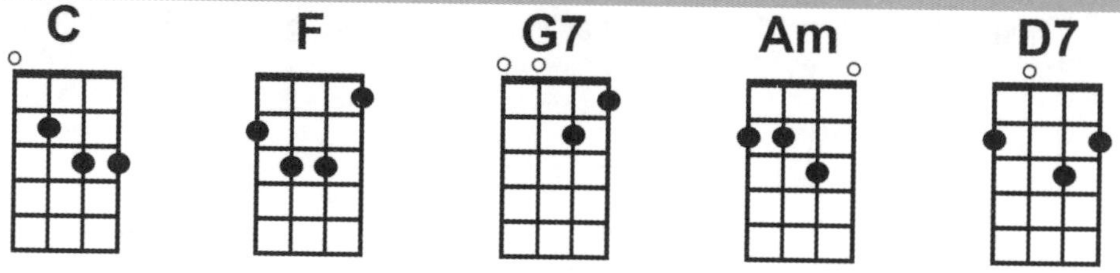
C
F
G7
Am
D7

Banjo

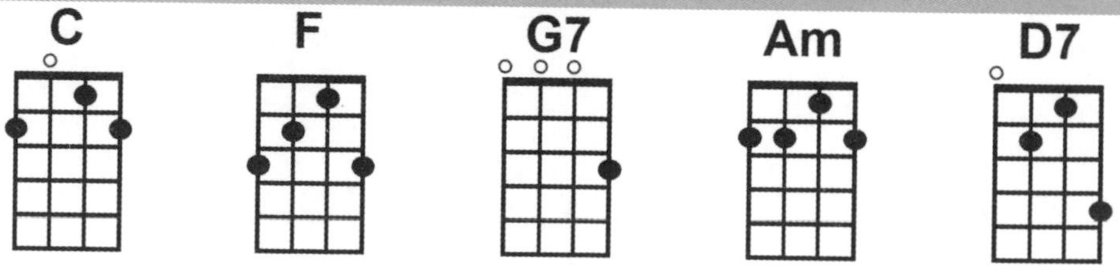
C
F
G7
Am
D7

The Blue Bells of Scotland

Words and Music attributed to Mrs. Jordon

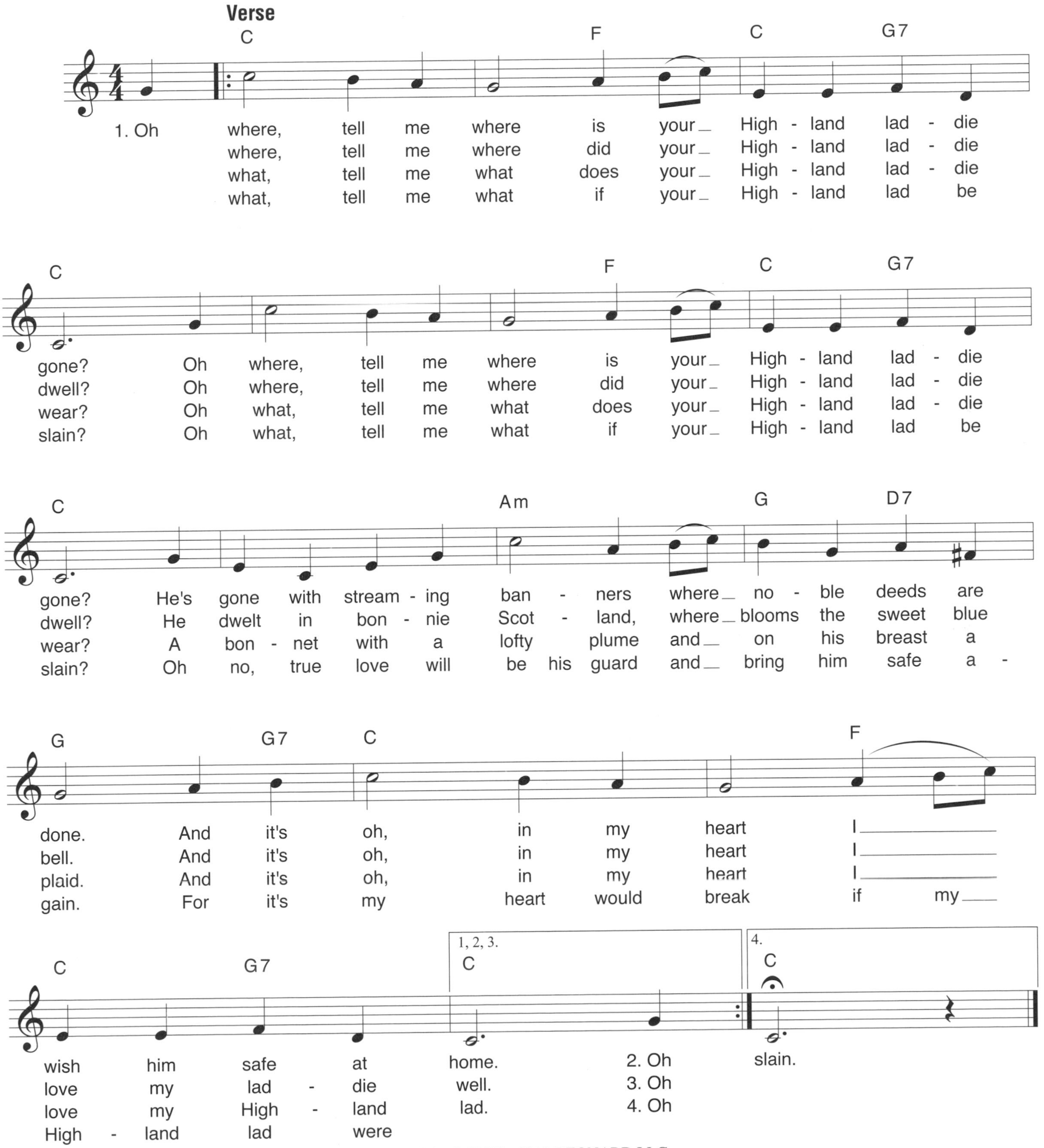
Verse
C F C G7
1. Oh where, tell me where is your_ High - land lad - die
where, tell me where did your_ High - land lad - die
what, tell me what does your_ High - land lad - die
what, tell me what if your_ High - land lad be
C F C G7
gone? Oh where, tell me where is your_ High - land lad - die
dwell? Oh where, tell me where did your_ High - land lad - die
wear? Oh what, tell me what does your_ High - land lad - die
slain? Oh what, tell me what if your_ High - land lad be
C Am G D7
gone? He's gone with stream - ing ban - ners where_ no - ble deeds are
dwell? He dwelt in bon - nie Scot - land, where_ blooms the sweet blue
wear? A bon - net with a lofty plume and_ on his breast a
slain? Oh no, true love will be his guard and_ bring him safe a -
G G7 C F
done. And it's oh, in my heart I_
bell. And it's oh, in my heart I_
plaid. And it's oh, in my heart I_
gain. For it's my heart would break if my_
C G7 1, 2, 3. C 4. C
wish him safe at home. 2. Oh slain.
love my lad - die well. 3. Oh
love my High - land lad. 4. Oh
High - land lad were

Standard Ukulele

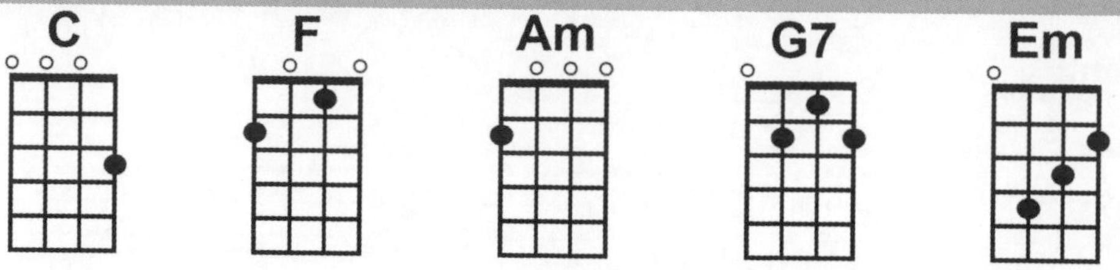
C
F
Am
G7
Em

Baritone Ukulele

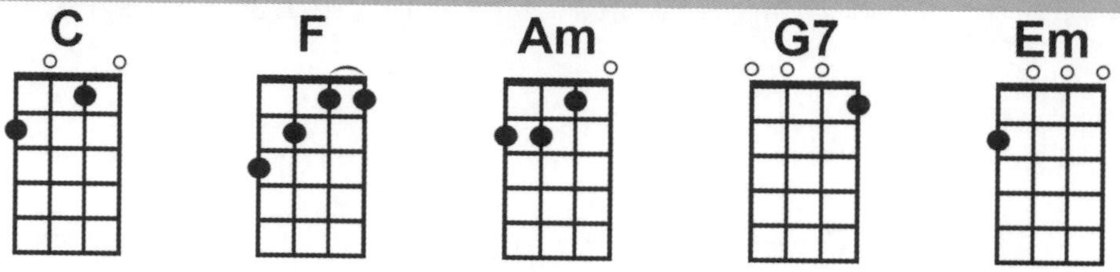
C
F
Am
G7
Em

Guitar

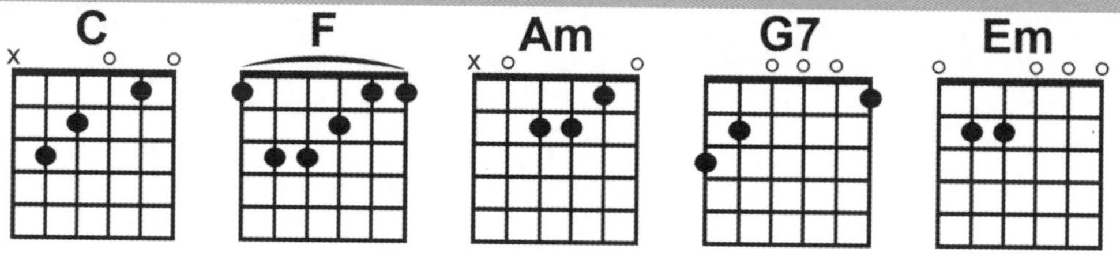
C
F
Am
G7
Em

Mandolin

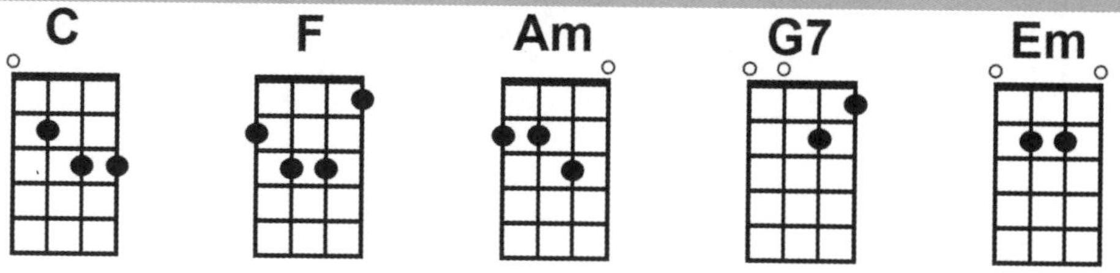
C
F
Am
G7
Em

Banjo

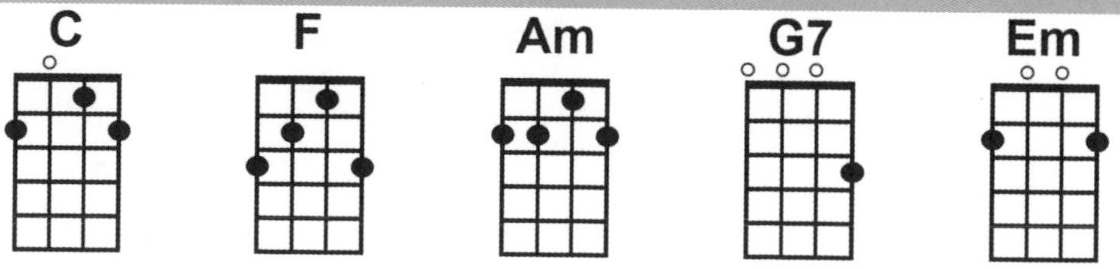
C
F
Am
G7
Em

Brennan on the Moor

Traditional

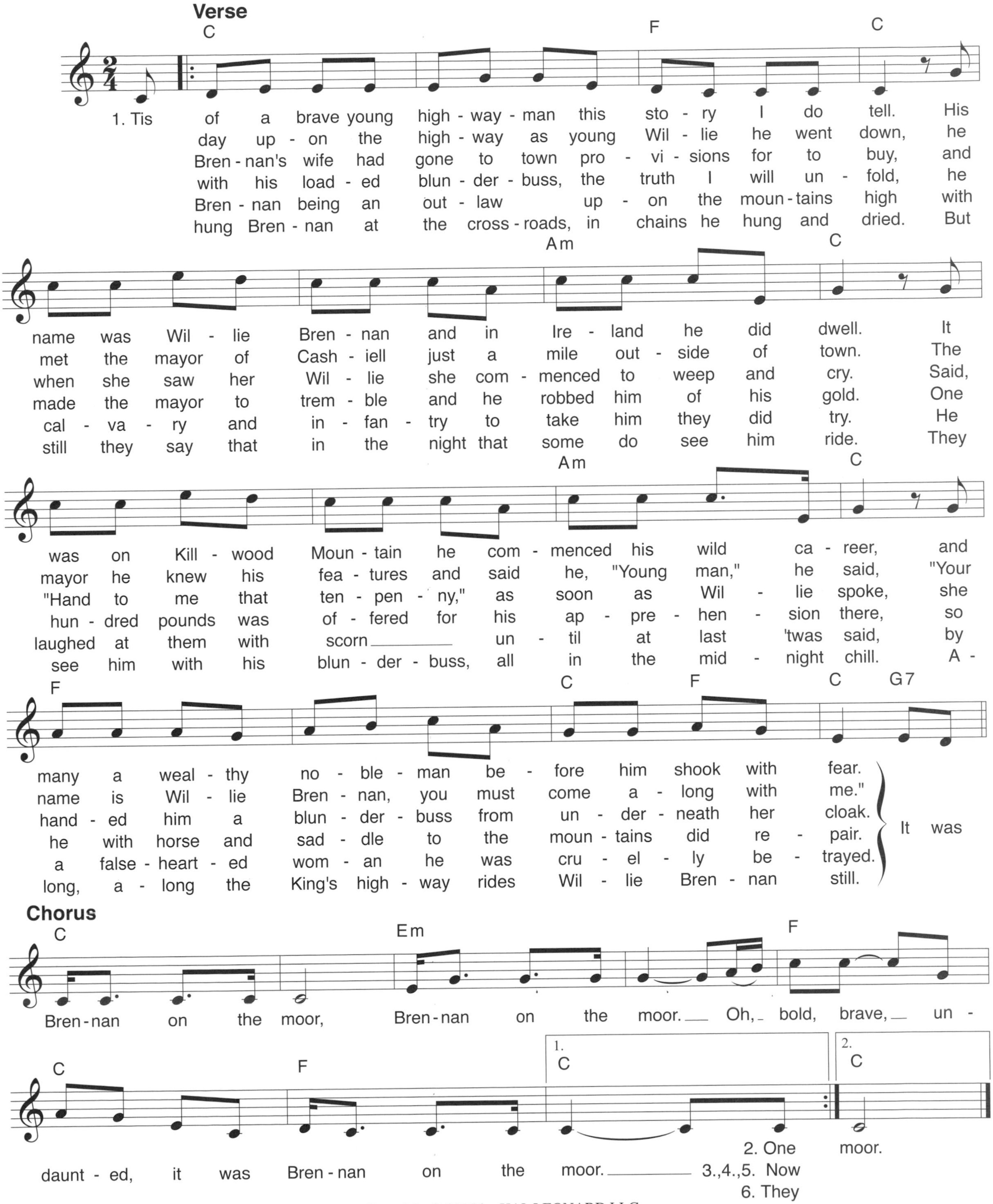

Verse
C F C
1. Tis of a brave young high - way - man this sto - ry I do tell. His
day up - on the high - way as young Wil - lie he went down, he
Bren - nan's wife had gone to town pro - vi - sions for to buy, and
with his load - ed blun - der - buss, the truth I will un - fold, he
Bren - nan being an out - law up - on the moun - tains high with
hung Bren - nan at the cross - roads, in chains he hung and dried. But
Am C
name was Wil - lie Bren - nan and in Ire - land he did dwell. It
met the mayor of Cash - iell just a mile out - side of town. The
when she saw her Wil - lie she com - menced to weep and cry. Said,
made the mayor to trem - ble and he robbed him of his gold. One
cal - va - ry and in - fan - try to take him they did try. He
still they say that in the night that some do see him ride. They
Am C
was on Kill - wood Moun - tain he com - menced his wild ca - reer, and
mayor he knew his fea - tures and said he, "Young man," he said, "Your
"Hand to me that ten - pen - ny," as soon as Wil - lie spoke, she
hun - dred pounds was of - fered for his ap - pre - hen - sion there, so
laughed at them with scorn un - til at last 'twas said, by
see him with his blun - der - buss, all in the mid - night chill. A -
F C F C G7
many a weal - thy no - ble - man be - fore him shook with fear.
name is Wil - lie Bren - nan, you must come a - long with me."
hand - ed him a blun - der - buss from un - der - neath her cloak.
he with horse and sad - dle to the moun - tains did re - pair.
a false - heart - ed wom - an he was cru - el - ly be - trayed.
long, a - long the King's high - way rides Wil - lie Bren - nan still.
It was
Chorus
C Em F
Bren - nan on the moor, Bren - nan on the moor. Oh, bold, brave, un -
C F 1. C 2. C
daunt - ed, it was Bren - nan on the moor.
2. One moor.
3.,4.,5. Now
6. They

Standard Ukulele

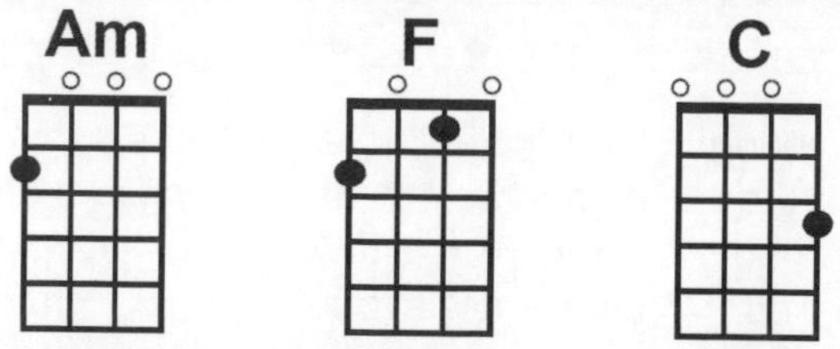

Baritone Ukulele

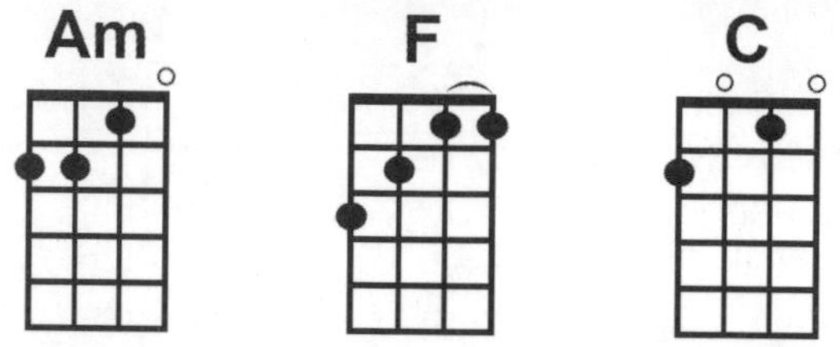

Guitar

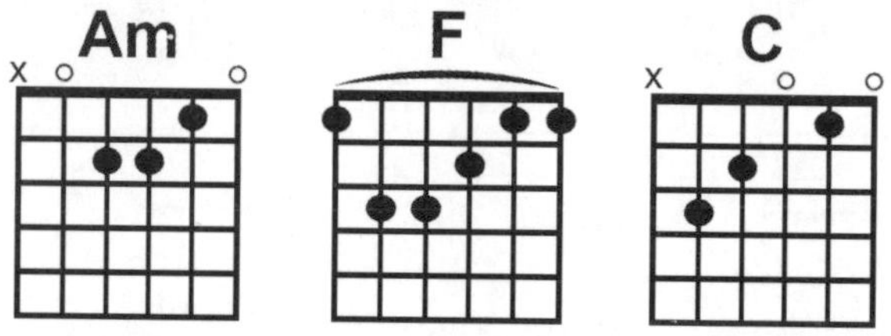

Mandolin

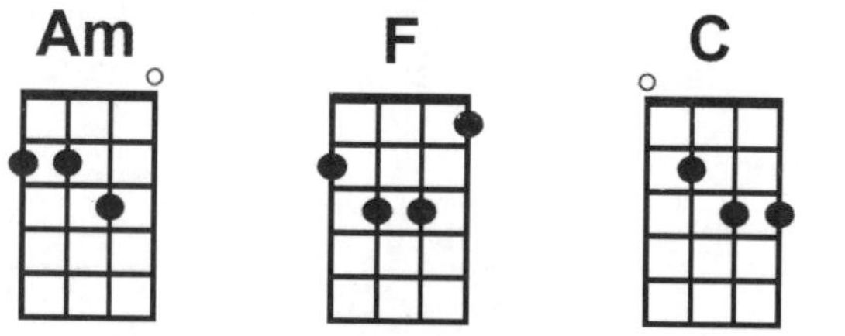

Banjo

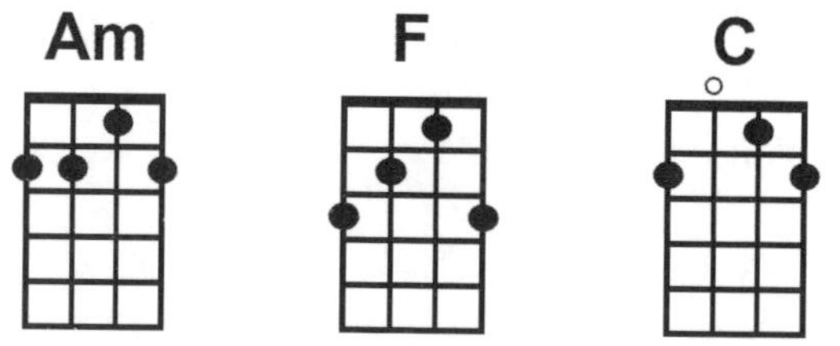

Byker Hill

Traditional

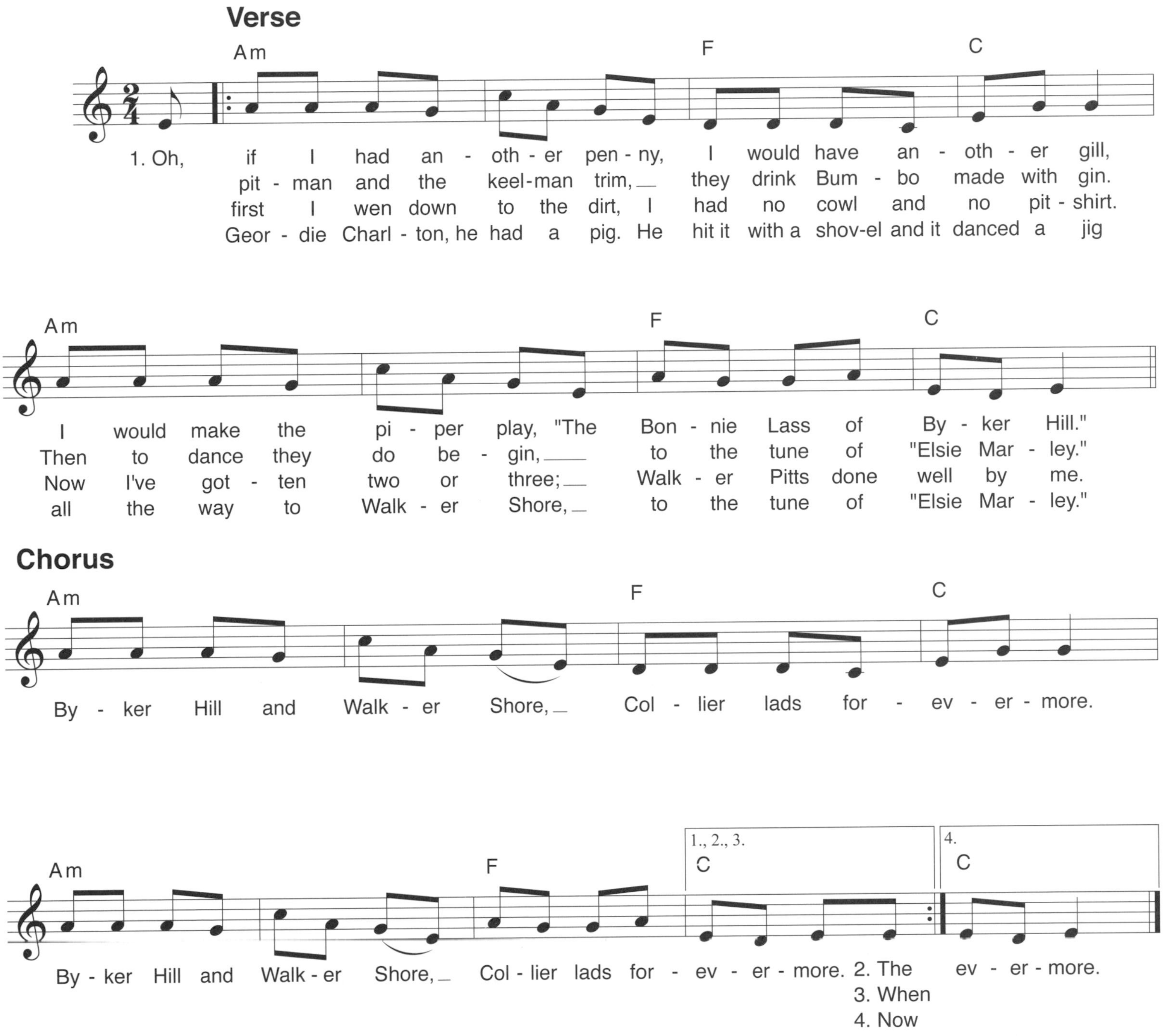
Verse
Am F C
1. Oh, if I had an - oth - er pen - ny, I would have an - oth - er gill,
pit - man and the keel-man trim,__ they drink Bum - bo made with gin.
first I wen down to the dirt, I had no cowl and no pit - shirt.
Geor - die Charl - ton, he had a pig. He hit it with a shov-el and it danced a jig
Am F C
I would make the pi - per play, "The Bon - nie Lass of By - ker Hill."
Then to dance they do be - gin,__ to the tune of "Elsie Mar - ley."
Now I've got - ten two or three;__ Walk - er Pitts done well by me.
all the way to Walk - er Shore,__ to the tune of "Elsie Mar - ley."
Chorus
Am F C
By - ker Hill and Walk - er Shore,__ Col - lier lads for - ev - er - more.
Am F
1., 2., 3.
C
4.
C
By - ker Hill and Walk - er Shore,__ Col - lier lads for - ev - er - more. 2. The ev - er - more.
3. When
4. Now

Standard Ukulele

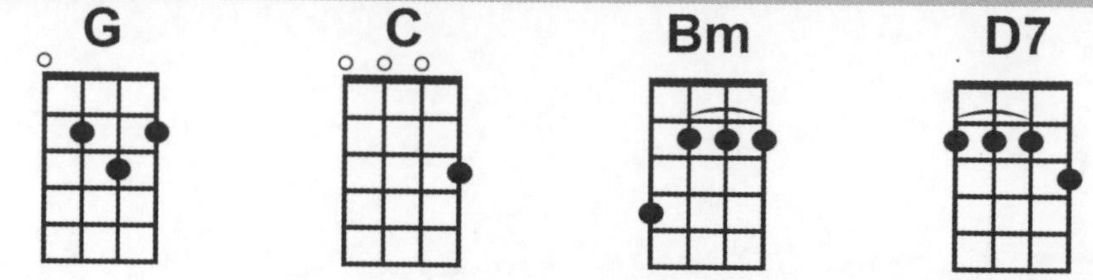
G
C
Bm
D7

Baritone Ukulele

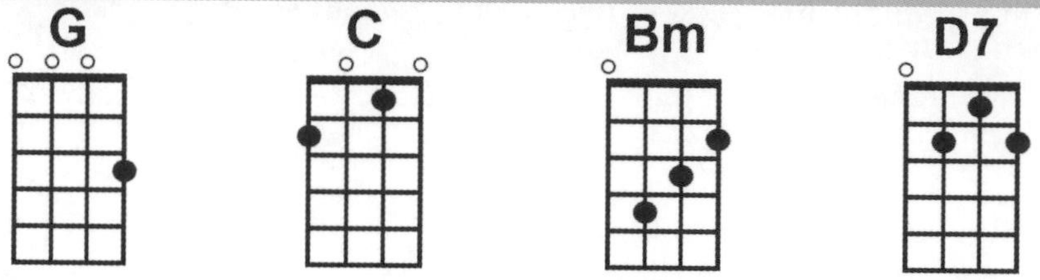
G
C
Bm
D7

Guitar

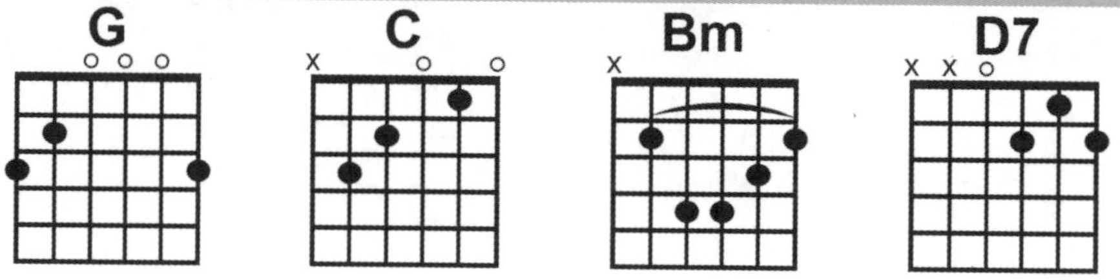
G
C
Bm
D7

Mandolin

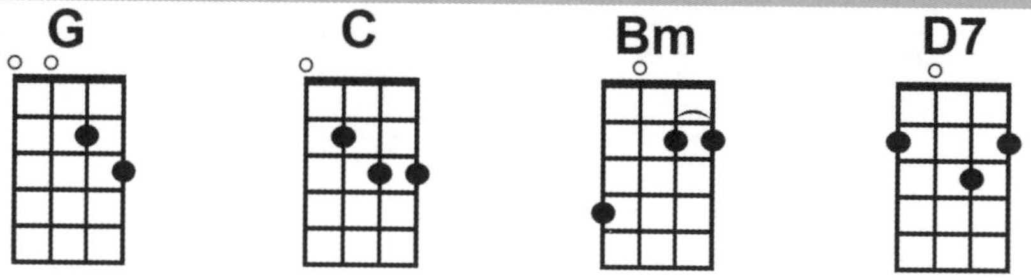
G
C
Bm
D7

Banjo

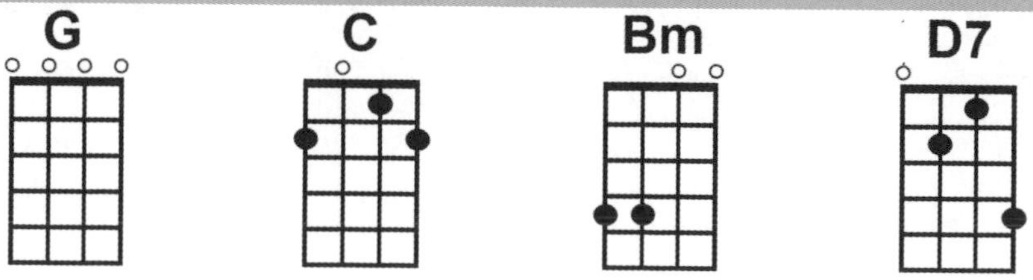
G
C
Bm
D7

Come to the Hills

Irish Folk Song

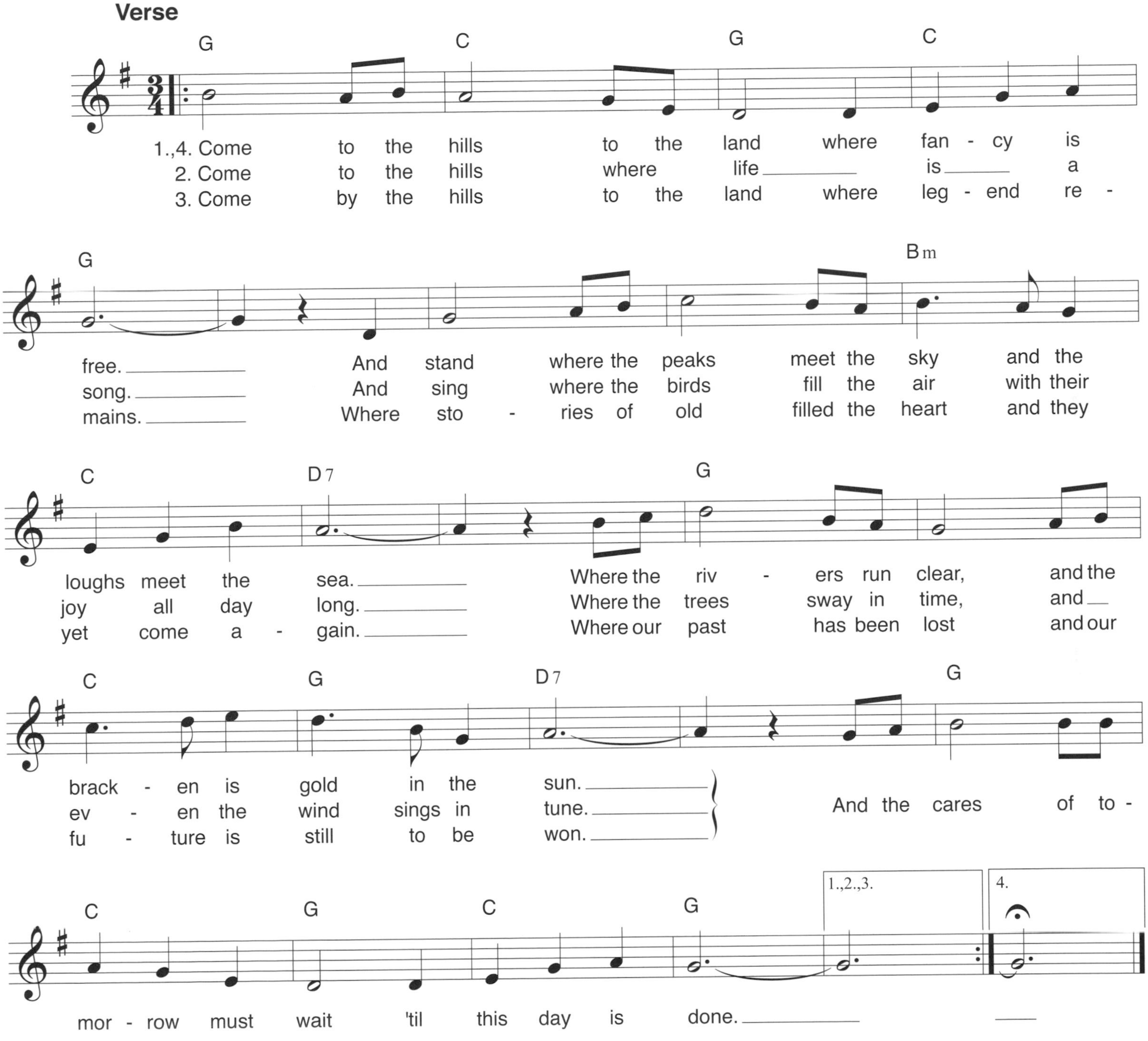
Verse
G C G C
1.,4. Come to the hills to the land where fan - cy is
2. Come to the hills where life ___ is ___ a
3. Come by the hills to the land where leg - end re -
G Bm
free. ___ And stand where the peaks meet the sky and the
song. ___ And sing where the birds fill the air with their
mains. ___ Where sto - ries of old filled the heart and they
C D7 G
loughs meet the sea. ___ Where the riv - ers run clear, and the
joy all day long. ___ Where the trees sway in time, and ___
yet come a - gain. ___ Where our past has been lost and our
C G D7 G
brack - en is gold in the sun. ___
ev - en the wind sings in tune. ___
fu - ture is still to be won. ___
And the cares of to -
C G C G
1.,2.,3.
4.
mor - row must wait 'til this day is done. ___ ___

Standard Ukulele

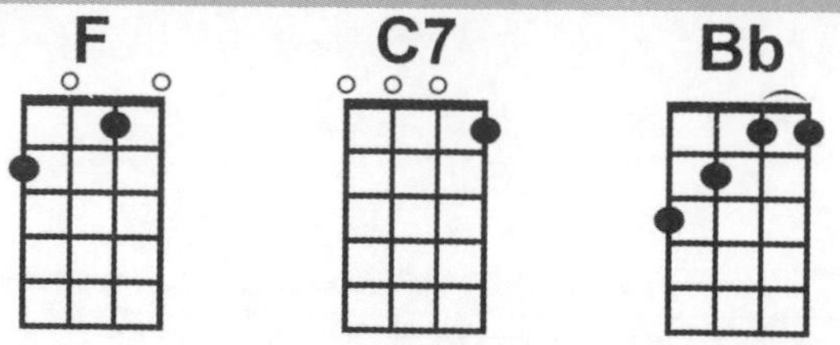
F
C7
Bb

Baritone Ukulele

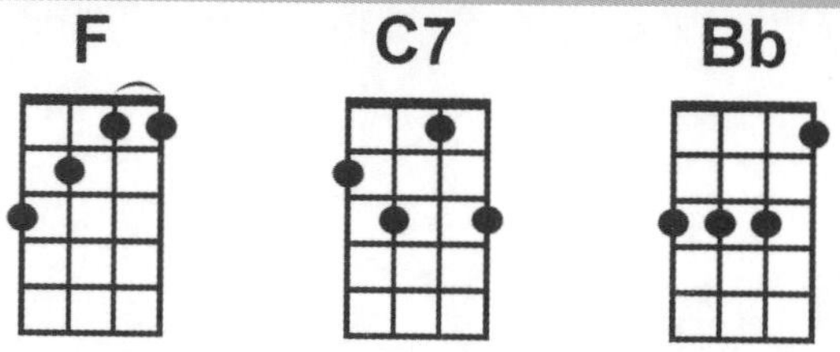
F
C7
Bb

Guitar

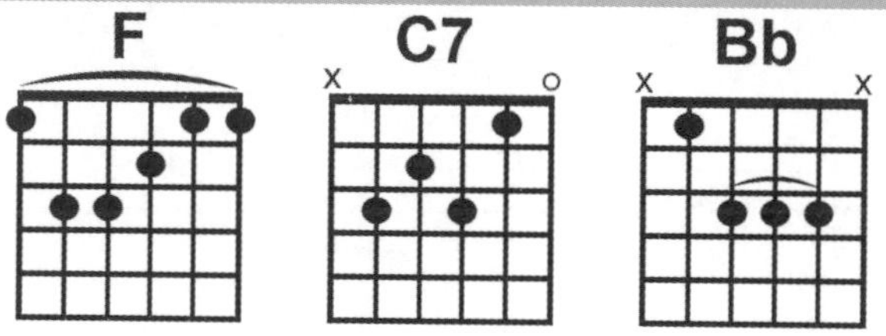
F
C7
Bb

Mandolin

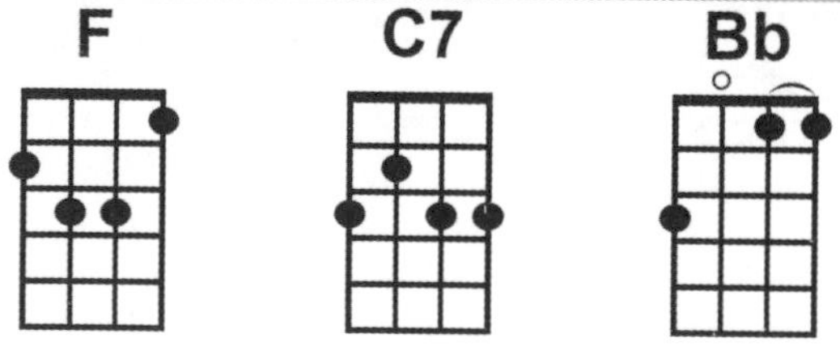
F
C7
Bb

Banjo

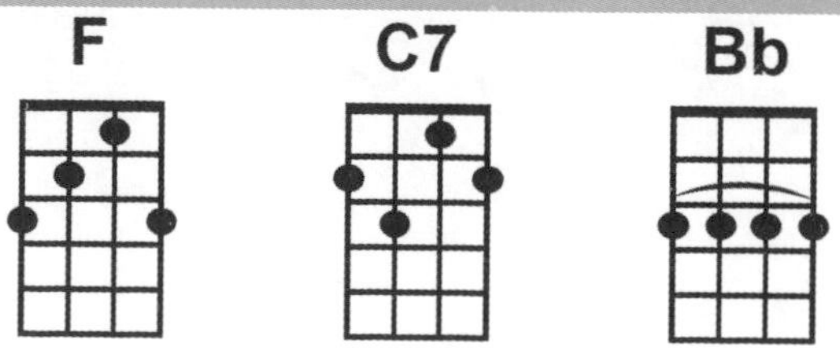
F
C7
Bb

Comin' Through the Rye

By Robert Burns

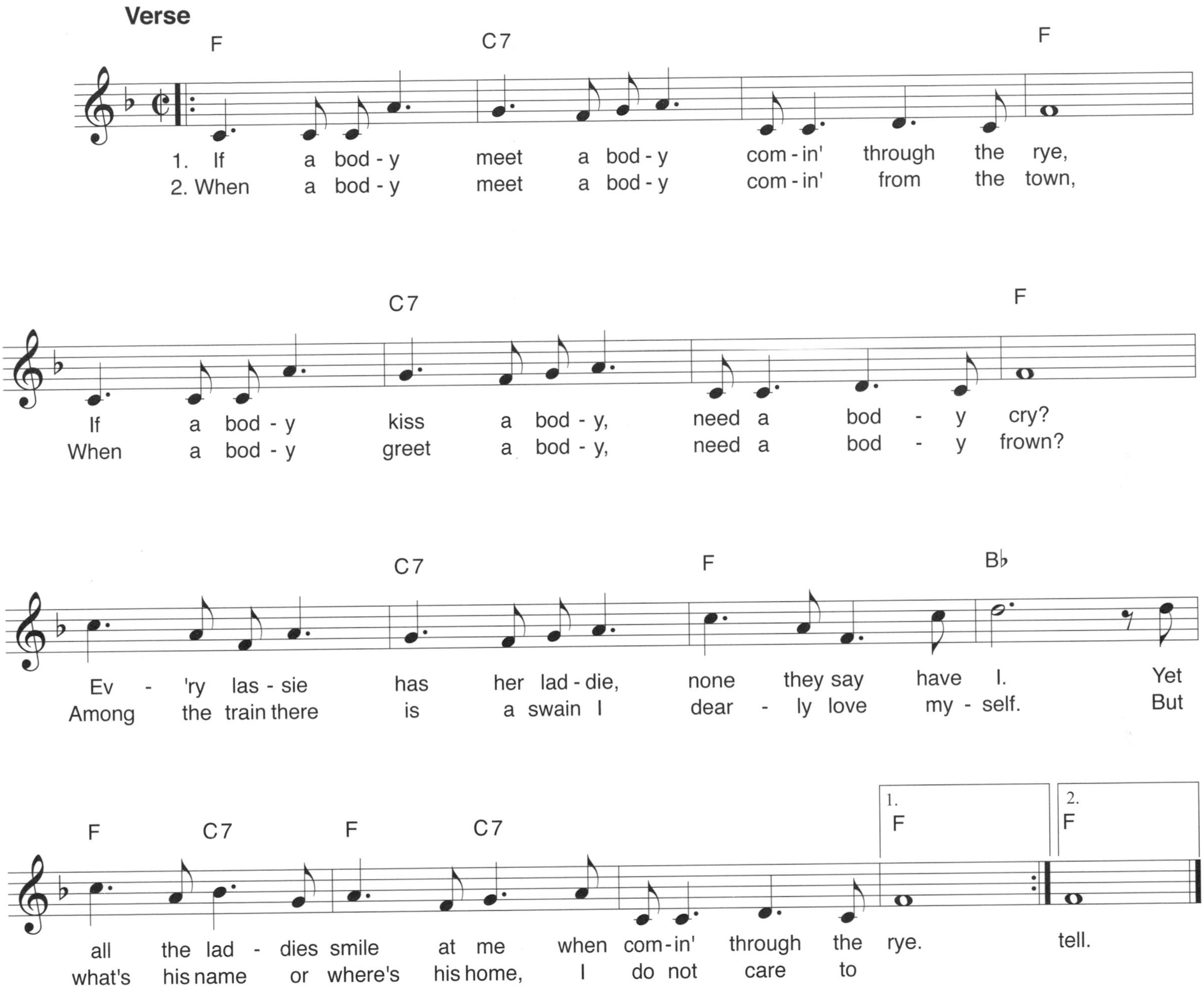
Verse
F C7 F
1. If a bod - y meet a bod - y com - in' through the rye,
2. When a bod - y meet a bod - y com - in' from the town,
C7 F
If a bod - y kiss a bod - y, need a bod - y cry?
When a bod - y greet a bod - y, need a bod - y frown?
C7 F B♭
Ev - 'ry las - sie has her lad - die, none they say have I. Yet
Among the train there is a swain I dear - ly love my - self. But
F C7 F C7 1. F 2. F
all the lad - dies smile at me when com - in' through the rye. tell.
what's his name or where's his home, I do not care to

Standard Ukulele

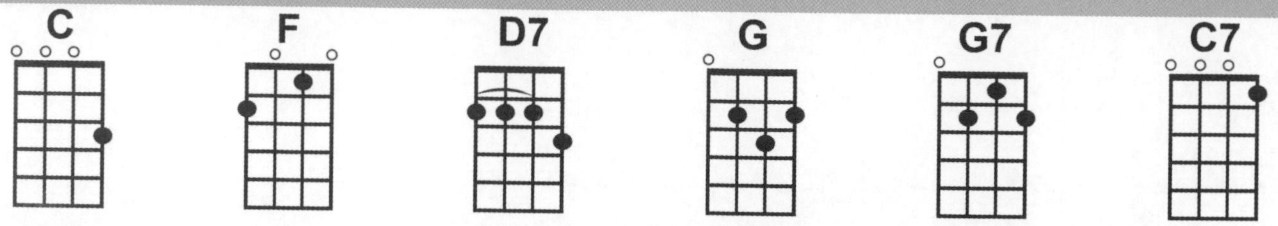
C
F
D7
G
G7
C7

Baritone Ukulele

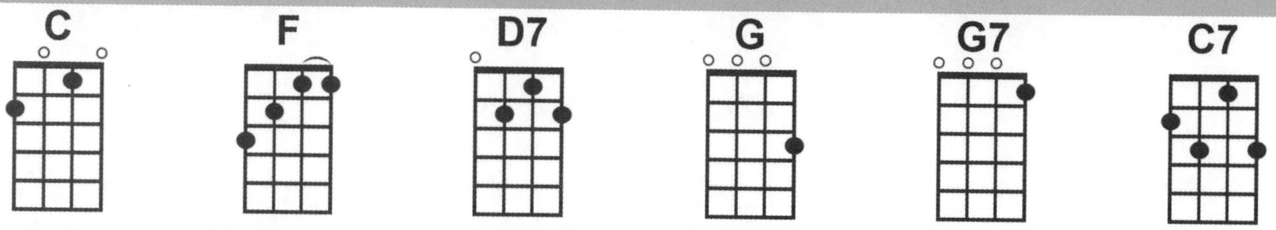
C
F
D7
G
G7
C7

Guitar

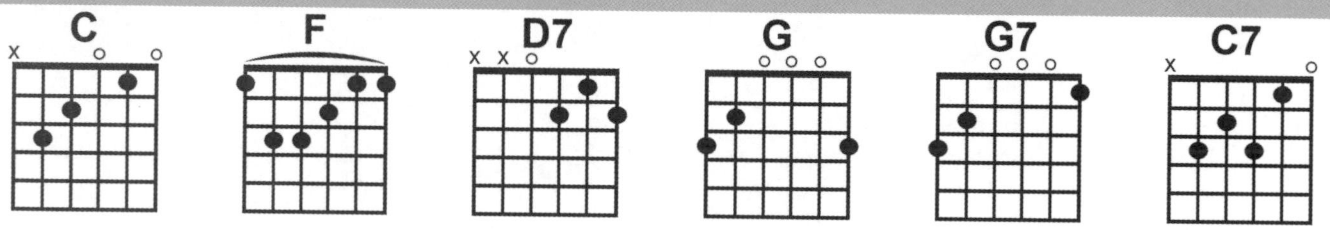
C
F
D7
G
G7
C7

Mandolin

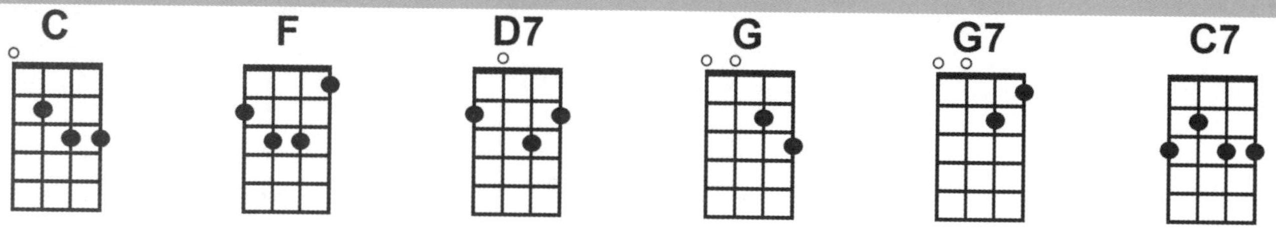
C
F
D7
G
G7
C7

Banjo

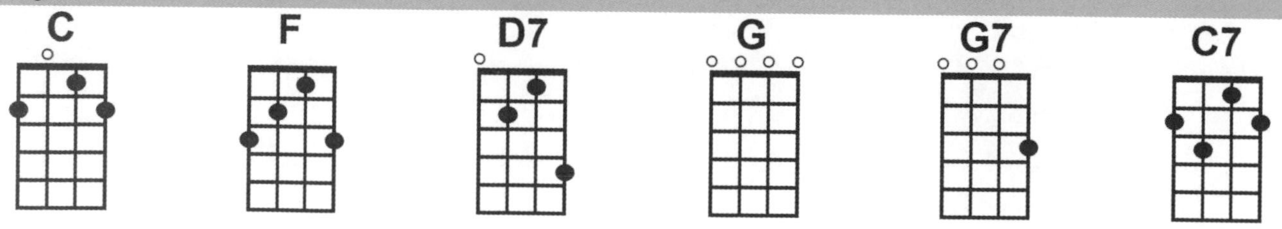
C
F
D7
G
G7
C7

Danny Boy

Words by Frederick Edward Weatherly
Tradition Irish Folk Melody

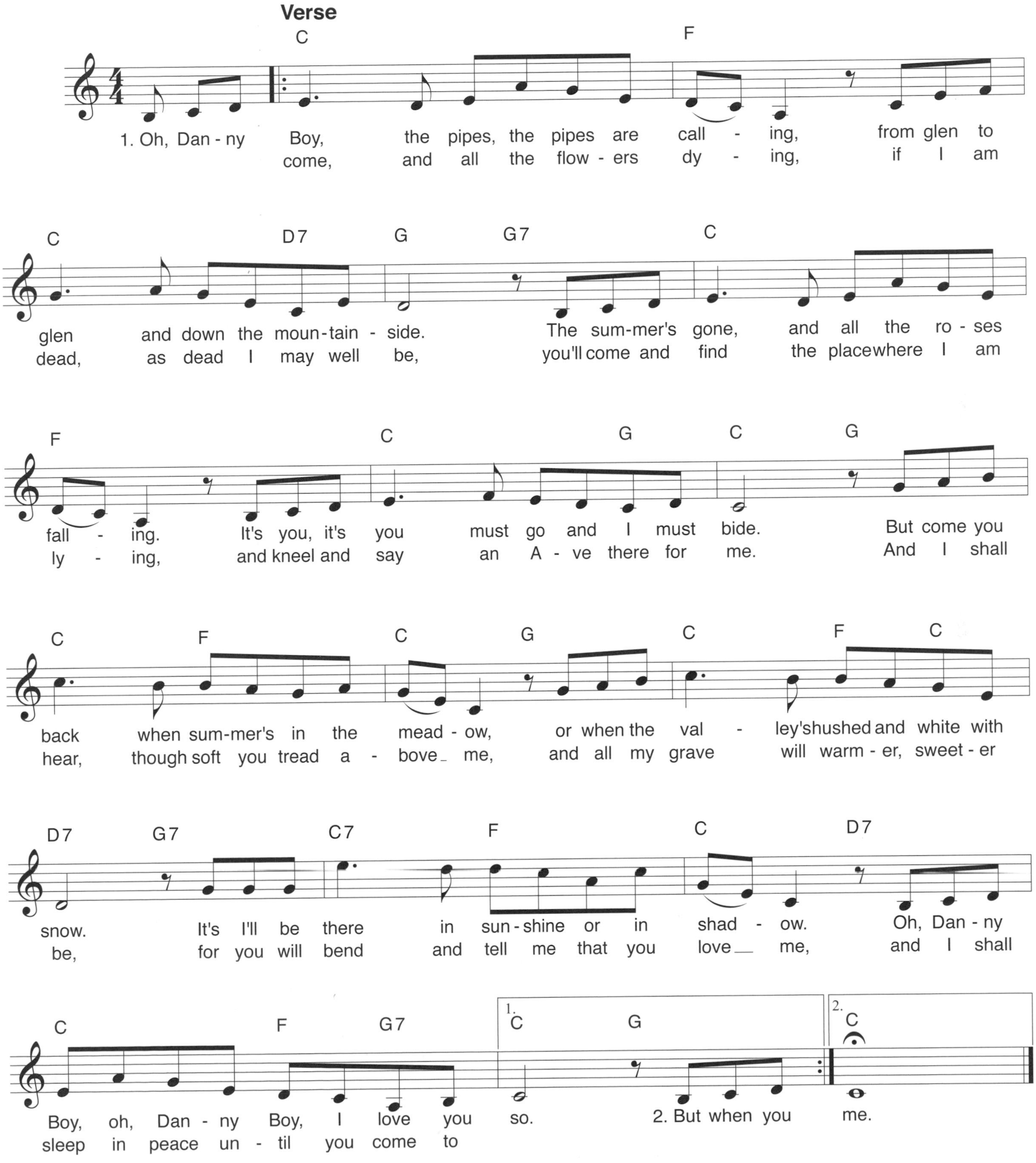
Verse
C F
1. Oh, Dan - ny Boy, the pipes, the pipes are call - ing, from glen to
come, and all the flow - ers dy - ing, if I am
C D7 G G7 C
glen and down the moun - tain - side. The sum - mer's gone, and all the ro - ses
dead, as dead I may well be, you'll come and find the place where I am
F C G C G
fall - ing. It's you, it's you must go and I must bide. But come you
ly - ing, and kneel and say an A - ve there for me. And I shall
C F C G C F C
back when sum - mer's in the mead - ow, or when the val - ley's hushed and white with
hear, though soft you tread a - bove me, and all my grave will warm - er, sweet - er
D7 G7 C7 F C D7
snow. It's I'll be there in sun - shine or in shad - ow. Oh, Dan - ny
be, for you will bend and tell me that you love me, and I shall
C F G7 1. C G 2. C
Boy, oh, Dan - ny Boy, I love you so. 2. But when you me.
sleep in peace un - til you come to

Standard Ukulele

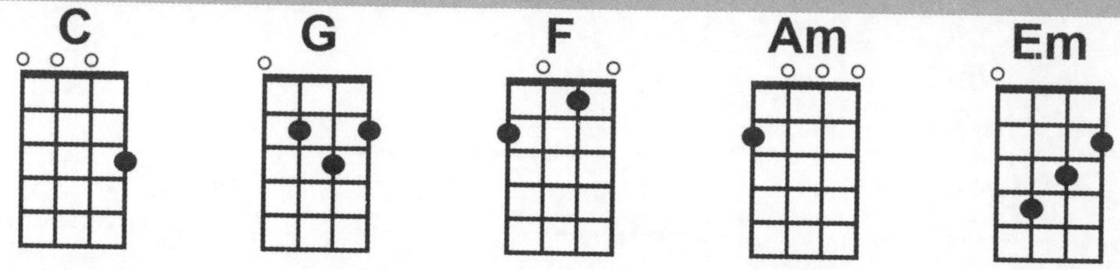
C
G
F
Am
Em

Baritone Ukulele

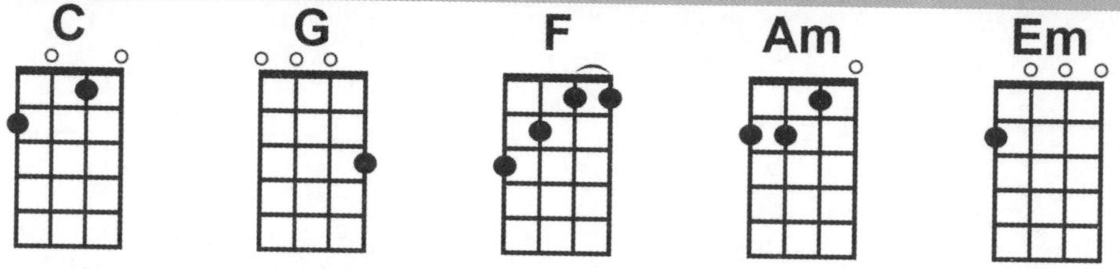
C
G
F
Am
Em

Guitar

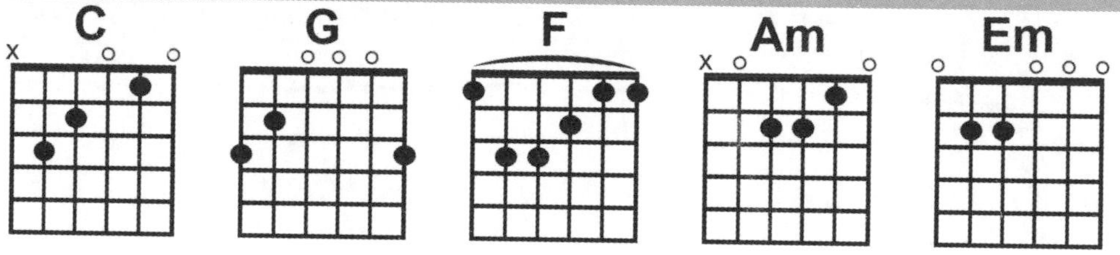
C
G
F
Am
Em

Mandolin

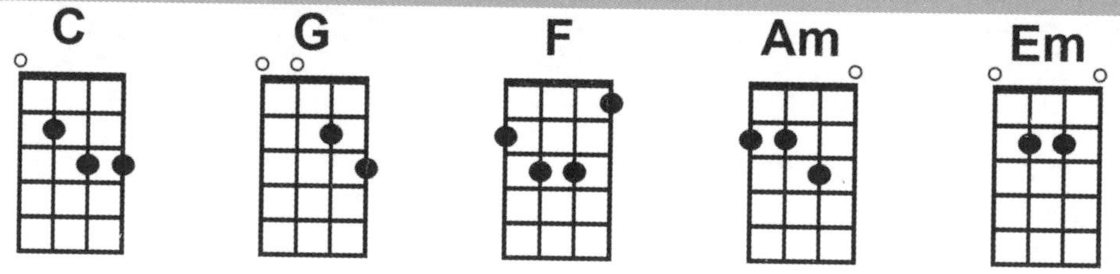
C
G
F
Am
Em

Banjo

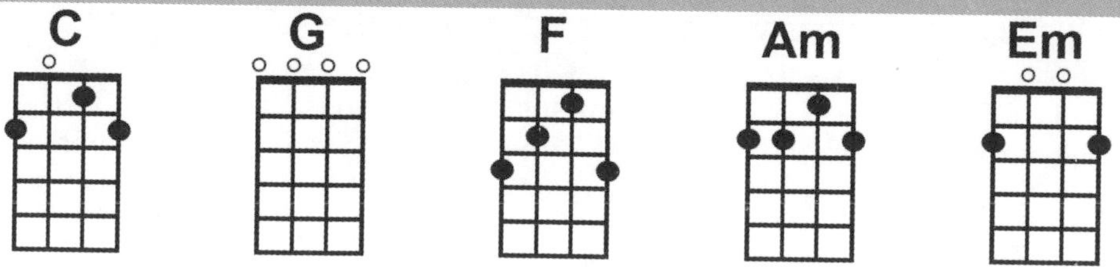
C
G
F
Am
Em

Down by the Salley Gardens

Traditional Irish Folk Song

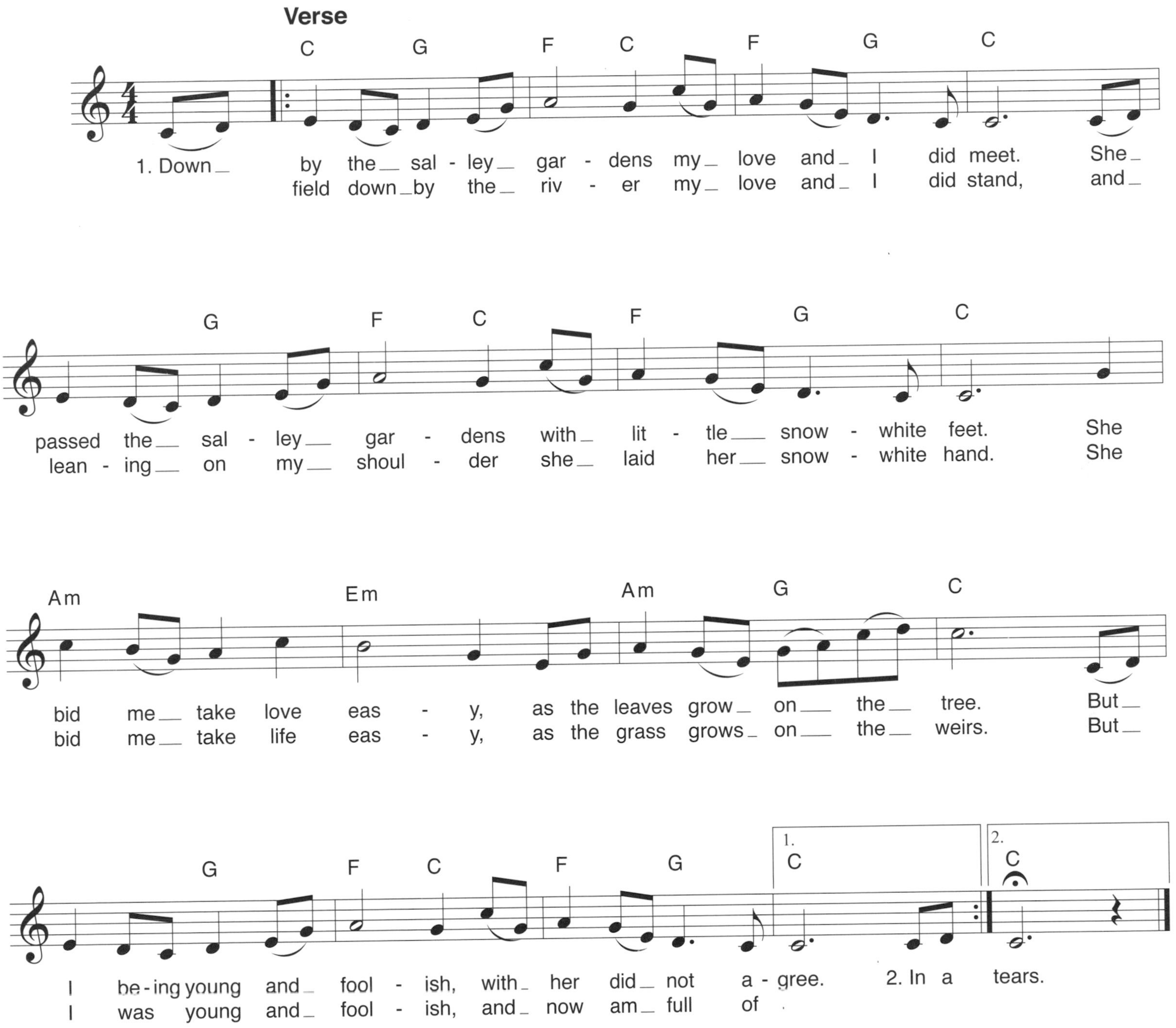
Verse
C G F C F G C
1. Down_ by the_ sal - ley_ gar - dens my_ love and_ I did meet. She_
field down_by the_ riv - er my_ love and_ I did stand, and_
G F C F G C
passed the_ sal - ley_ gar - dens with_ lit - tle_ snow - white feet. She
lean - ing_ on my_ shoul - der she_ laid her_ snow - white hand. She
Am Em Am G C
bid me_ take love eas - y, as the leaves grow_ on_ the_ tree. But_
bid me_ take life eas - y, as the grass grows_ on_ the_ weirs. But_
G F C F G 1. C 2. C
I be - ing young and_ fool - ish, with_ her did_ not a - gree. 2. In a tears.
I was young and_ fool - ish, and_ now am_ full of

Standard Ukulele

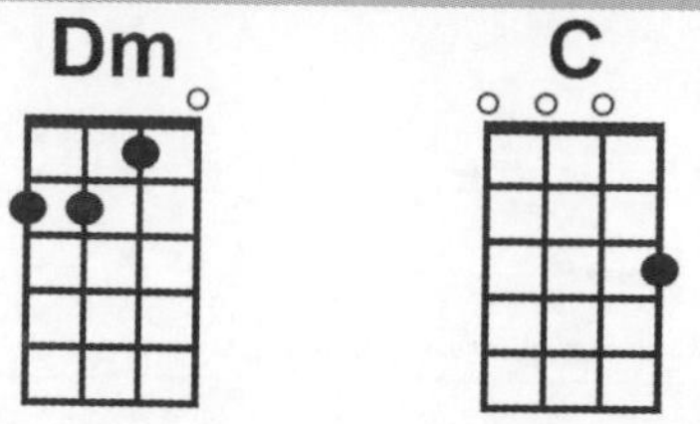

Baritone Ukulele

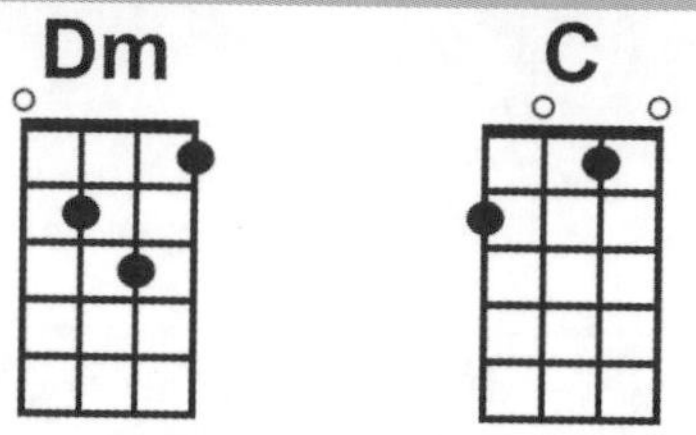

Guitar

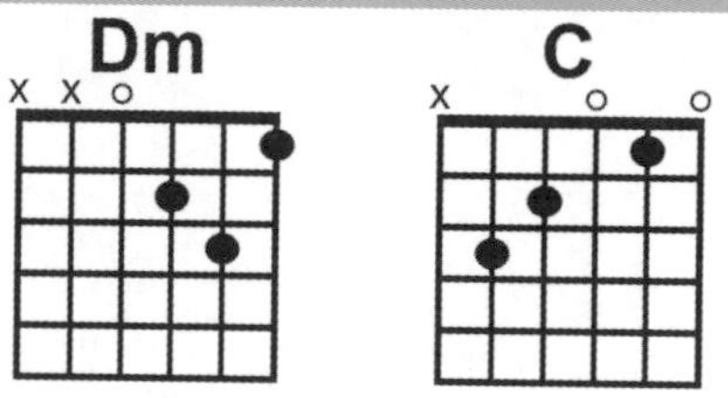

Mandolin

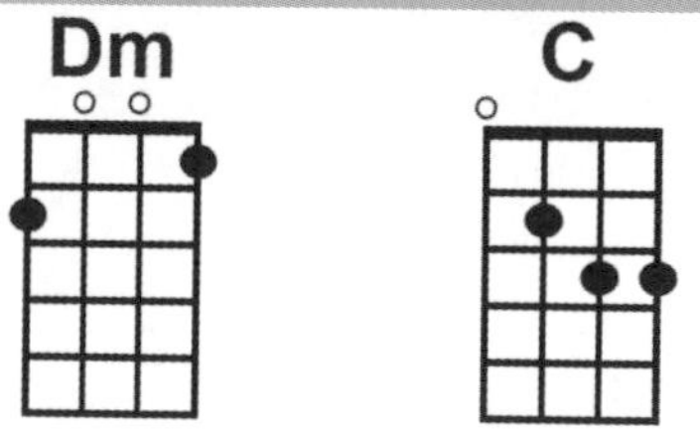

Banjo

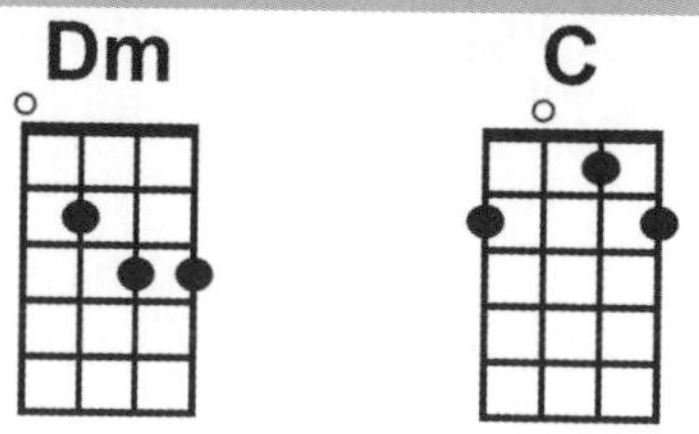

The Drunken Sailor

Sea Chanty

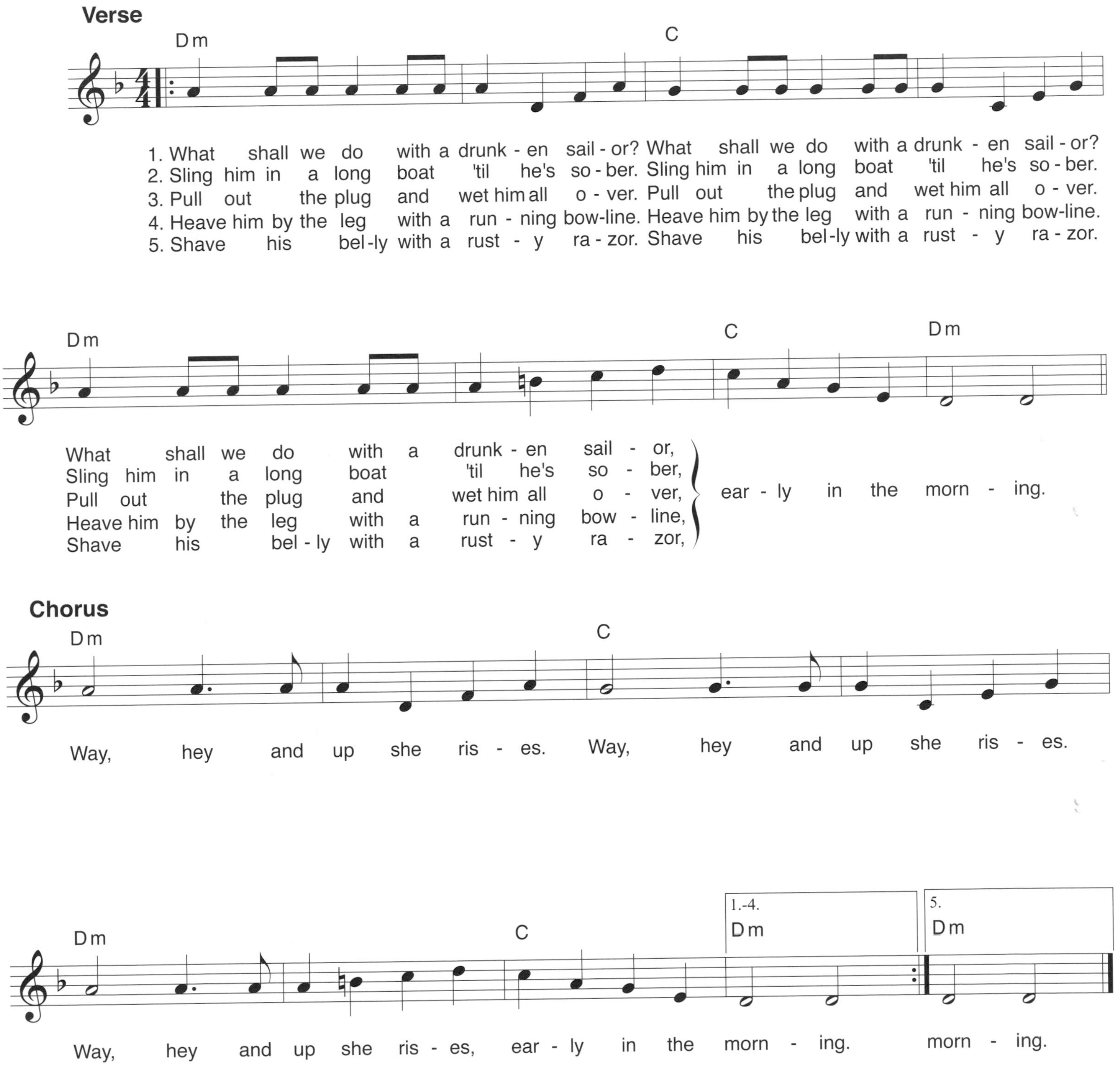
Verse
Dm
C
1. What shall we do with a drunk - en sail - or? What shall we do with a drunk - en sail - or?
2. Sling him in a long boat 'til he's so - ber. Sling him in a long boat 'til he's so - ber.
3. Pull out the plug and wet him all o - ver. Pull out the plug and wet him all o - ver.
4. Heave him by the leg with a run - ning bow-line. Heave him by the leg with a run - ning bow-line.
5. Shave his bel-ly with a rust - y ra - zor. Shave his bel-ly with a rust - y ra - zor.
Dm
C
Dm
What shall we do with a drunk - en sail - or,
Sling him in a long boat 'til he's so - ber,
Pull out the plug and wet him all o - ver,
Heave him by the leg with a run - ning bow - line,
Shave his bel - ly with a rust - y ra - zor,
ear - ly in the morn - ing.
Chorus
Dm
C
Way, hey and up she ris - es. Way, hey and up she ris - es.
Dm
C
1.-4.
Dm
5.
Dm
Way, hey and up she ris - es, ear - ly in the morn - ing. morn - ing.

Standard Ukulele

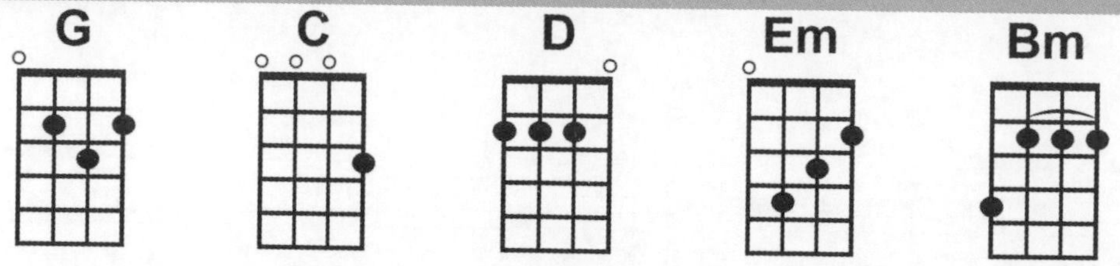
G
C
D
Em
Bm

Baritone Ukulele

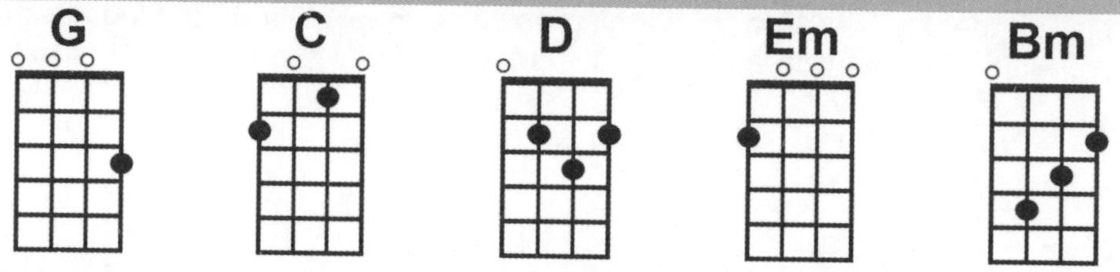
G
C
D
Em
Bm

Guitar

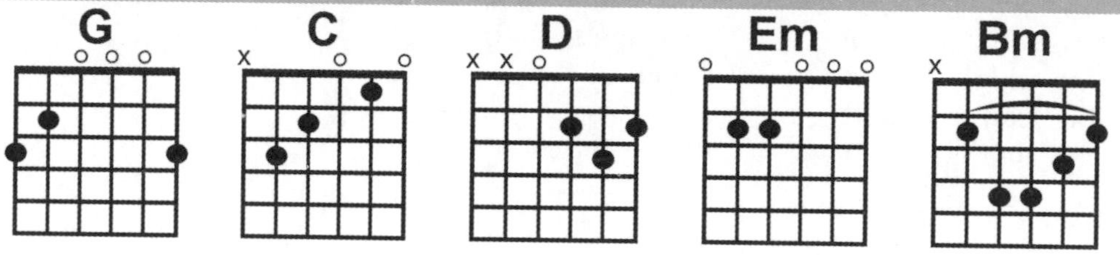
G
C
D
Em
Bm

Mandolin

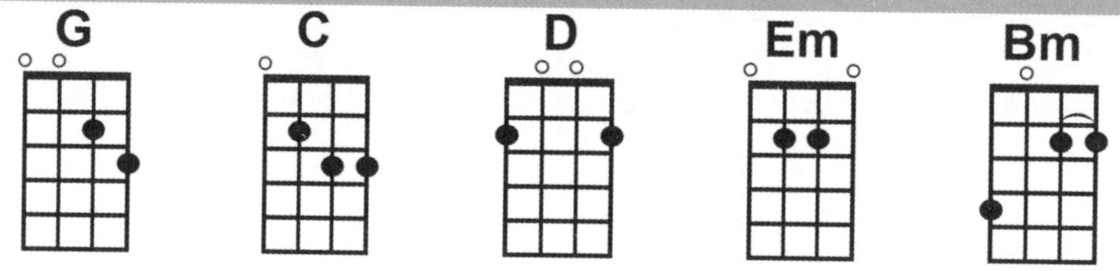
G
C
D
Em
Bm

Banjo

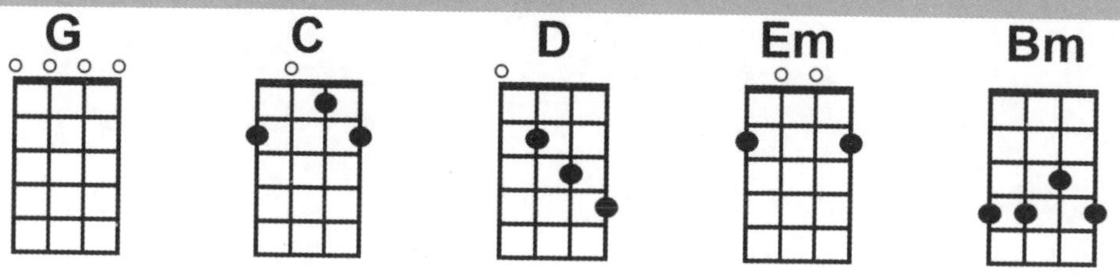
G
C
D
Em
Bm

Eileen Aroon

Words by Gerald Griffin
Music by Lady Caroline Keppel

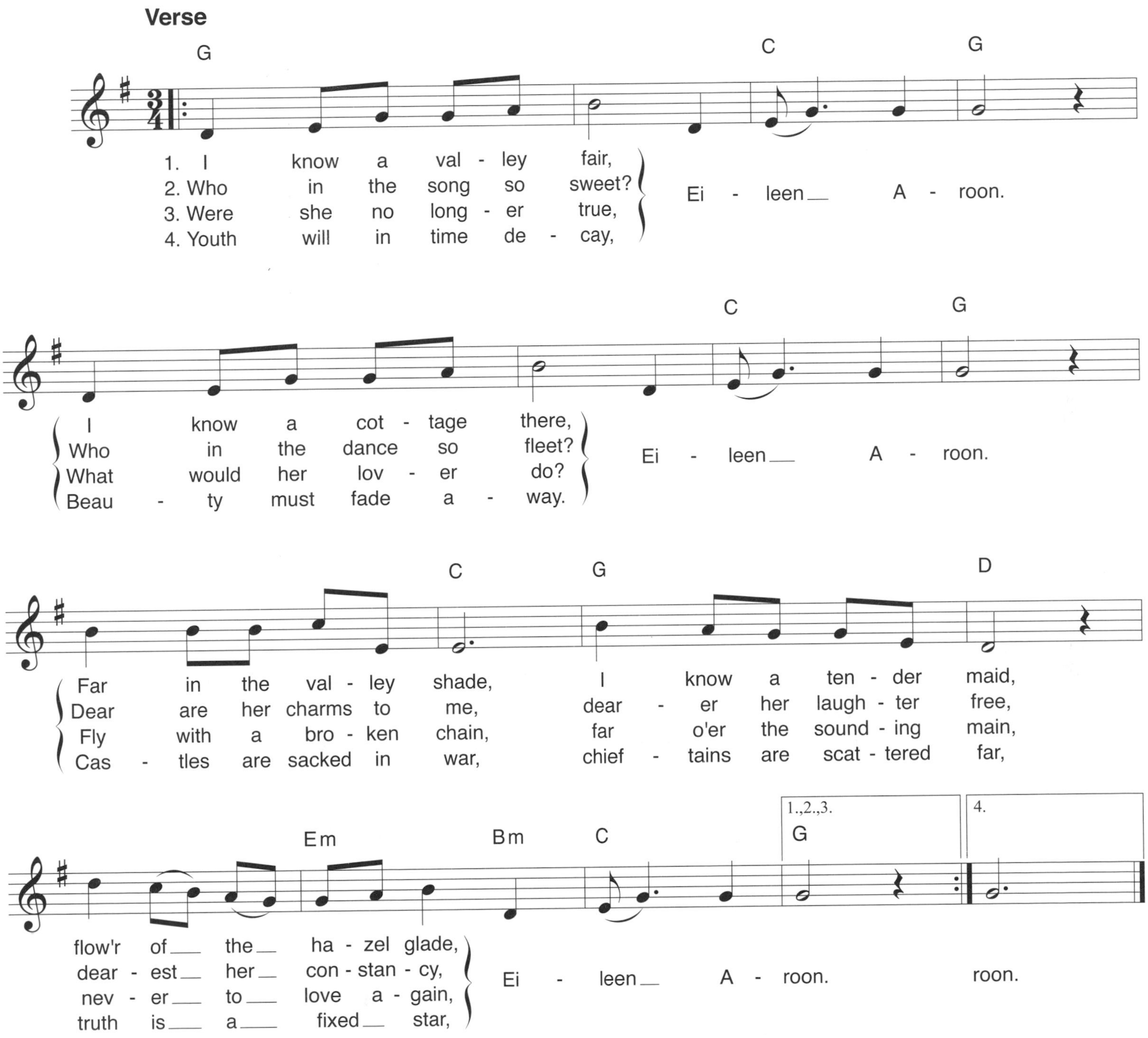
Verse
G
C
G
1. I know a val - ley fair,
2. Who in the song so sweet?
3. Were she no long - er true,
4. Youth will in time de - cay,
Ei - leen A - roon.
C
G
I know a cot - tage there,
Who in the dance so fleet?
What would her lov - er do?
Beau - ty must fade a - way.
Ei - leen A - roon.
C
G
D
Far in the val - ley shade, I know a ten - der maid,
Dear are her charms to me, dear - er her laugh - ter free,
Fly with a bro - ken chain, far o'er the sound - ing main,
Cas - tles are sacked in war, chief - tains are scat - tered far,
Em
Bm
C
1.,2.,3.
G
4.
flow'r of the ha - zel glade,
dear - est her con - stan - cy,
nev - er to love a - gain,
truth is a fixed star,
Ei - leen A - roon.
roon.

Standard Ukulele

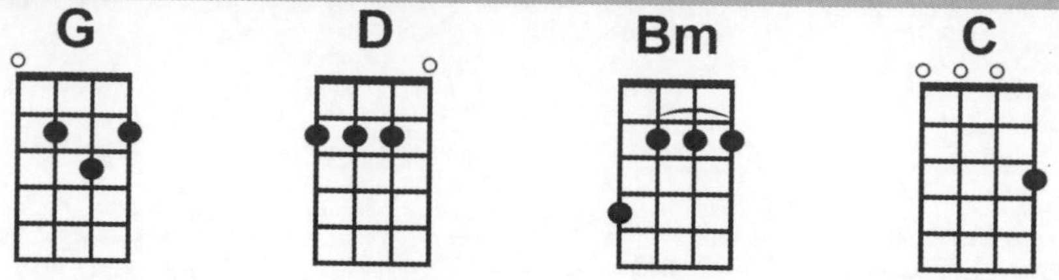

Baritone Ukulele

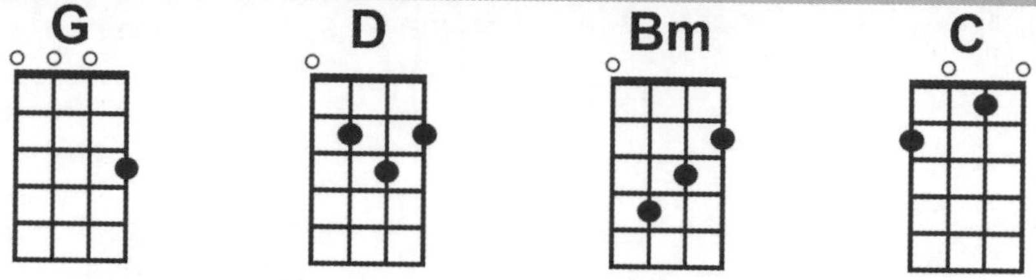

Guitar

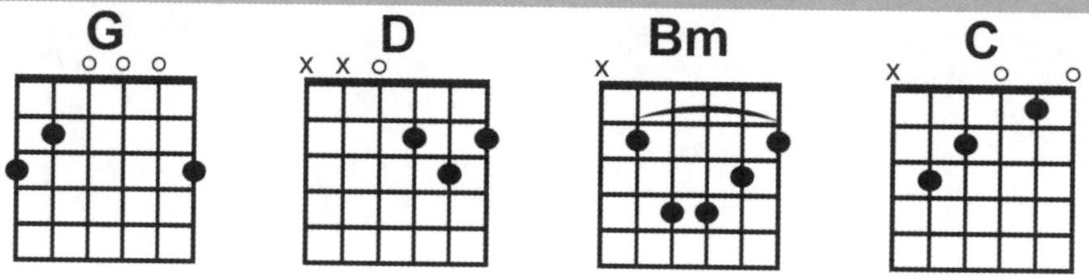

Mandolin

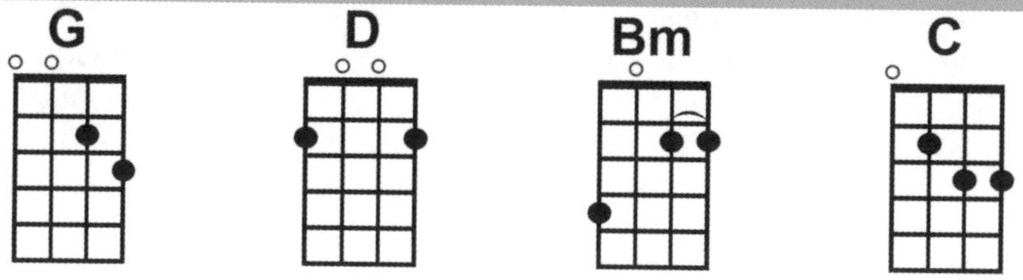

Banjo

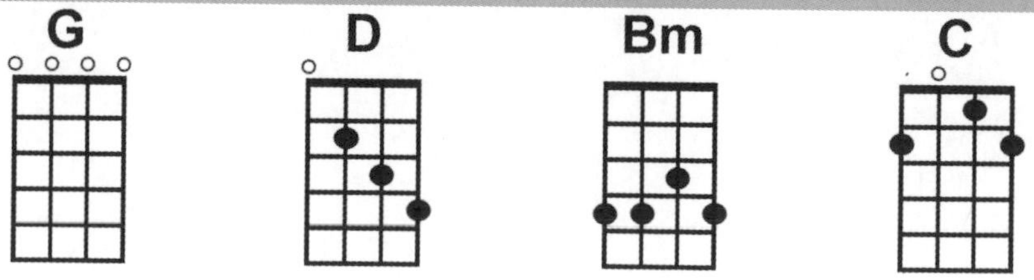

An Eriskay Love Lilt

Traditional Scottish

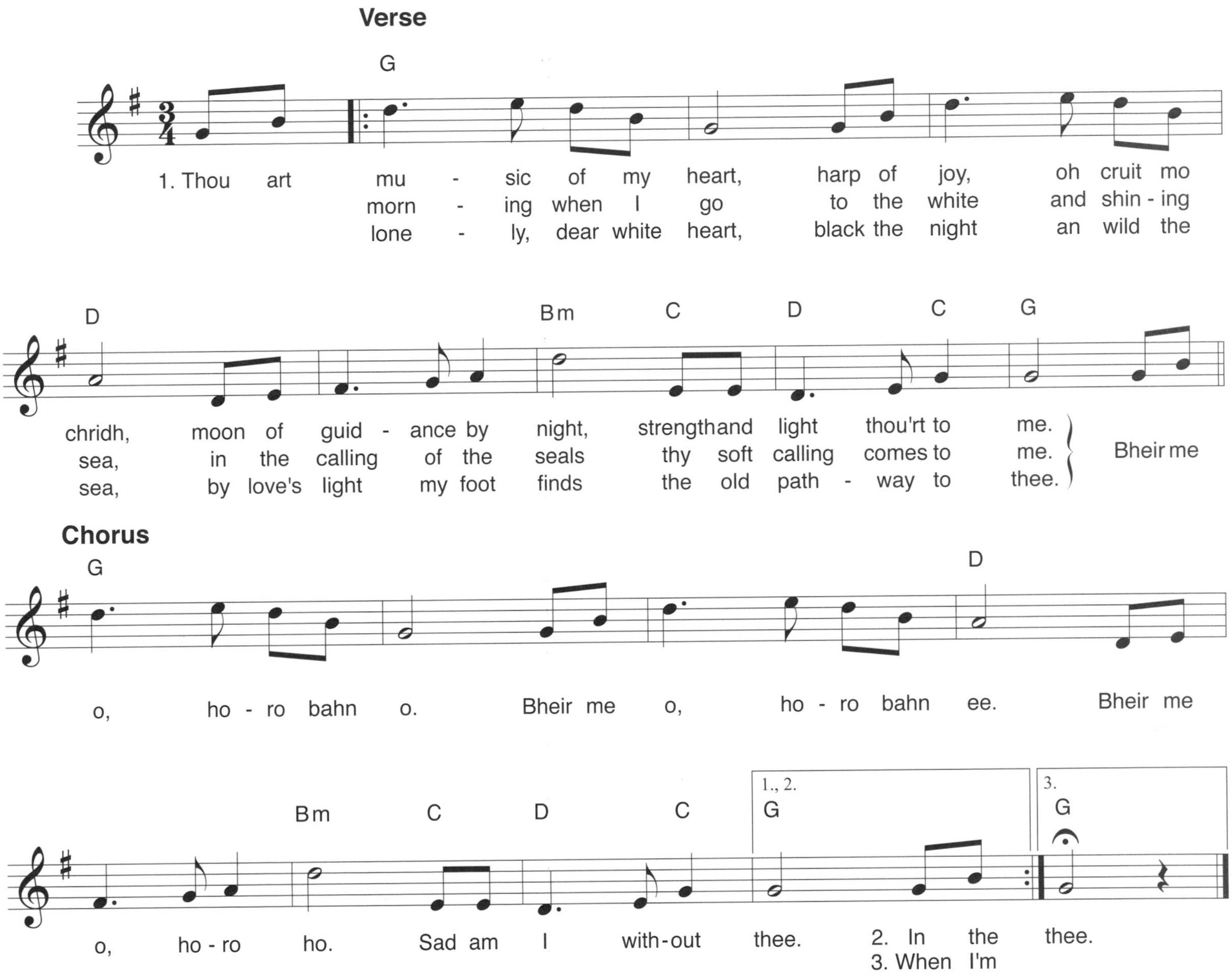
Verse
G
1. Thou art mu - sic of my heart, harp of joy, oh cruit mo
morn - ing when I go to the white and shin - ing
lone - ly, dear white heart, black the night an wild the
D Bm C D C G
chridh, moon of guid - ance by night, strength and light thou'rt to me.
sea, in the calling of the seals thy soft calling comes to me.
sea, by love's light my foot finds the old path - way to thee.
Bheir me
Chorus
G D
o, ho - ro bahn o. Bheir me o, ho - ro bahn ee. Bheir me
Bm C D C
1., 2.
G
3.
G
o, ho - ro ho. Sad am I with-out thee.
2. In the
3. When I'm
thee.

Standard Ukulele

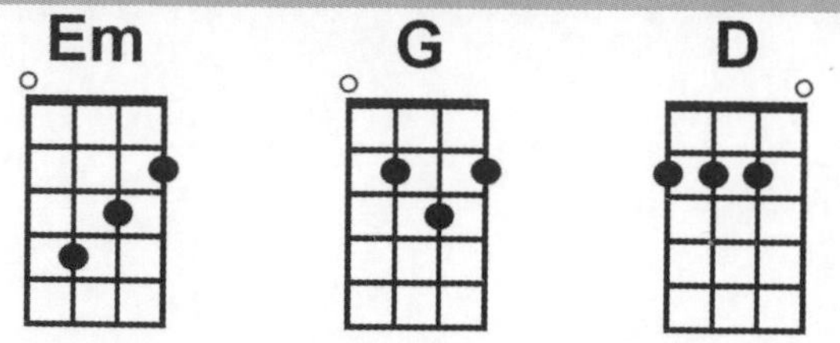

Baritone Ukulele

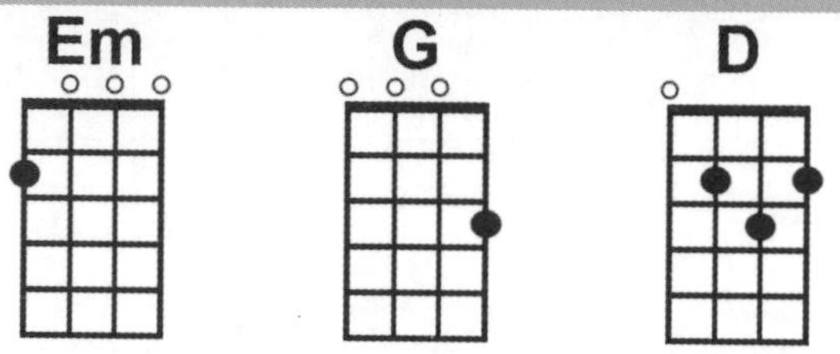

Guitar

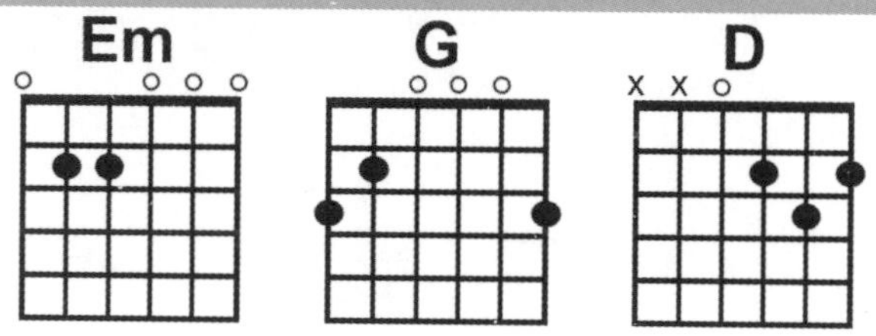

Mandolin

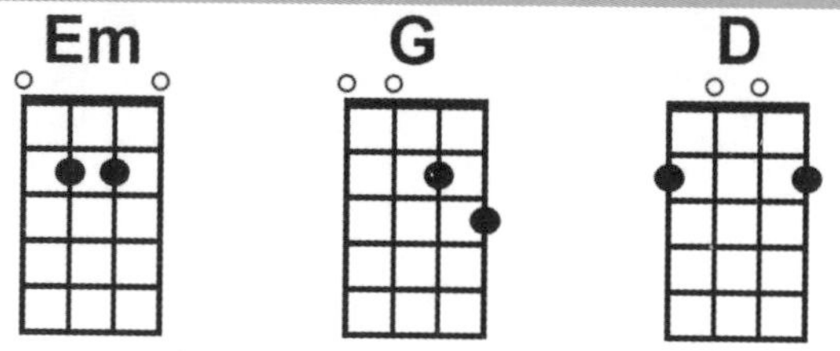

Banjo

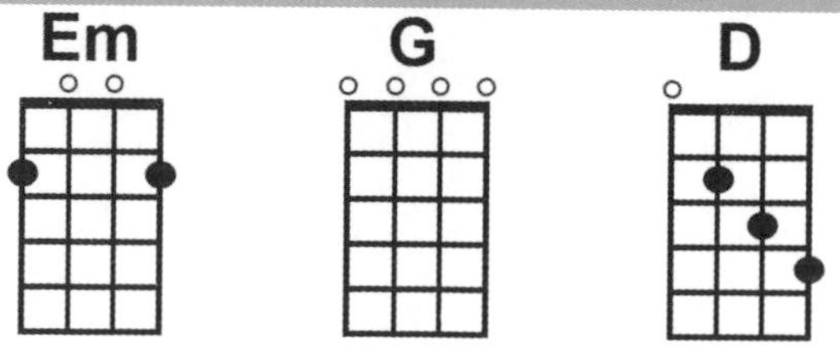

Filimioorioriay

Irish-American Folk Song

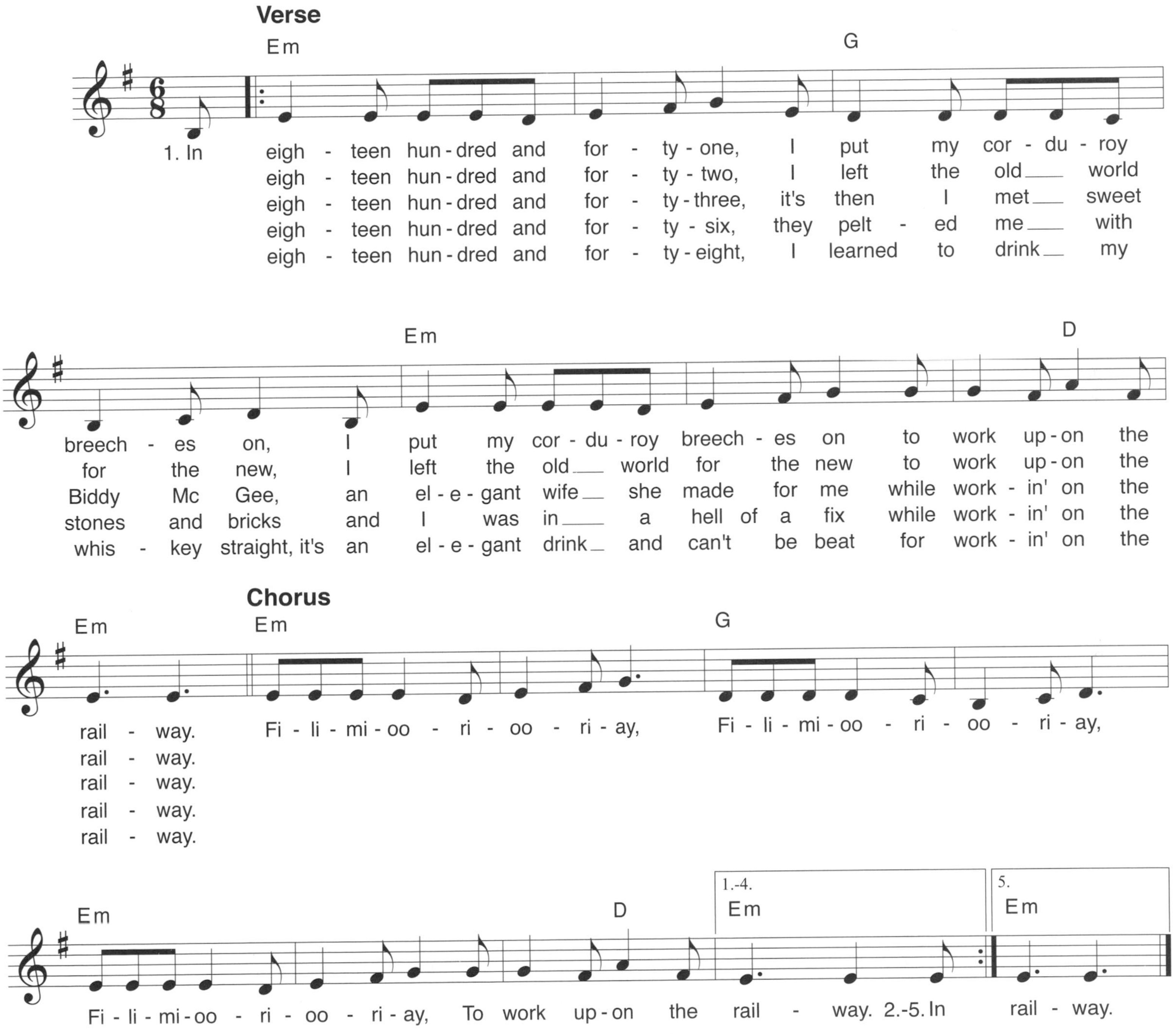
Verse
Em
G
1. In eigh - teen hun - dred and for - ty - one, I put my cor - du - roy
eigh - teen hun - dred and for - ty - two, I left the old world
eigh - teen hun - dred and for - ty - three, it's then I met sweet
eigh - teen hun - dred and for - ty - six, they pelt - ed me with
eigh - teen hun - dred and for - ty - eight, I learned to drink my
Em
D
breech - es on, I put my cor - du - roy breech - es on to work up - on the
for the new, I left the old world for the new to work up - on the
Biddy Mc Gee, an el - e - gant wife she made for me while work - in' on the
stones and bricks and I was in a hell of a fix while work - in' on the
whis - key straight, it's an el - e - gant drink and can't be beat for work - in' on the
Chorus
Em
Em
G
rail - way. Fi - li - mi - oo - ri - oo - ri - ay, Fi - li - mi - oo - ri - oo - ri - ay,
rail - way.
rail - way.
rail - way.
rail - way.
Em
D
1.-4.
Em
5.
Em
Fi - li - mi - oo - ri - oo - ri - ay, To work up - on the rail - way. 2.-5. In rail - way.

Standard Ukulele

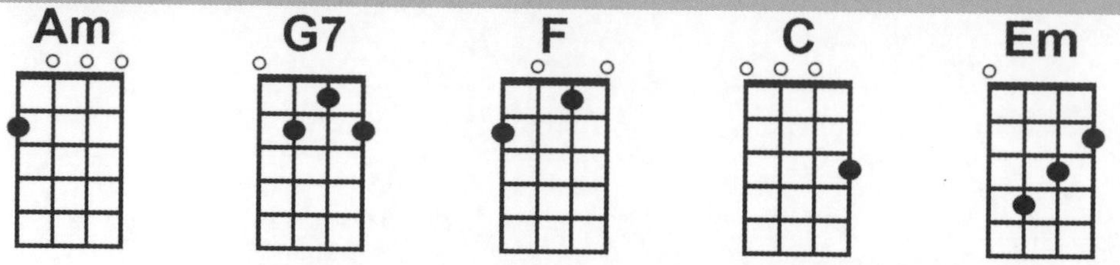
Am
G7
F
C
Em

Baritone Ukulele

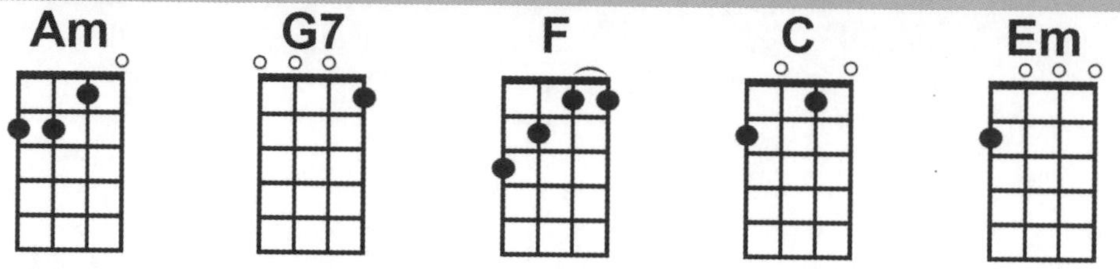
Am
G7
F
C
Em

Guitar

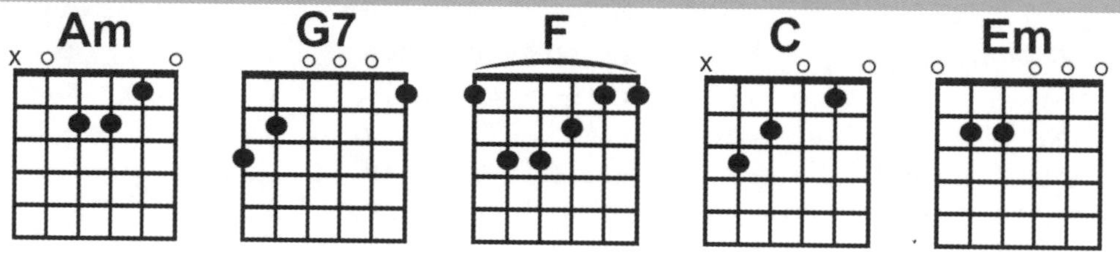
Am
G7
F
C
Em

Mandolin

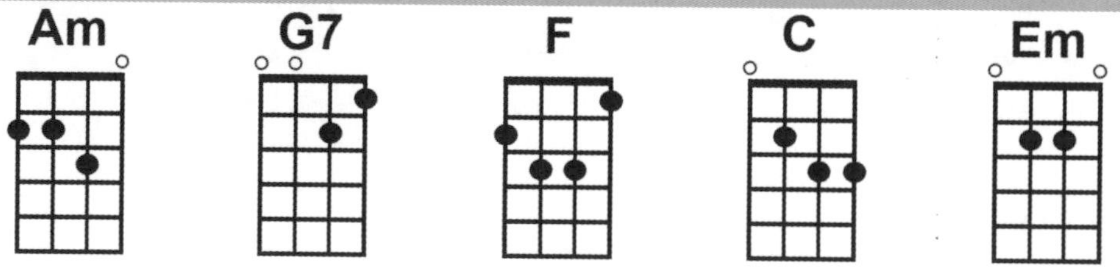
Am
G7
F
C
Em

Banjo

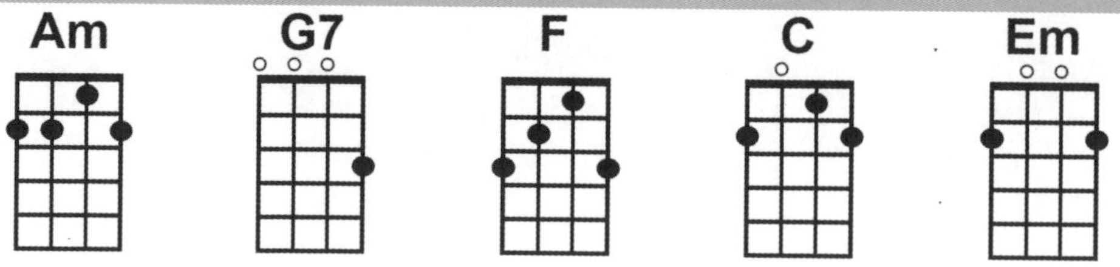
Am
G7
F
C
Em

Finnegan's Wake

Traditional Irish Folk Song

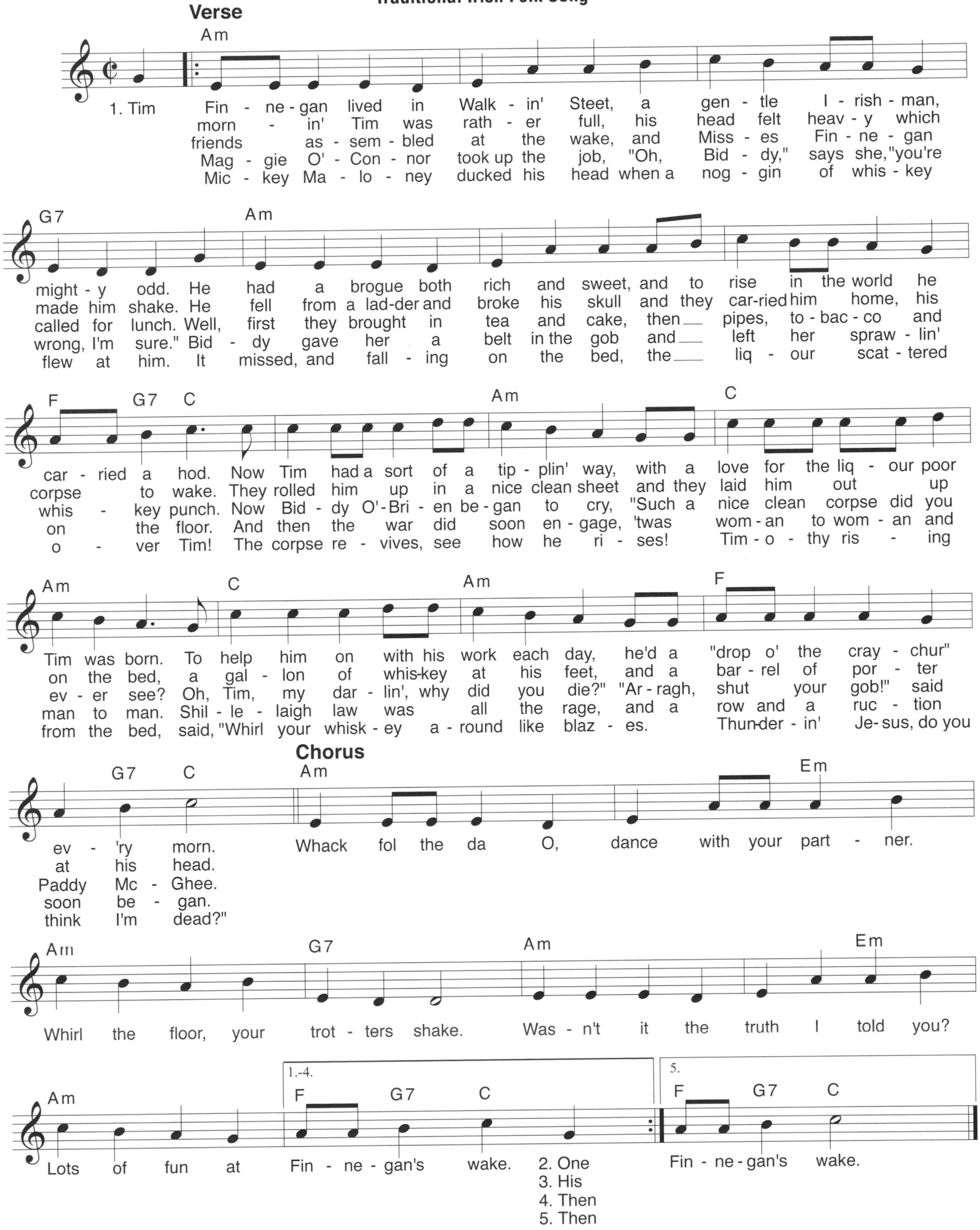
Verse
Chorus
Am
G7
C
F
Em
1. Tim Fin - ne - gan lived in Walk - in' Steet, a gen - tle I - rish - man,
morn - in' Tim was rath - er full, his head felt heav - y which
friends as - sem - bled at the wake, and Miss - es Fin - ne - gan
Mag - gie O' - Con - nor took up the job, "Oh, Bid - dy," says she,"you're
Mic - key Ma - lo - ney ducked his head when a nog - gin of whis - key
might - y odd. He had a brogue both rich and sweet, and to rise in the world he
made him shake. He fell from a lad-der and broke his skull and they car-ried him home, his
called for lunch. Well, first they brought in tea and cake, then pipes, to - bac - co and
wrong, I'm sure." Bid - dy gave her a belt in the gob and left her spraw - lin'
flew at him. It missed, and fall - ing on the bed, the liq - our scat - tered
car - ried a hod. Now Tim had a sort of a tip - plin' way, with a love for the liq - our poor
corpse to wake. They rolled him up in a nice clean sheet and they laid him out up
whis - key punch. Now Bid - dy O'-Bri - en be - gan to cry, "Such a nice clean corpse did you
on the floor. And then the war did soon en - gage, 'twas wom - an to wom - an and
o - ver Tim! The corpse re - vives, see how he ri - ses! Tim - o - thy ris - ing
Tim was born. To help him on with his work each day, he'd a "drop o' the cray - chur"
on the bed, a gal - lon of whis-key at his feet, and a bar - rel of por - ter
ev - er see? Oh, Tim, my dar - lin', why did you die?" "Ar - ragh, shut your gob!" said
man to man. Shil - le - laigh law was all the rage, and a row and a ruc - tion
from the bed, said, "Whirl your whisk - ey a - round like blaz - es. Thun-der - in' Je-sus, do you
ev - 'ry morn.
at his head.
Paddy Mc - Ghee.
soon be - gan.
think I'm dead?"
Whack fol the da O, dance with your part - ner.
Whirl the floor, your trot - ters shake. Was - n't it the truth I told you?
Lots of fun at Fin - ne - gan's wake. 2. One
3. His
4. Then
5. Then
1.-4.
5.
Fin - ne - gan's wake.

Standard Ukulele

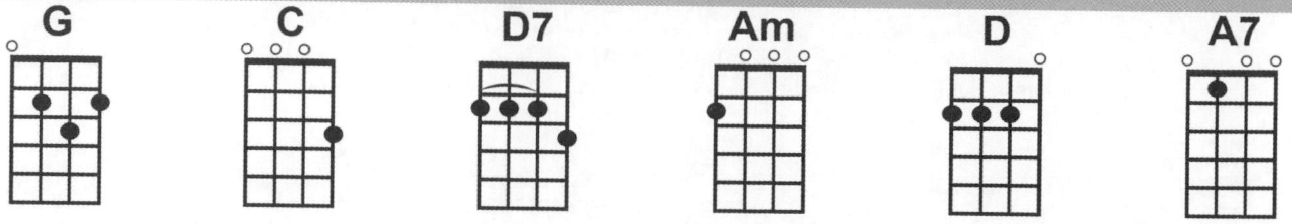
G
C
D7
Am
D
A7

Baritone Ukulele

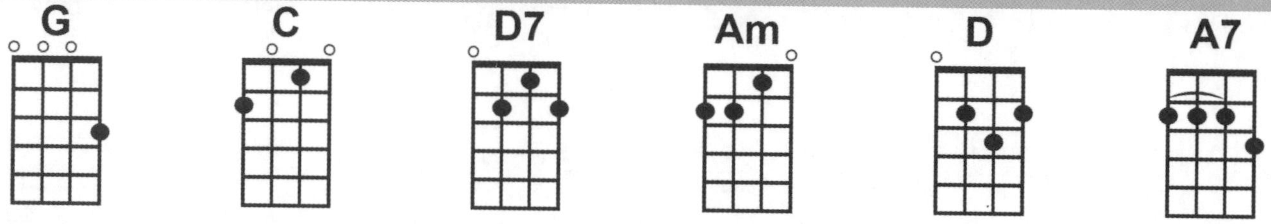
G
C
D7
Am
D
A7

Guitar

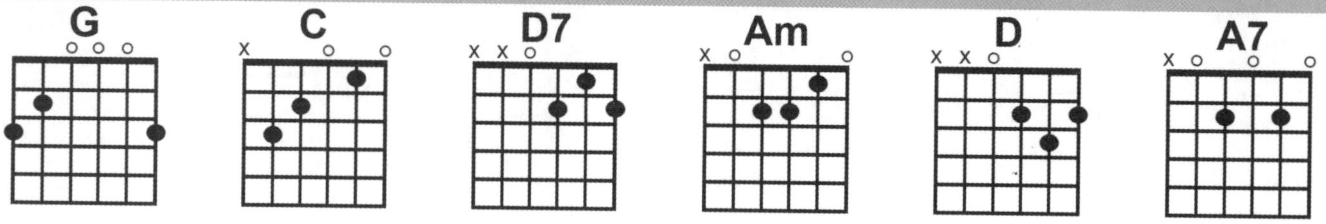
G
C
D7
Am
D
A7

Mandolin

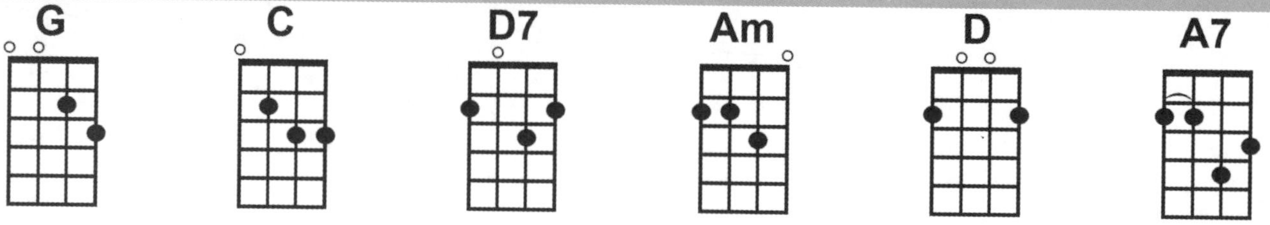
G
C
D7
Am
D
A7

Banjo

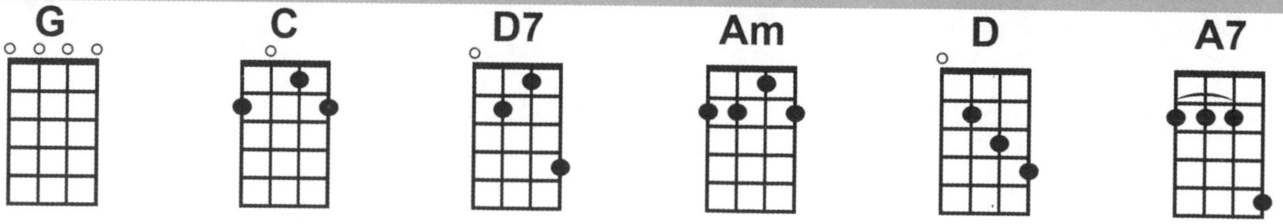
G
C
D7
Am
D
A7

Flow Gently, Sweet Afton

Lyrics by Robert Burns
Music by Alexander Hume

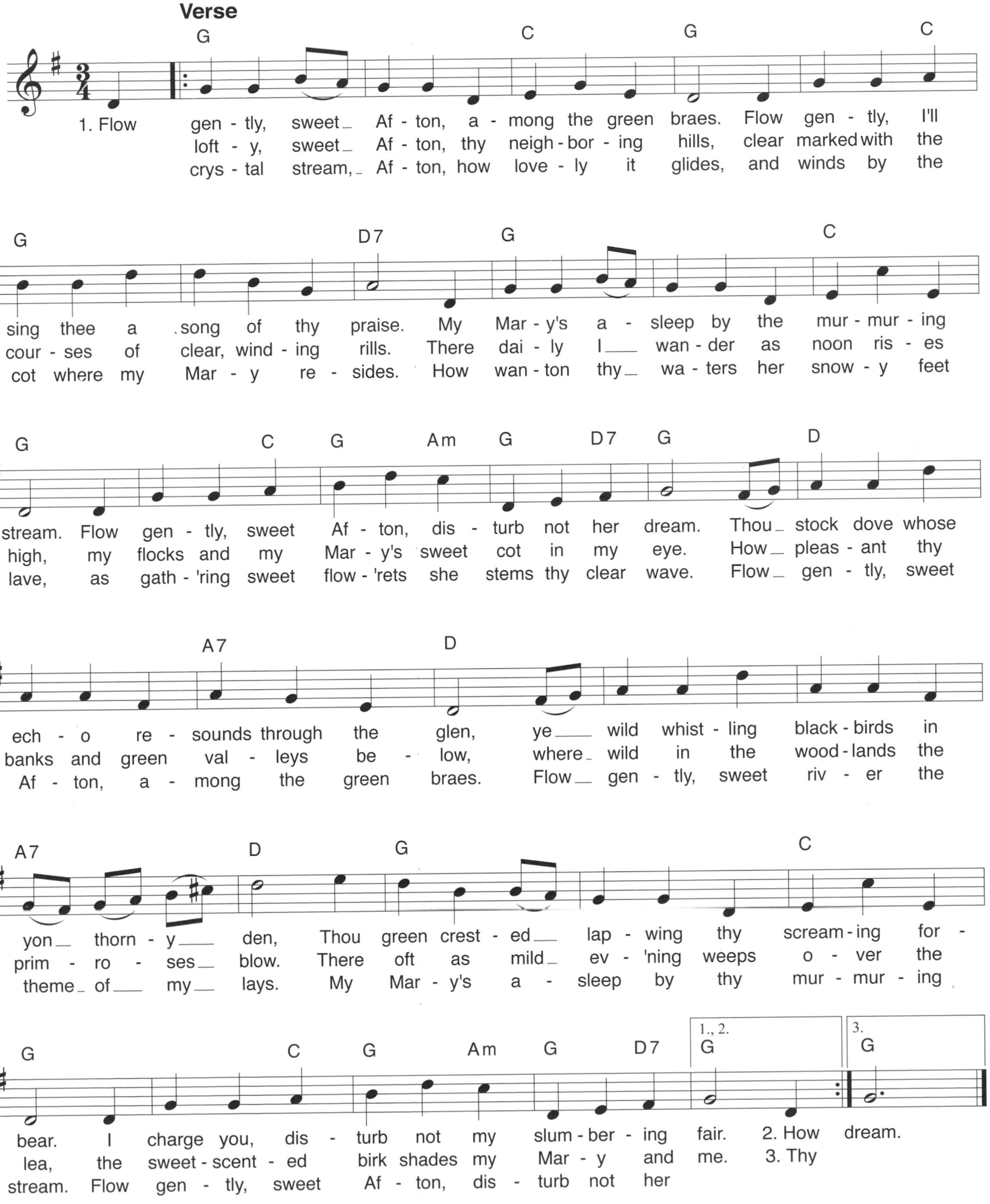
Verse
G C G C
1. Flow gen - tly, sweet_ Af - ton, a - mong the green braes. Flow gen - tly, I'll
loft - y, sweet_ Af - ton, thy neigh - bor - ing hills, clear marked with the
crys - tal stream,_ Af - ton, how love - ly it glides, and winds by the
G D7 G C
sing thee a song of thy praise. My Mar - y's a - sleep by the mur - mur - ing
cour - ses of clear, wind - ing rills. There dai - ly I___ wan - der as noon ris - es
cot where my Mar - y re - sides. How wan - ton thy_ wa - ters her snow - y feet
G C G Am G D7 G D
stream. Flow gen - tly, sweet Af - ton, dis - turb not her dream. Thou_ stock dove whose
high, my flocks and my Mar - y's sweet cot in my eye. How_ pleas - ant thy
lave, as gath - 'ring sweet flow - 'rets she stems thy clear wave. Flow_ gen - tly, sweet
A7 D
ech - o re - sounds through the glen, ye___ wild whist - ling black - birds in
banks and green val - leys be - low, where_ wild in the wood - lands the
Af - ton, a - mong the green braes. Flow__ gen - tly, sweet riv - er the
A7 D G C
yon_ thorn - y___ den, Thou green crest - ed__ lap - wing thy scream - ing for -
prim - ro - ses_ blow. There oft as mild_ ev - 'ning weeps o - ver the
theme_ of___ my_ lays. My Mar - y's a - sleep by thy mur - mur - ing
G C G Am G D7 1., 2. G 3. G
bear. I charge you, dis - turb not my slum - ber - ing fair. 2. How dream.
lea, the sweet - scent - ed birk shades my Mar - y and me. 3. Thy
stream. Flow gen - tly, sweet Af - ton, dis - turb not her

Standard Ukulele

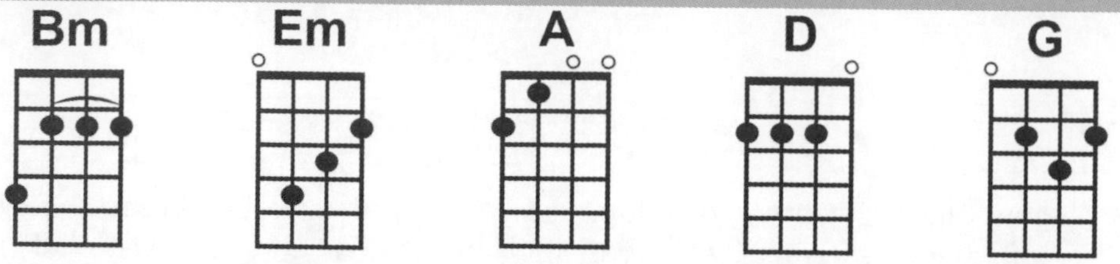
Bm
Em
A
D
G

Baritone Ukulele

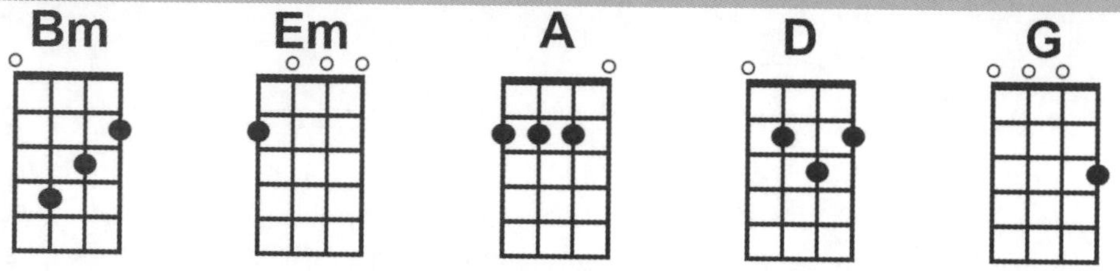
Bm
Em
A
D
G

Guitar

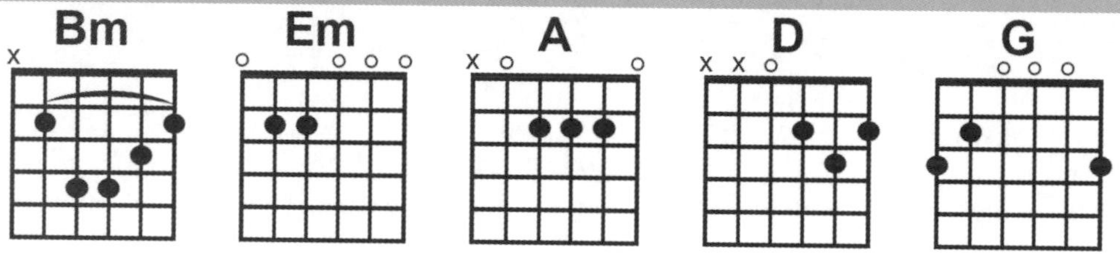
Bm
Em
A
D
G

Mandolin

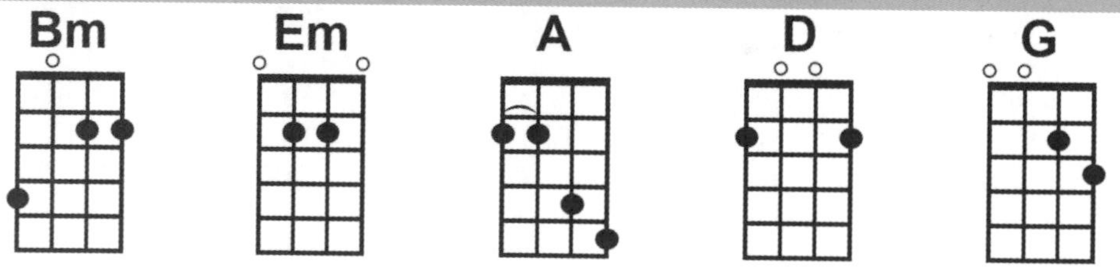
Bm
Em
A
D
G

Banjo

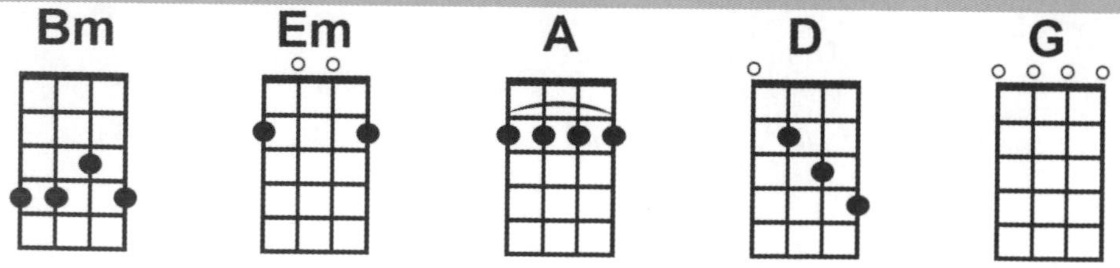
Bm
Em
A
D
G

The Foggy Dew

Traditional Irish Folk Song

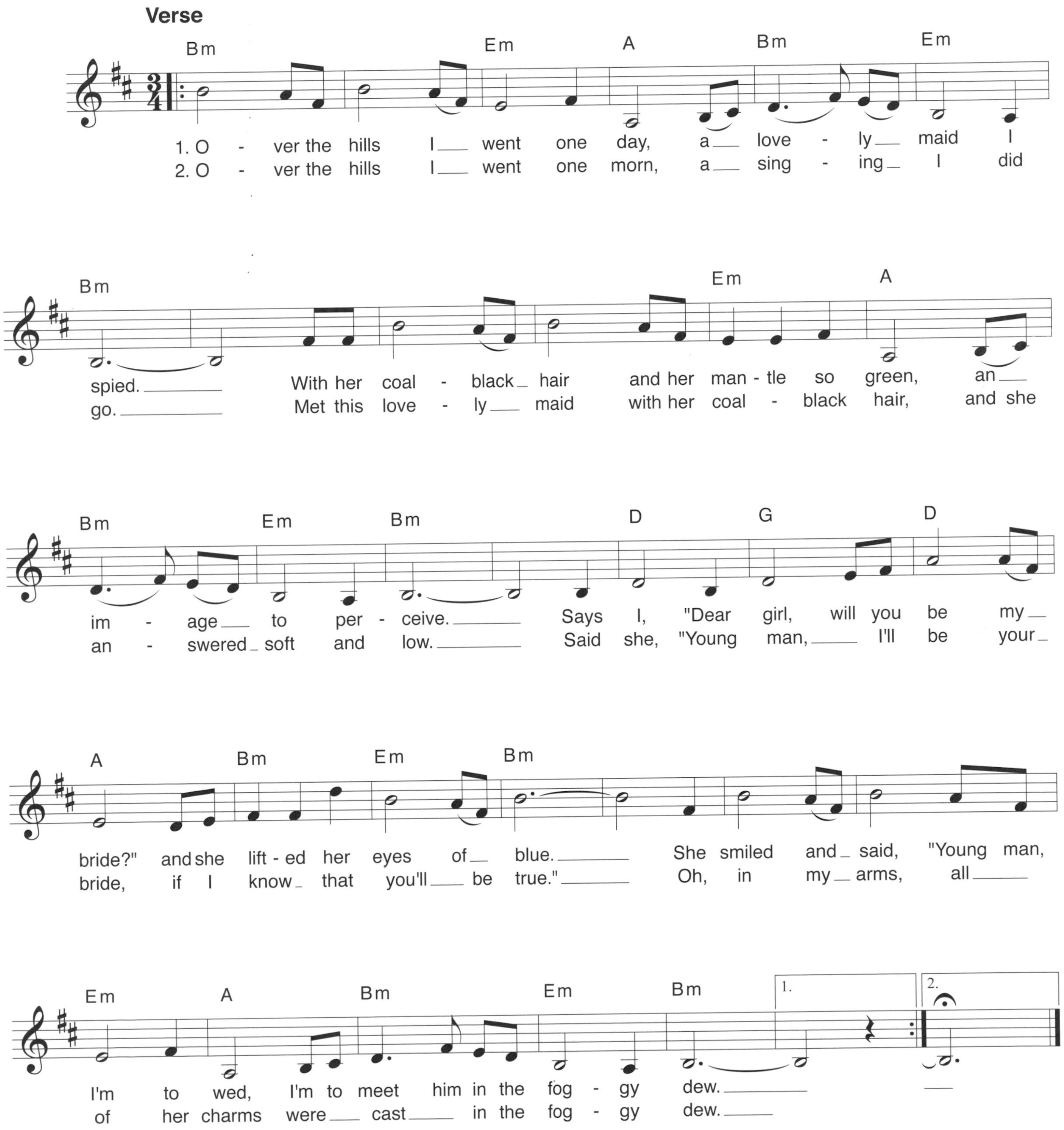
Verse
Bm Em A Bm Em
1. O - ver the hills I__ went one day, a__ love - ly__ maid I
2. O - ver the hills I__ went one morn, a__ sing - ing__ I did
Bm Em A
spied.__ With her coal - black__ hair and her man - tle so green, an__
go.__ Met this love - ly__ maid with her coal - black hair, and she
Bm Em Bm D G D
im - age__ to per - ceive.__ Says I, "Dear girl, will you be my__
an - swered__ soft and low.__ Said she, "Young man,__ I'll be your__
A Bm Em Bm
bride?" and she lift - ed her eyes of__ blue.__ She smiled and__ said, "Young man,
bride, if I know__ that you'll__ be true."__ Oh, in my__ arms, all__
Em A Bm Em Bm
1. 2.
I'm to wed, I'm to meet him in the fog - gy dew.__ __
of her charms were__ cast__ in the fog - gy dew.__

Standard Ukulele

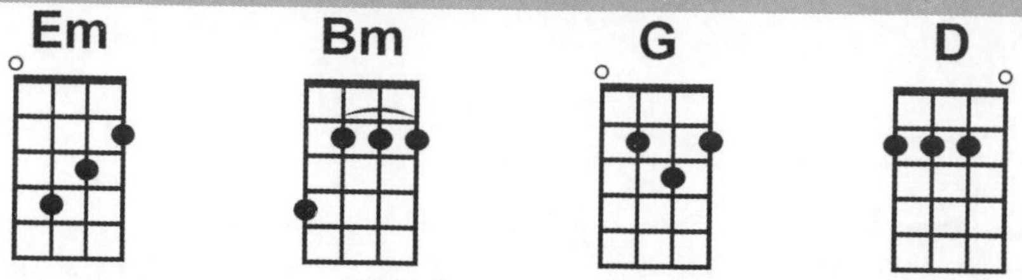
Em
Bm
G
D

Baritone Ukulele

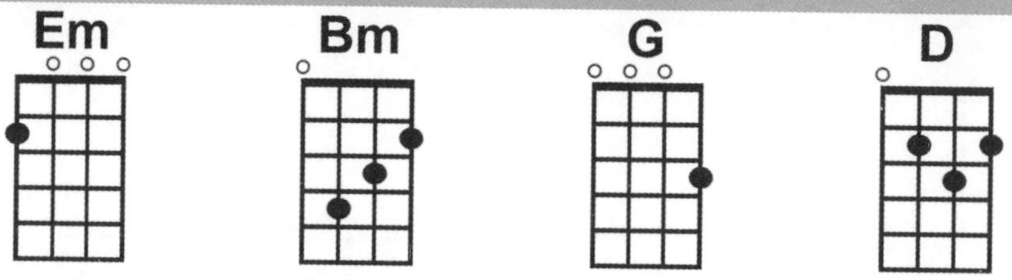
Em
Bm
G
D

Guitar

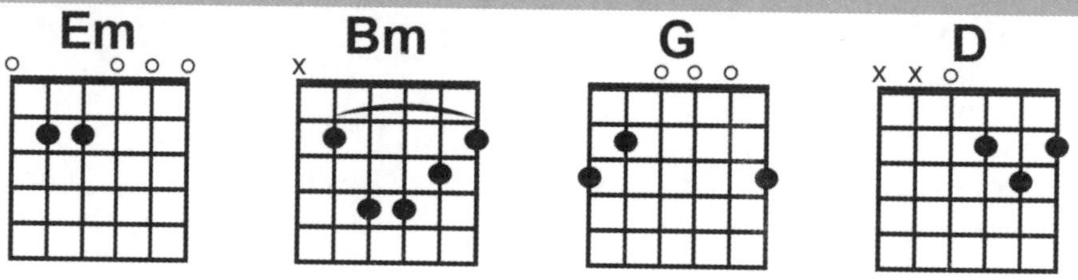
Em
Bm
G
D

Mandolin

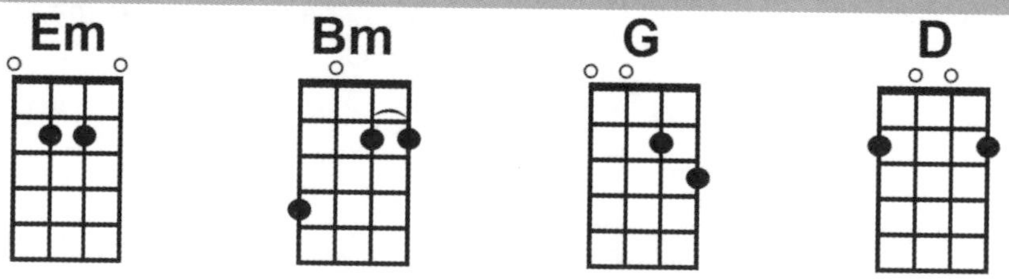
Em
Bm
G
D

Banjo

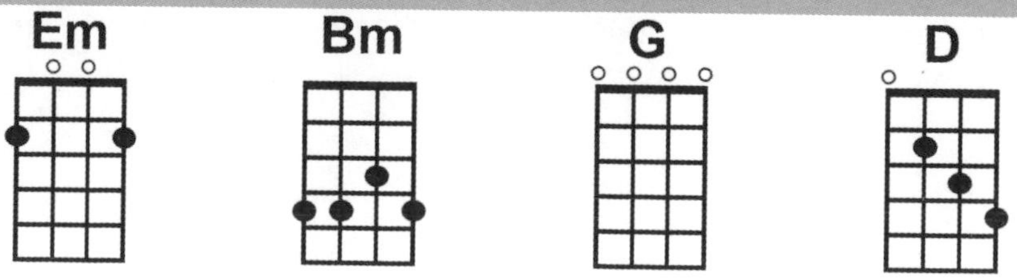
Em
Bm
G
D

Follow Me Up to Carlow

Traditional Irish Folk Song

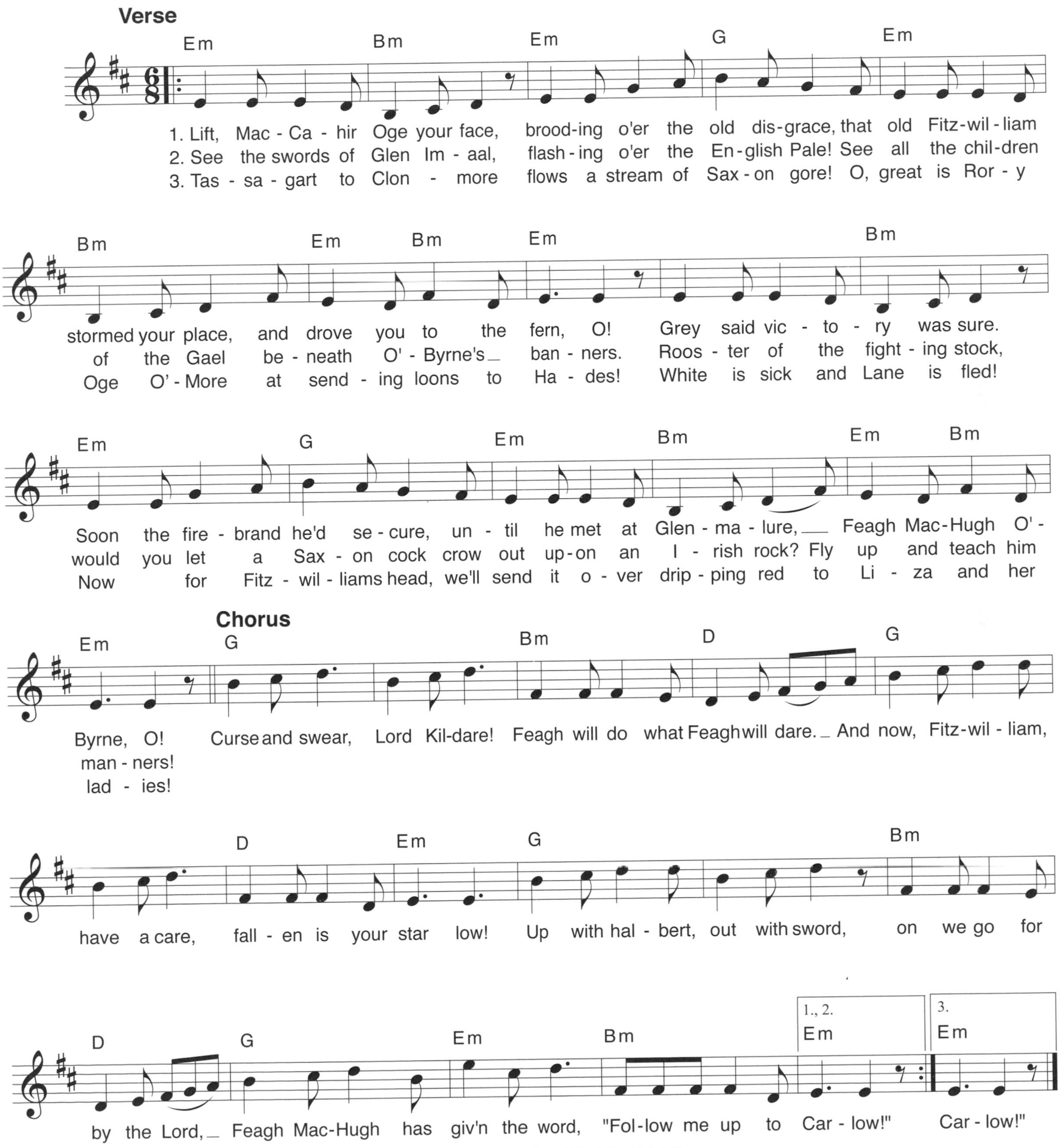
Verse
Em Bm Em G Em
1. Lift, Mac - Ca - hir Oge your face, brood-ing o'er the old dis-grace, that old Fitz-wil - liam
2. See the swords of Glen Im - aal, flash - ing o'er the En-glish Pale! See all the chil-dren
3. Tas - sa - gart to Clon - more flows a stream of Sax - on gore! O, great is Ror - y
Bm Em Bm Em Bm
stormed your place, and drove you to the fern, O! Grey said vic - to - ry was sure.
of the Gael be - neath O' - Byrne's_ ban - ners. Roos - ter of the fight - ing stock,
Oge O' - More at send - ing loons to Ha - des! White is sick and Lane is fled!
Em G Em Bm Em Bm
Soon the fire - brand he'd se - cure, un - til he met at Glen - ma - lure,___ Feagh Mac-Hugh O' -
would you let a Sax - on cock crow out up-on an I - rish rock? Fly up and teach him
Now for Fitz - wil - liams head, we'll send it o - ver drip - ping red to Li - za and her
Chorus
Em G Bm D G
Byrne, O! Curse and swear, Lord Kil-dare! Feagh will do what Feagh will dare._ And now, Fitz-wil - liam,
man - ners!
lad - ies!
D Em G Bm
have a care, fall - en is your star low! Up with hal - bert, out with sword, on we go for
1., 2. 3.
D G Em Bm Em Em
by the Lord,_ Feagh Mac-Hugh has giv'n the word, "Fol-low me up to Car - low!" Car - low!"

Standard Ukulele

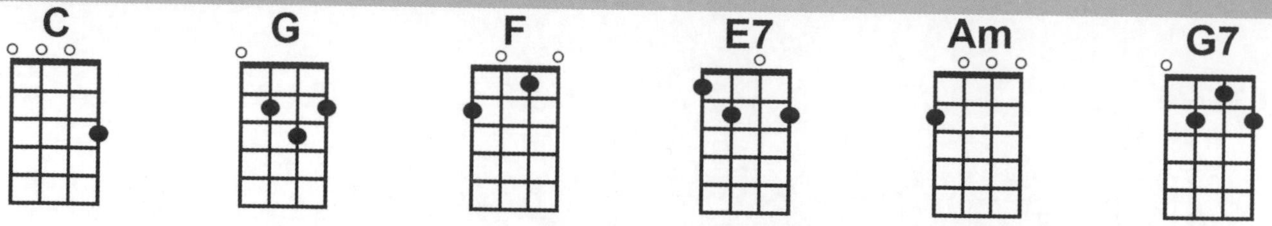
C
G
F
E7
Am
G7

Baritone Ukulele

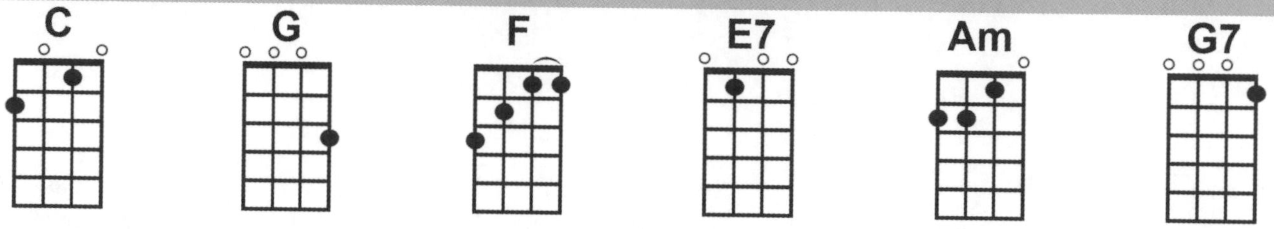
C
G
F
E7
Am
G7

Guitar

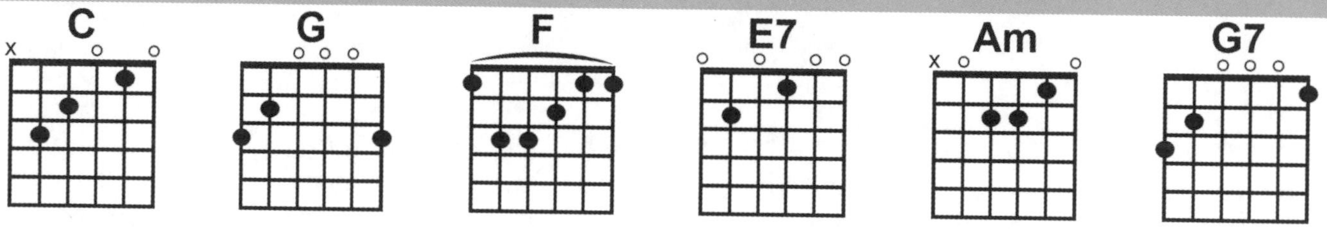
C
G
F
E7
Am
G7

Mandolin

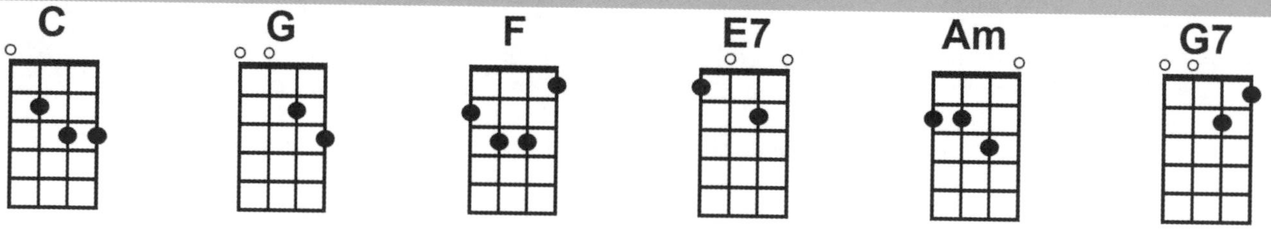
C
G
F
E7
Am
G7

Banjo

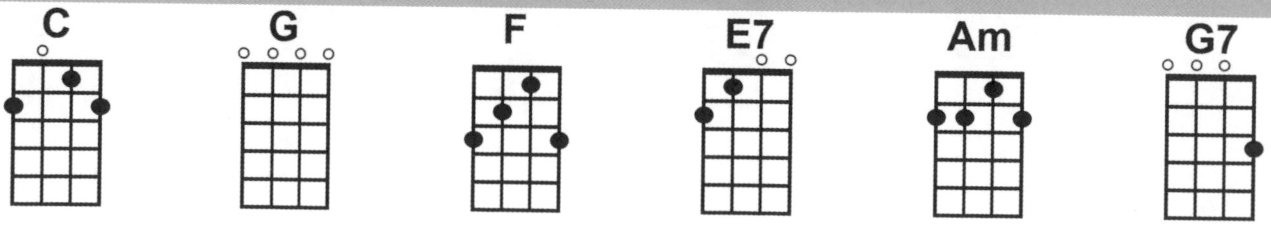
C
G
F
E7
Am
G7

Garryowen

Irish Folk Song

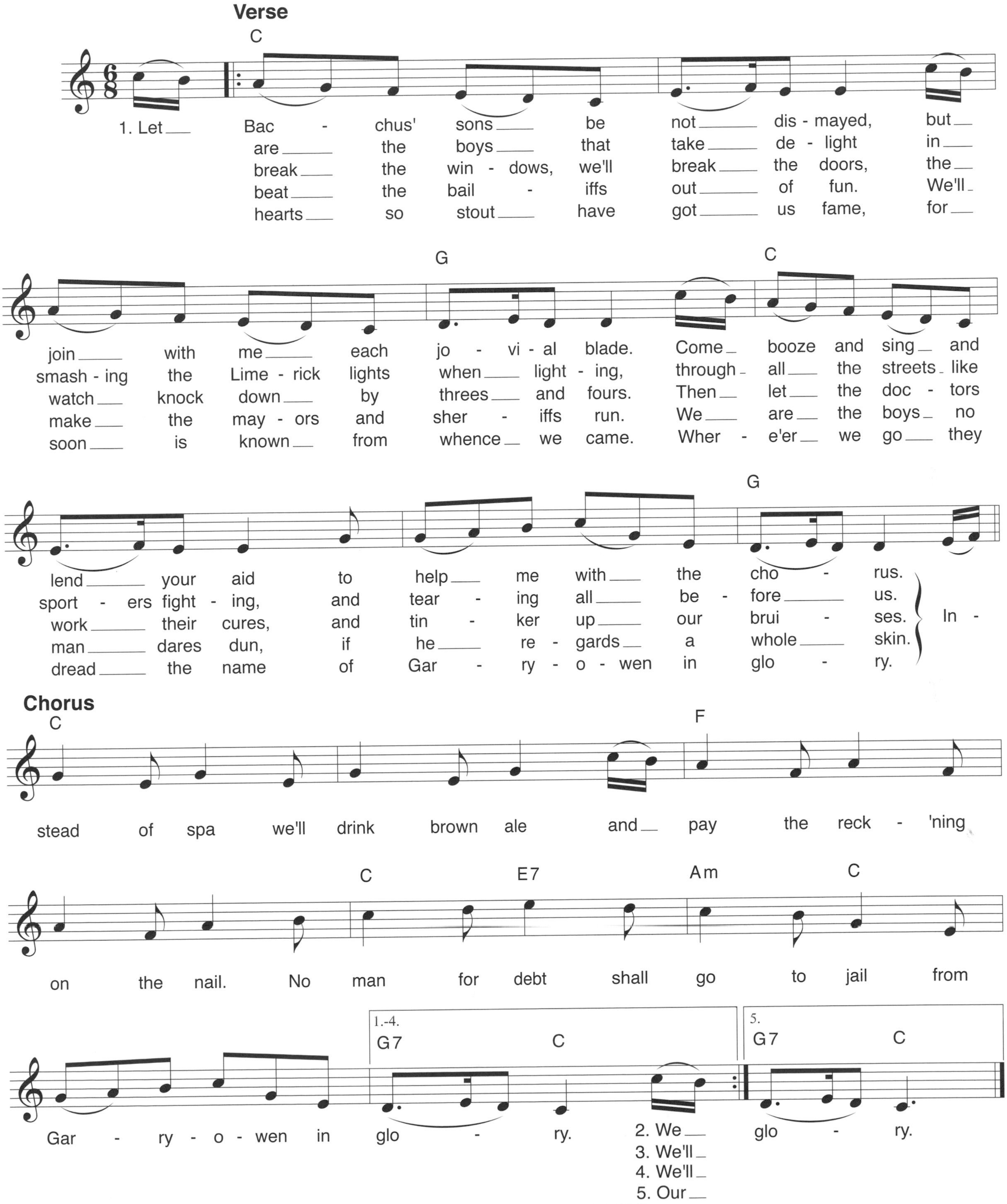
Verse
C G C G
1. Let Bac - chus' sons be not dis - mayed, but join with me each jo - vi - al blade. Come booze and sing and lend your aid to help me with the cho - rus.
are the boys that take de - light in smash - ing the Lime - rick lights when light - ing, through all the streets like sport - ers fight - ing, and tear - ing all be - fore us.
break the win - dows, we'll break the doors, the watch knock down by threes and fours. Then let the doc - tors work their cures, and tin - ker up our brui - ses.
beat the bail - iffs out of fun. We'll make the may - ors and sher - iffs run. We are the boys no man dares dun, if he re - gards a whole skin.
hearts so stout have got us fame, for soon is known from whence we came. Wher - e'er we go they dread the name of Gar - ry - o - wen in glo - ry.
Chorus
C F C E7 Am C
In - stead of spa we'll drink brown ale and pay the reck - 'ning on the nail. No man for debt shall go to jail from Gar - ry - o - wen in
1.-4.
G7 C
glo - ry.
2. We
3. We'll
4. We'll
5. Our
5.
G7 C
glo - ry.

Standard Ukulele

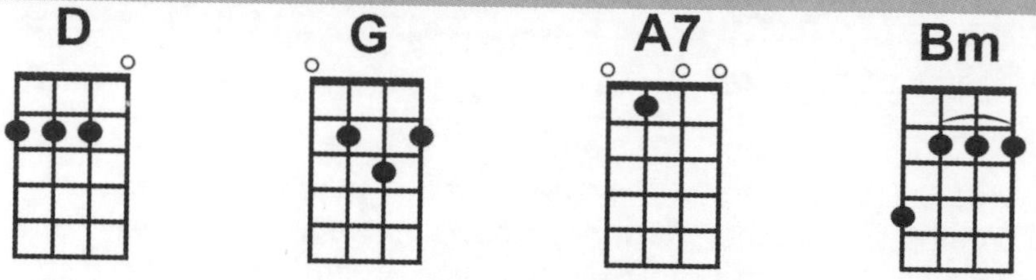
D
G
A7
Bm

Baritone Ukulele

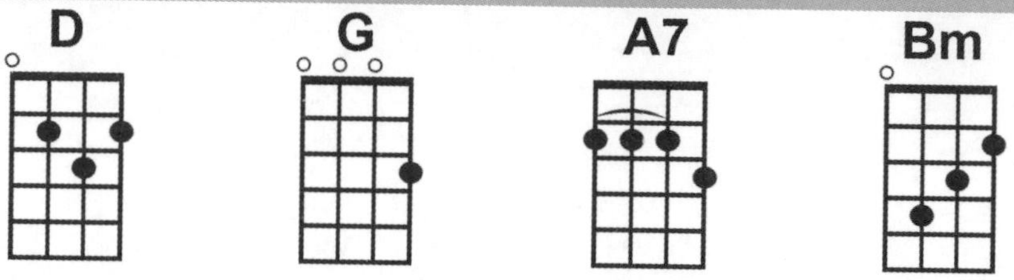
D
G
A7
Bm

Guitar

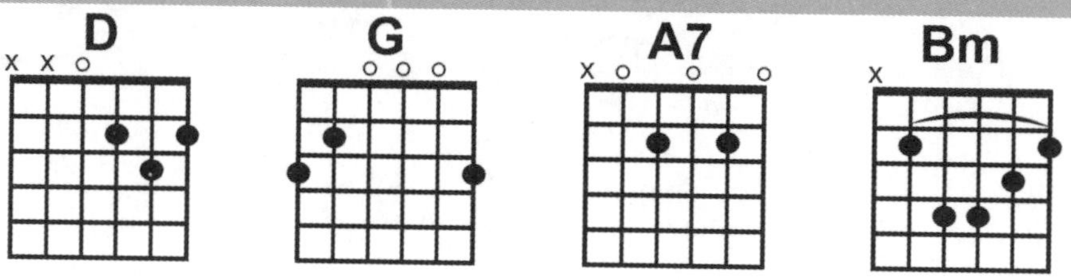
D
G
A7
Bm

Mandolin

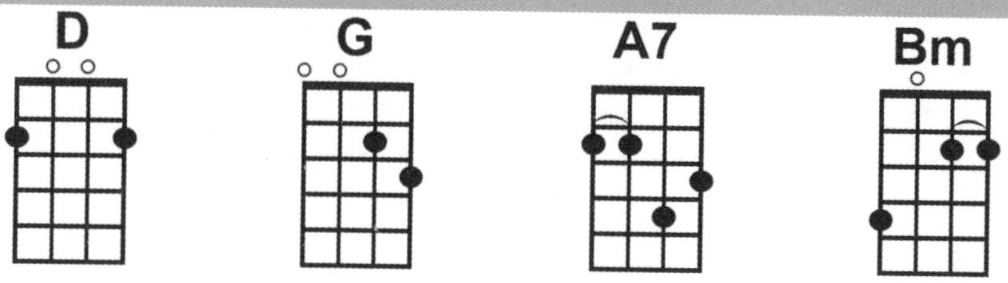
D
G
A7
Bm

Banjo

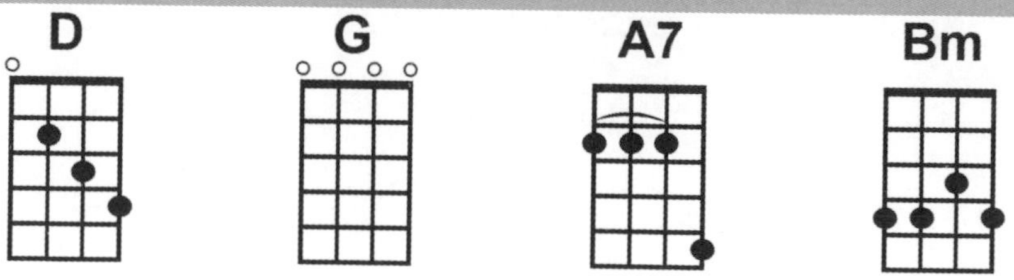
D
G
A7
Bm

Girl I Left Behind Me

Traditional Irish Folk Song

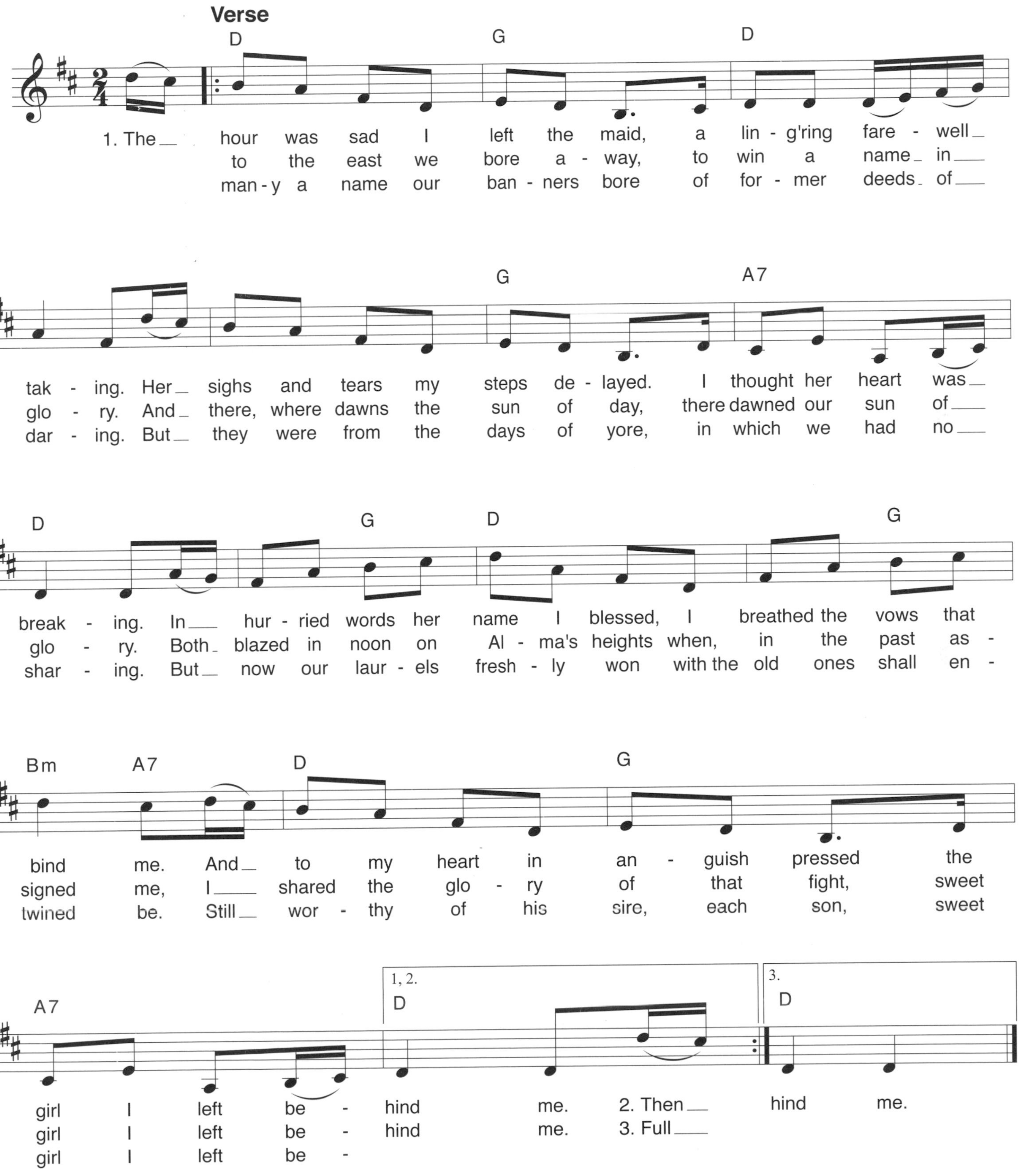
Verse
D G D
1. The hour was sad I left the maid, a lin - g'ring fare - well
to the east we bore a - way, to win a name in
man - y a name our ban - ners bore of for - mer deeds of
G A7
tak - ing. Her sighs and tears my steps de - layed. I thought her heart was
glo - ry. And there, where dawns the sun of day, there dawned our sun of
dar - ing. But they were from the days of yore, in which we had no
D G D G
break - ing. In hur - ried words her name I blessed, I breathed the vows that
glo - ry. Both blazed in noon on Al - ma's heights when, in the past as -
shar - ing. But now our laur - els fresh - ly won with the old ones shall en -
Bm A7 D G
bind me. And to my heart in an - guish pressed the
signed me, I shared the glo - ry of that fight, sweet
twined be. Still wor - thy of his sire, each son, sweet
A7
1, 2.
D
3.
D
girl I left be - hind me. 2. Then hind me.
girl I left be - hind me. 3. Full
girl I left be -

Standard Ukulele

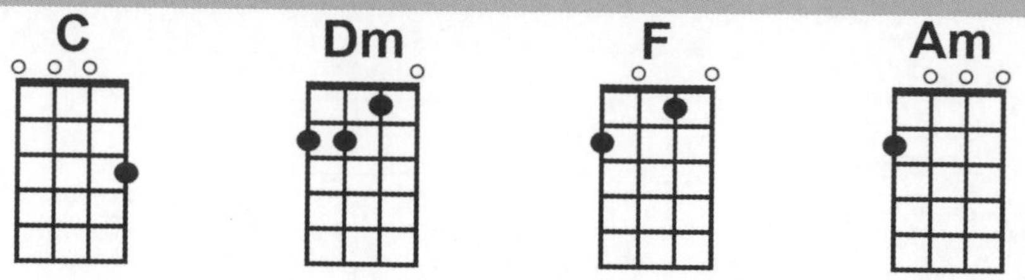

Baritone Ukulele

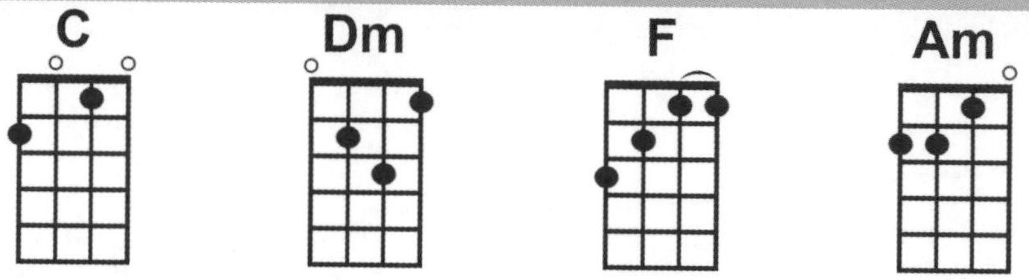

Guitar

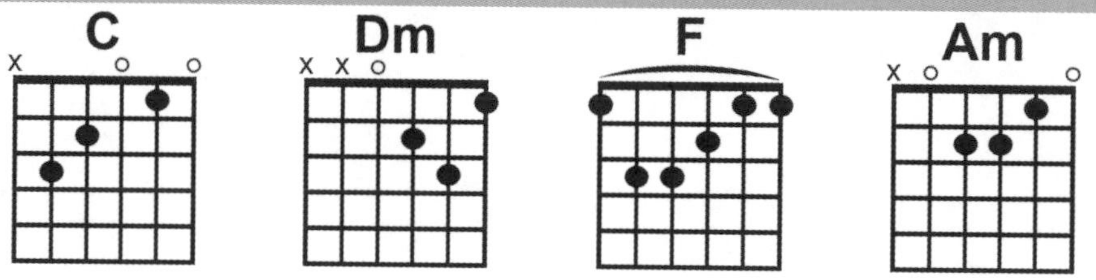

Mandolin

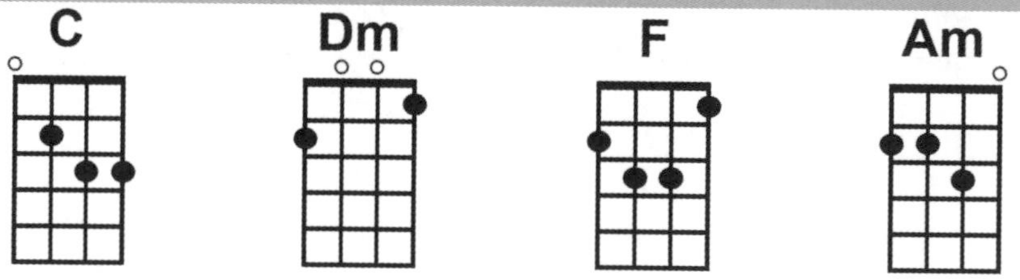

Banjo

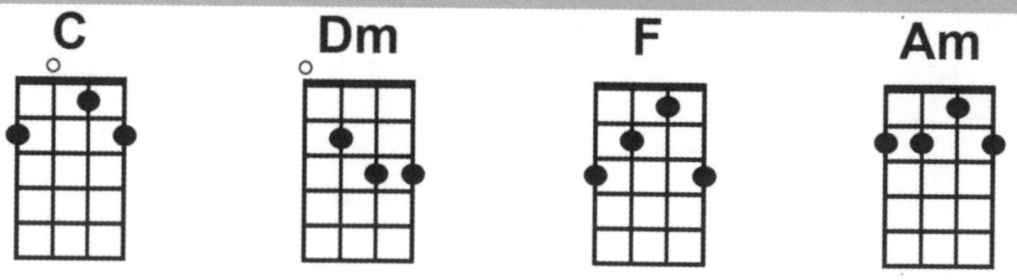

Green Grow the Rushes, O

Traditional Irish Folk Song

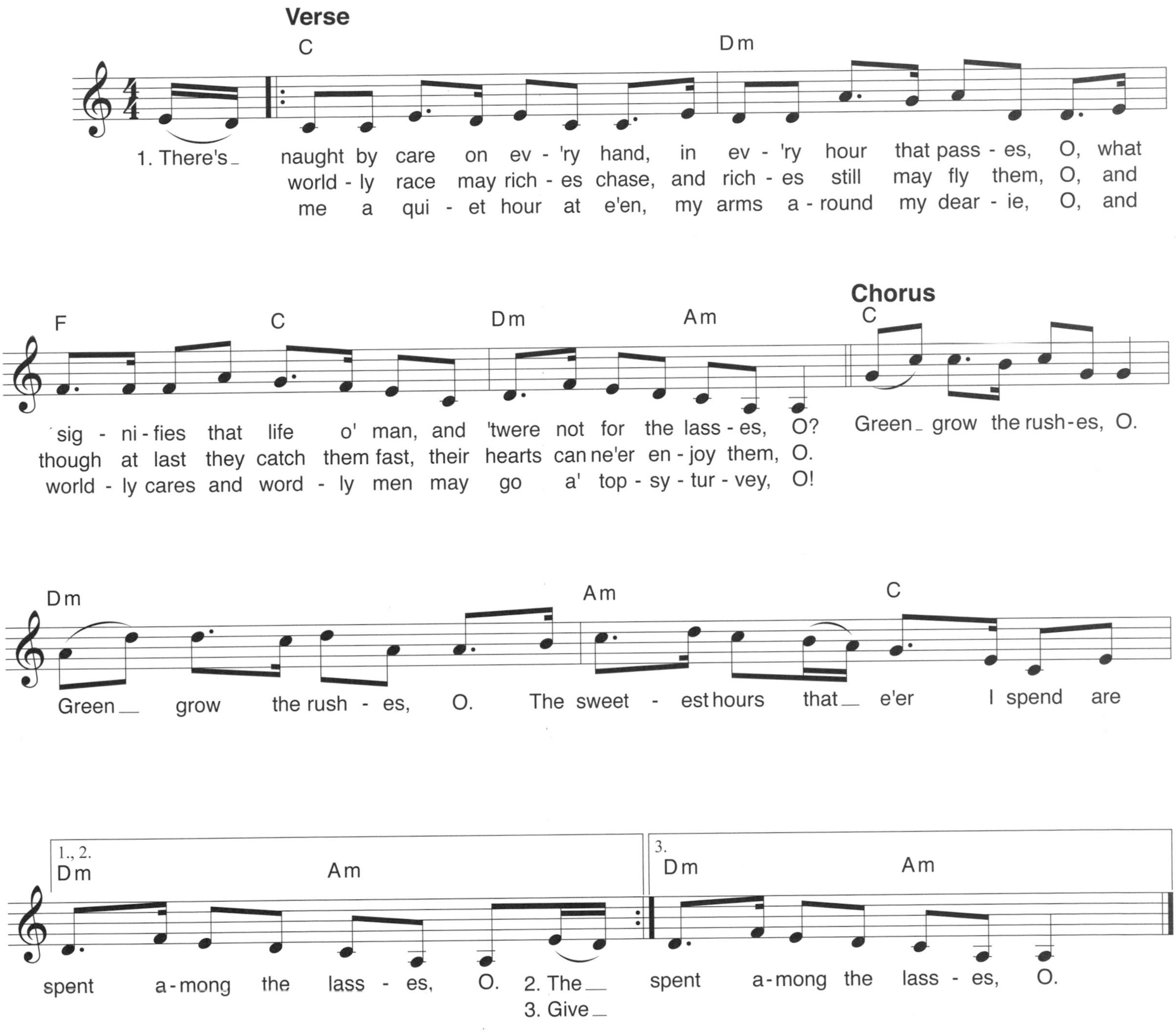
Verse
C
Dm
1. There's naught by care on ev - 'ry hand, in ev - 'ry hour that pass - es, O, what
world - ly race may rich - es chase, and rich - es still may fly them, O, and
me a qui - et hour at e'en, my arms a - round my dear - ie, O, and
F
C
Dm
Am
sig - ni - fies that life o' man, and 'twere not for the lass - es, O?
though at last they catch them fast, their hearts can ne'er en - joy them, O.
world - ly cares and word - ly men may go a' top - sy - tur - vey, O!
Chorus
C
Green grow the rush - es, O.
Dm
Am
C
Green grow the rush - es, O. The sweet - est hours that e'er I spend are
1., 2.
Dm
Am
spent a - mong the lass - es, O. 2. The
3. Give
3.
Dm
Am
spent a - mong the lass - es, O.

Standard Ukulele

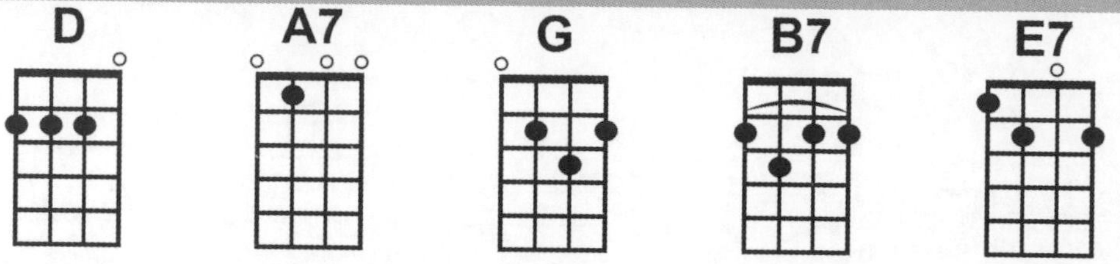
D
A7
G
B7
E7

Baritone Ukulele

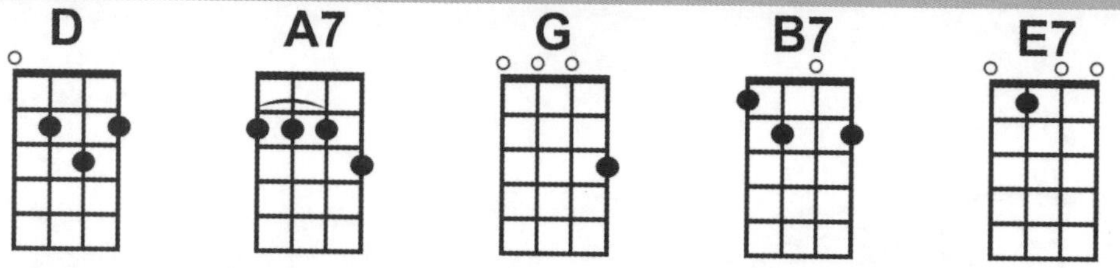
D
A7
G
B7
E7

Guitar

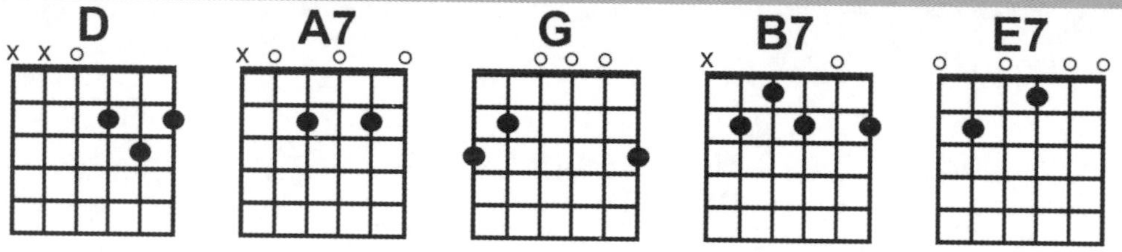
D
A7
G
B7
E7

Mandolin

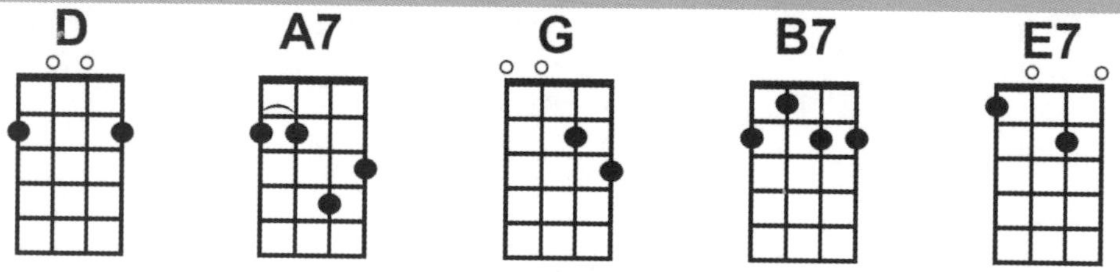
D
A7
G
B7
E7

Banjo

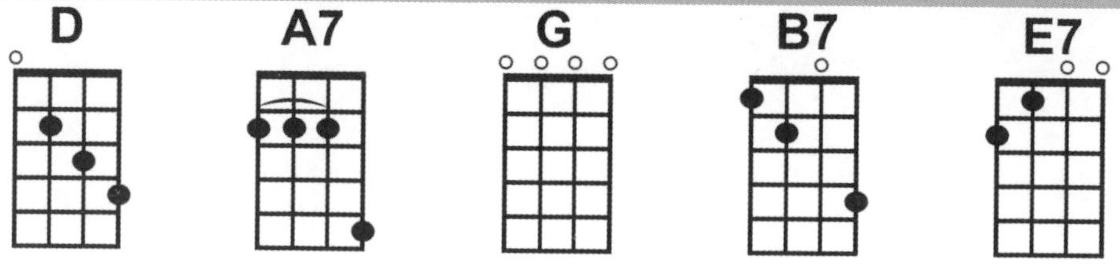
D
A7
G
B7
E7

Green Grows the Laurel

Traditional Irish Folk Song

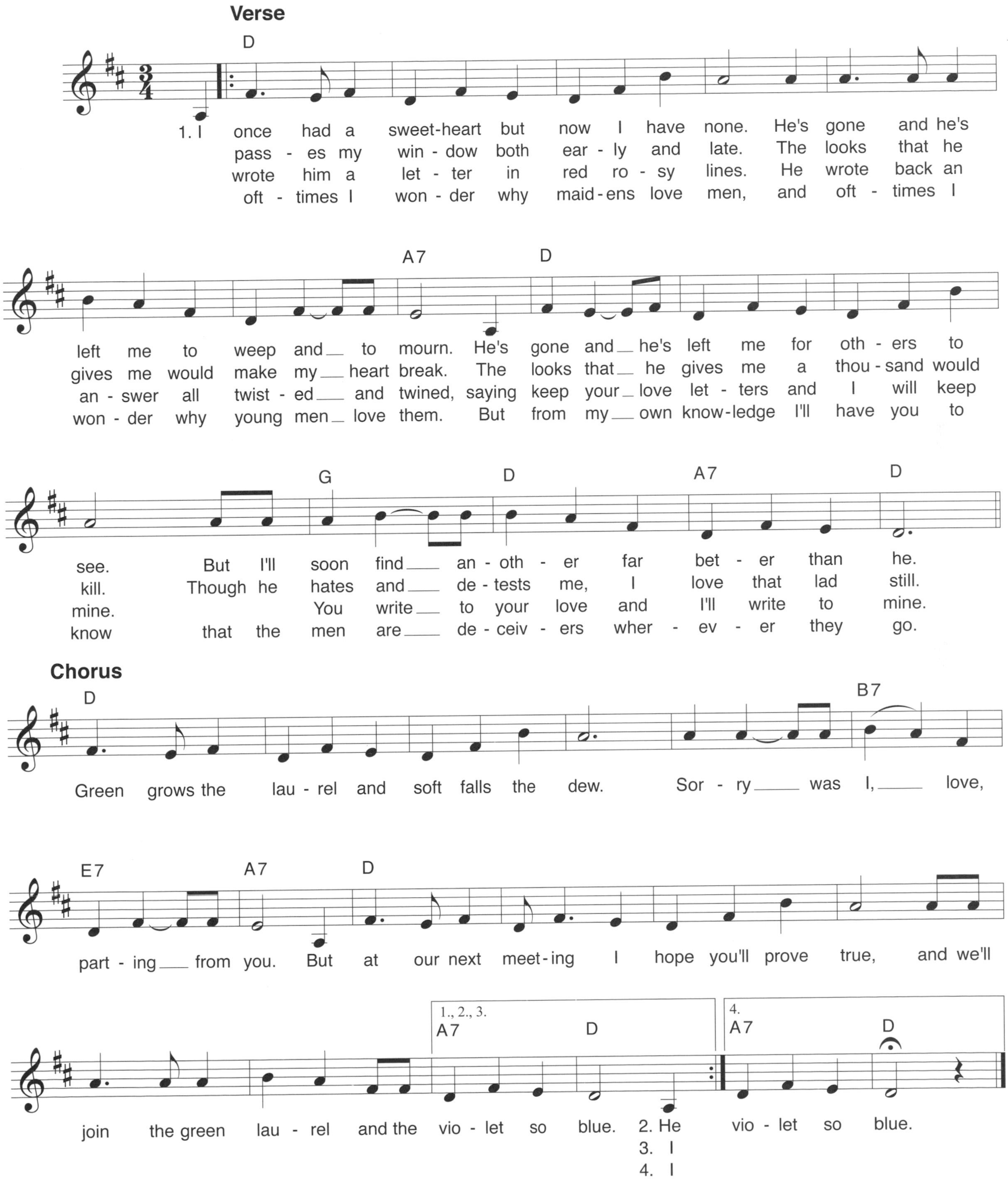
Verse
D
1. I once had a sweet-heart but now I have none. He's gone and he's left me to weep and to mourn. He's gone and he's left me for oth - ers to see. But I'll soon find an - oth - er far bet - er than he.
pass - es my win - dow both ear - ly and late. The looks that he gives me would make my heart break. The looks that he gives me a thou - sand would kill. Though he hates and de - tests me, I love that lad still.
wrote him a let - ter in red ro - sy lines. He wrote back an an - swer all twist - ed and twined, saying keep your love let - ters and I will keep mine. You write to your love and I'll write to mine.
oft - times I won - der why maid - ens love men, and oft - times I won - der why young men love them. But from my own know - ledge I'll have you to know that the men are de - ceiv - ers wher - ev - er they go.
A7
D
G
D
A7
D
Chorus
D
Green grows the lau - rel and soft falls the dew. Sor - ry was I, love,
B7
E7
A7
D
part - ing from you. But at our next meet - ing I hope you'll prove true, and we'll
join the green lau - rel and the vio - let so blue.
1., 2., 3.
A7
D
2. He
3. I
4. I
4.
A7
D
vio - let so blue.

Standard Ukulele

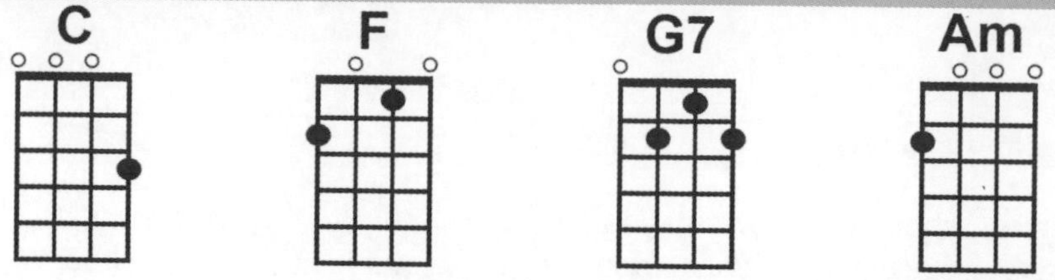
C
F
G7
Am

Baritone Ukulele

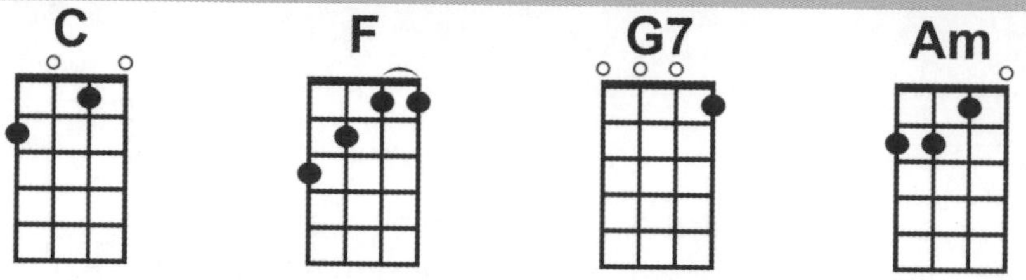
C
F
G7
Am

Guitar

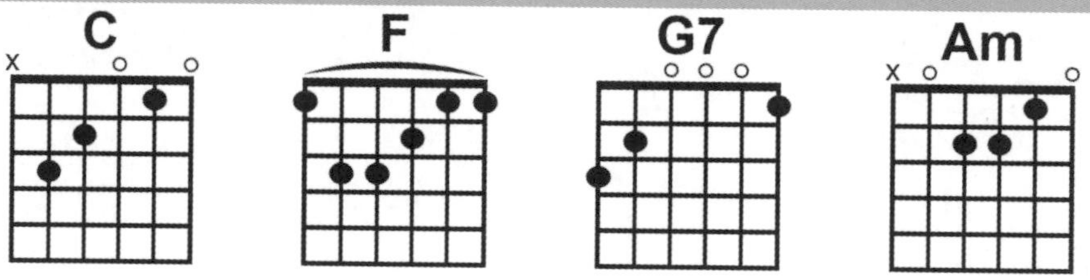
C
F
G7
Am

Mandolin

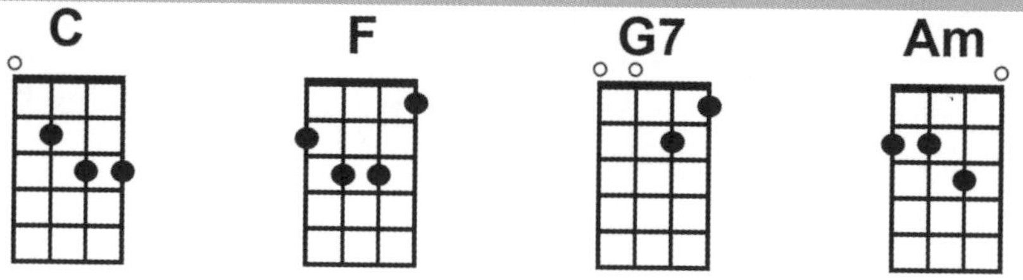
C
F
G7
Am

Banjo

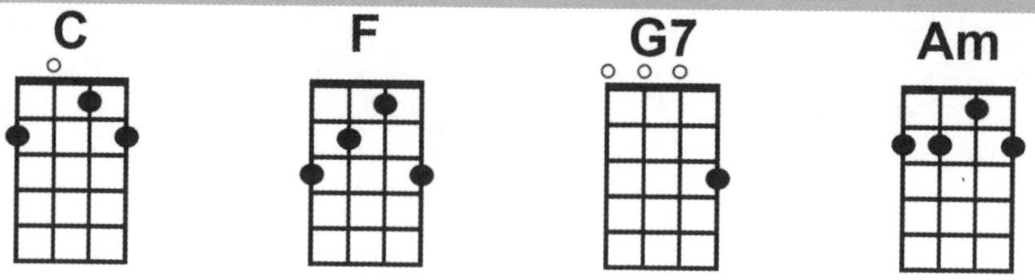
C
F
G7
Am

The Harp That Once

Traditional Irish Folk Song

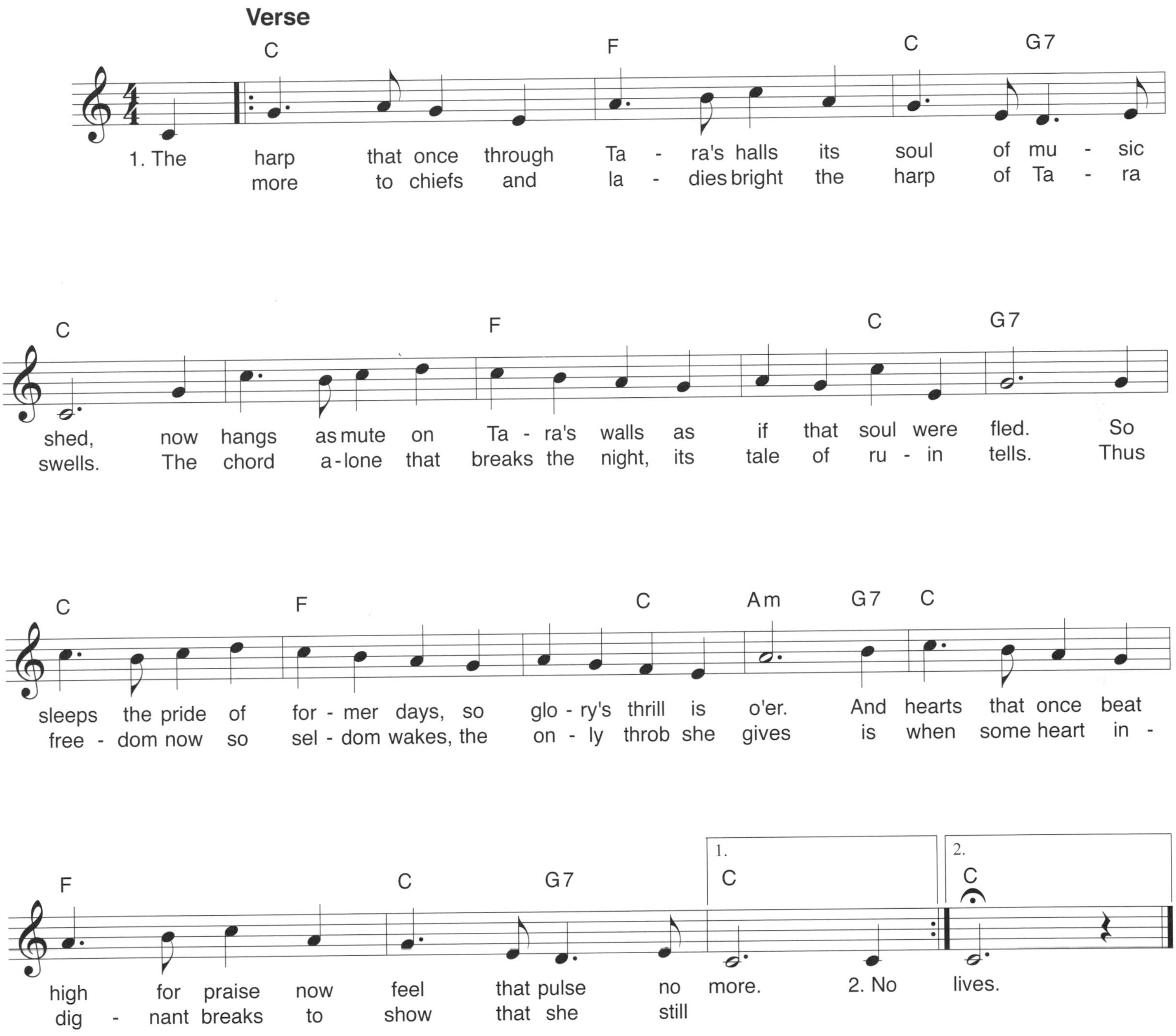
Verse
C F C G7
1. The harp that once through Ta - ra's halls its soul of mu - sic
more to chiefs and la - dies bright the harp of Ta - ra
C F C G7
shed, now hangs as mute on Ta - ra's walls as if that soul were fled. So
swells. The chord a - lone that breaks the night, its tale of ru - in tells. Thus
C F C Am G7 C
sleeps the pride of for - mer days, so glo - ry's thrill is o'er. And hearts that once beat
free - dom now so sel - dom wakes, the on - ly throb she gives is when some heart in -
F C G7
1. C
2. C
high for praise now feel that pulse no more. 2. No lives.
dig - nant breaks to show that she still

Standard Ukulele

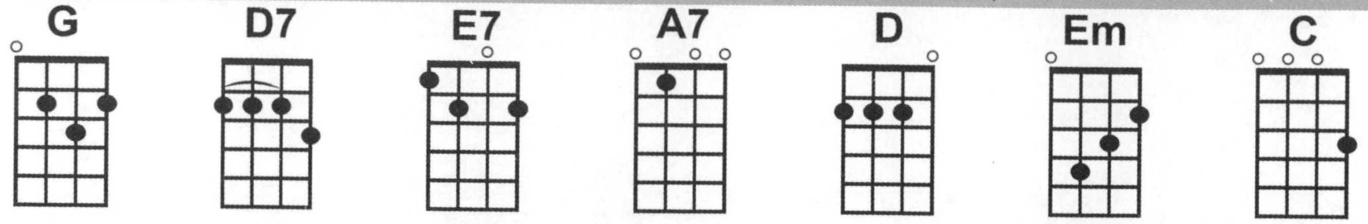
G
D7
E7
A7
D
Em
C

Baritone Ukulele

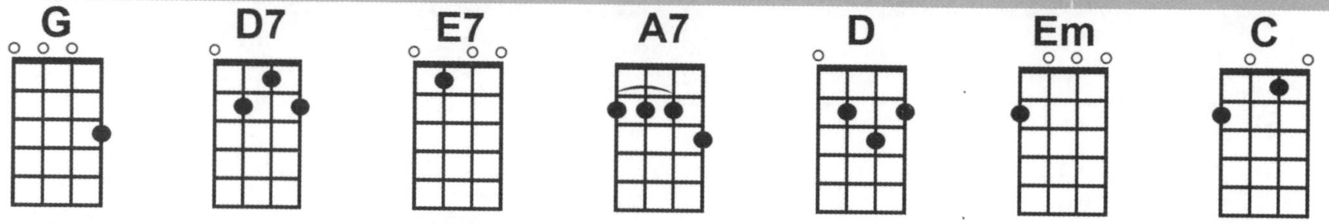
G
D7
E7
A7
D
Em
C

Guitar

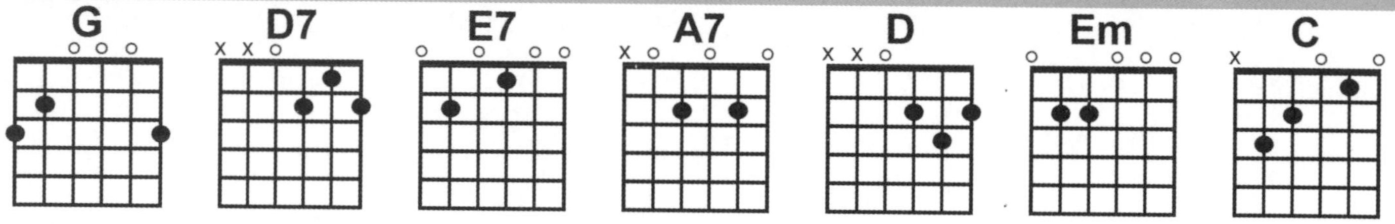
G
D7
E7
A7
D
Em
C

Mandolin

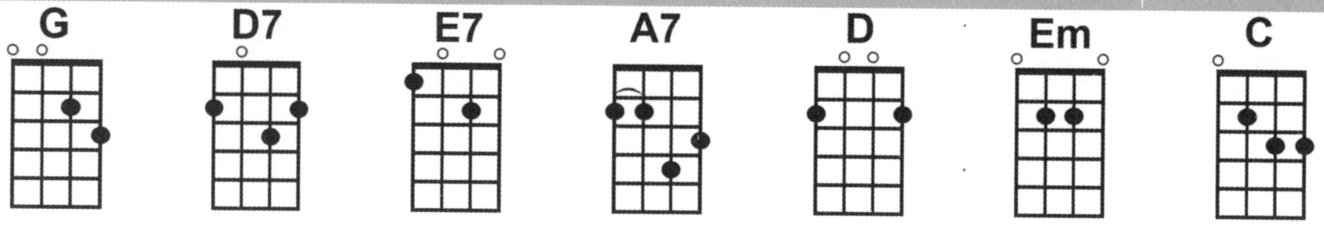
G
D7
E7
A7
D
Em
C

Banjo

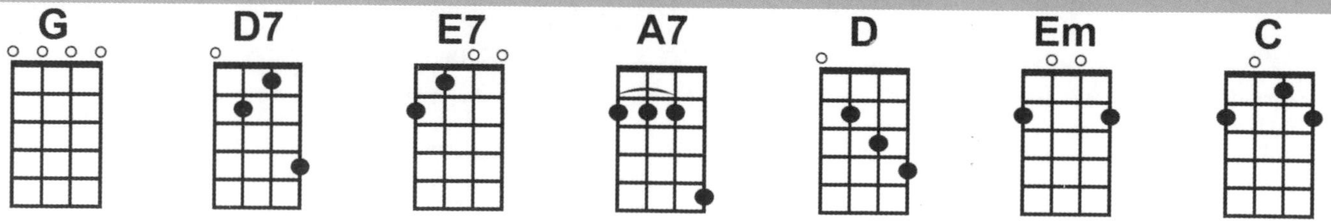
G
D7
E7
A7
D
Em
C

Has Anybody Here Seen Kelly?

Words and Music by C.W. Murphy, Will Letters and William J. McKenna

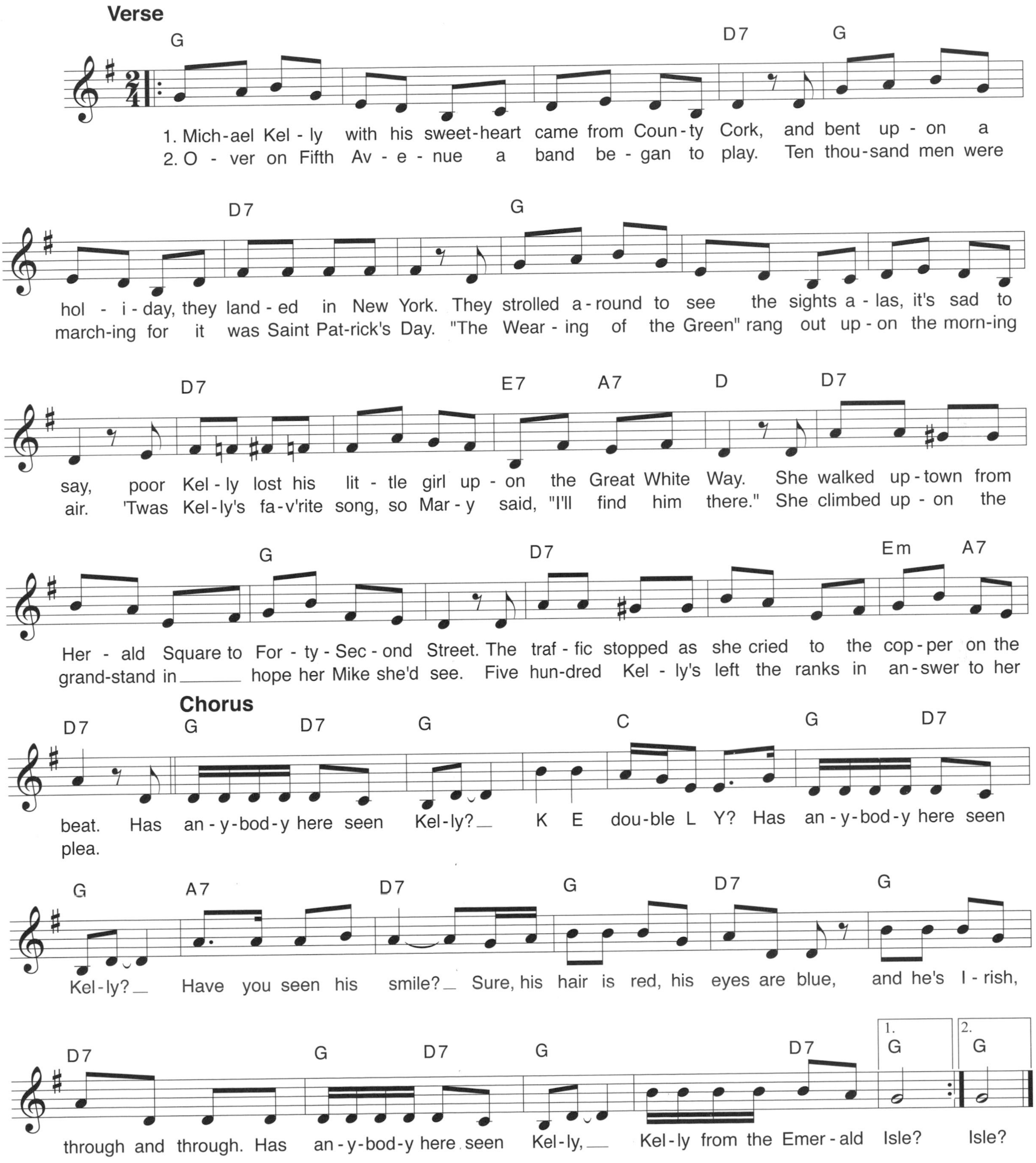
Verse
G D7 G
1. Mich-ael Kel - ly with his sweet-heart came from Coun - ty Cork, and bent up - on a
2. O - ver on Fifth Av - e - nue a band be - gan to play. Ten thou-sand men were
D7 G
hol - i - day, they land - ed in New York. They strolled a - round to see the sights a - las, it's sad to
march-ing for it was Saint Pat-rick's Day. "The Wear - ing of the Green" rang out up - on the morn-ing
D7 E7 A7 D D7
say, poor Kel - ly lost his lit - tle girl up - on the Great White Way. She walked up - town from
air. 'Twas Kel-ly's fa-v'rite song, so Mar - y said, "I'll find him there." She climbed up - on the
G D7 Em A7
Her - ald Square to For - ty - Sec - ond Street. The traf - fic stopped as she cried to the cop-per on the
grand-stand in____ hope her Mike she'd see. Five hun-dred Kel - ly's left the ranks in an-swer to her
Chorus
D7 G D7 G C G D7
beat. Has an - y - bod - y here seen Kel-ly?__ K E dou-ble L Y? Has an - y - bod - y here seen
plea.
G A7 D7 G D7 G
Kel-ly?__ Have you seen his smile?__ Sure, his hair is red, his eyes are blue, and he's I - rish,
D7 G D7 G D7 1. G 2. G
through and through. Has an - y - bod - y here seen Kel-ly,__ Kel-ly from the Emer - ald Isle? Isle?

Standard Ukulele

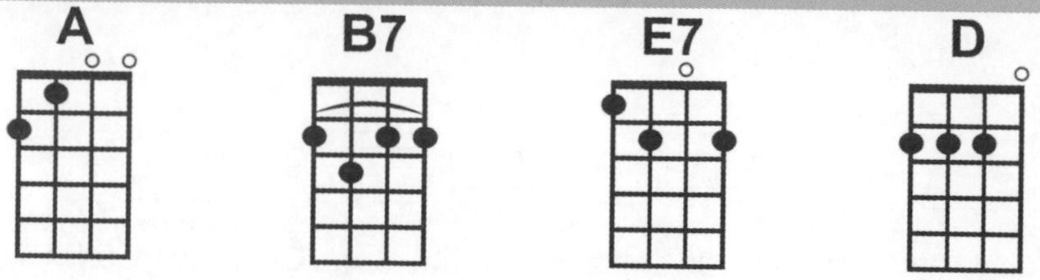
A
B7
E7
D

Baritone Ukulele

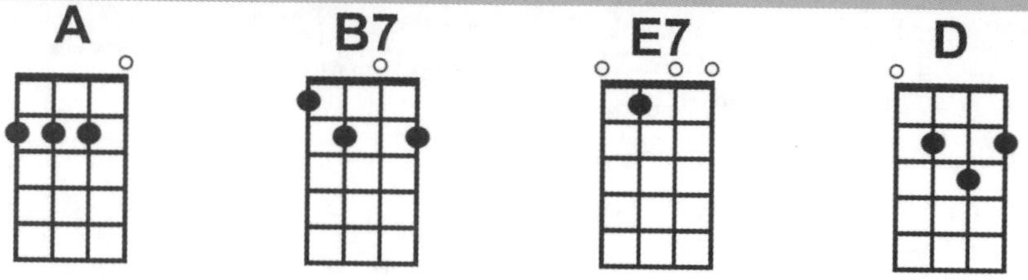
A
B7
E7
D

Guitar

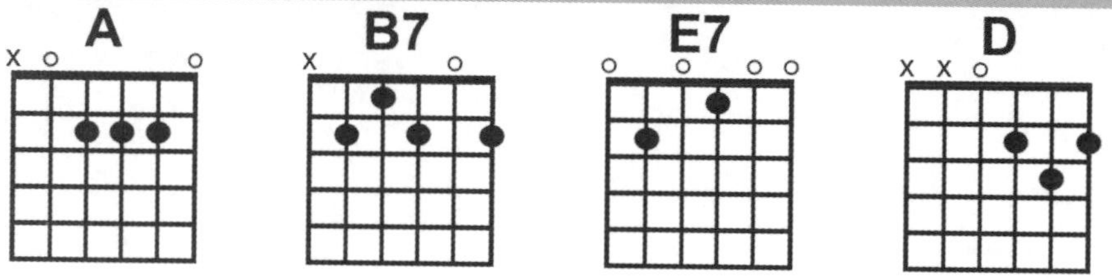
A
B7
E7
D

Mandolin

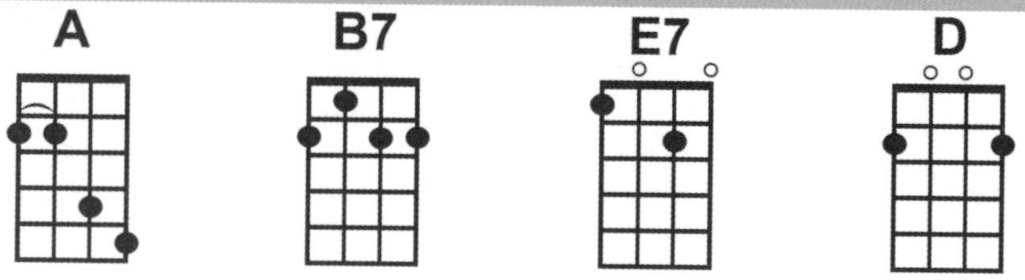
A
B7
E7
D

Banjo

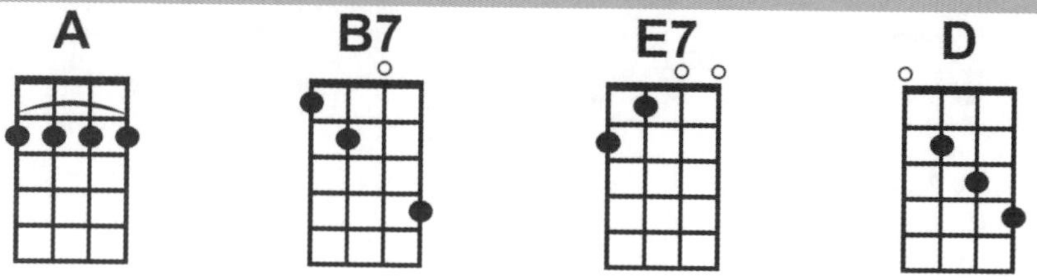
A
B7
E7
D

A Highland Lad My Love Was Born

Traditional Folk Melody
Lyrics by Robert Burns

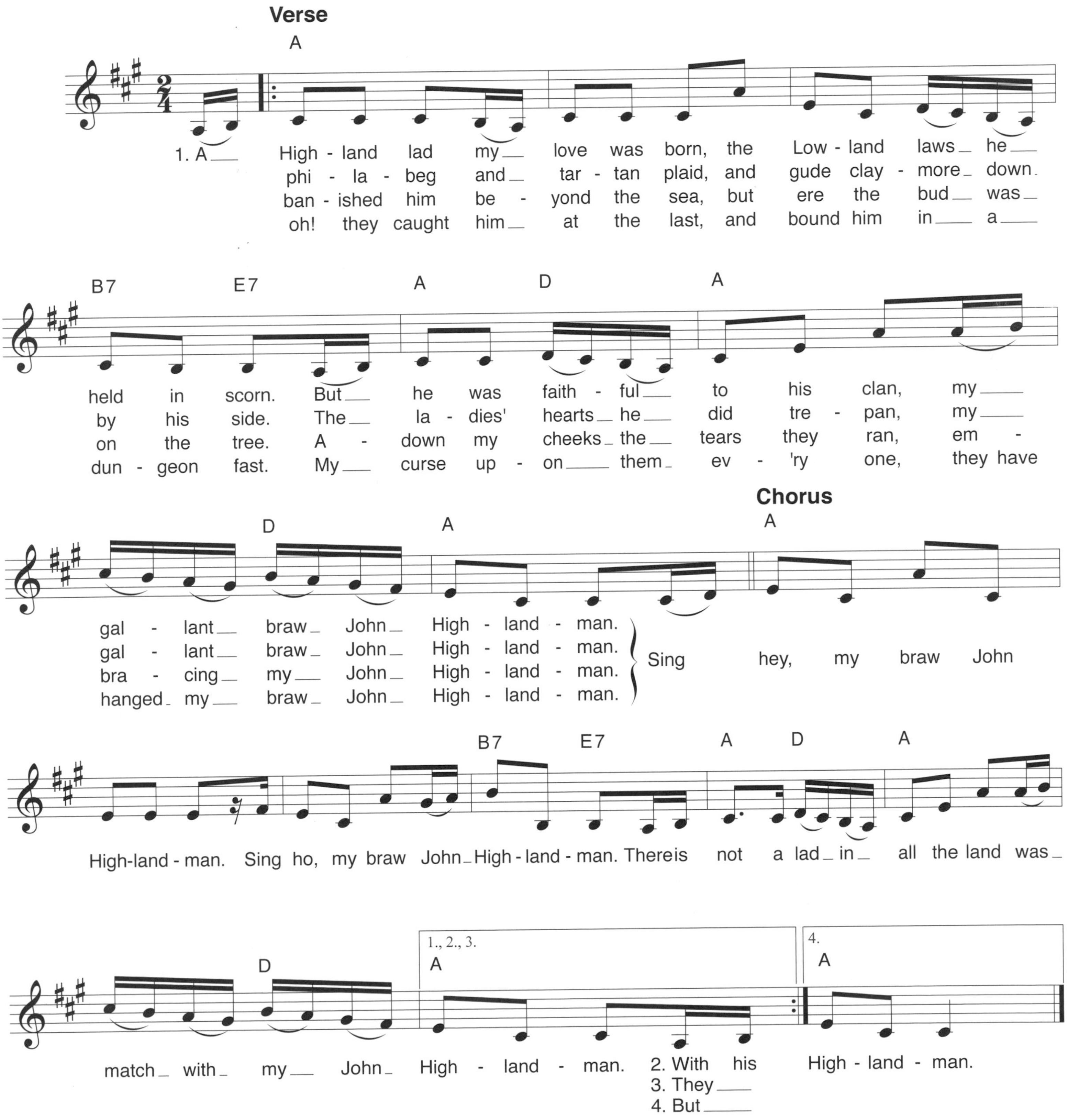
Verse
A
1. A High - land lad my love was born, the Low - land laws he
phi - la - beg and tar - tan plaid, and gude clay - more down
ban - ished him be - yond the sea, but ere the bud was
oh! they caught him at the last, and bound him in a
B7 E7 A D A
held in scorn. But he was faith - ful to his clan, my
by his side. The la - dies' hearts he did tre - pan, my
on the tree. A - down my cheeks the tears they ran, em -
dun - geon fast. My curse up - on them ev - 'ry one, they have
D A
gal - lant braw John High - land - man.
gal - lant braw John High - land - man.
bra - cing my John High - land - man.
hanged my braw John High - land - man.
Chorus
A
Sing hey, my braw John
B7 E7 A D A
High-land - man. Sing ho, my braw John High - land - man. Thereis not a lad in all the land was
D
1., 2., 3.
A
4.
A
match with my John High - land - man. 2. With his
3. They
4. But
High - land - man.

Standard Ukulele

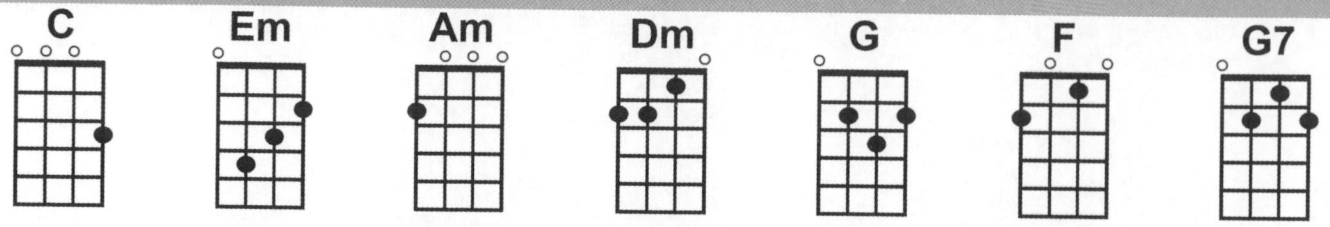
C
Em
Am
Dm
G
F
G7

Baritone Ukulele

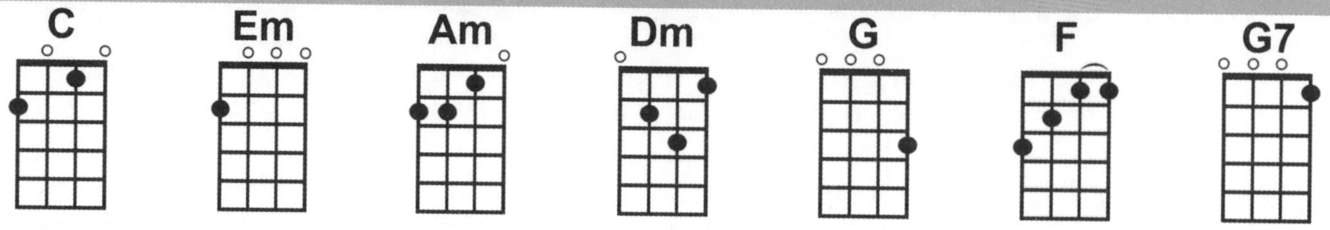
C
Em
Am
Dm
G
F
G7

Guitar

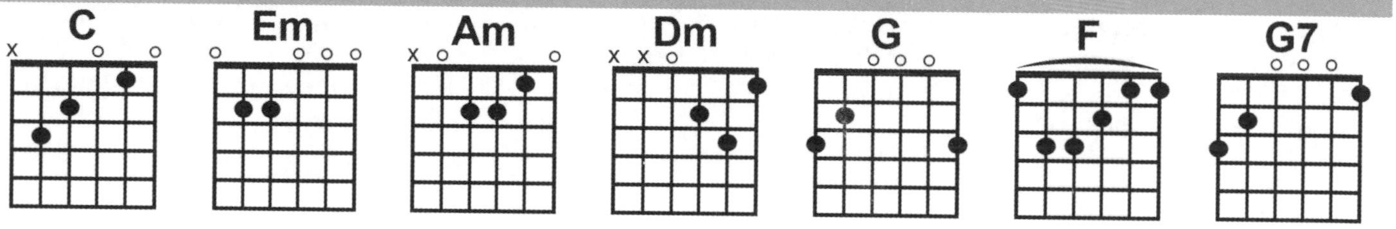
C
Em
Am
Dm
G
F
G7

Mandolin

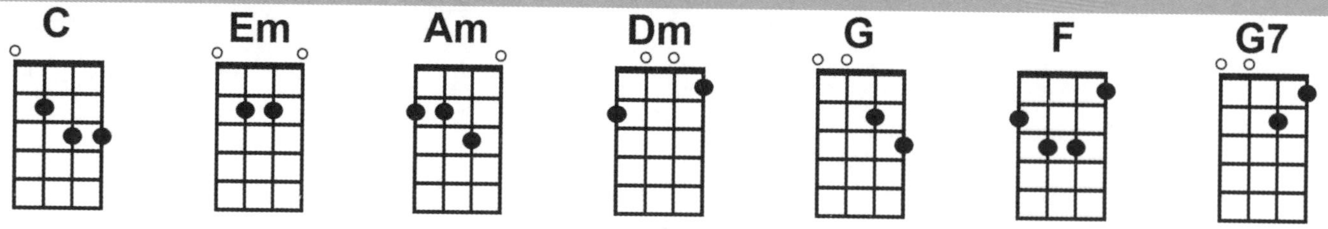
C
Em
Am
Dm
G
F
G7

Banjo

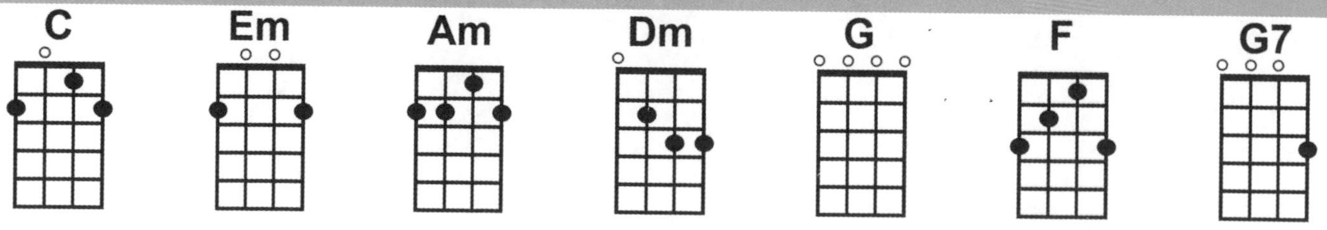
C
Em
Am
Dm
G
F
G7

I Know Where I'm Goin'

Folksong

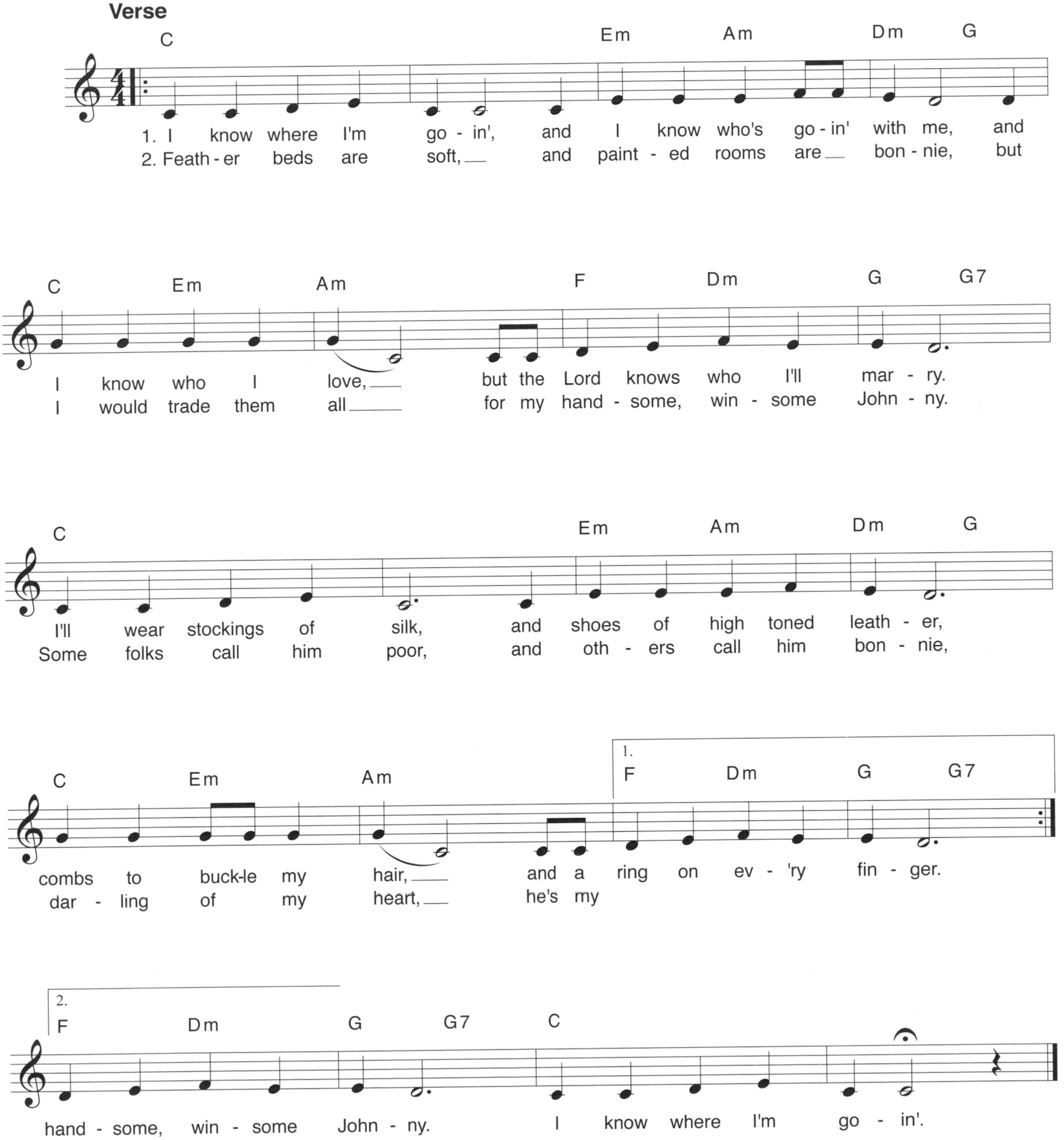
Verse
C Em Am Dm G
1. I know where I'm go - in', and I know who's go - in' with me, and
2. Feath - er beds are soft, and paint - ed rooms are bon - nie, but
C Em Am F Dm G G7
I know who I love, but the Lord knows who I'll mar - ry.
I would trade them all for my hand - some, win - some John - ny.
C Em Am Dm G
I'll wear stockings of silk, and shoes of high toned leath - er,
Some folks call him poor, and oth - ers call him bon - nie,
C Em Am
combs to buck-le my hair, and a
dar - ling of my heart, he's my
1.
F Dm G G7
ring on ev - 'ry fin - ger.
2.
F Dm G G7 C
hand - some, win - some John - ny. I know where I'm go - in'.

Standard Ukulele

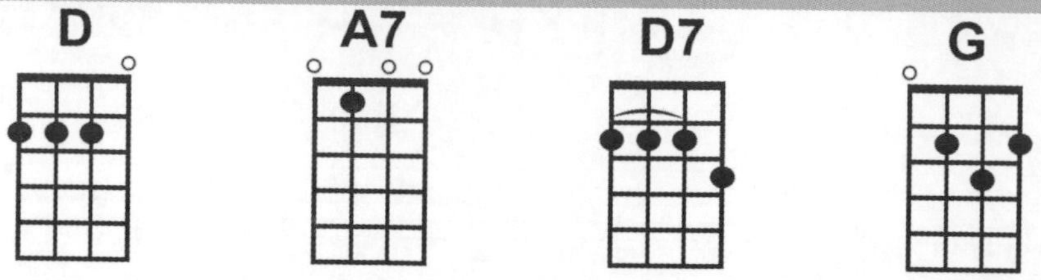
D
A7
D7
G

Baritone Ukulele

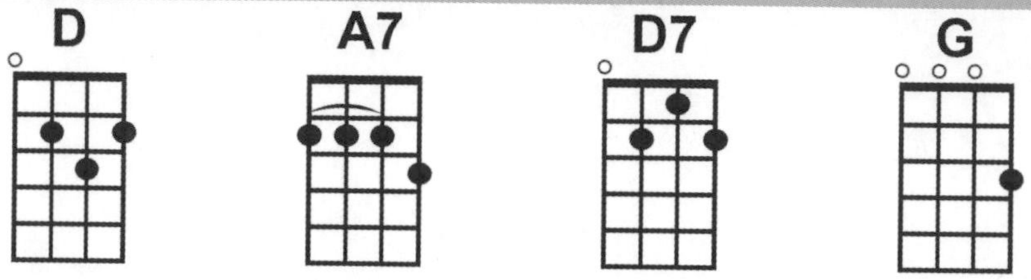
D
A7
D7
G

Guitar

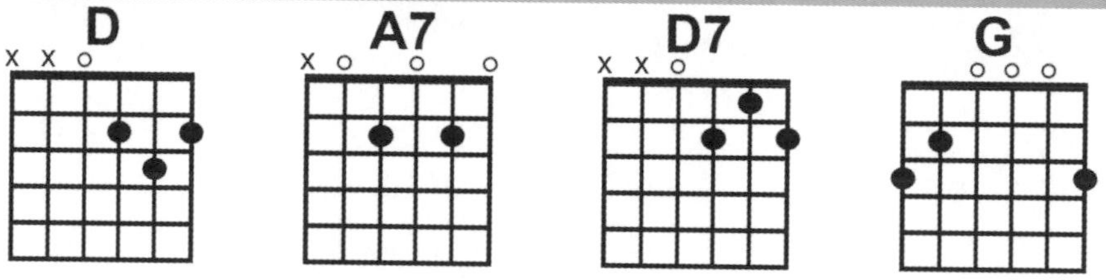
D
A7
D7
G

Mandolin

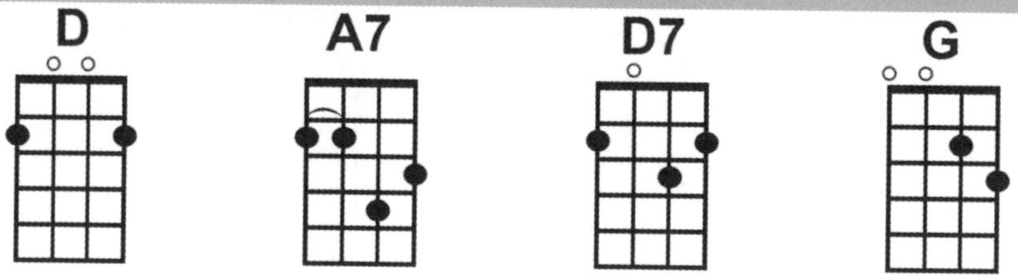
D
A7
D7
G

Banjo

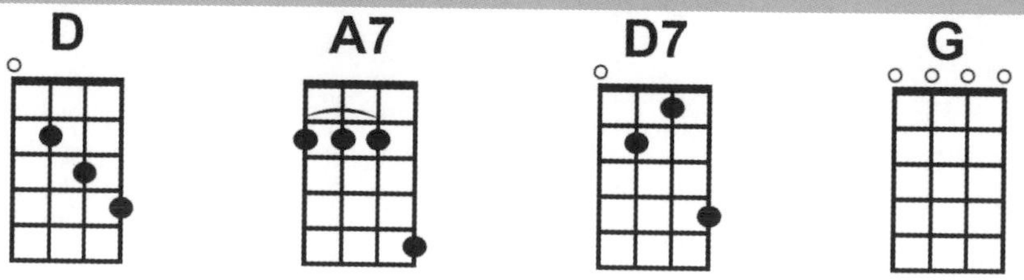
D
A7
D7
G

I Never Will Marry

Irish Folk Song

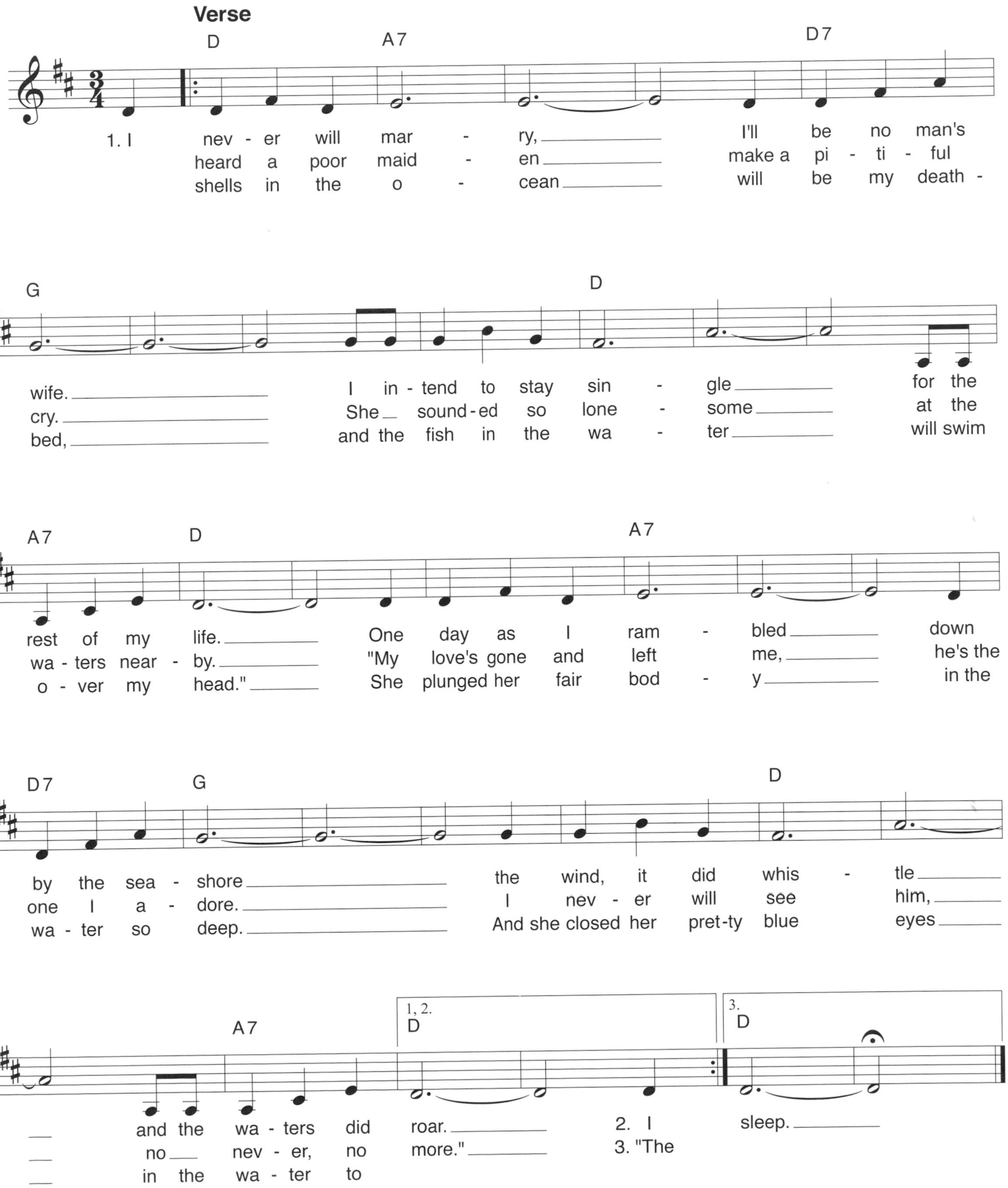
Verse
D A7 D7
1. I nev - er will mar - ry, I'll be no man's
heard a poor maid - en make a pi - ti - ful
shells in the o - cean will be my death -
G D
wife. I in - tend to stay sin - gle for the
cry. She sound - ed so lone - some at the
bed, and the fish in the wa - ter will swim
A7 D A7
rest of my life. One day as I ram - bled down
wa - ters near - by. "My love's gone and left me, he's the
o - ver my head." She plunged her fair bod - y in the
D7 G D
by the sea - shore the wind, it did whis - tle
one I a - dore. I nev - er will see him,
wa - ter so deep. And she closed her pret-ty blue eyes
A7 1, 2. D 3. D
and the wa - ters did roar. 2. I sleep.
no nev - er, no more." 3. "The
in the wa - ter to

Standard Ukulele

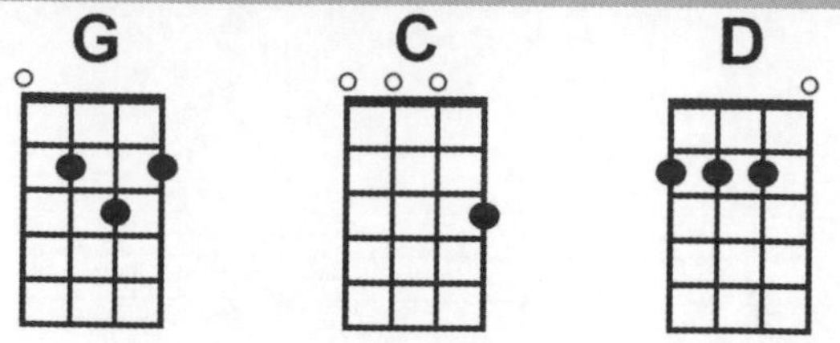

Baritone Ukulele

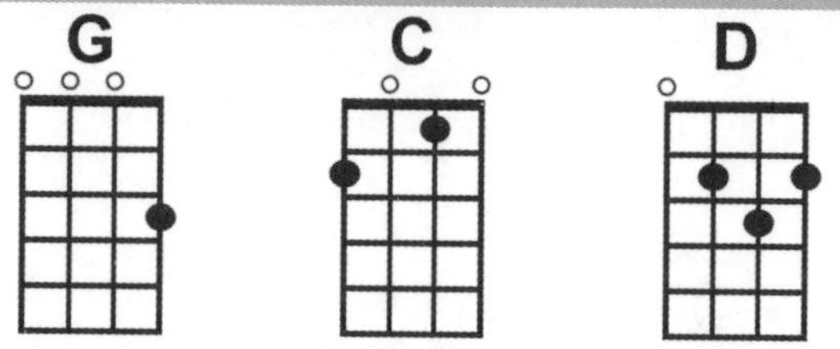

Guitar

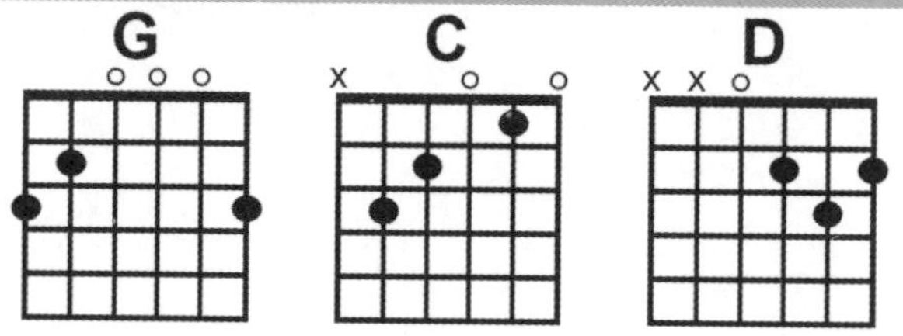

Mandolin

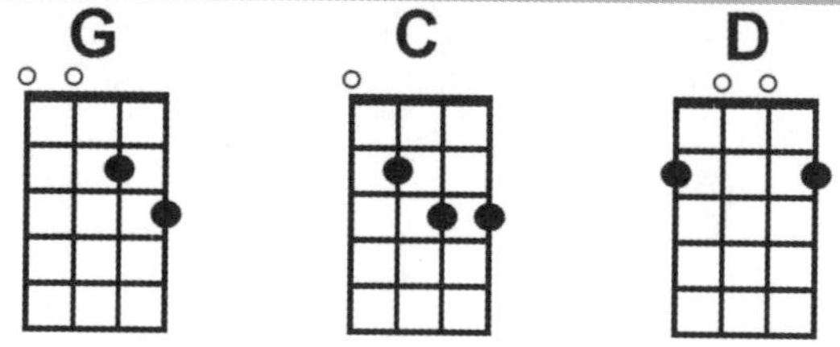

Banjo

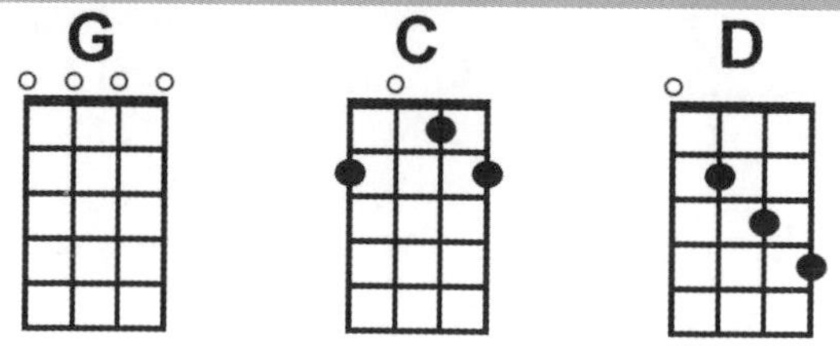

I Wish I Had Someone to Love Me

Irish Folk Song

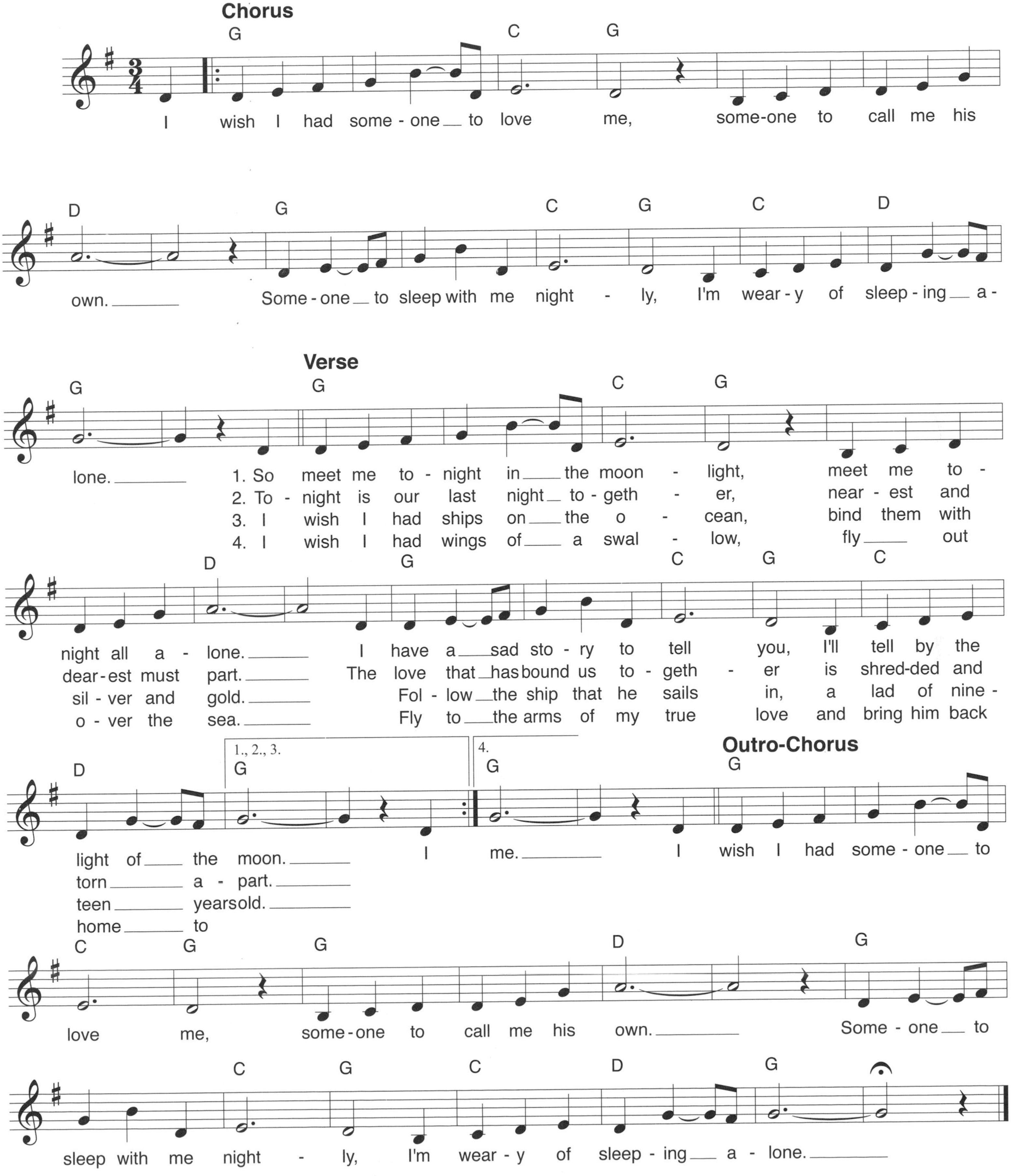
Chorus
G C G
I wish I had some - one to love me, some-one to call me his
D G C G C D
own. Some - one to sleep with me night - ly, I'm wear - y of sleep - ing a -
Verse
G G C G
lone. 1. So meet me to - night in the moon - light, meet me to -
2. To - night is our last night to - geth - er, near - est and
3. I wish I had ships on the o - cean, bind them with
4. I wish I had wings of a swal - low, fly out
D G C G C
night all a - lone. I have a sad sto - ry to tell you, I'll tell by the
dear - est must part. The love that has bound us to - geth - er is shred - ded and
sil - ver and gold. Fol - low the ship that he sails in, a lad of nine -
o - ver the sea. Fly to the arms of my true love and bring him back
1., 2., 3.
4.
Outro-Chorus
D G G G
light of the moon. I me. I wish I had some - one to
torn a - part.
teen years old.
home to
C G G D G
love me, some-one to call me his own. Some - one to
C G C D G
sleep with me night - ly, I'm wear - y of sleep - ing a - lone.

Standard Ukulele

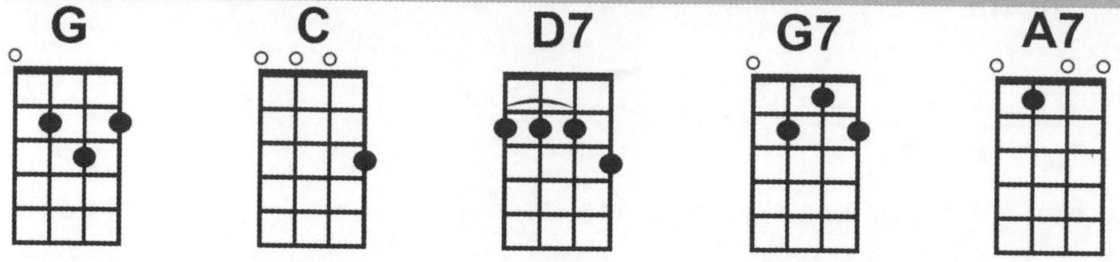
G
C
D7
G7
A7

Baritone Ukulele

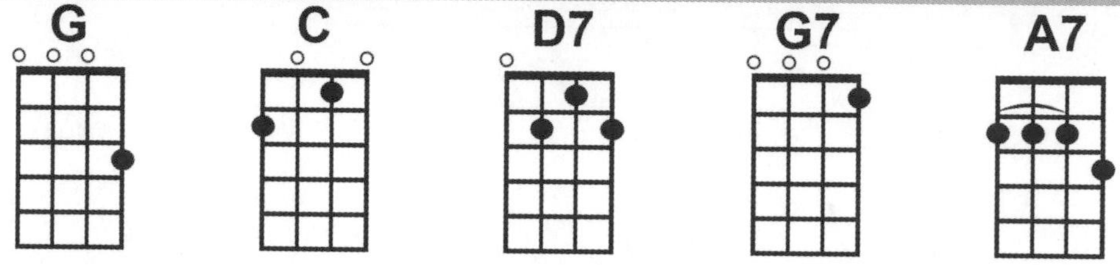
G
C
D7
G7
A7

Guitar

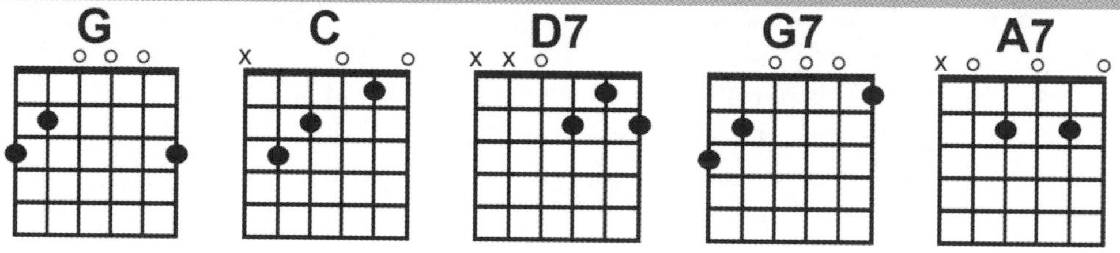
G
C
D7
G7
A7

Mandolin

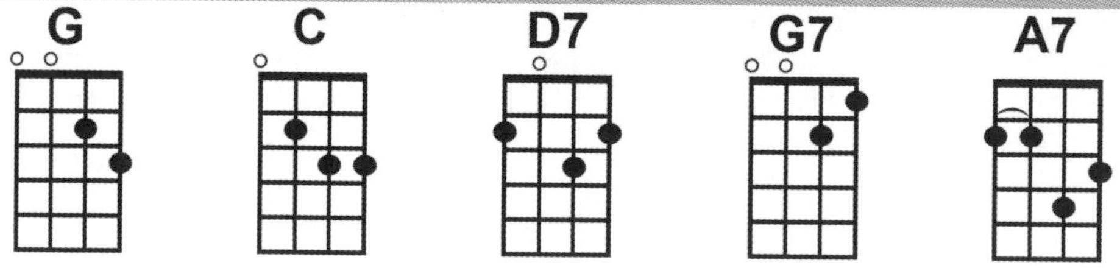
G
C
D7
G7
A7

Banjo

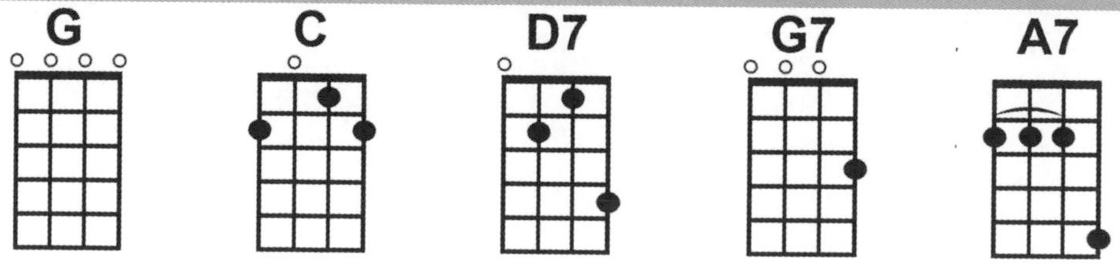
G
C
D7
G7
A7

I'll Tell My Ma

Irish Folk Song

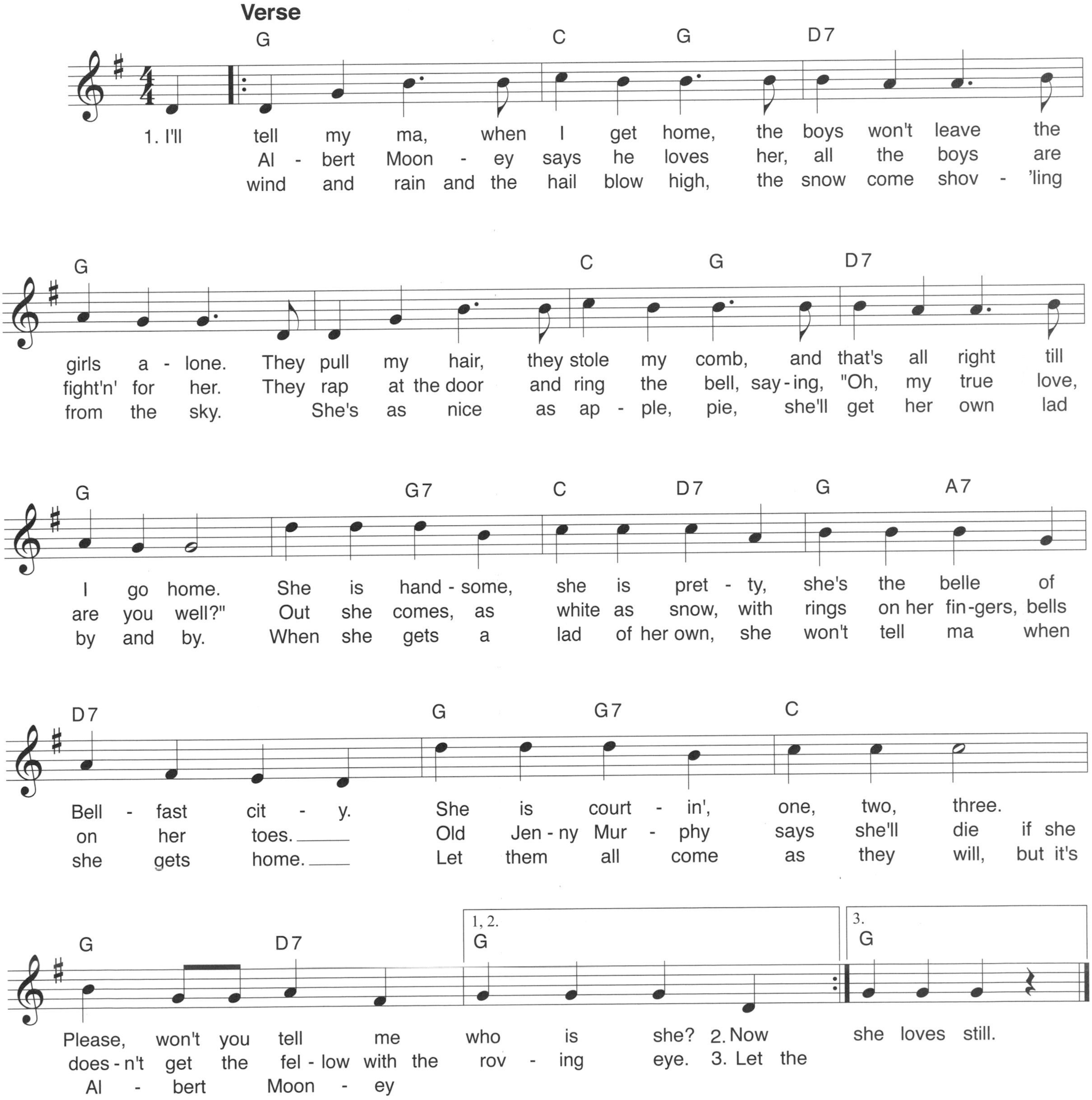
Verse
G C G D7
1. I'll tell my ma, when I get home, the boys won't leave the
Al - bert Moon - ey says he loves her, all the boys are
wind and rain and the hail blow high, the snow come shov - 'ling
G C G D7
girls a - lone. They pull my hair, they stole my comb, and that's all right till
fight'n' for her. They rap at the door and ring the bell, say - ing, "Oh, my true love,
from the sky. She's as nice as ap - ple, pie, she'll get her own lad
G G7 C D7 G A7
I go home. She is hand - some, she is pret - ty, she's the belle of
are you well?" Out she comes, as white as snow, with rings on her fin-gers, bells
by and by. When she gets a lad of her own, she won't tell ma when
D7 G G7 C
Bell - fast cit - y. She is court - in', one, two, three.
on her toes. Old Jen - ny Mur - phy says she'll die if she
she gets home. Let them all come as they will, but it's
1, 2.
3.
G D7 G G
Please, won't you tell me who is she? 2. Now she loves still.
does - n't get the fel - low with the rov - ing eye. 3. Let the
Al - bert Moon - ey

Standard Ukulele

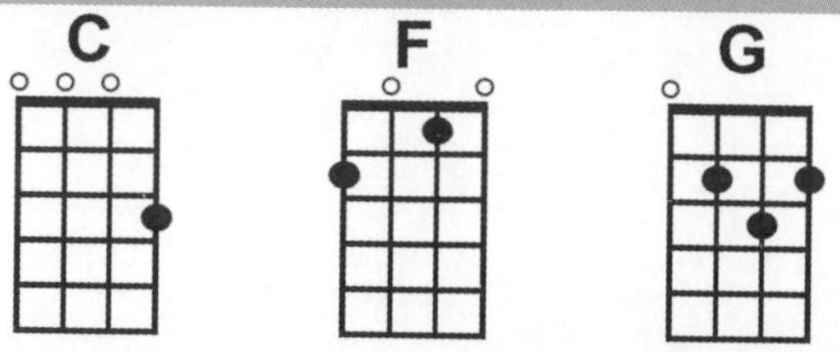

Baritone Ukulele

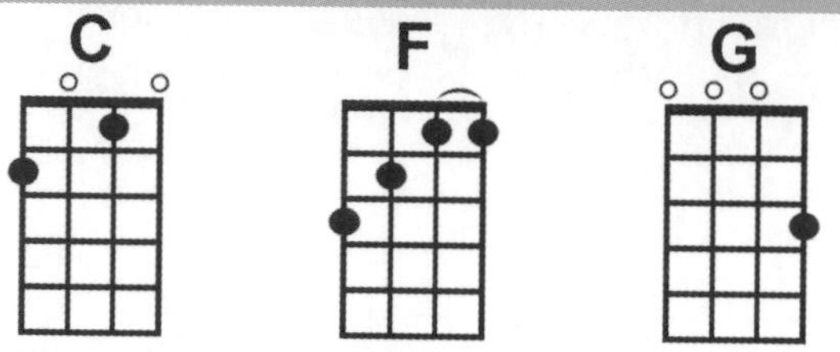

Guitar

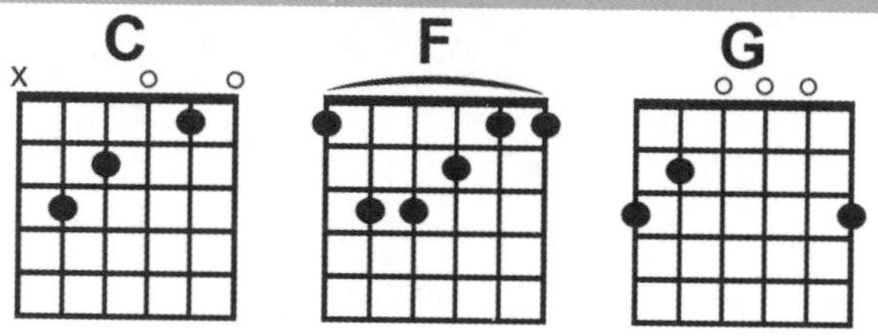

Mandolin

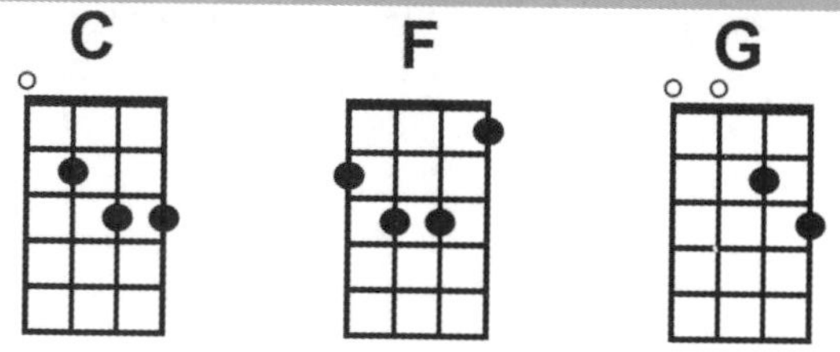

Banjo

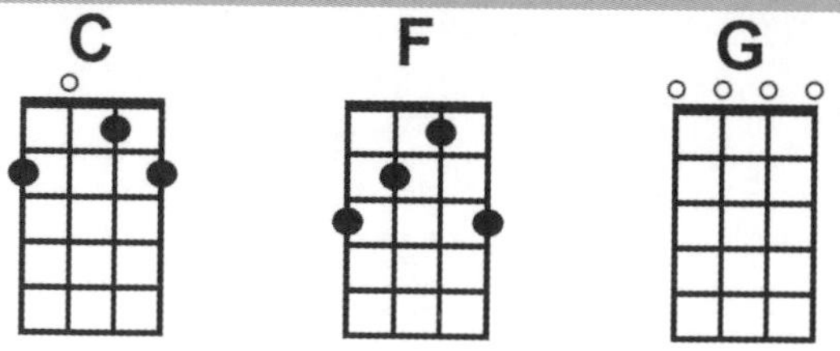

The Irish Rover

Traditional Irish Folk Song

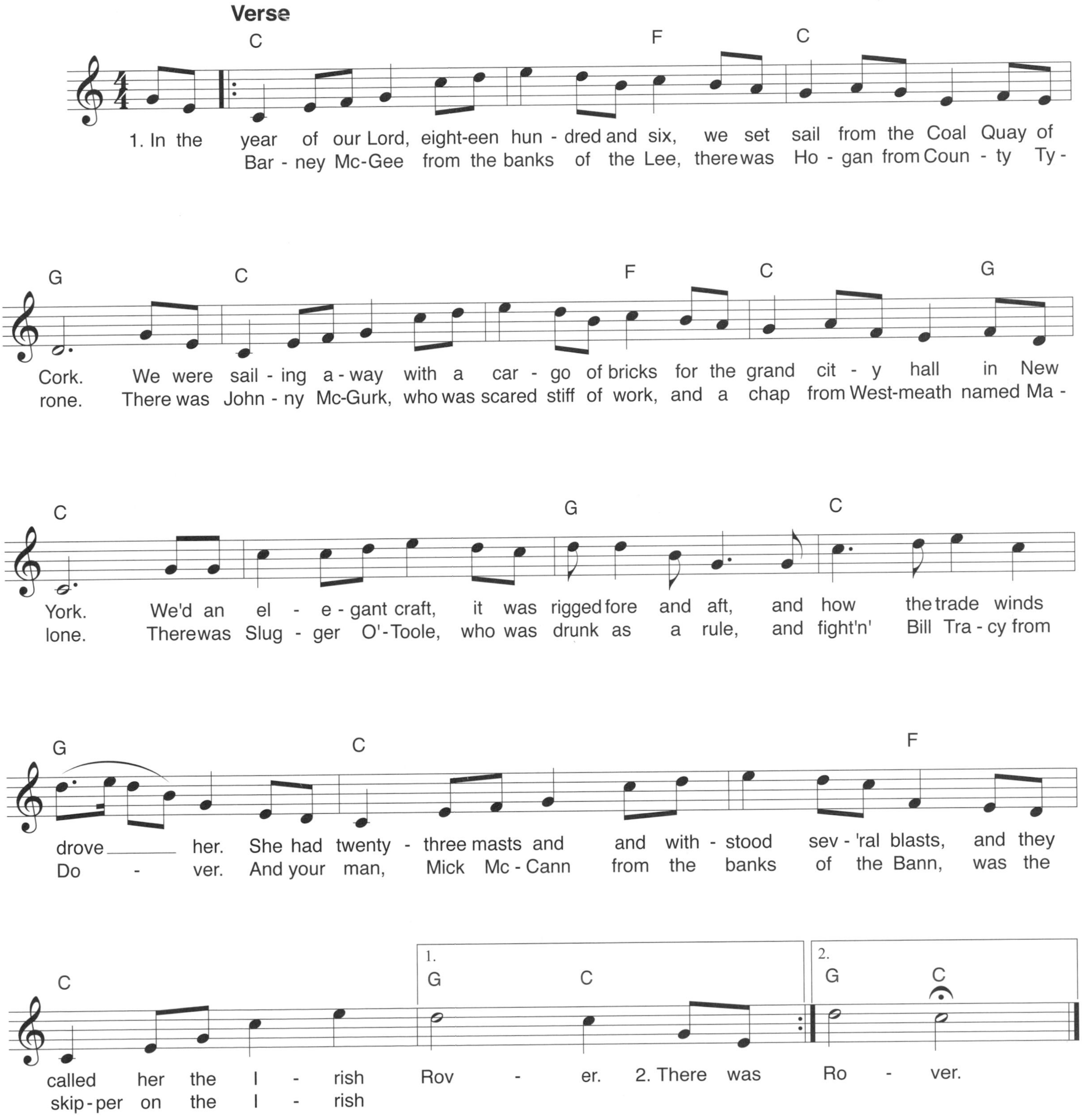
Verse
C F C
1. In the year of our Lord, eight-een hun - dred and six, we set sail from the Coal Quay of
Bar - ney Mc-Gee from the banks of the Lee, there was Ho - gan from Coun - ty Ty -
G C F C G
Cork. We were sail - ing a - way with a car - go of bricks for the grand cit - y hall in New
rone. There was John - ny Mc-Gurk, who was scared stiff of work, and a chap from West-meath named Ma -
C G C
York. We'd an el - e - gant craft, it was rigged fore and aft, and how the trade winds
lone. There was Slug - ger O'-Toole, who was drunk as a rule, and fight'n' Bill Tra - cy from
G C F
drove her. She had twenty - three masts and and with - stood sev - 'ral blasts, and they
Do - ver. And your man, Mick Mc - Cann from the banks of the Bann, was the
C 1. G C 2. G C
called her the I - rish Rov - er. 2. There was Ro - ver.
skip - per on the I - rish

Standard Ukulele

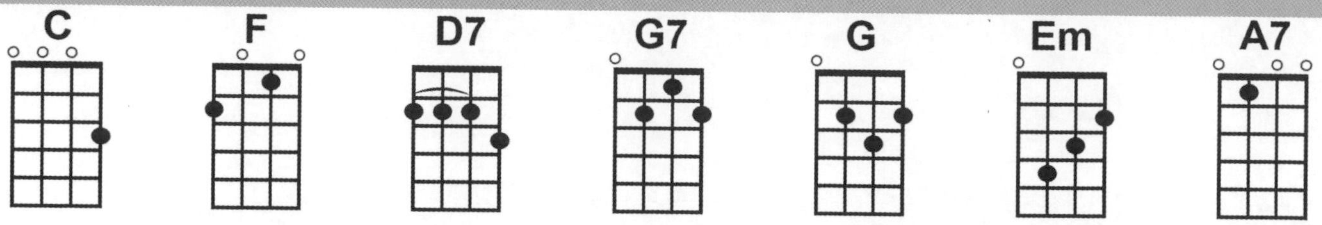
C
F
D7
G7
G
Em
A7

Baritone Ukulele

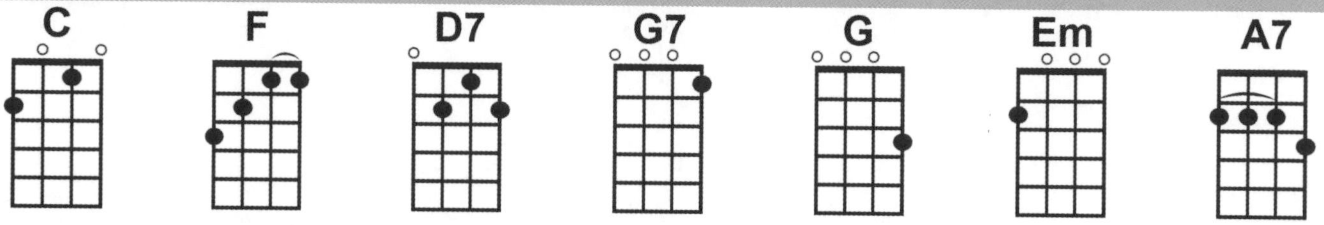
C
F
D7
G7
G
Em
A7

Guitar

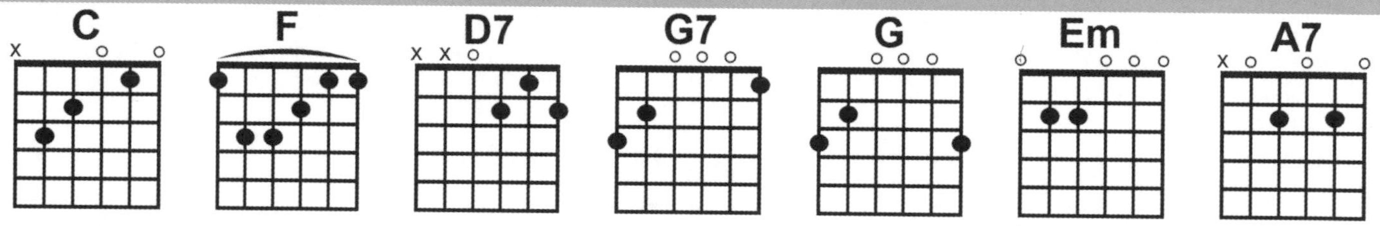
C
F
D7
G7
G
Em
A7

Mandolin

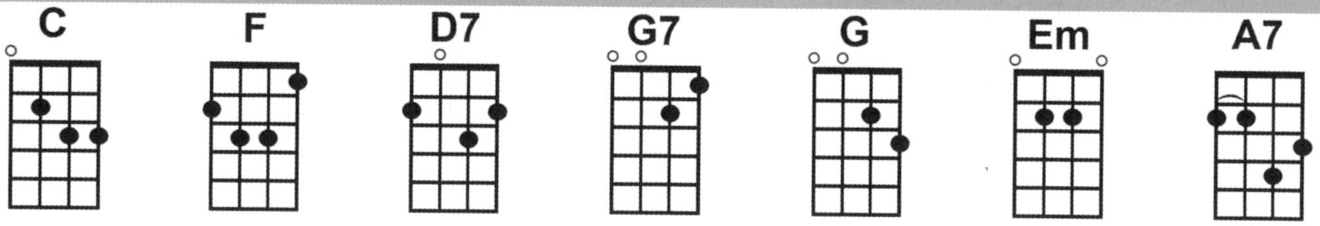
C
F
D7
G7
G
Em
A7

Banjo

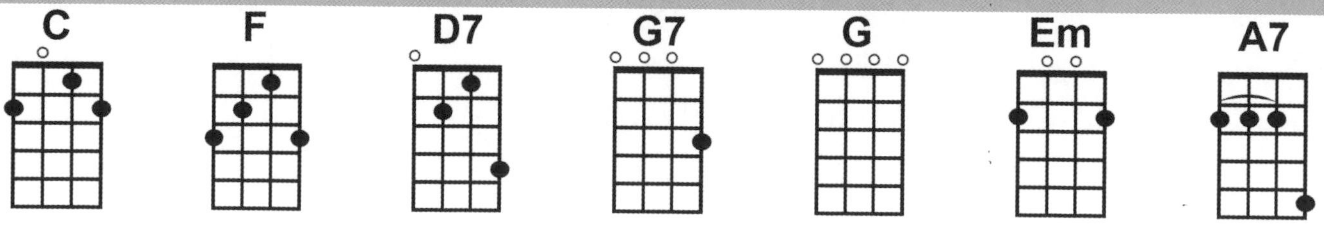
C
F
D7
G7
G
Em
A7

Kerry Dance

By J.L. Molloy

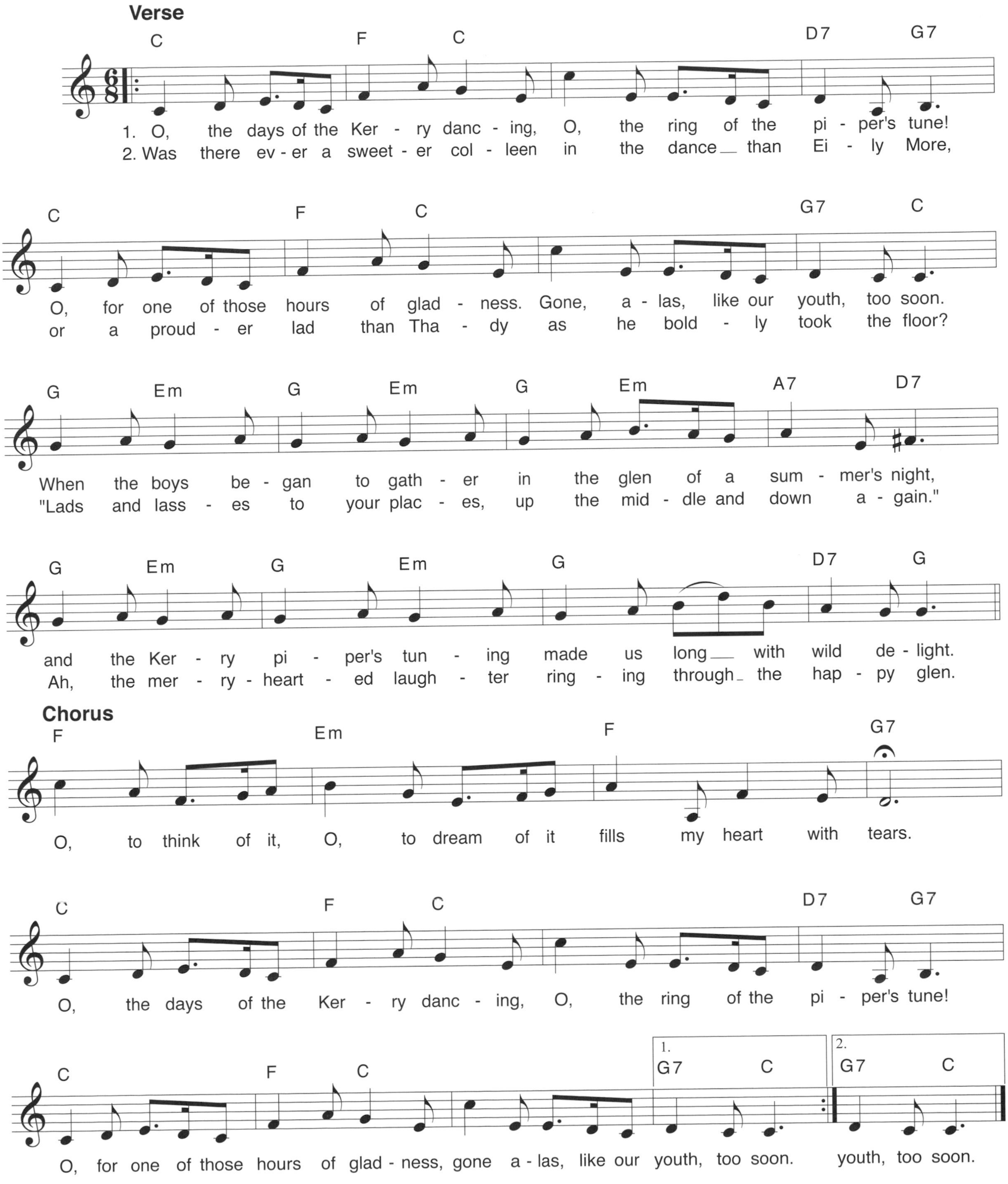
Verse
C F C D7 G7
1. O, the days of the Ker - ry danc - ing, O, the ring of the pi - per's tune!
2. Was there ev - er a sweet - er col - leen in the dance than Ei - ly More,
C F C G7 C
O, for one of those hours of glad - ness. Gone, a - las, like our youth, too soon.
or a proud - er lad than Tha - dy as he bold - ly took the floor?
G Em G Em G Em A7 D7
When the boys be - gan to gath - er in the glen of a sum - mer's night,
"Lads and lass - es to your plac - es, up the mid - dle and down a - gain."
G Em G Em G D7 G
and the Ker - ry pi - per's tun - ing made us long with wild de - light.
Ah, the mer - ry - heart - ed laugh - ter ring - ing through the hap - py glen.
Chorus
F Em F G7
O, to think of it, O, to dream of it fills my heart with tears.
C F C D7 G7
O, the days of the Ker - ry danc - ing, O, the ring of the pi - per's tune!
C F C
1. G7 C
2. G7 C
O, for one of those hours of glad - ness, gone a - las, like our youth, too soon.
youth, too soon.

Standard Ukulele

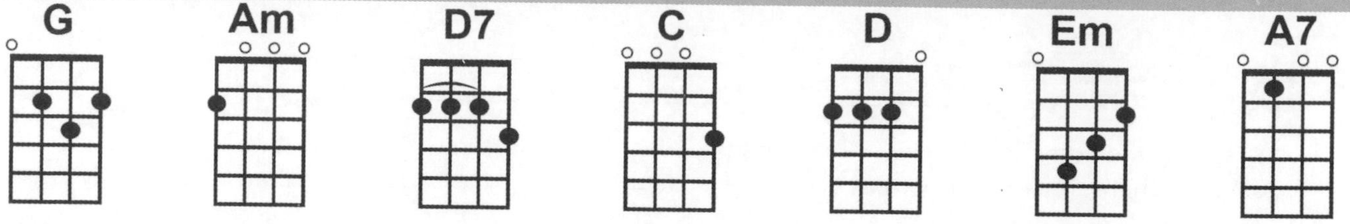
G
Am
D7
C
D
Em
A7

Baritone Ukulele

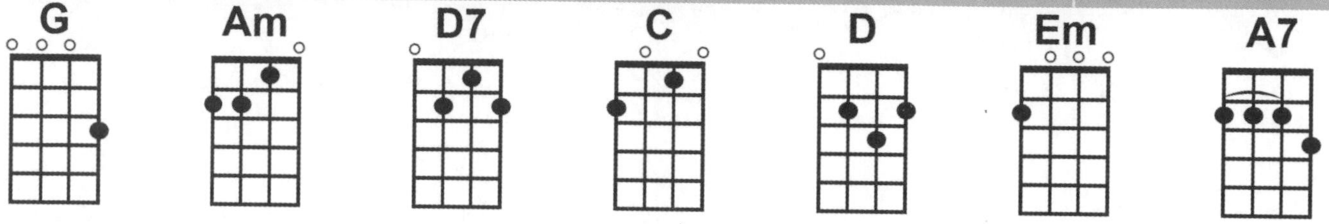
G
Am
D7
C
D
Em
A7

Guitar

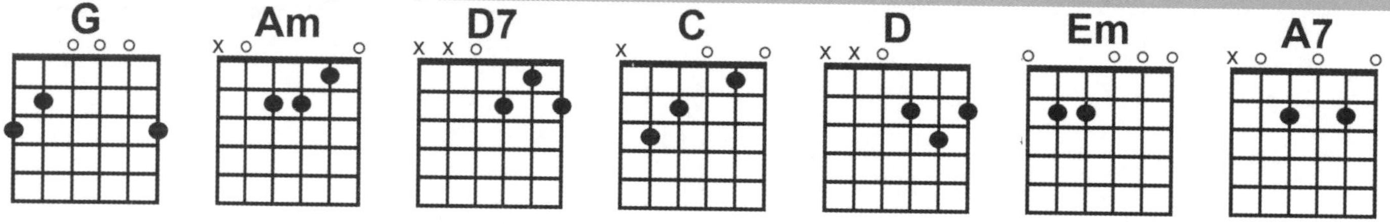
G
Am
D7
C
D
Em
A7

Mandolin

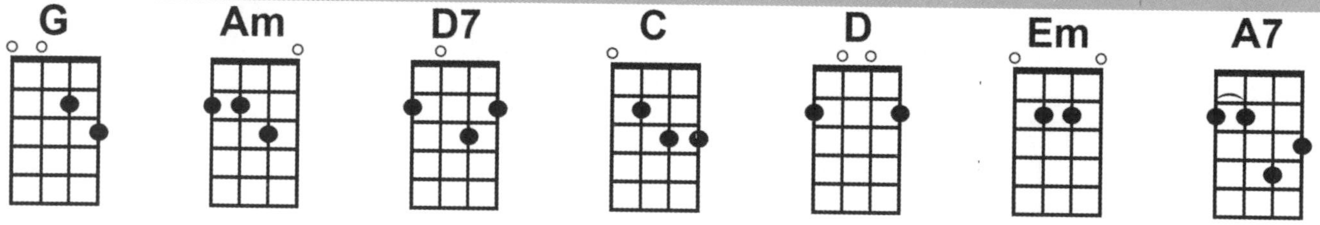
G
Am
D7
C
D
Em
A7

Banjo

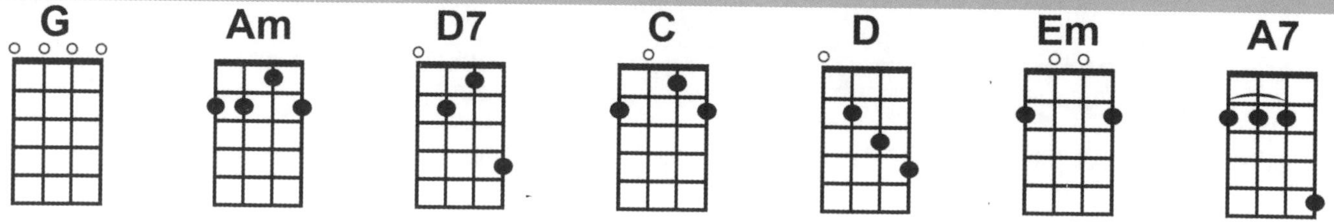
G
Am
D7
C
D
Em
A7

Kitty of Coleraine

Irish Folk Song

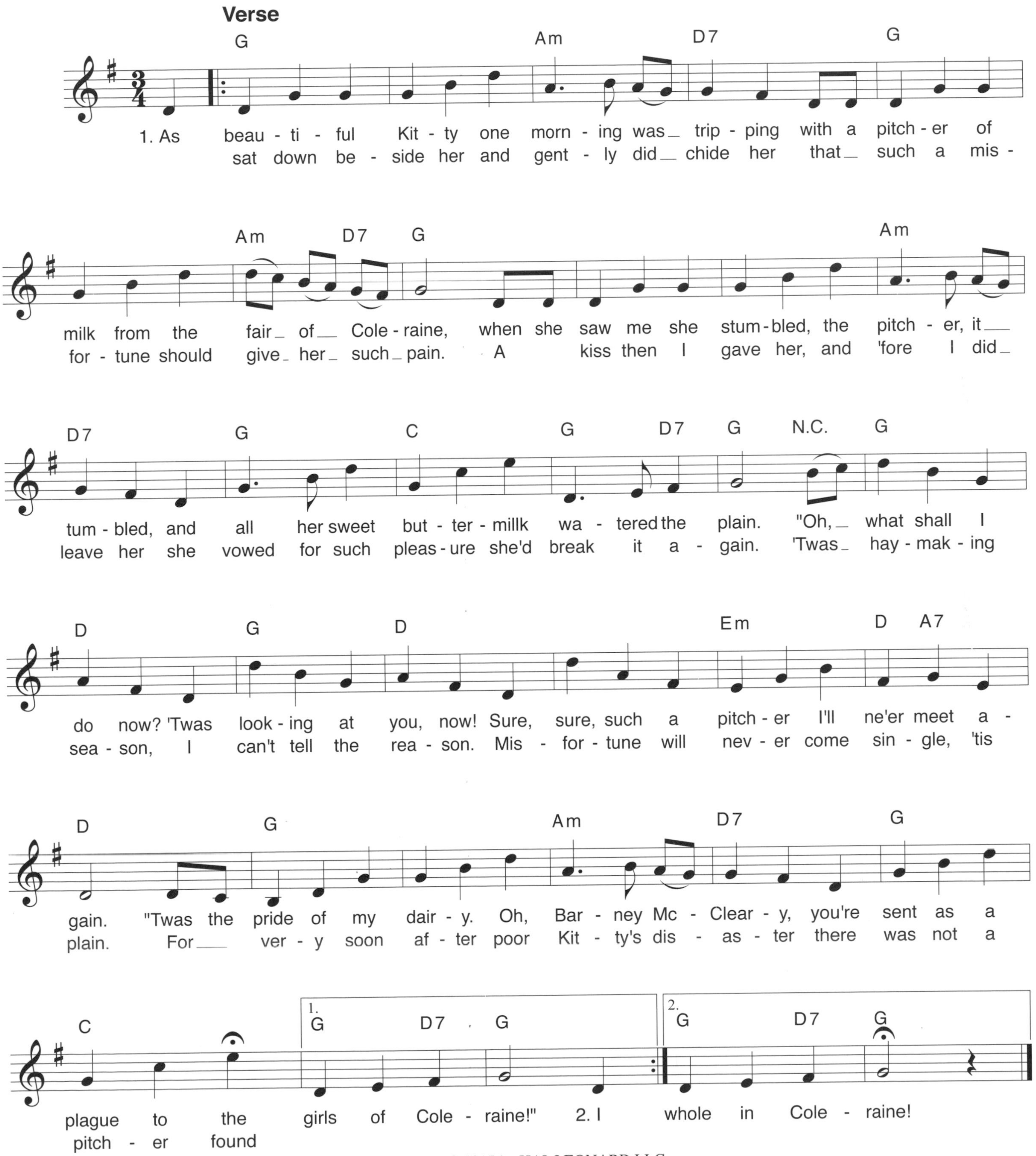
Verse
G Am D7 G
1. As beau - ti - ful Kit - ty one morn - ing was_ trip - ping with a pitch - er of
sat down be - side her and gent - ly did_ chide her that_ such a mis -
Am D7 G Am
milk from the fair_ of_ Cole - raine, when she saw me she stum - bled, the pitch - er, it_
for - tune should give_ her_ such_pain. A kiss then I gave her, and 'fore I did_
D7 G C G D7 G N.C. G
tum - bled, and all her sweet but - ter - millk wa - tered the plain. "Oh,_ what shall I
leave her she vowed for such pleas - ure she'd break it a - gain. 'Twas_ hay - mak - ing
D G D Em D A7
do now? 'Twas look - ing at you, now! Sure, sure, such a pitch - er I'll ne'er meet a -
sea - son, I can't tell the rea - son. Mis - for - tune will nev - er come sin - gle, 'tis
D G Am D7 G
gain. "Twas the pride of my dair - y. Oh, Bar - ney Mc - Clear - y, you're sent as a
plain. For_ ver - y soon af - ter poor Kit - ty's dis - as - ter there was not a
C 1. G D7 G 2. G D7 G
plague to the girls of Cole - raine!" 2. I whole in Cole - raine!
pitch - er found

Standard Ukulele

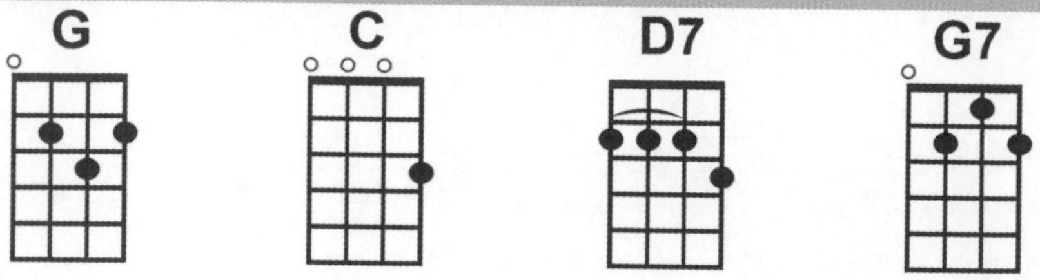
G
C
D7
G7

Baritone Ukulele

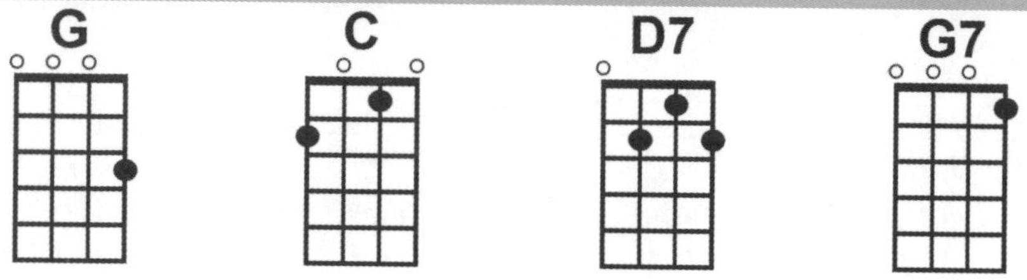
G
C
D7
G7

Guitar

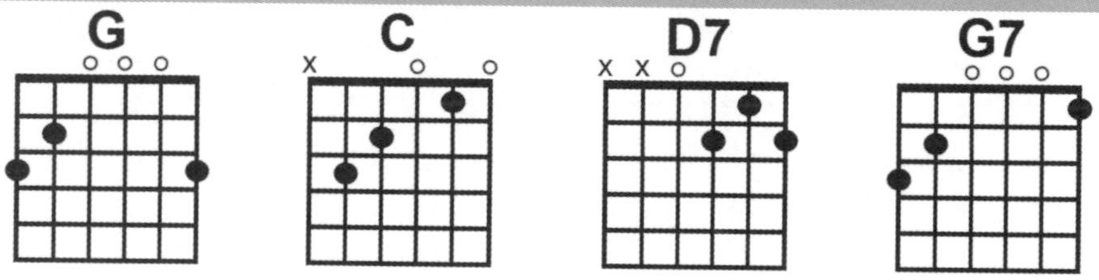
G
C
D7
G7

Mandolin

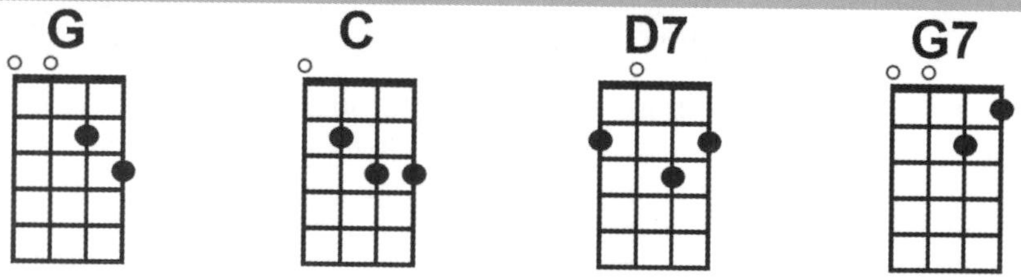
G
C
D7
G7

Banjo

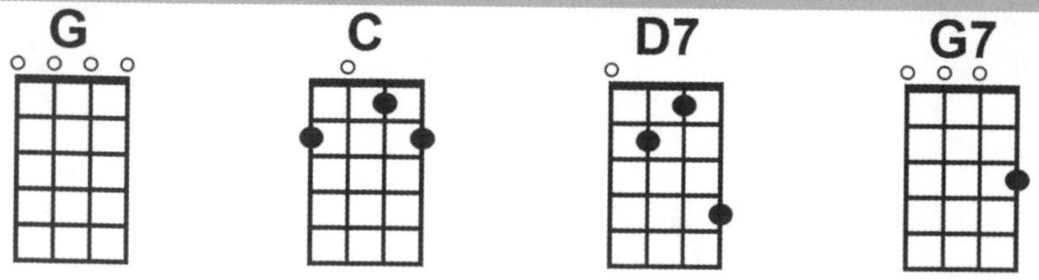
G
C
D7
G7

The Lark in the Clear Air

Words and Music by Sir Samuel Ferguson

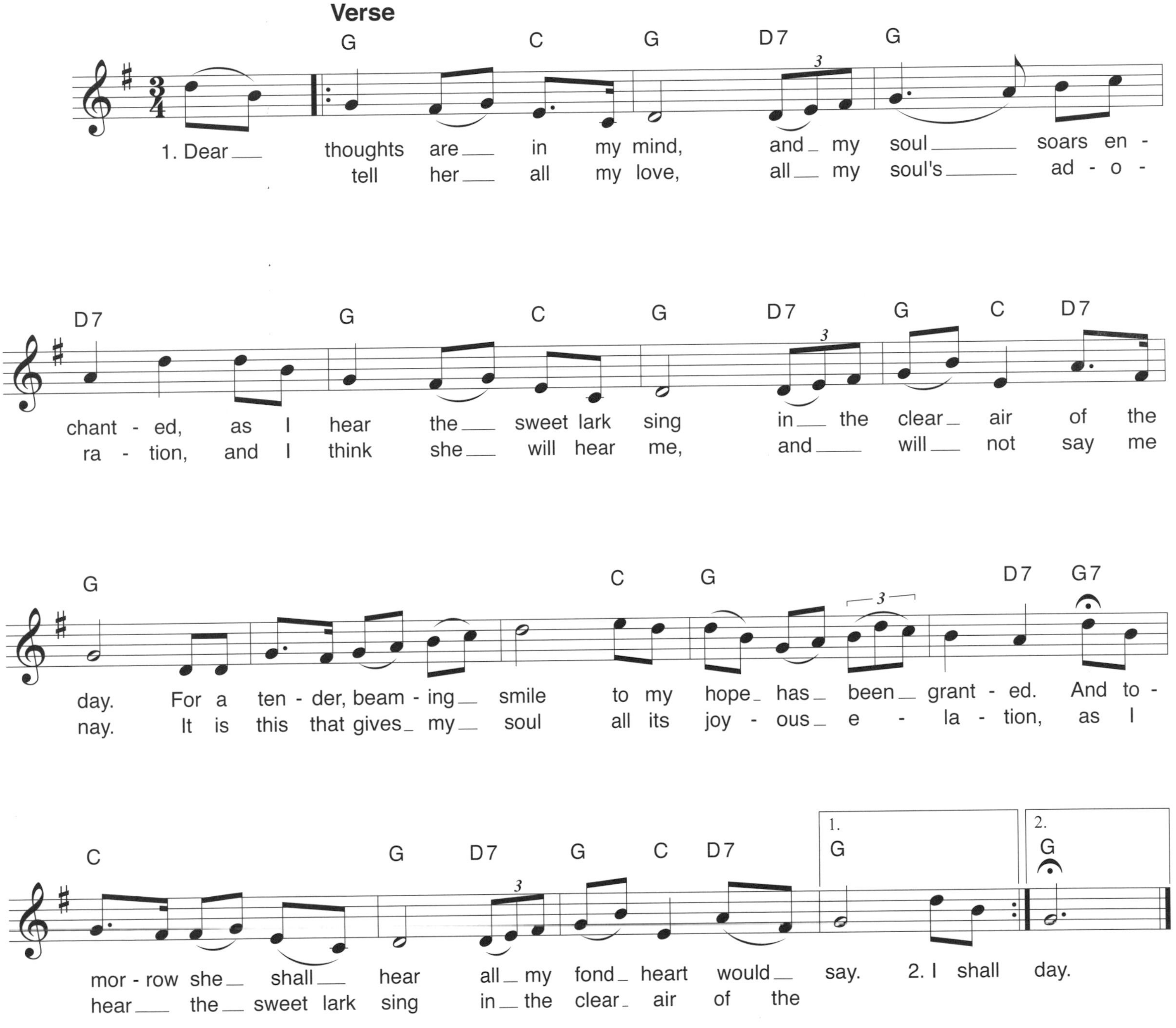
Verse
G C G D7 G
1. Dear thoughts are in my mind, and my soul soars en -
tell her all my love, all my soul's ad - o -
D7 G C G D7 G C D7
chant - ed, as I hear the sweet lark sing in the clear air of the
ra - tion, and I think she will hear me, and will not say me
G C G D7 G7
day. For a ten - der, beam - ing smile to my hope has been grant - ed. And to -
nay. It is this that gives my soul all its joy - ous e - la - tion, as I
C G D7 G C D7
mor - row she shall hear all my fond heart would say. 2. I shall
hear the sweet lark sing in the clear air of the
1. G
2. G
day.

Standard Ukulele

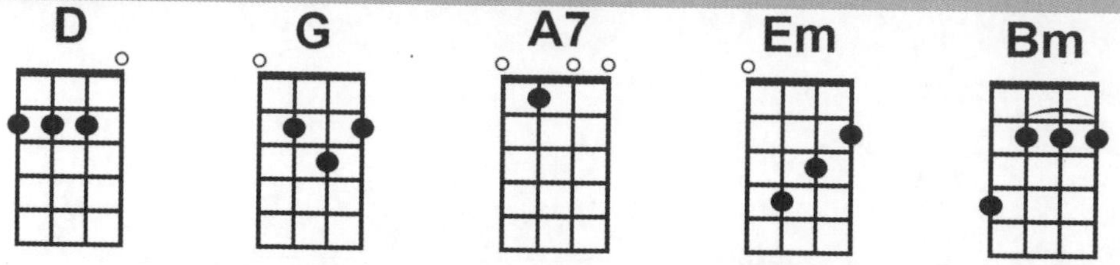
D
G
A7
Em
Bm

Baritone Ukulele

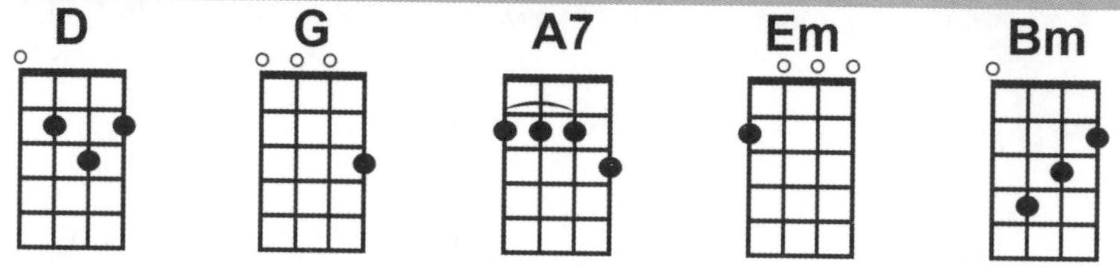
D
G
A7
Em
Bm

Guitar

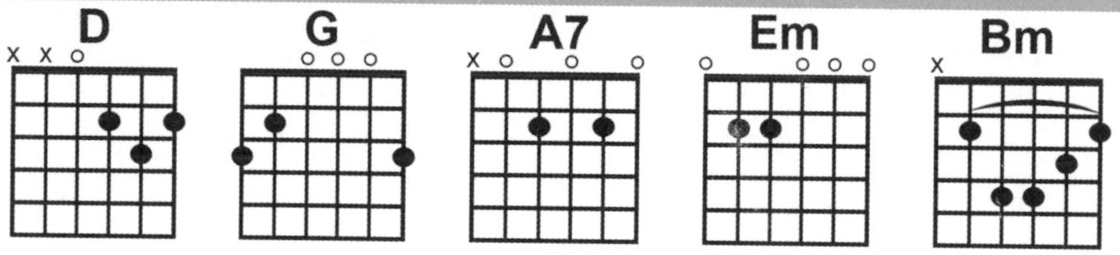
D
G
A7
Em
Bm

Mandolin

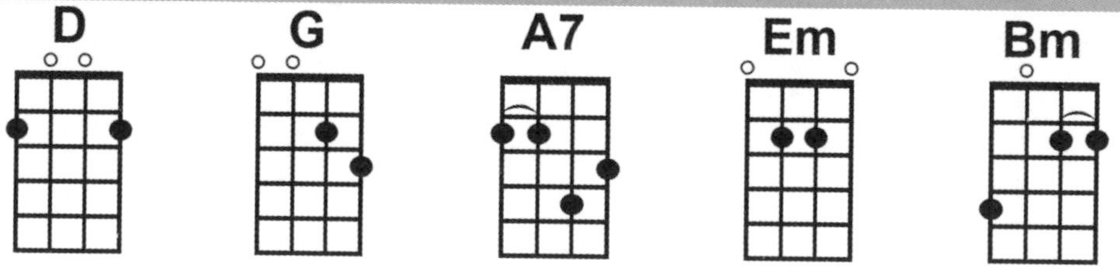
D
G
A7
Em
Bm

Banjo

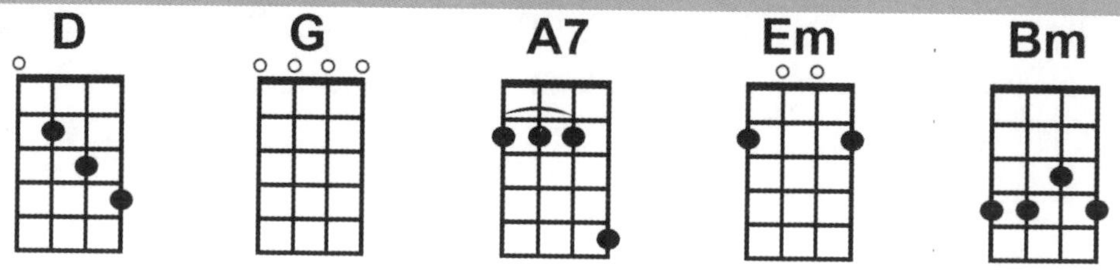
D
G
A7
Em
Bm

Let Erin Remember the Days of Old

Lyrics by Thomas Moore
Folk Melody "The Red Fox"

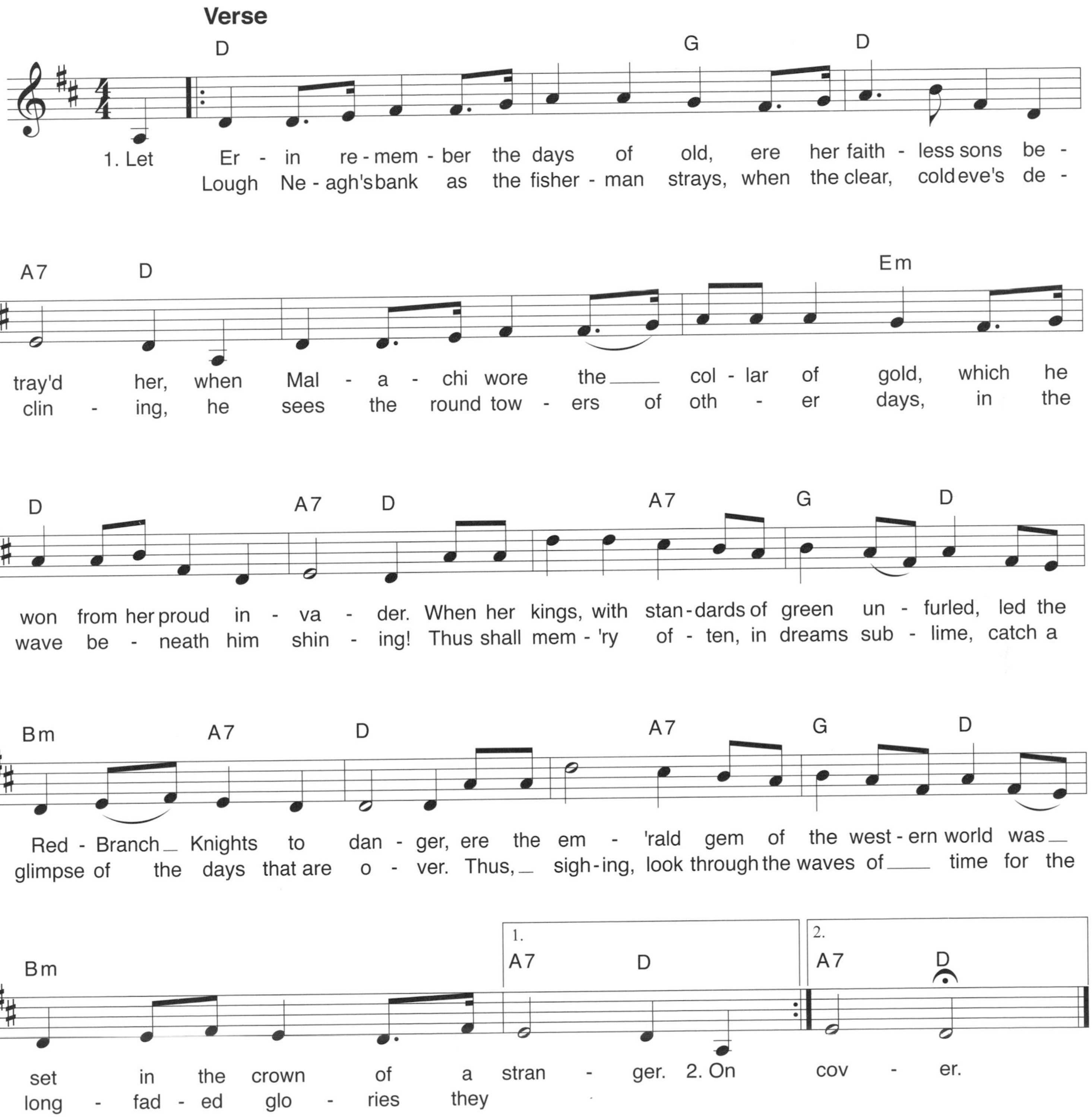
Verse
D G D
1. Let Er - in re - mem - ber the days of old, ere her faith - less sons be -
Lough Ne - agh's bank as the fisher - man strays, when the clear, cold eve's de -
A7 D Em
tray'd her, when Mal - a - chi wore the col - lar of gold, which he
clin - ing, he sees the round tow - ers of oth - er days, in the
D A7 D A7 G D
won from her proud in - va - der. When her kings, with stan - dards of green un - furled, led the
wave be - neath him shin - ing! Thus shall mem - 'ry of - ten, in dreams sub - lime, catch a
Bm A7 D A7 G D
Red - Branch Knights to dan - ger, ere the em - 'rald gem of the west - ern world was
glimpse of the days that are o - ver. Thus, sigh - ing, look through the waves of time for the
Bm 1. A7 D 2. A7 D
set in the crown of a stran - ger. 2. On cov - er.
long - fad - ed glo - ries they

Standard Ukulele

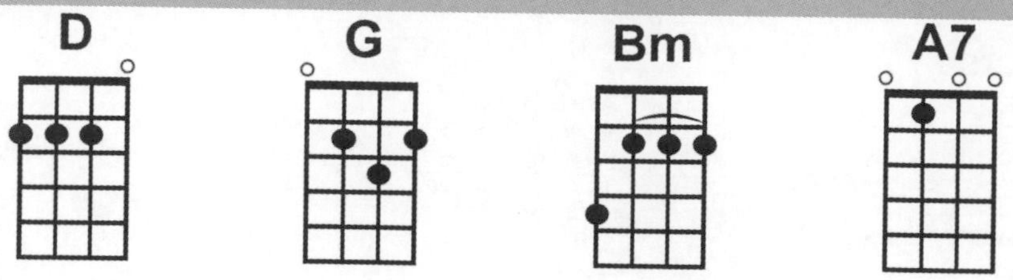
D
G
Bm
A7

Baritone Ukulele

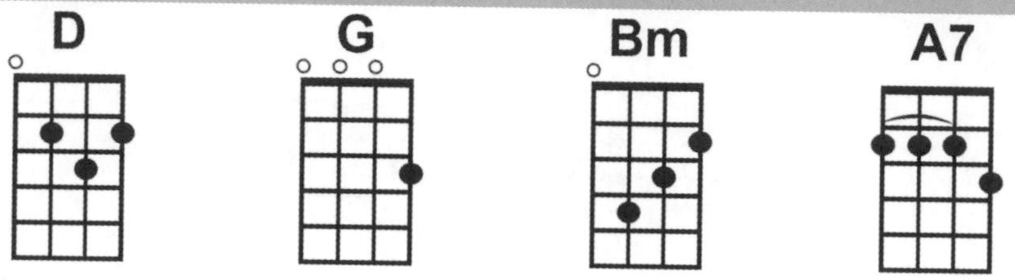
D
G
Bm
A7

Guitar

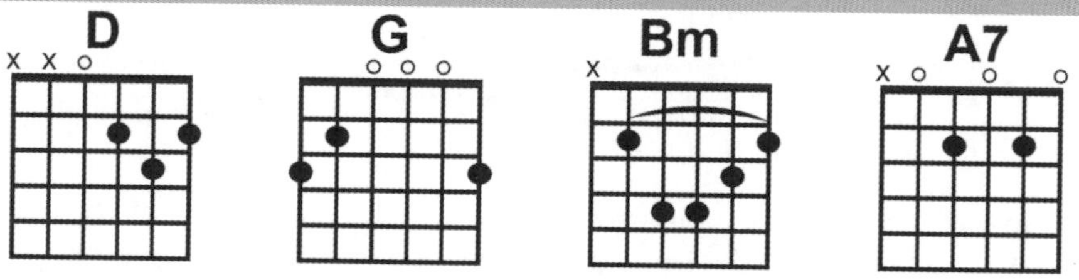
D
G
Bm
A7

Mandolin

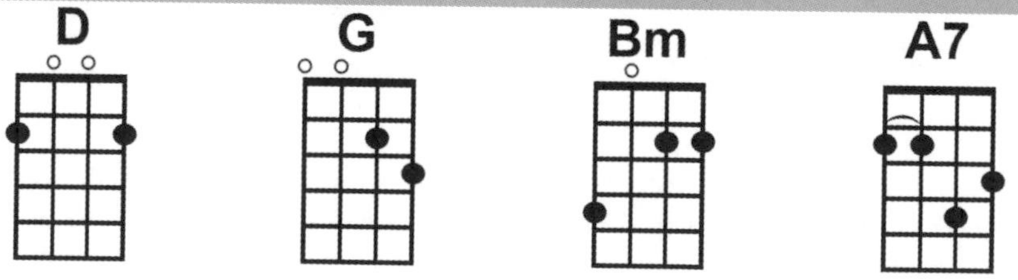
D
G
Bm
A7

Banjo

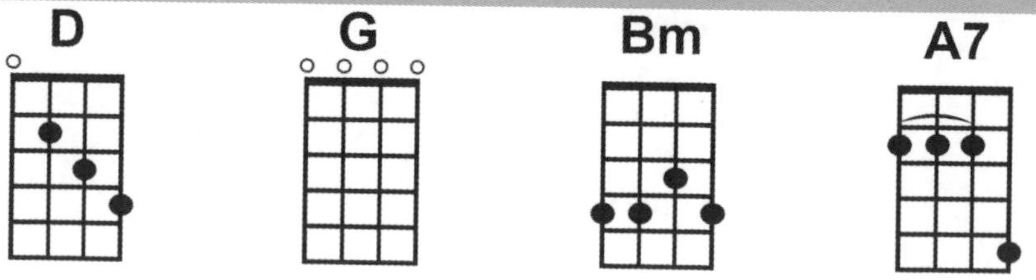
D
G
Bm
A7

Limerick Is Beautiful

Traditional Irish Melody
Words by M. Scanlan

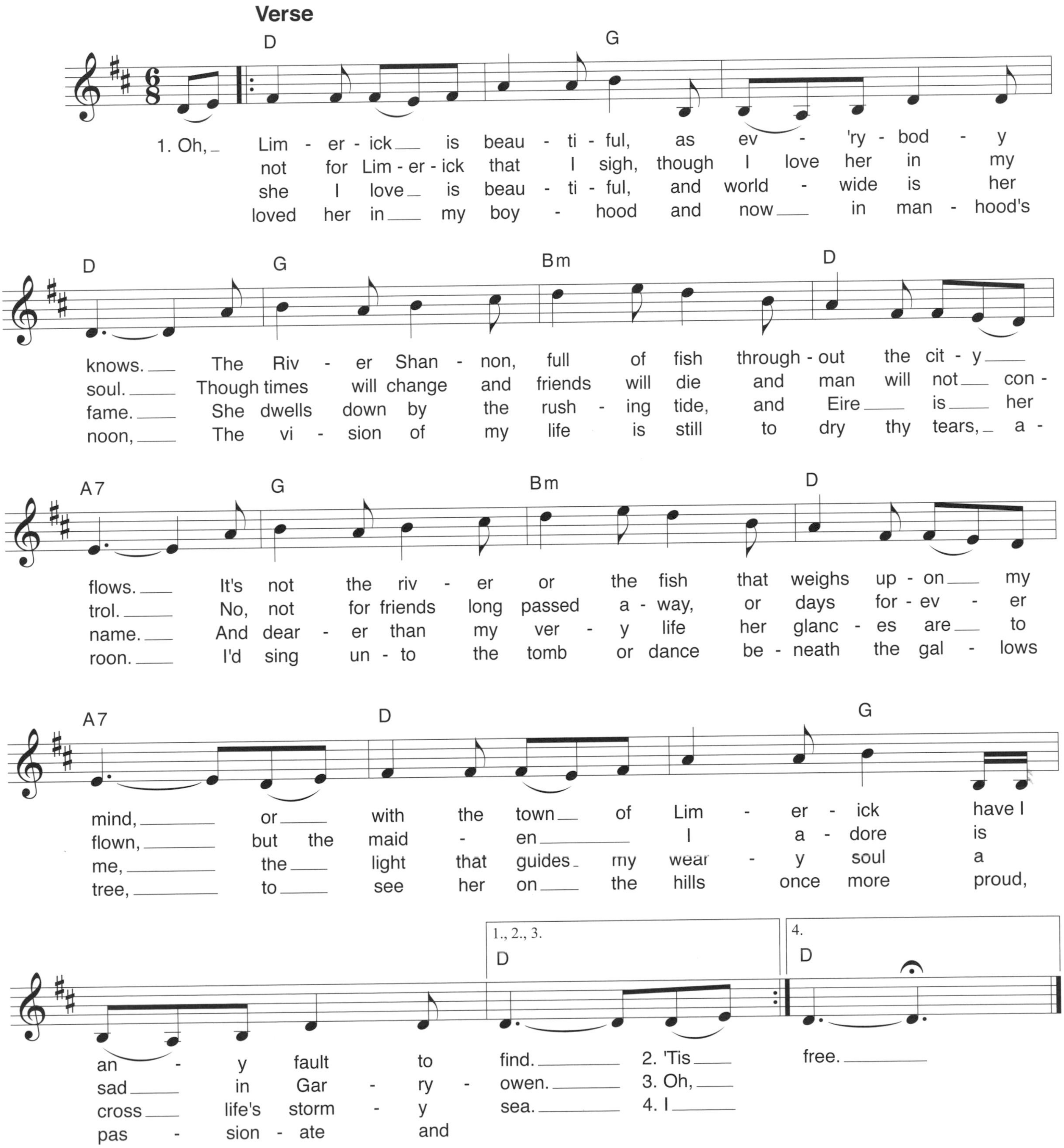
Verse
D G
1. Oh, Lim - er - ick is beau - ti - ful, as ev - 'ry - bod - y
not for Lim - er - ick that I sigh, though I love her in my
she I love is beau - ti - ful, and world - wide is her
loved her in my boy - hood and now in man - hood's
D G Bm D
knows. The Riv - er Shan - non, full of fish through - out the cit - y
soul. Though times will change and friends will die and man will not con -
fame. She dwells down by the rush - ing tide, and Eire is her
noon, The vi - sion of my life is still to dry thy tears, a -
A7 G Bm D
flows. It's not the riv - er or the fish that weighs up - on my
trol. No, not for friends long passed a - way, or days for - ev - er
name. And dear - er than my ver - y life her glanc - es are to
roon. I'd sing un - to the tomb or dance be - neath the gal - lows
A7 D G
mind, or with the town of Lim - er - ick have I
flown, but the maid - en I a - dore is
me, the light that guides my wear - y soul a
tree, to see her on the hills once more proud,
1., 2., 3. D 4. D
an - y fault to find. 2. 'Tis free.
sad in Gar - ry - owen. 3. Oh,
cross life's storm - y sea. 4. I
pas - sion - ate and

Standard Ukulele

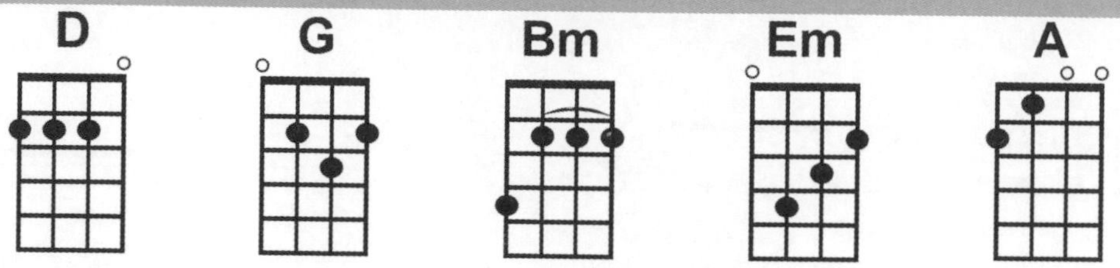
D
G
Bm
Em
A

Baritone Ukulele

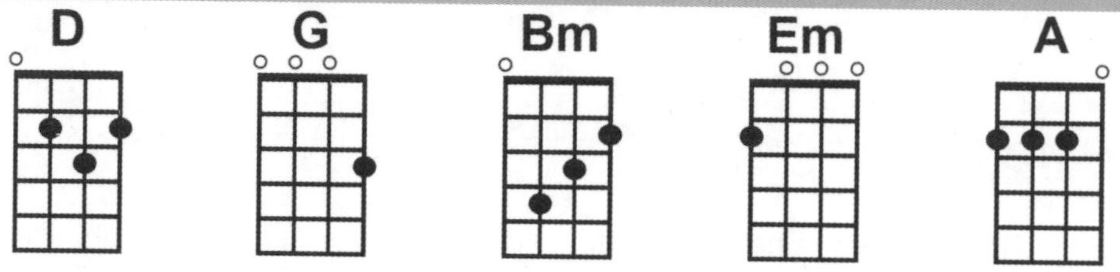
D
G
Bm
Em
A

Guitar

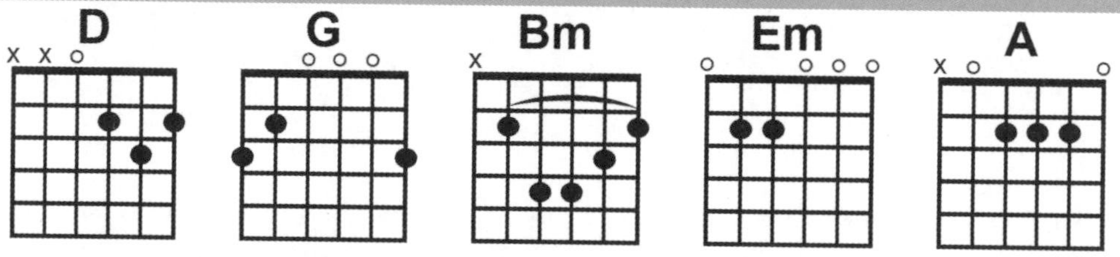
D
G
Bm
Em
A

Mandolin

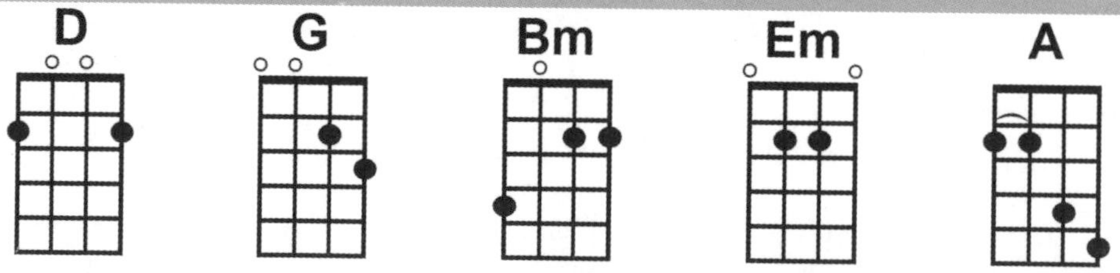
D
G
Bm
Em
A

Banjo

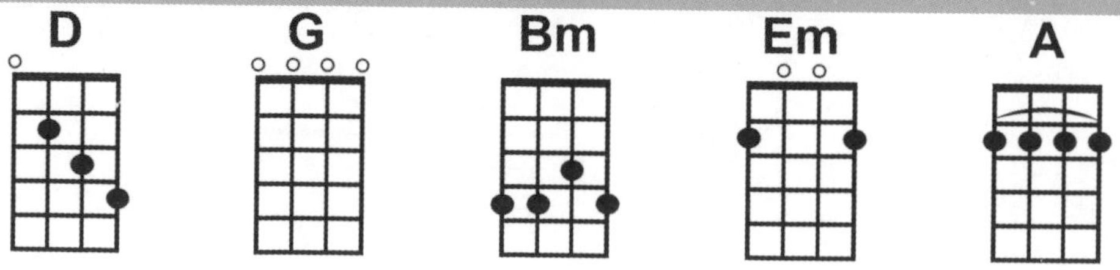
D
G
Bm
Em
A

Loch Lomond

Scottish Folk Song

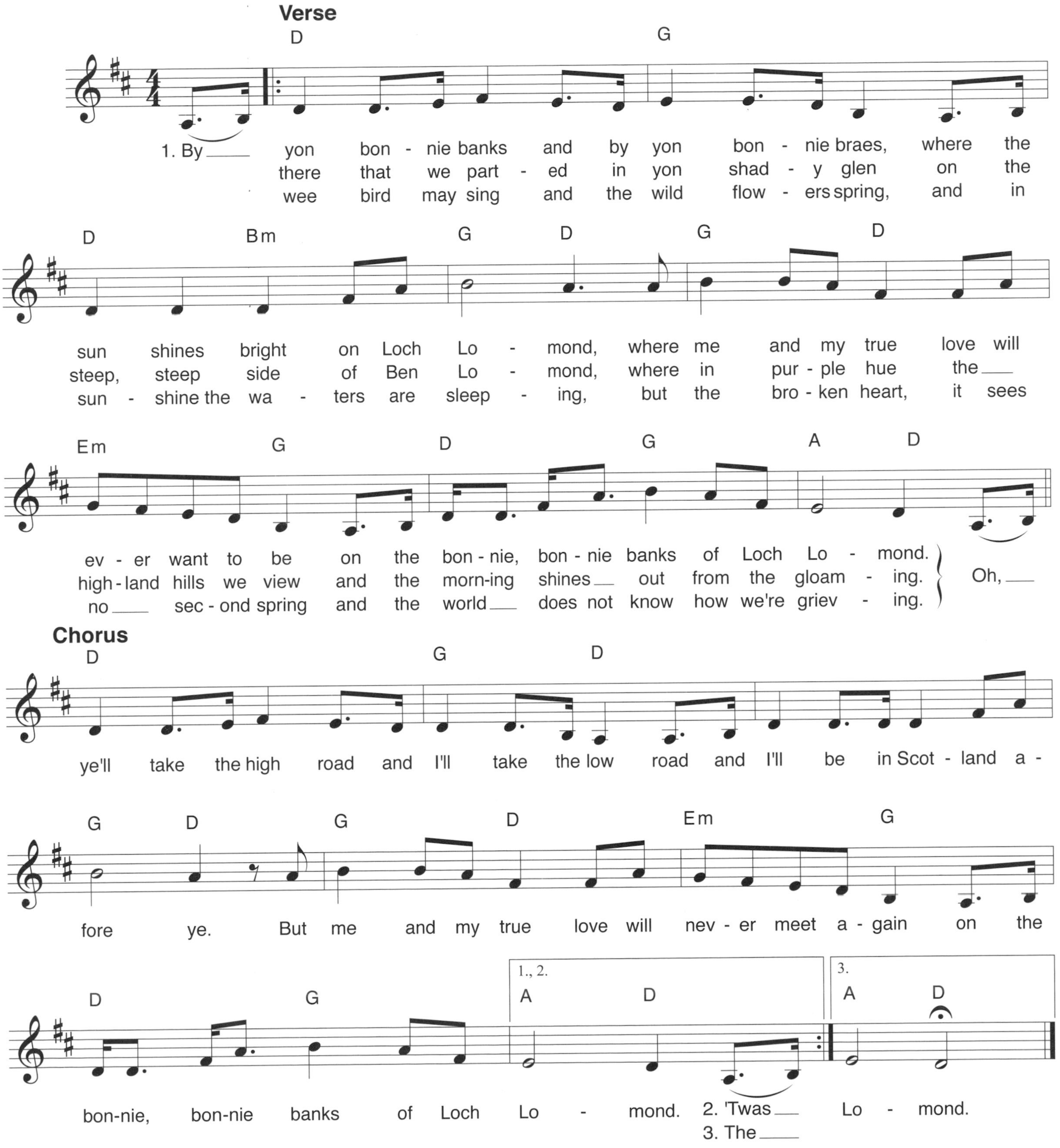
Verse
D G
1. By yon bon - nie banks and by yon bon - nie braes, where the
there that we part - ed in yon shad - y glen on the
wee bird may sing and the wild flow - ers spring, and in
D Bm G D G D
sun shines bright on Loch Lo - mond, where me and my true love will
steep, steep side of Ben Lo - mond, where in pur - ple hue the
sun - shine the wa - ters are sleep - ing, but the bro - ken heart, it sees
Em G D G A D
ev - er want to be on the bon - nie, bon - nie banks of Loch Lo - mond.
high - land hills we view and the morn - ing shines out from the gloam - ing.
no sec - ond spring and the world does not know how we're griev - ing.
Oh,
Chorus
D G D
ye'll take the high road and I'll take the low road and I'll be in Scot - land a -
G D G D Em G
fore ye. But me and my true love will nev - er meet a - gain on the
D G
bon - nie, bon - nie banks of Loch
1., 2.
A D
Lo - mond.
2. 'Twas
3. The
3.
A D
Lo - mond.

Standard Ukulele

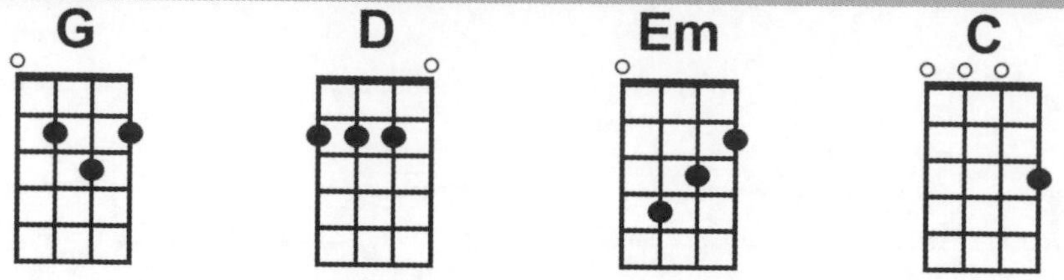

Baritone Ukulele

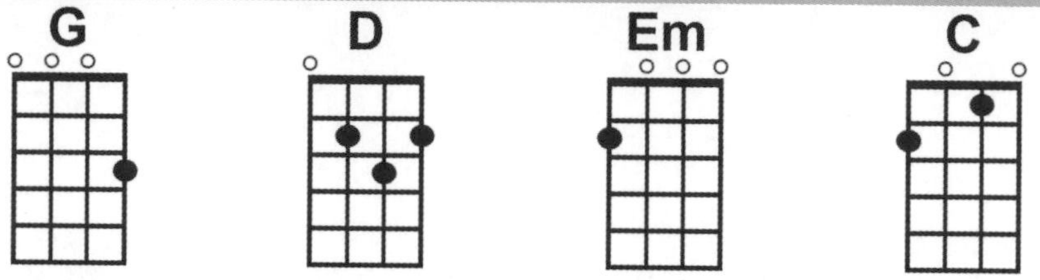

Guitar

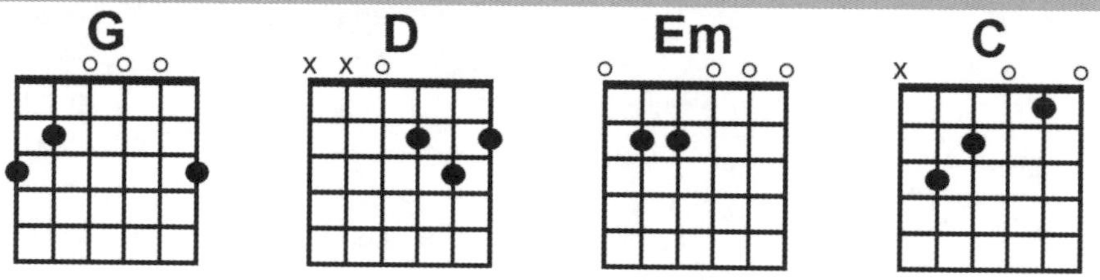

Mandolin

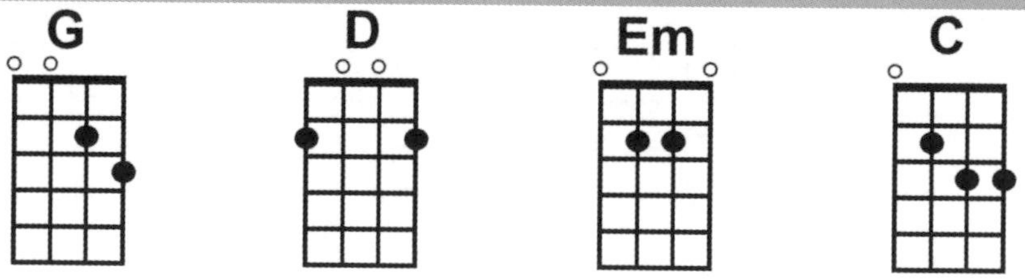

Banjo

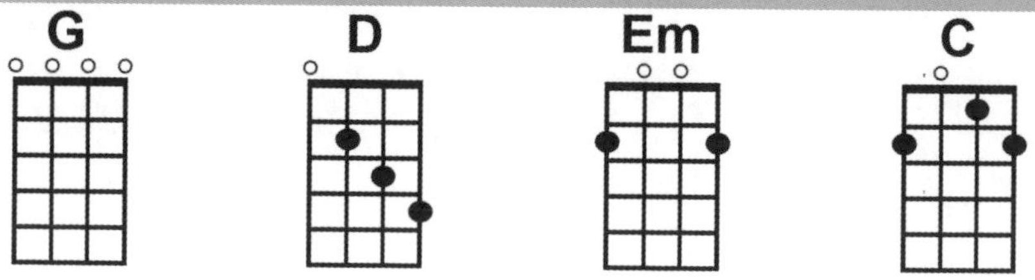

MacPherson's Farewell

By Robert Burns

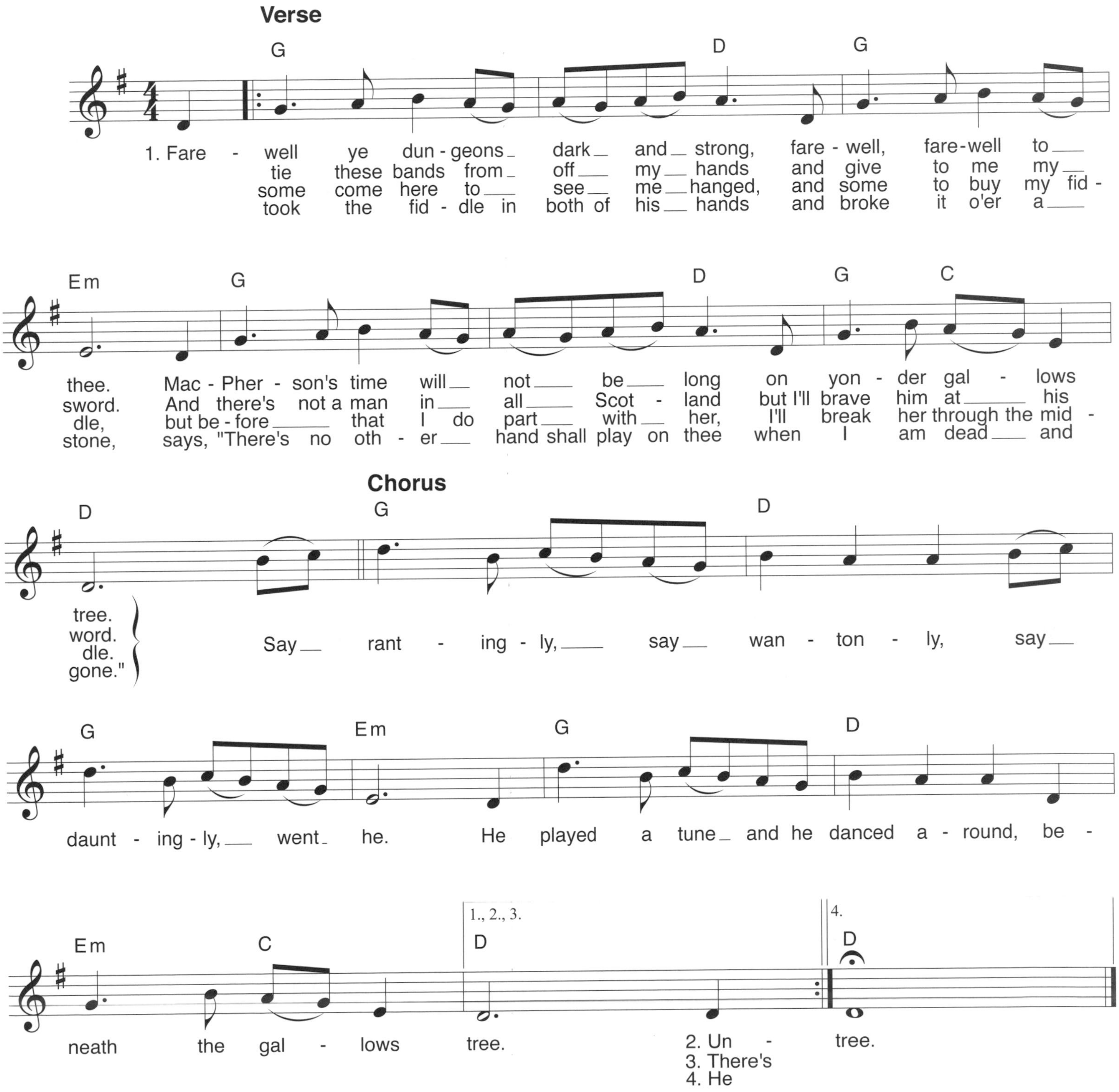
Verse
G D G
1. Fare - well ye dun - geons dark and strong, fare - well, fare-well to
tie these bands from off my hands and give to me my
some come here to see me hanged, and some to buy my fid -
took the fid - dle in both of his hands and broke it o'er a
Em G D G C
thee. Mac - Pher - son's time will not be long on yon - der gal - lows
sword. And there's not a man in all Scot - land but I'll brave him at his
dle, but be - fore that I do part with her, I'll break her through the mid -
stone, says, "There's no oth - er hand shall play on thee when I am dead and
Chorus
D G D
tree.
word.
dle.
gone."
Say rant - ing - ly, say wan - ton - ly, say
G Em G D
daunt - ing - ly, went he. He played a tune and he danced a - round, be -
Em C
1., 2., 3.
D
4.
D
neath the gal - lows tree.
2. Un -
3. There's
4. He
tree.

Standard Ukulele

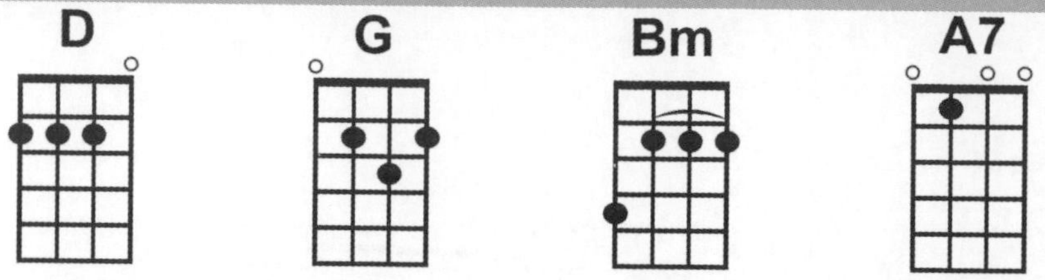
D
G
Bm
A7

Baritone Ukulele

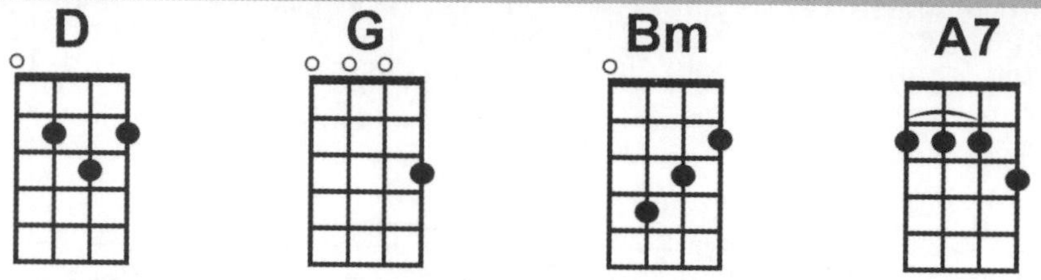
D
G
Bm
A7

Guitar

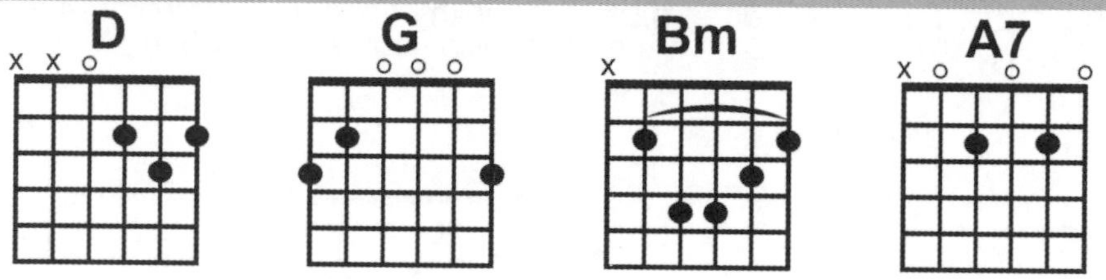
D
G
Bm
A7

Mandolin

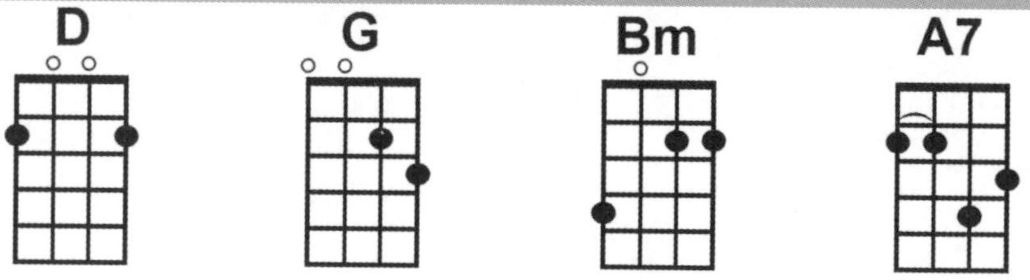
D
G
Bm
A7

Banjo

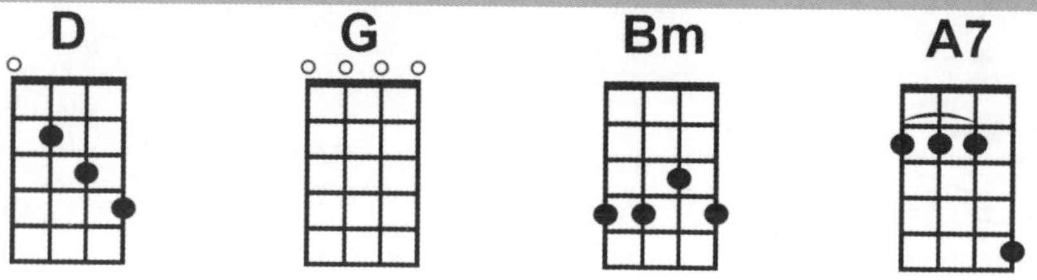
D
G
Bm
A7

The Men of the West

Irish Folk Song

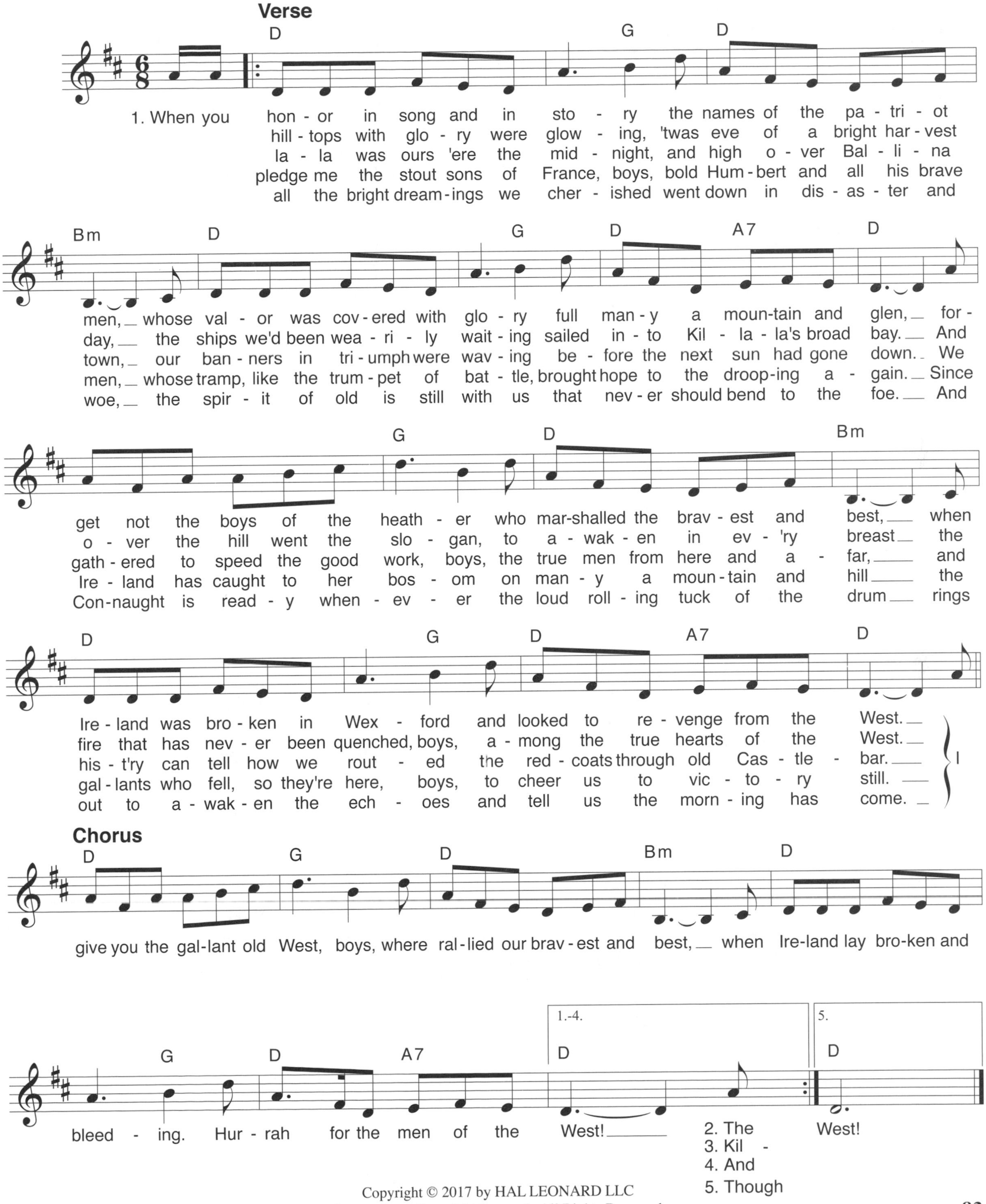
Verse
D G D
1. When you hon - or in song and in sto - ry the names of the pa - tri - ot
hill - tops with glo - ry were glow - ing, 'twas eve of a bright har - vest
la - la was ours 'ere the mid - night, and high o - ver Bal - li - na
pledge me the stout sons of France, boys, bold Hum - bert and all his brave
all the bright dream - ings we cher - ished went down in dis - as - ter and
Bm D G D A7 D
men, whose val - or was cov - ered with glo - ry full man - y a moun - tain and glen, for -
day, the ships we'd been wea - ri - ly wait - ing sailed in - to Kil - la - la's broad bay. And
town, our ban - ners in tri - umph were wav - ing be - fore the next sun had gone down. We
men, whose tramp, like the trum - pet of bat - tle, brought hope to the droop - ing a - gain. Since
woe, the spir - it of old is still with us that nev - er should bend to the foe. And
G D Bm
get not the boys of the heath - er who mar - shalled the brav - est and best, when
o - ver the hill went the slo - gan, to a - wak - en in ev - 'ry breast the
gath - ered to speed the good work, boys, the true men from here and a - far, and
Ire - land has caught to her bos - om on man - y a moun - tain and hill the
Con - naught is read - y when - ev - er the loud roll - ing tuck of the drum rings
D G D A7 D
Ire - land was bro - ken in Wex - ford and looked to re - venge from the West.
fire that has nev - er been quenched, boys, a - mong the true hearts of the West.
his - t'ry can tell how we rout - ed the red - coats through old Cas - tle - bar.
gal - lants who fell, so they're here, boys, to cheer us to vic - to - ry still.
out to a - wak - en the ech - oes and tell us the morn - ing has come.
I
Chorus
D G D Bm D
give you the gal - lant old West, boys, where ral - lied our brav - est and best, when Ire - land lay bro - ken and
G D A7
1.-4.
D
5.
D
bleed - ing. Hur - rah for the men of the West!
2. The
3. Kil -
4. And
5. Though
West!

Standard Ukulele

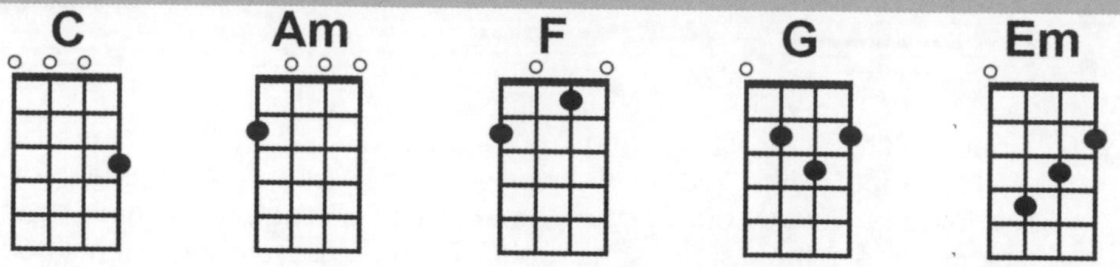
C
Am
F
G
Em

Baritone Ukulele

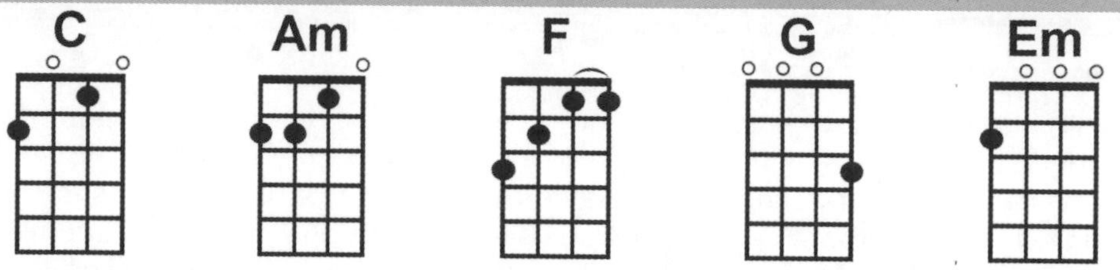
C
Am
F
G
Em

Guitar

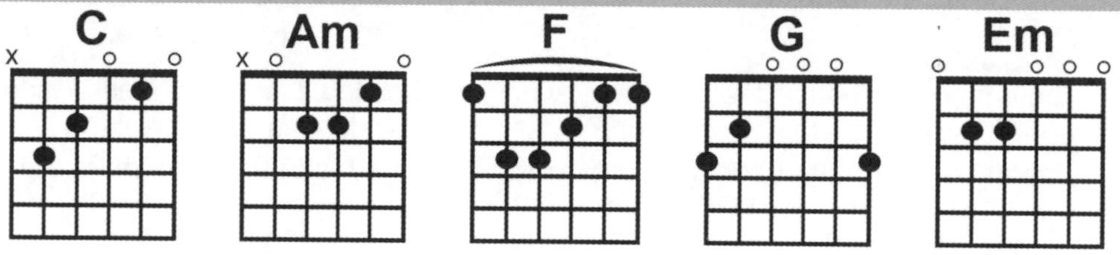
C
Am
F
G
Em

Mandolin

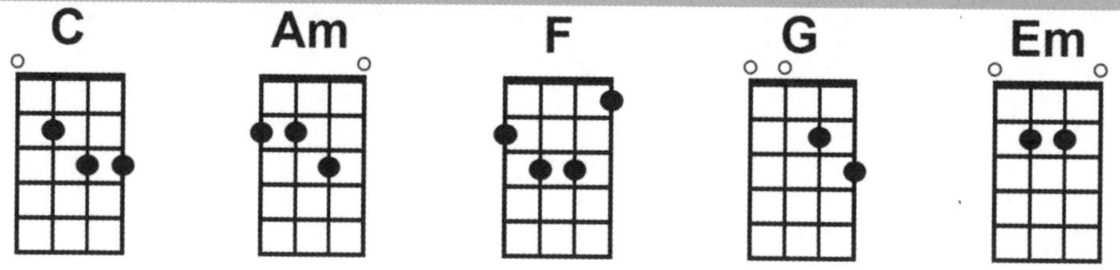
C
Am
F
G
Em

Banjo

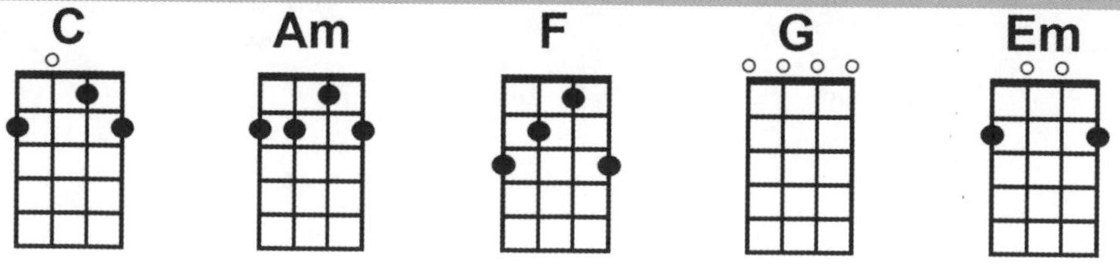
C
Am
F
G
Em

Minstrel Boy

Traditional

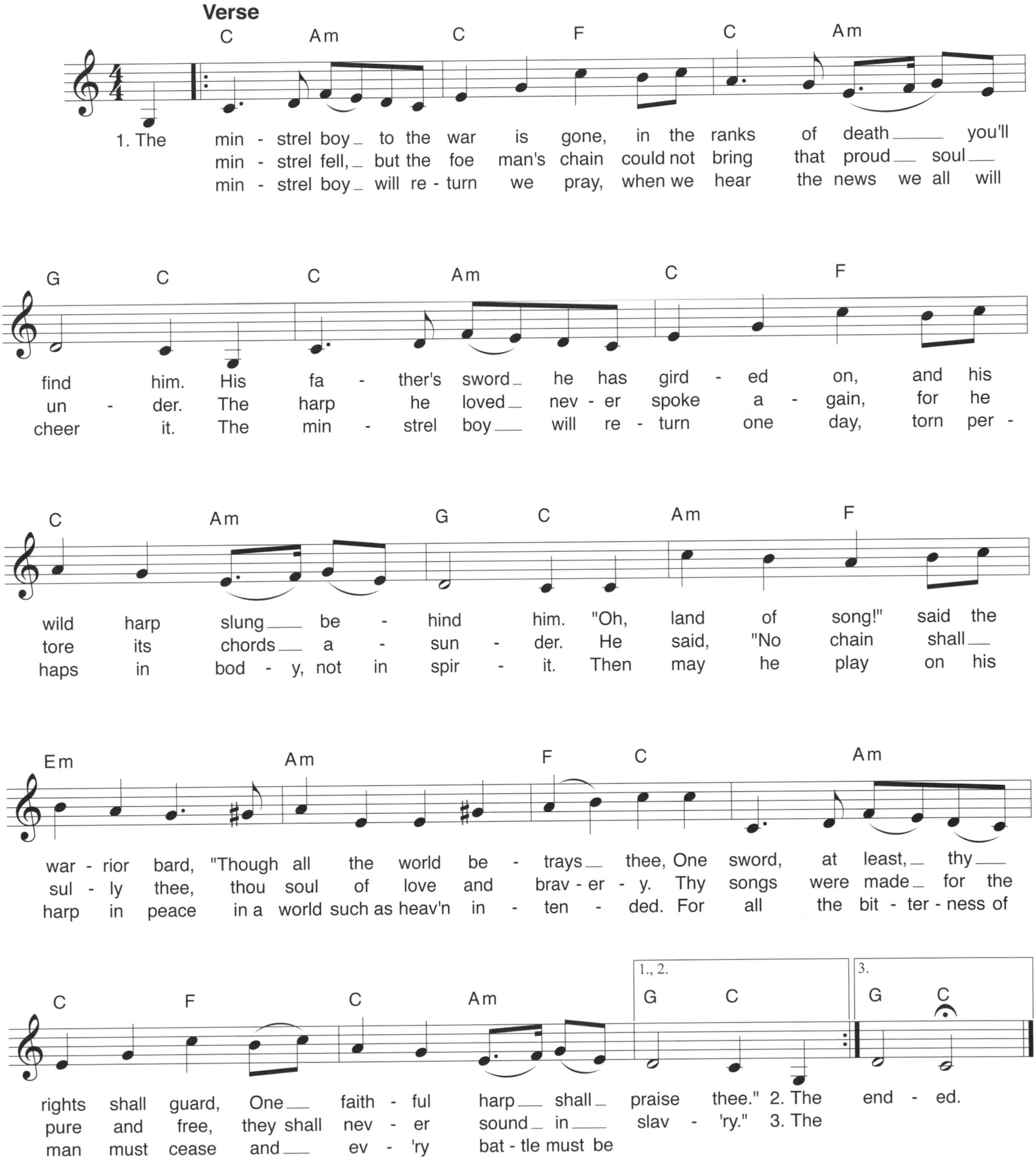
Verse
C Am C F C Am
1. The min - strel boy to the war is gone, in the ranks of death you'll
min - strel fell, but the foe man's chain could not bring that proud soul
min - strel boy will re - turn we pray, when we hear the news we all will
G C C Am C F
find him. His fa - ther's sword he has gird - ed on, and his
un - der. The harp he loved nev - er spoke a - gain, for he
cheer it. The min - strel boy will re - turn one day, torn per -
C Am G C Am F
wild harp slung be - hind him. "Oh, land of song!" said the
tore its chords a - sun - der. He said, "No chain shall
haps in bod - y, not in spir - it. Then may he play on his
Em Am F C Am
war - rior bard, "Though all the world be - trays thee, One sword, at least, thy
sul - ly thee, thou soul of love and brav - er - y. Thy songs were made for the
harp in peace in a world such as heav'n in - ten - ded. For all the bit - ter - ness of
C F C Am
1., 2. G C
3. G C
rights shall guard, One faith - ful harp shall praise thee." 2. The end - ed.
pure and free, they shall nev - er sound in slav - 'ry." 3. The
man must cease and ev - 'ry bat - tle must be

Standard Ukulele

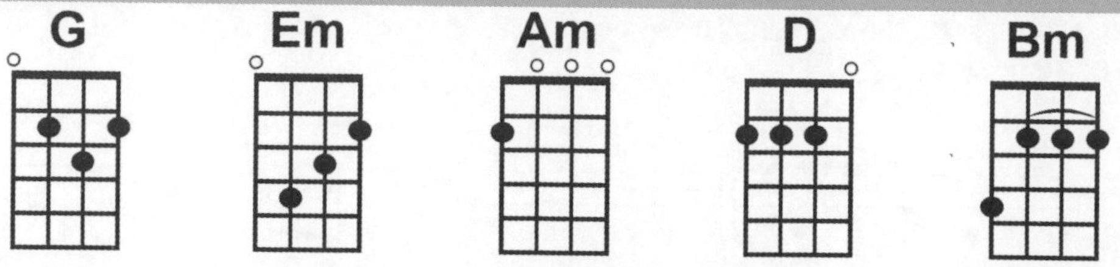
G
Em
Am
D
Bm

Baritone Ukulele

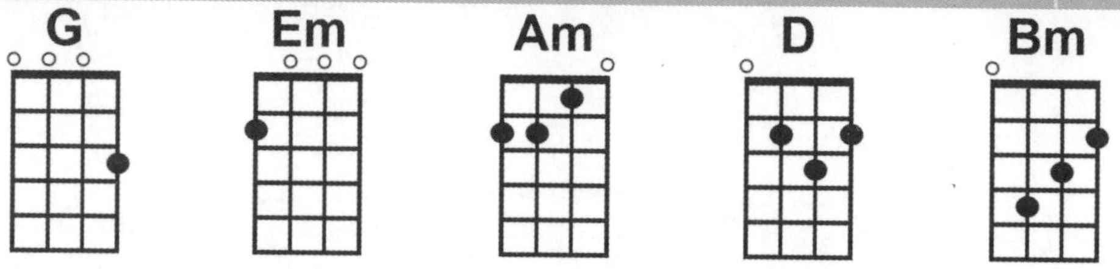
G
Em
Am
D
Bm

Guitar

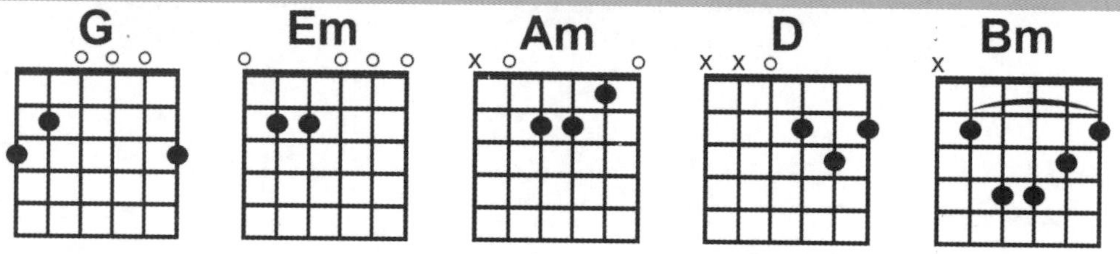
G
Em
Am
D
Bm

Mandolin

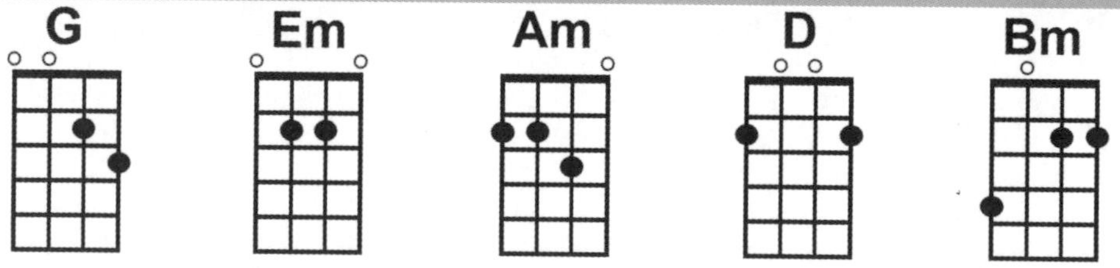
G
Em
Am
D
Bm

Banjo

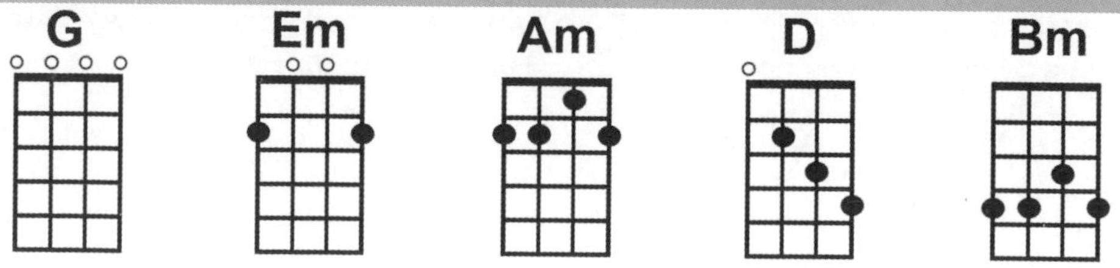
G
Em
Am
D
Bm

Molly Malone
(Cockles & Mussels)
Irish Folk Song

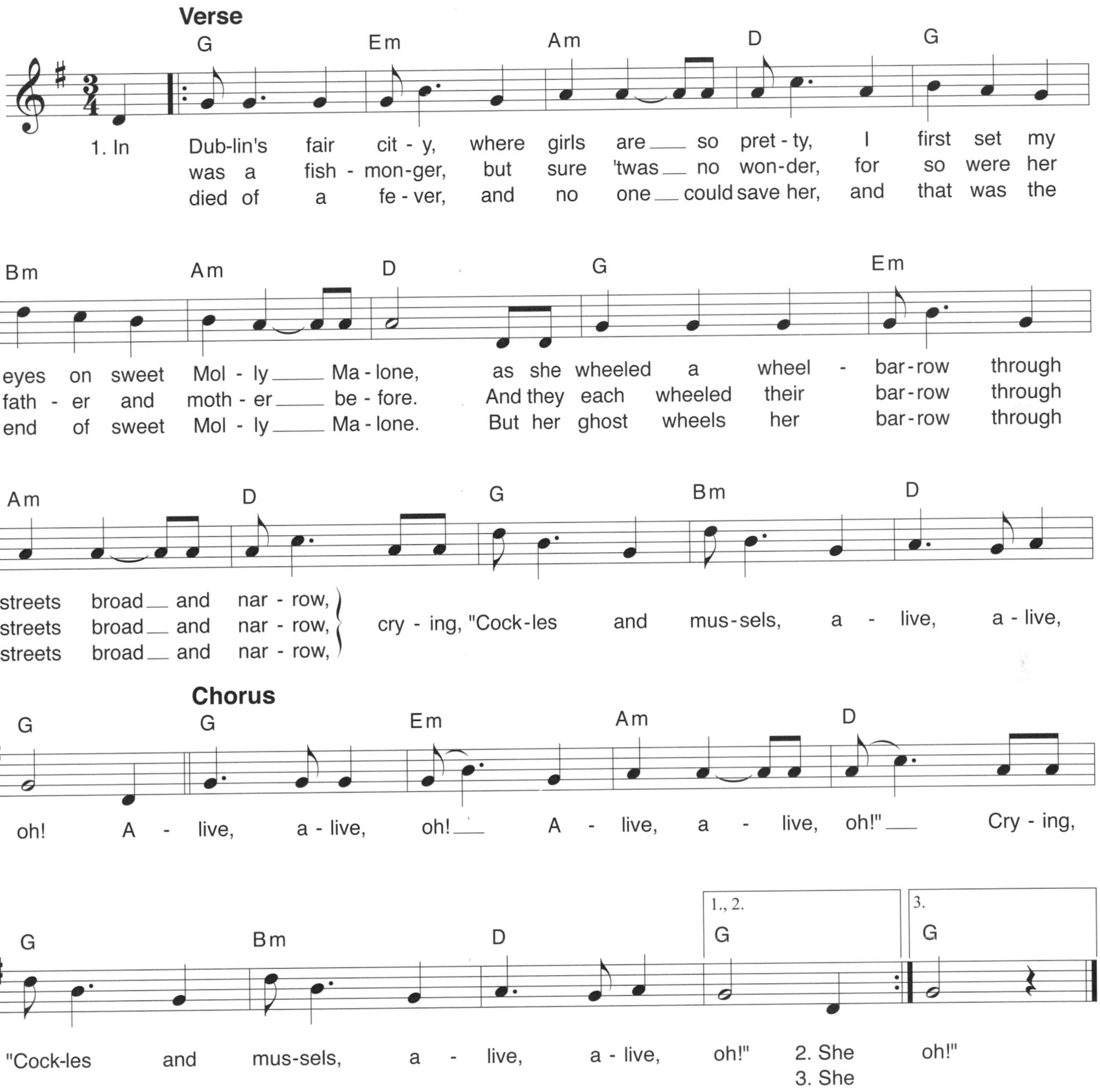
Verse
G Em Am D G
1. In Dub-lin's fair cit - y, where girls are so pret - ty, I first set my
was a fish - mon-ger, but sure 'twas no won-der, for so were her
died of a fe - ver, and no one could save her, and that was the
Bm Am D G Em
eyes on sweet Mol - ly Ma - lone, as she wheeled a wheel - bar-row through
fath - er and moth - er be - fore. And they each wheeled their bar-row through
end of sweet Mol - ly Ma - lone. But her ghost wheels her bar-row through
Am D G Bm D
streets broad and nar - row,
streets broad and nar - row,
streets broad and nar - row,
cry - ing, "Cock-les and mus-sels, a - live, a - live,
Chorus
G G Em Am D
oh! A - live, a - live, oh! A - live, a - live, oh!" Cry - ing,
G Bm D
1., 2. G
3. G
"Cock-les and mus-sels, a - live, a - live, oh!" 2. She oh!"
3. She

Standard Ukulele

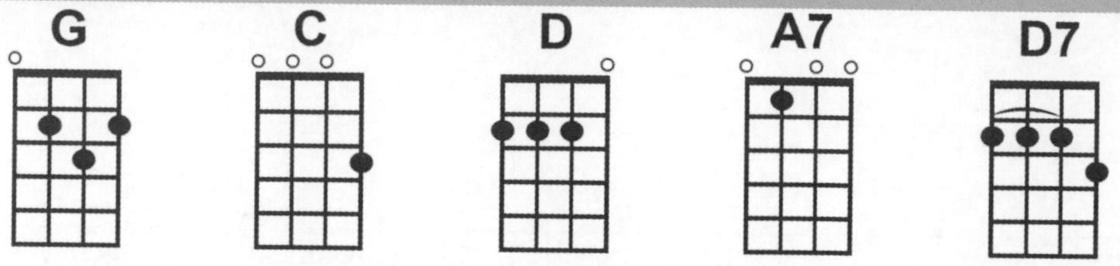
G
C
D
A7
D7

Baritone Ukulele

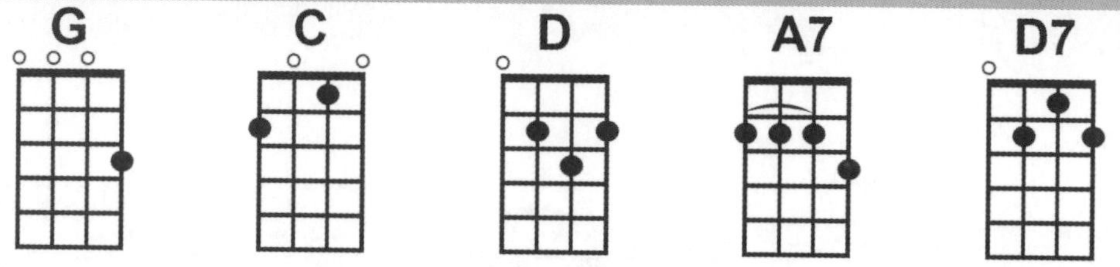
G
C
D
A7
D7

Guitar

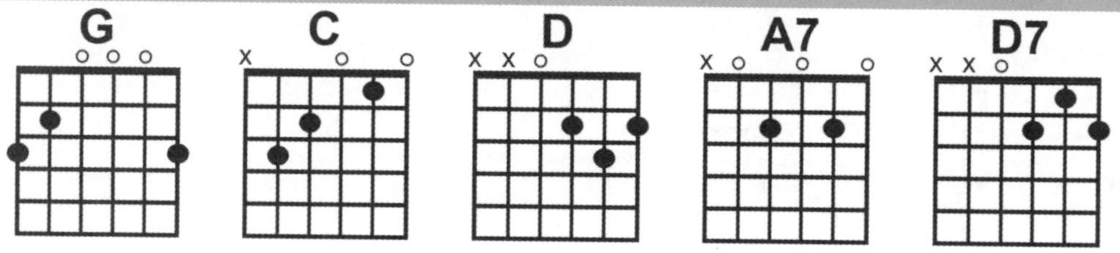
G
C
D
A7
D7

Mandolin

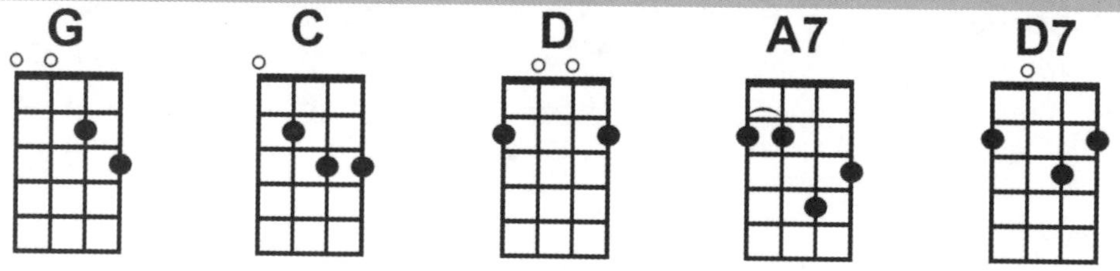
G
C
D
A7
D7

Banjo

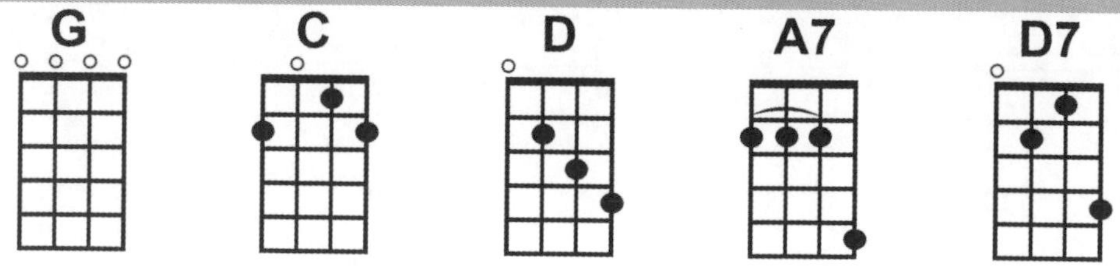
G
C
D
A7
D7

The Mountains of Mourne

Words by Percy French
Traditional Irish Melody

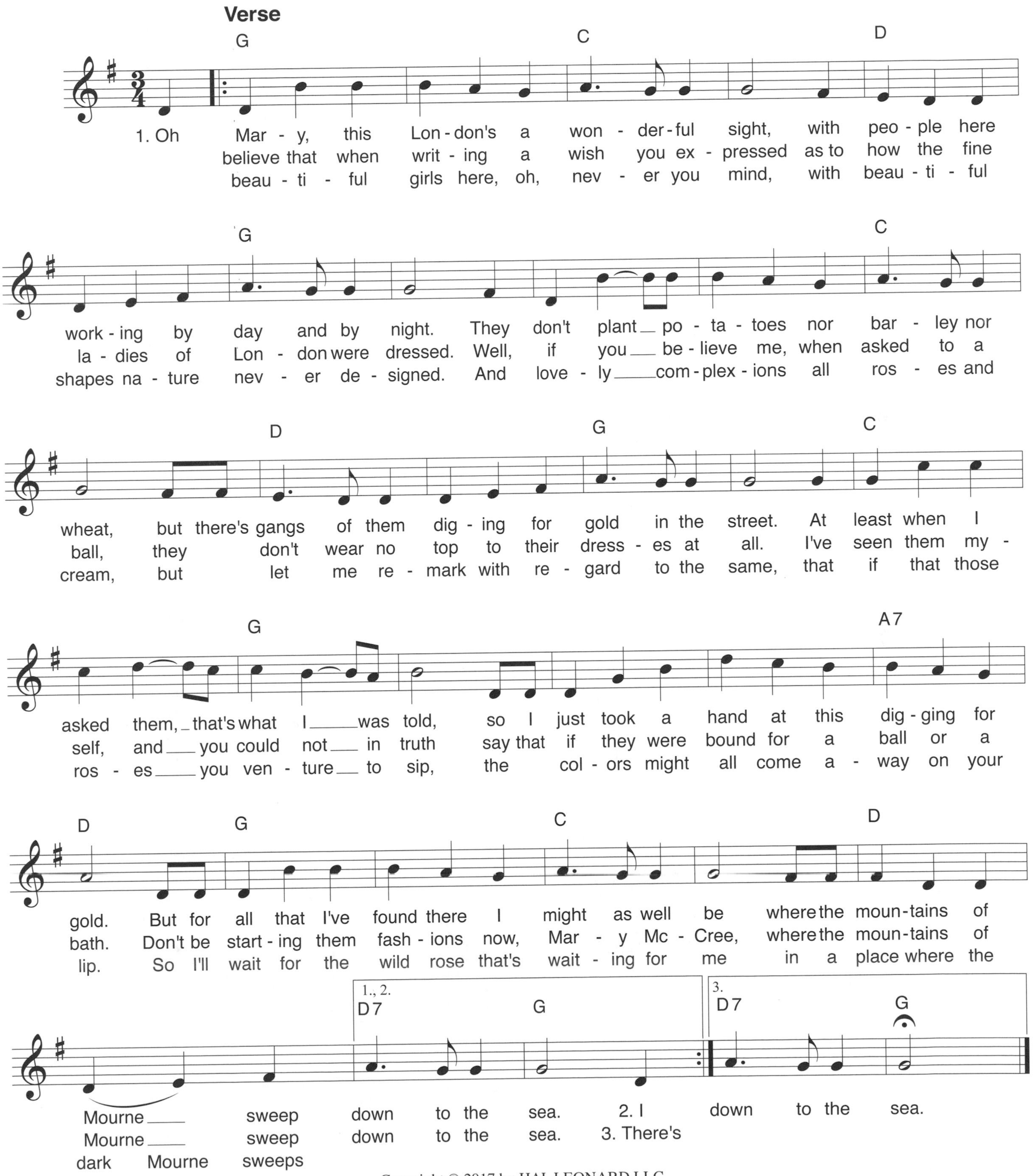
Verse
G C D
1. Oh Mar - y, this Lon - don's a won - der - ful sight, with peo - ple here
believe that when writ - ing a wish you ex - pressed as to how the fine
beau - ti - ful girls here, oh, nev - er you mind, with beau - ti - ful
G C
work - ing by day and by night. They don't plant po - ta - toes nor bar - ley nor
la - dies of Lon - don were dressed. Well, if you be - lieve me, when asked to a
shapes na - ture nev - er de - signed. And love - ly com - plex - ions all ros - es and
D G C
wheat, but there's gangs of them dig - ing for gold in the street. At least when I
ball, they don't wear no top to their dress - es at all. I've seen them my -
cream, but let me re - mark with re - gard to the same, that if that those
G A7
asked them, that's what I was told, so I just took a hand at this dig - ging for
self, and you could not in truth say that if they were bound for a ball or a
ros - es you ven - ture to sip, the col - ors might all come a - way on your
D G C D
gold. But for all that I've found there I might as well be where the moun - tains of
bath. Don't be start - ing them fash - ions now, Mar - y Mc - Cree, where the moun - tains of
lip. So I'll wait for the wild rose that's wait - ing for me in a place where the
1., 2. D7 G 3. D7 G
Mourne sweep down to the sea. 2. I down to the sea.
Mourne sweep down to the sea. 3. There's
dark Mourne sweeps

Standard Ukulele

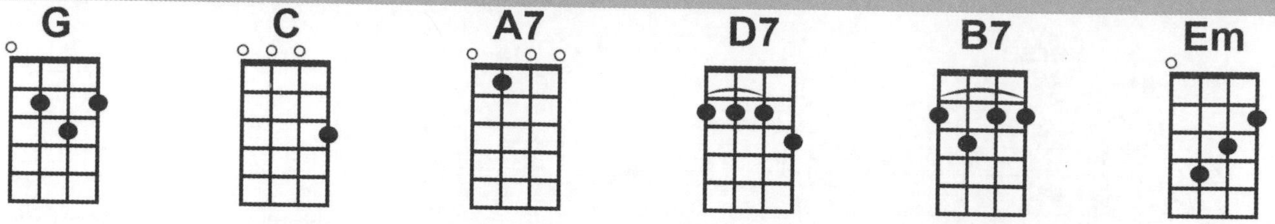
G
C
A7
D7
B7
Em

Baritone Ukulele

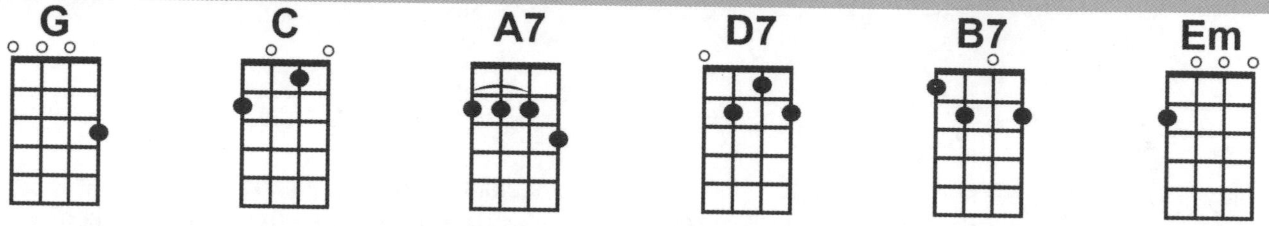
G
C
A7
D7
B7
Em

Guitar

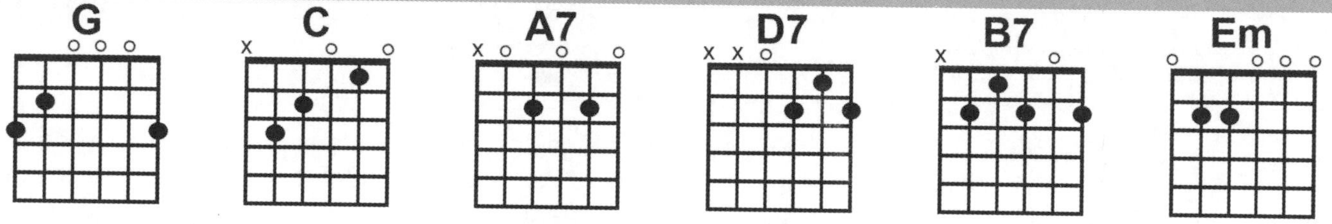
G
C
A7
D7
B7
Em

Mandolin

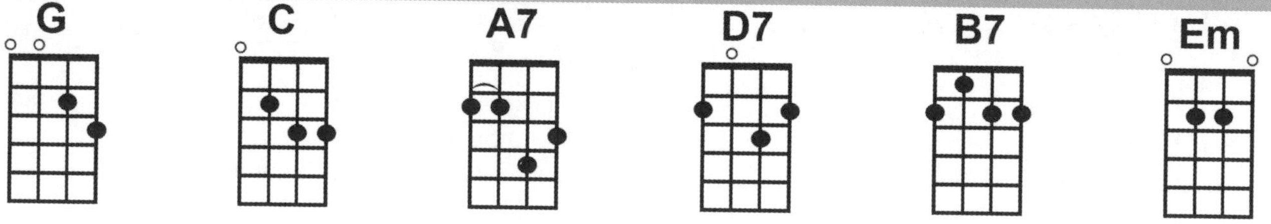
G
C
A7
D7
B7
Em

Banjo

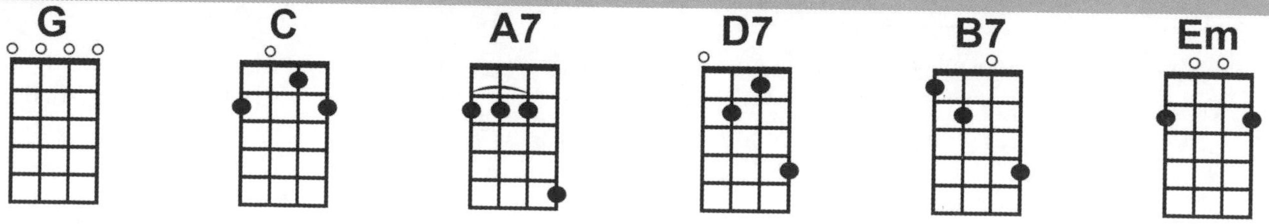
G
C
A7
D7
B7
Em

My Wild Irish Rose

Words and Music by Chauncey Olcott

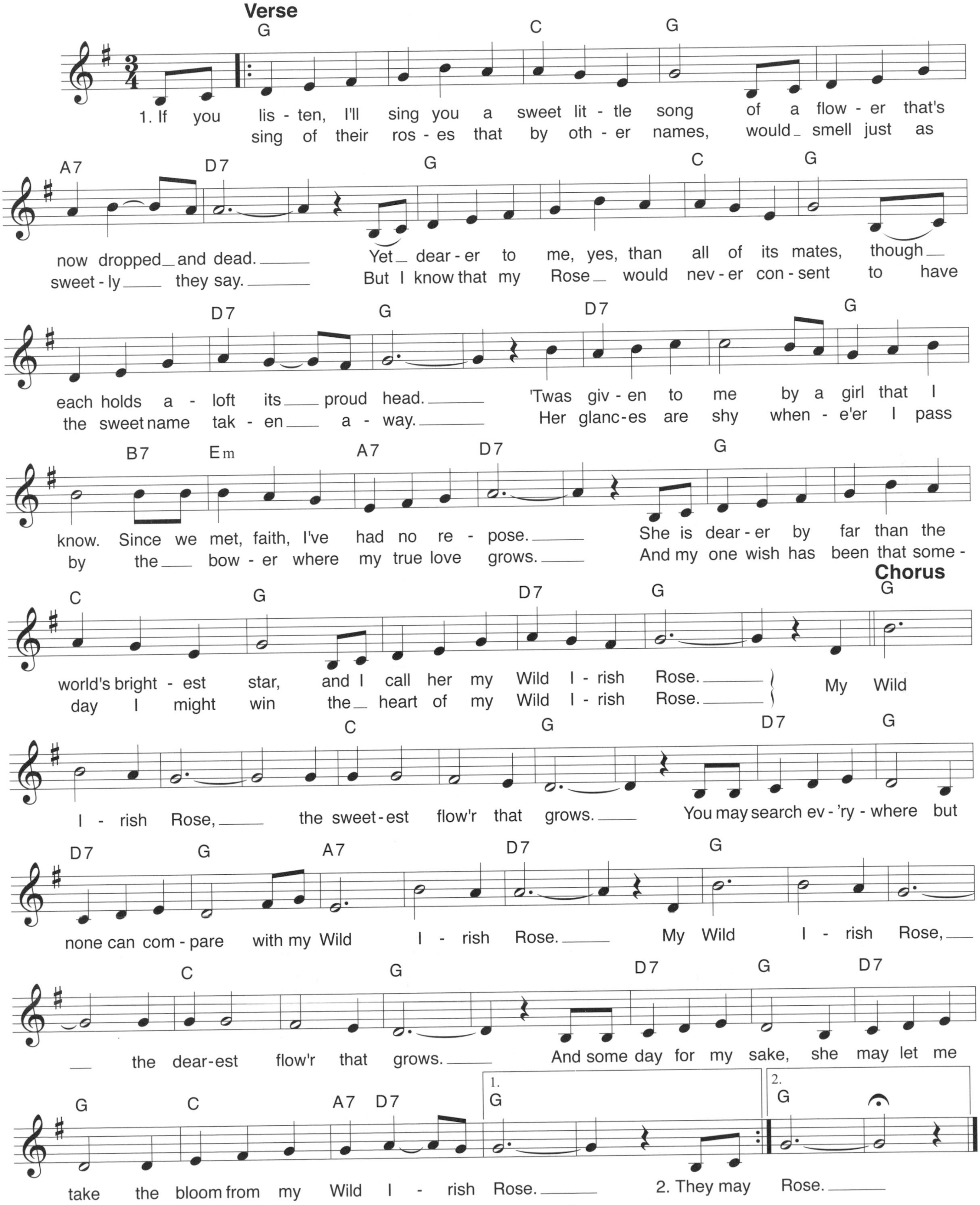
Verse
1. If you lis - ten, I'll sing you a sweet lit - tle song of a flow - er that's
sing of their ros - es that by oth - er names, would smell just as
now dropped and dead. Yet dear - er to me, yes, than all of its mates, though
sweet - ly they say. But I know that my Rose would nev - er con - sent to have
each holds a - loft its proud head. 'Twas giv - en to me by a girl that I
the sweet name tak - en a - way. Her glanc - es are shy when - e'er I pass
know. Since we met, faith, I've had no re - pose. She is dear - er by far than the
by the bow - er where my true love grows. And my one wish has been that some -
world's bright - est star, and I call her my Wild I - rish Rose.
day I might win the heart of my Wild I - rish Rose.
Chorus
My Wild I - rish Rose, the sweet - est flow'r that grows. You may search ev - 'ry - where but
none can com - pare with my Wild I - rish Rose. My Wild I - rish Rose,
the dear - est flow'r that grows. And some day for my sake, she may let me
take the bloom from my Wild I - rish Rose. 2. They may Rose.

Standard Ukulele

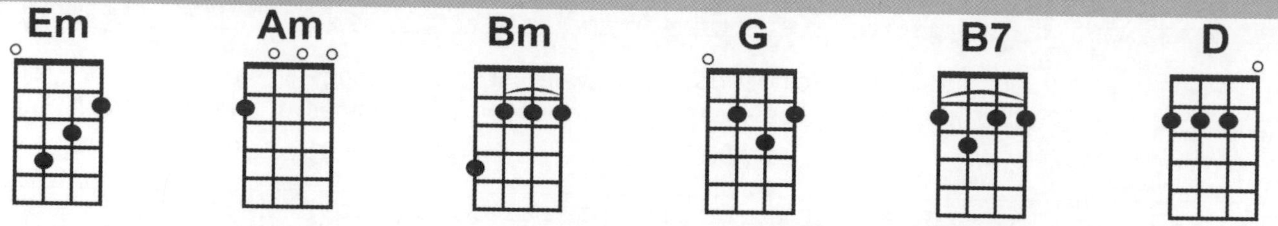
Em
Am
Bm
G
B7
D

Baritone Ukulele

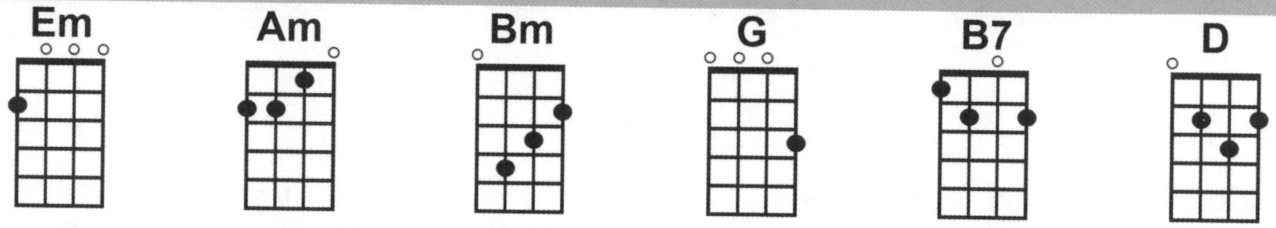
Em
Am
Bm
G
B7
D

Guitar

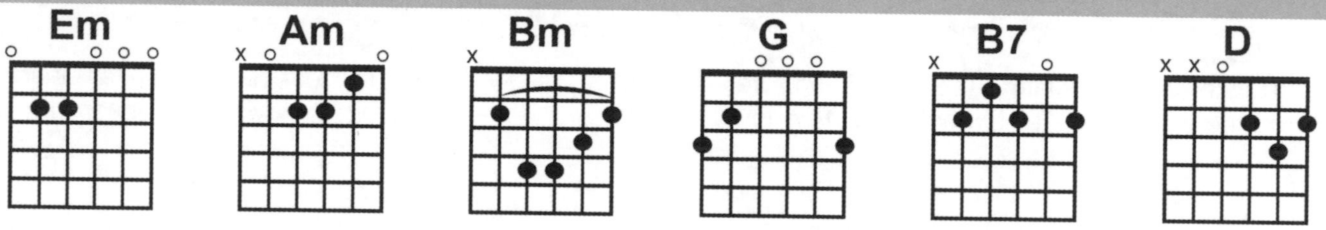
Em
Am
Bm
G
B7
D

Mandolin

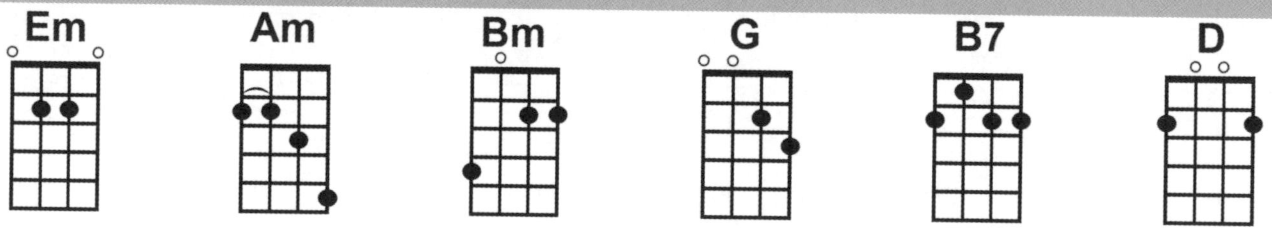
Em
Am
Bm
G
B7
D

Banjo

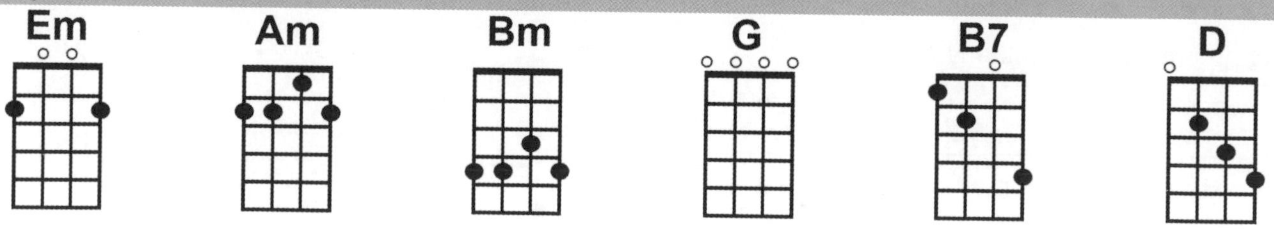
Em
Am
Bm
G
B7
D

The Next Market Day

Traditional Irish Folk Song

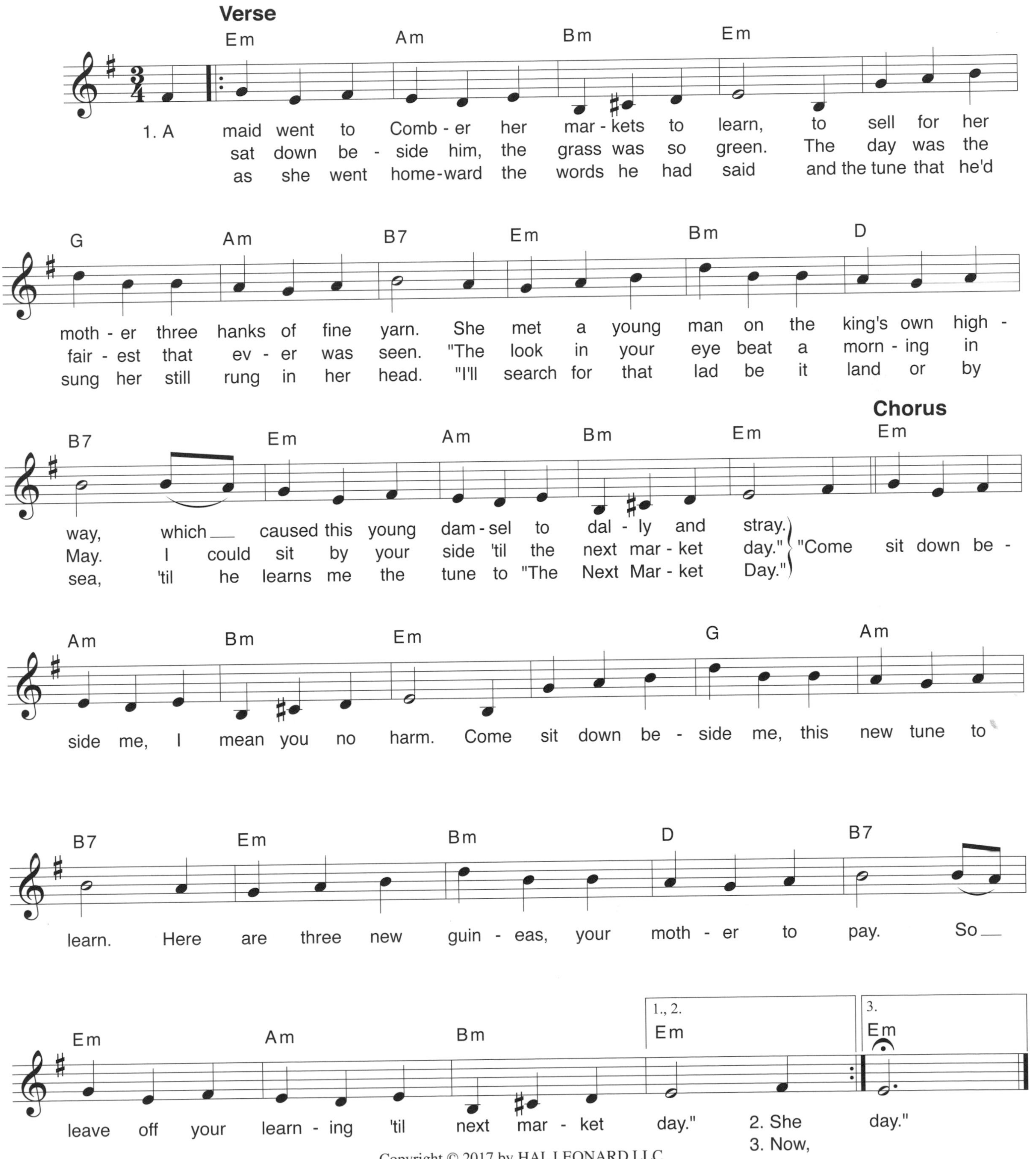
Verse
Em Am Bm Em
1. A maid went to Comb - er her mar - kets to learn, to sell for her
sat down be - side him, the grass was so green. The day was the
as she went home-ward the words he had said and the tune that he'd
G Am B7 Em Bm D
moth - er three hanks of fine yarn. She met a young man on the king's own high -
fair - est that ev - er was seen. "The look in your eye beat a morn - ing in
sung her still rung in her head. "I'll search for that lad be it land or by
Chorus
B7 Em Am Bm Em Em
way, which caused this young dam - sel to dal - ly and stray.
May. I could sit by your side 'til the next mar - ket day."
sea, 'til he learns me the tune to "The Next Mar - ket Day."
"Come sit down be -
Am Bm Em G Am
side me, I mean you no harm. Come sit down be - side me, this new tune to
B7 Em Bm D B7
learn. Here are three new guin - eas, your moth - er to pay. So
1., 2.
3.
Em Am Bm Em Em
leave off your learn - ing 'til next mar - ket day."
2. She
3. Now,
day."

Standard Ukulele

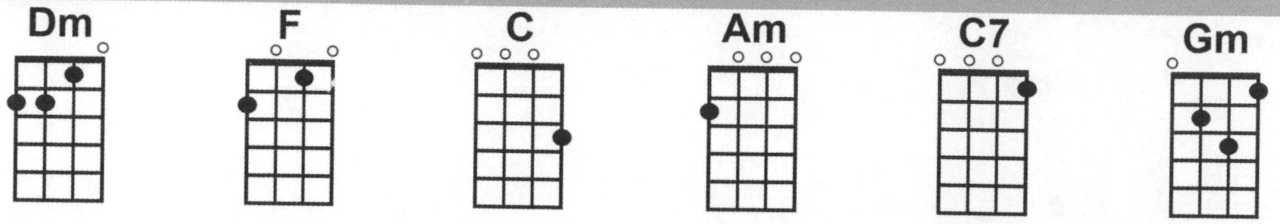
Dm
F
C
Am
C7
Gm

Baritone Ukulele

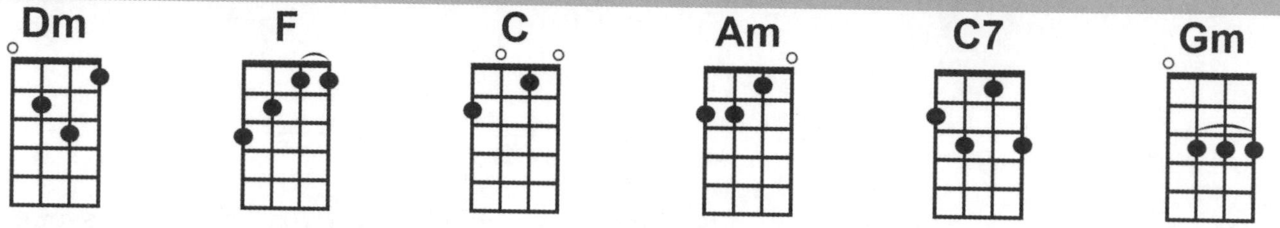
Dm
F
C
Am
C7
Gm

Guitar

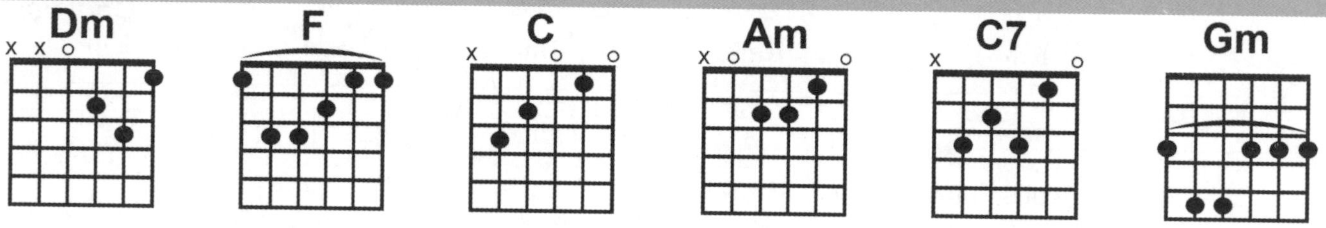
Dm
F
C
Am
C7
Gm

Mandolin

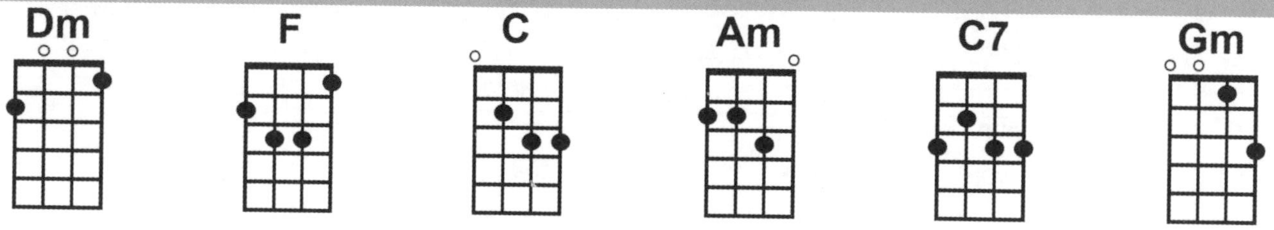
Dm
F
C
Am
C7
Gm

Banjo

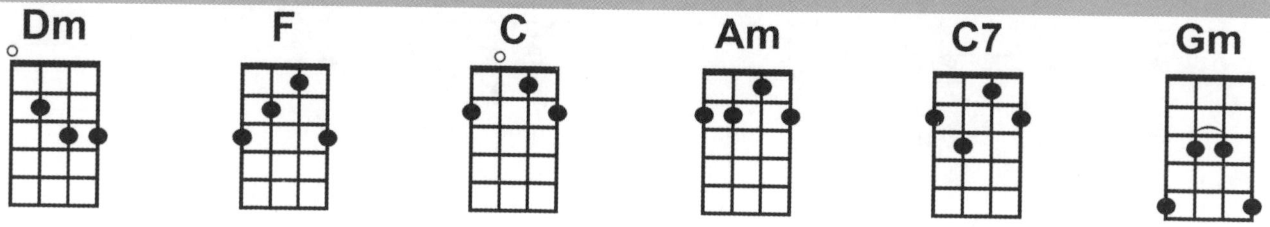
Dm
F
C
Am
C7
Gm

The Parting Glass

Irish Folk Song

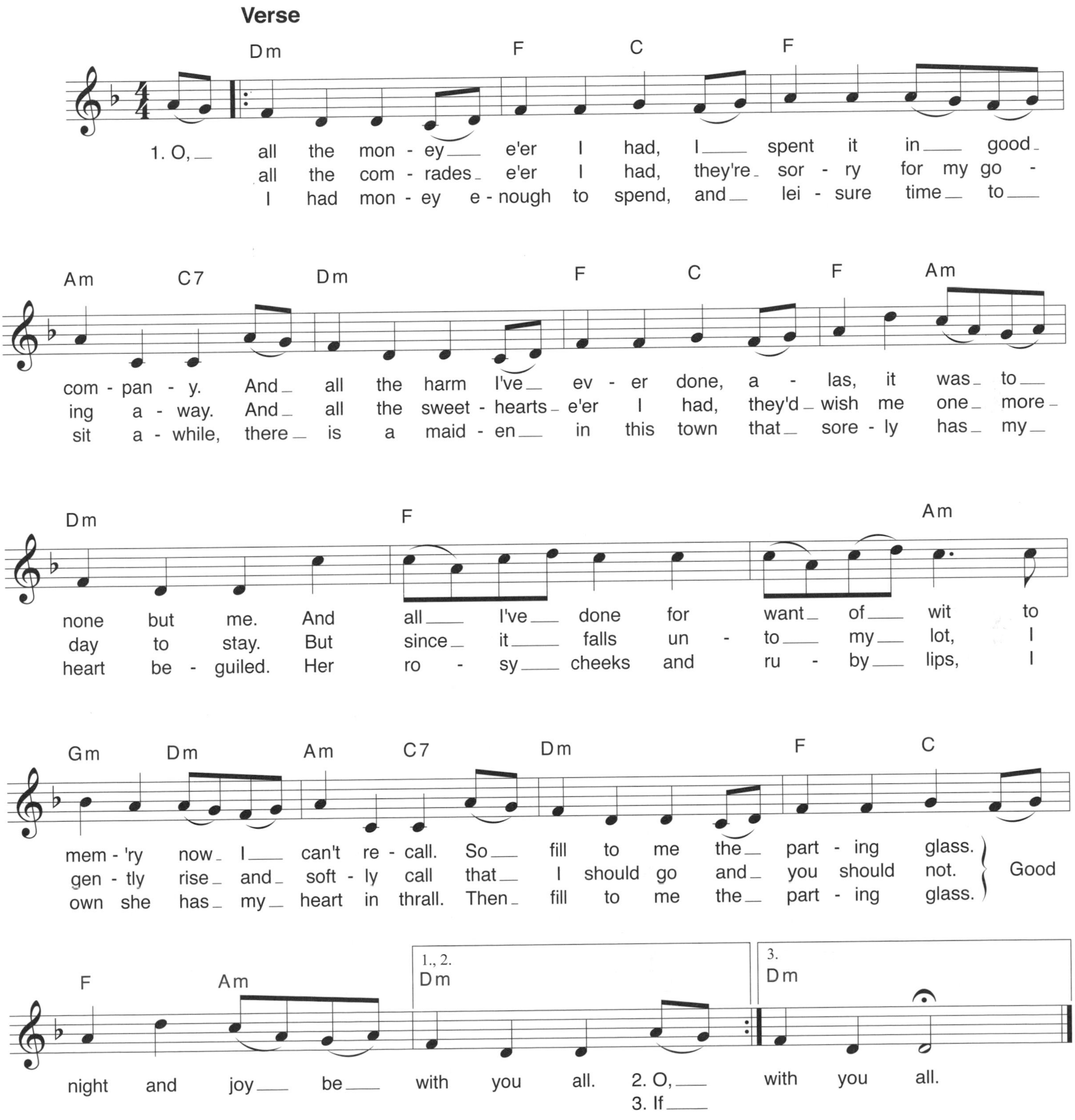
Verse
Dm F C F
1. O, all the mon - ey e'er I had, I spent it in good
all the com - rades e'er I had, they're sor - ry for my go -
I had mon - ey e - nough to spend, and lei - sure time to
Am C7 Dm F C F Am
com - pan - y. And all the harm I've ev - er done, a - las, it was to
ing a - way. And all the sweet - hearts e'er I had, they'd wish me one more
sit a - while, there is a maid - en in this town that sore - ly has my
Dm F Am
none but me. And all I've done for want of wit to
day to stay. But since it falls un - to my lot, I
heart be - guiled. Her ro - sy cheeks and ru - by lips, I
Gm Dm Am C7 Dm F C
mem - 'ry now I can't re - call. So fill to me the part - ing glass.
gen - tly rise and soft - ly call that I should go and you should not.
own she has my heart in thrall. Then fill to me the part - ing glass.
Good
F Am
night and joy be with you all.
1., 2.
Dm
with you all. 2. O,
3. If
3.
Dm
with you all.

Standard Ukulele

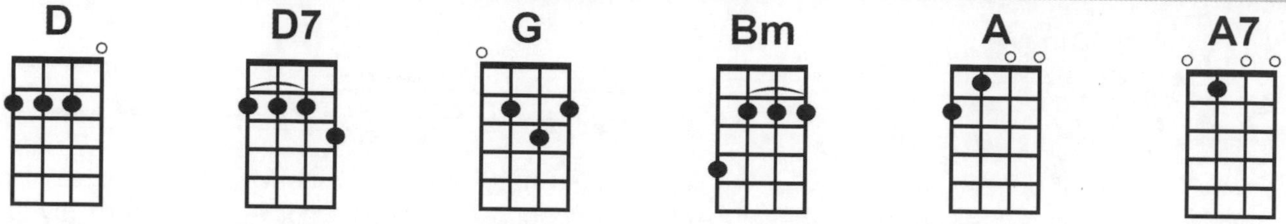
D
D7
G
Bm
A
A7

Baritone Ukulele

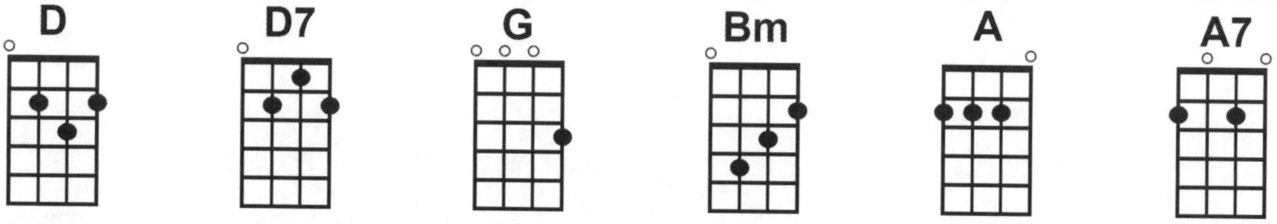
D
D7
G
Bm
A
A7

Guitar

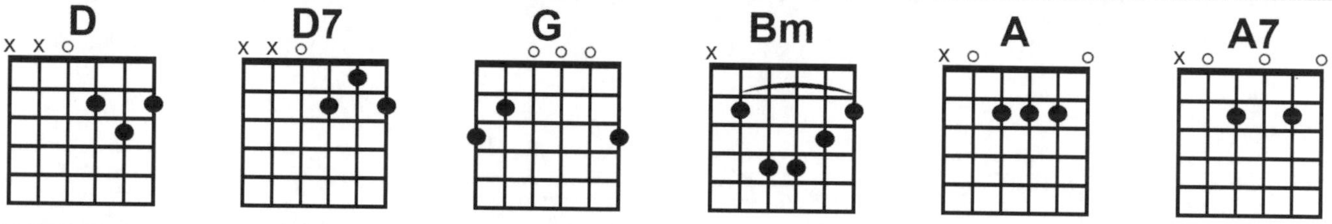
D
D7
G
Bm
A
A7

Mandolin

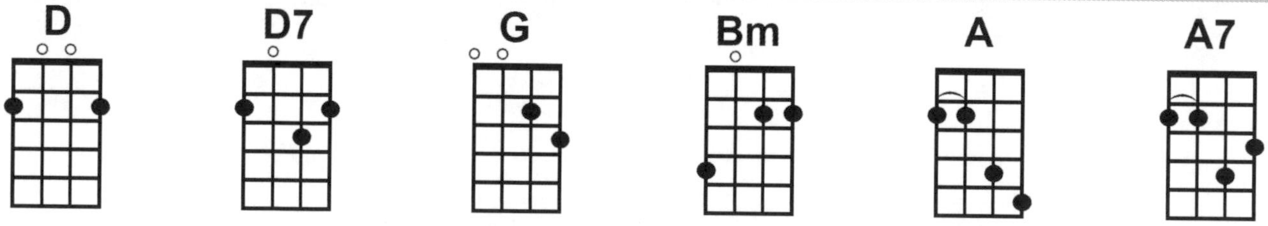
D
D7
G
Bm
A
A7

Banjo

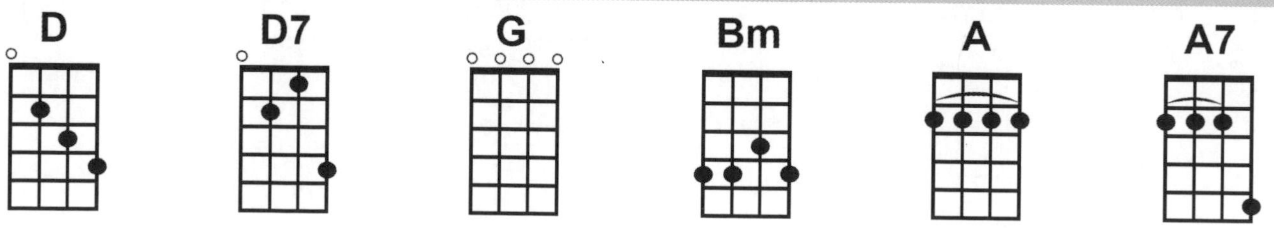
D
D7
G
Bm
A
A7

Raglan Road

Traditional Irish Folk Song

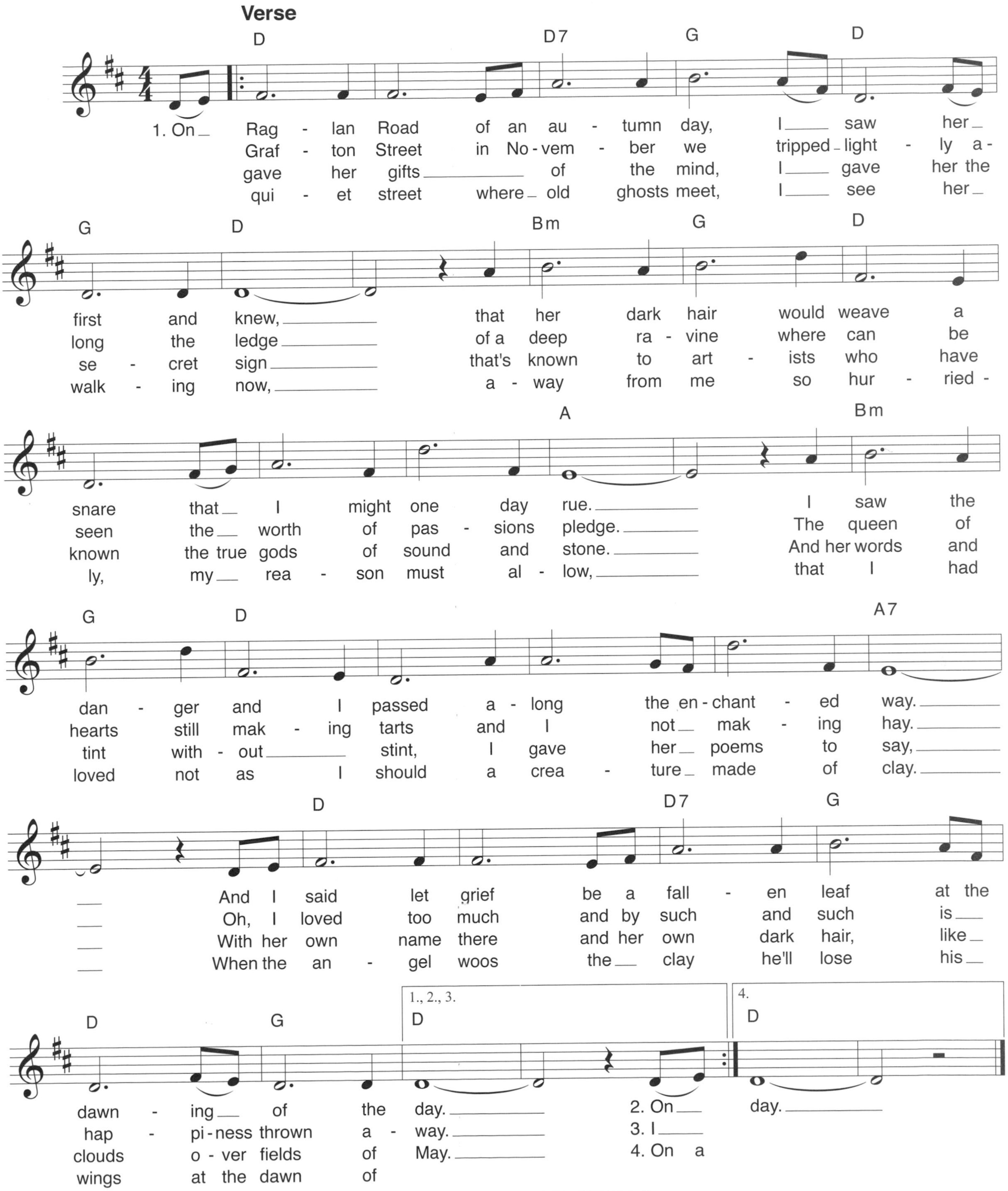
Verse
D D7 G D
1. On Rag - lan Road of an au - tumn day, I saw her
Graf - ton Street in No - vem - ber we tripped light - ly a -
gave her gifts of the mind, I gave her the
qui - et street where old ghosts meet, I see her
G D Bm G D
first and knew, that her dark hair would weave a
long the ledge of a deep ra - vine where can be
se - cret sign that's known to art - ists who have
walk - ing now, a - way from me so hur - ried -
A Bm
snare that I might one day rue. I saw the
seen the worth of pas - sions pledge. The queen of
known the true gods of sound and stone. And her words and
ly, my rea - son must al - low, that I had
G D A7
dan - ger and I passed a - long the en - chant - ed way.
hearts still mak - ing tarts and I not mak - ing hay.
tint with - out stint, I gave her poems to say,
loved not as I should a crea - ture made of clay.
D D7 G
And I said let grief be a fall - en leaf at the
Oh, I loved too much and by such and such is
With her own name there and her own dark hair, like
When the an - gel woos the clay he'll lose his
D G
dawn - ing of the day.
hap - pi - ness thrown a - way.
clouds o - ver fields of May.
wings at the dawn of
1., 2., 3.
D
2. On
3. I
4. On a
4.
D
day.

Standard Ukulele

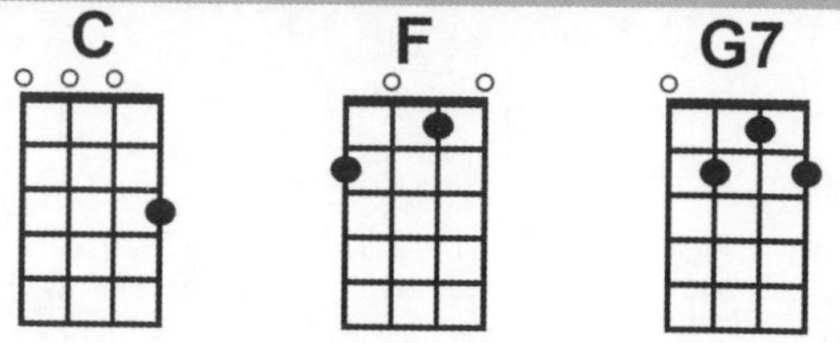

Baritone Ukulele

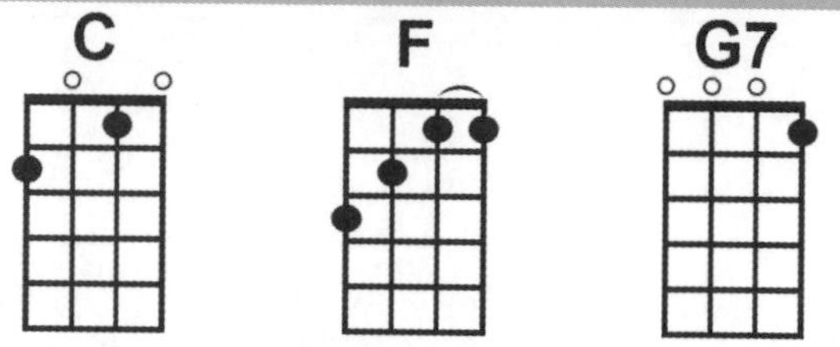

Guitar

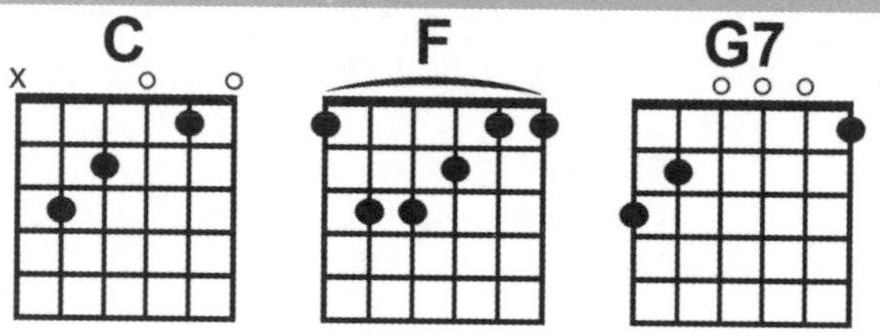

Mandolin

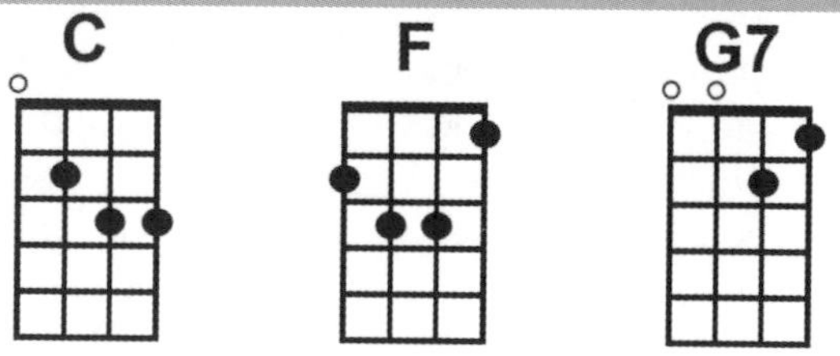

Banjo

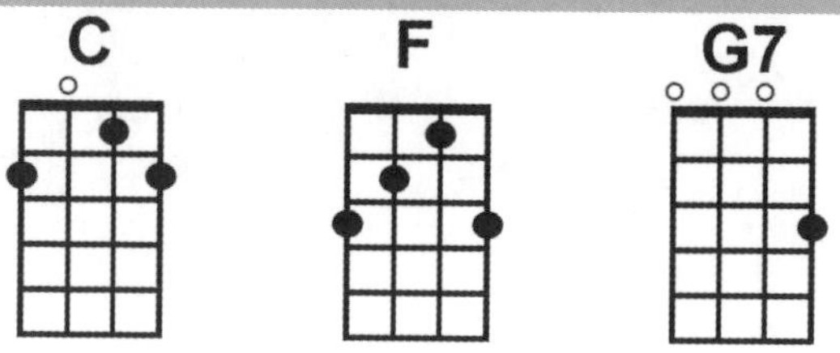

Rake and Rambling Boy

Irish Folk Song

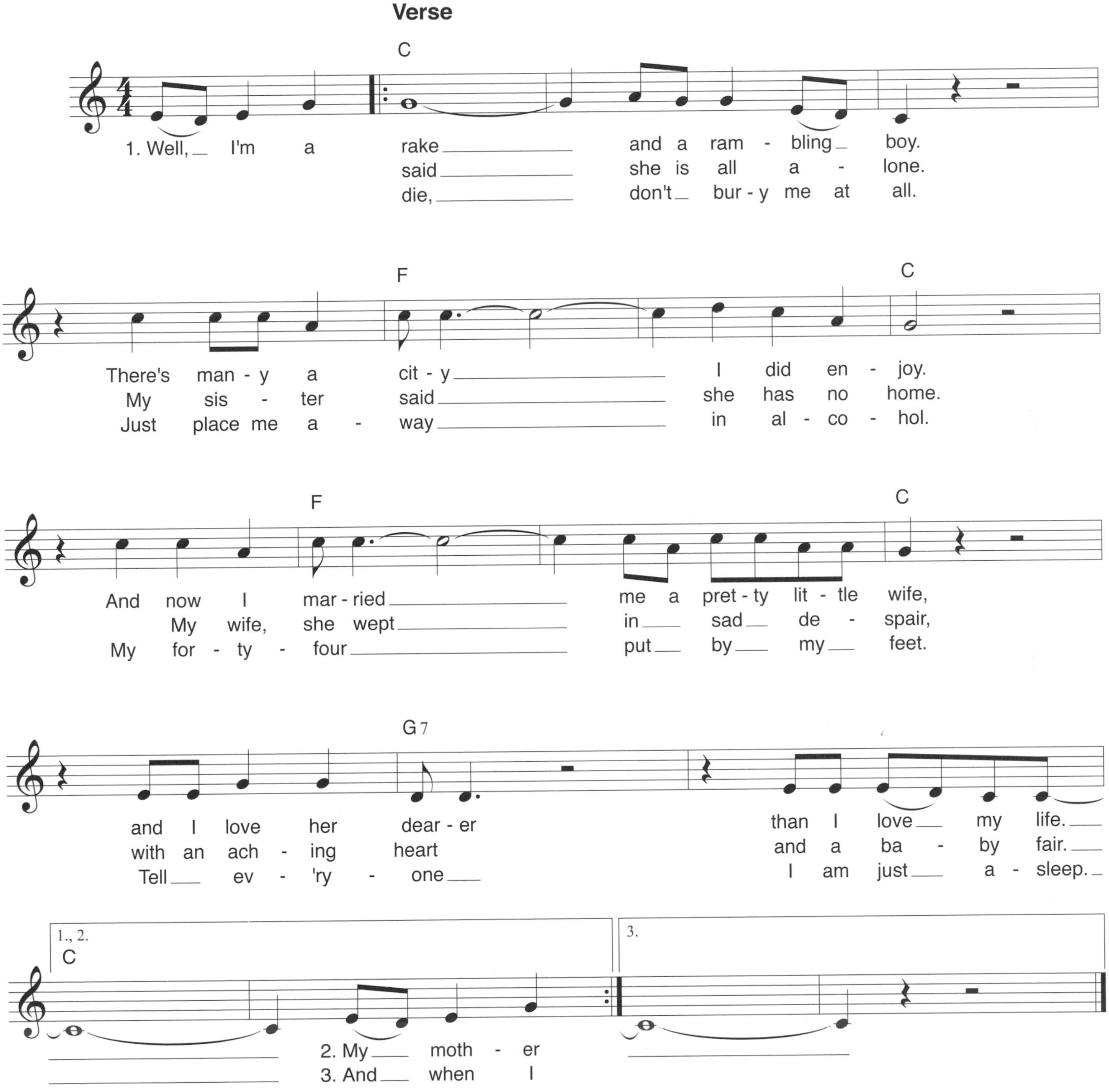
Verse
C
1. Well, I'm a rake and a ram - bling boy.
said she is all a - lone.
die, don't bur - y me at all.
F
C
There's man - y a cit - y I did en - joy.
My sis - ter said she has no home.
Just place me a - way in al - co - hol.
F
C
And now I mar - ried me a pret - ty lit - tle wife,
My wife, she wept in sad de - spair,
My for - ty - four put by my feet.
G7
and I love her dear - er than I love my life.
with an ach - ing heart and a ba - by fair.
Tell ev - 'ry - one I am just a - sleep.
1., 2.
C
2. My moth - er
3. And when I
3.

Standard Ukulele

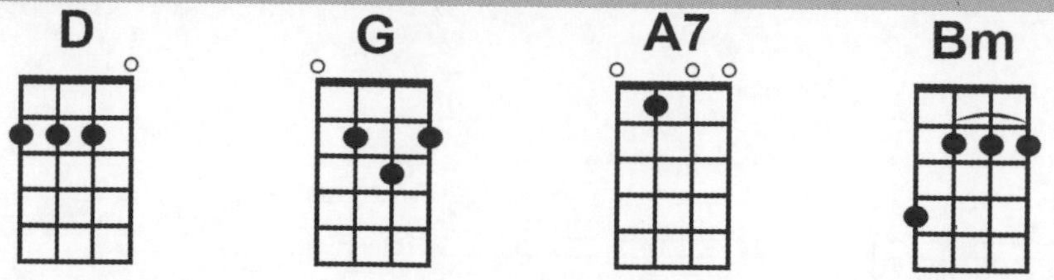

Baritone Ukulele

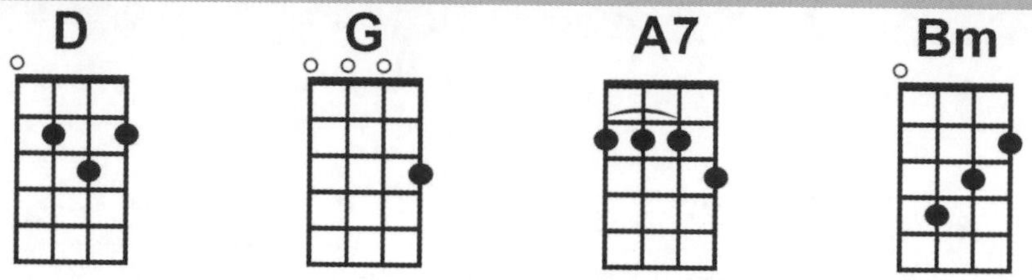

Guitar

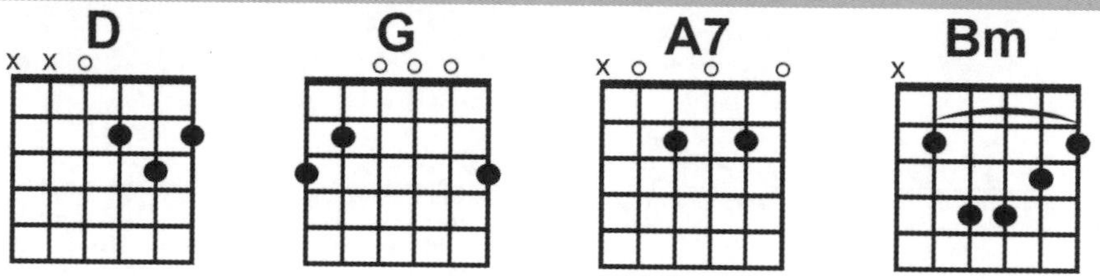

Mandolin

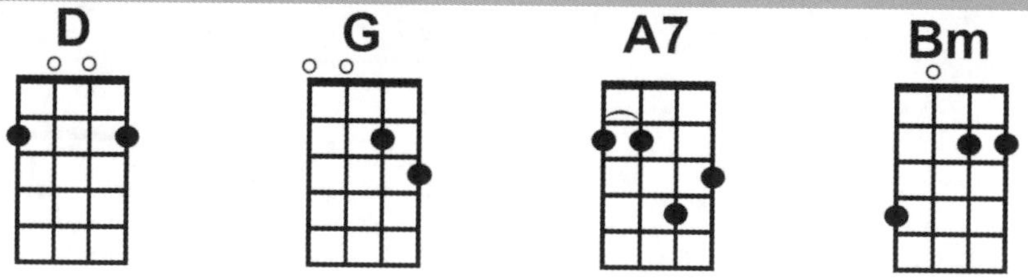

Banjo

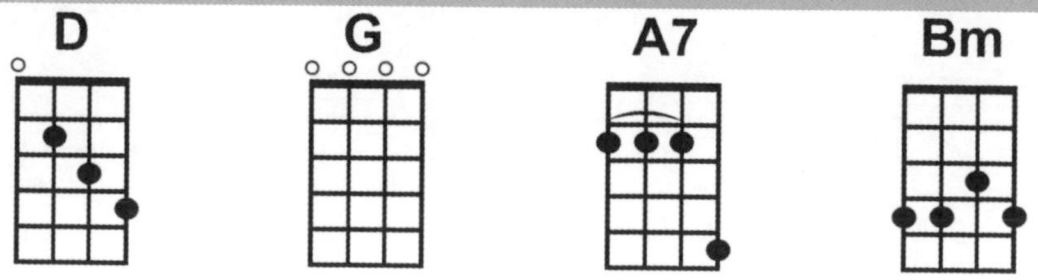

Real Old Mountain Dew

Irish Folk Song
Words by Edward Harrigan

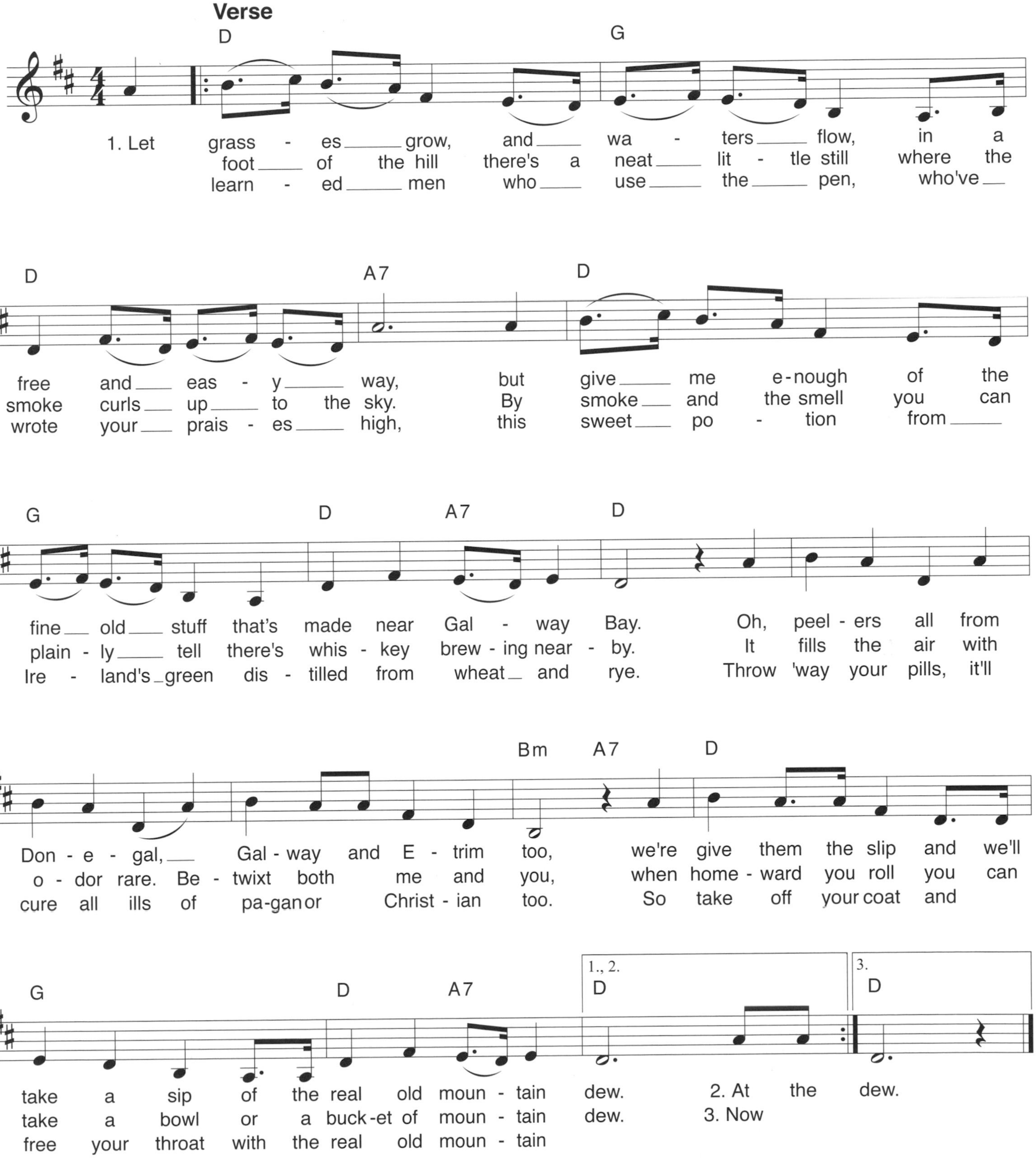
Verse
D G D A7 D G D A7 D Bm A7 D G D A7
1., 2.
3.
1. Let grass - es grow, and wa - ters flow, in a free and eas - y way, but give me e-nough of the fine old stuff that's made near Gal - way Bay. Oh, peel - ers all from Don - e - gal, Gal - way and E - trim too, we're give them the slip and we'll take a sip of the real old moun - tain dew. 2. At the
foot of the hill there's a neat lit - tle still where the smoke curls up to the sky. By smoke and the smell you can plain - ly tell there's whis - key brew - ing near - by. It fills the air with o - dor rare. Be - twixt both me and you, when home - ward you roll you can take a bowl or a buck - et of moun - tain dew. 3. Now
learn - ed men who use the pen, who've wrote your prais - es high, this sweet po - tion from Ire - land's green dis - tilled from wheat and rye. Throw 'way your pills, it'll cure all ills of pa - gan or Christ - ian too. So take off your coat and free your throat with the real old moun - tain dew.

Standard Ukulele

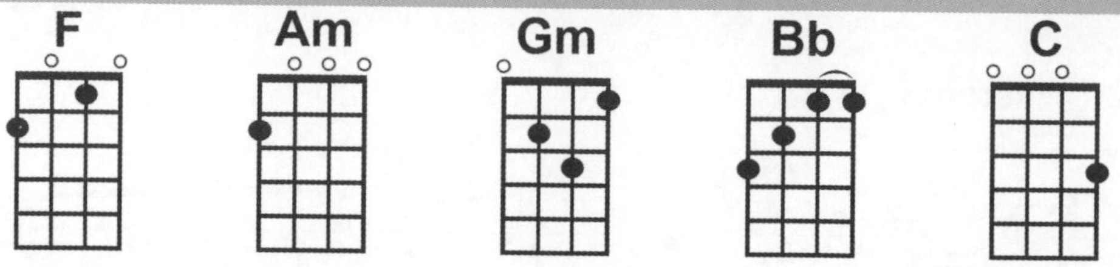
F
Am
Gm
Bb
C

Baritone Ukulele

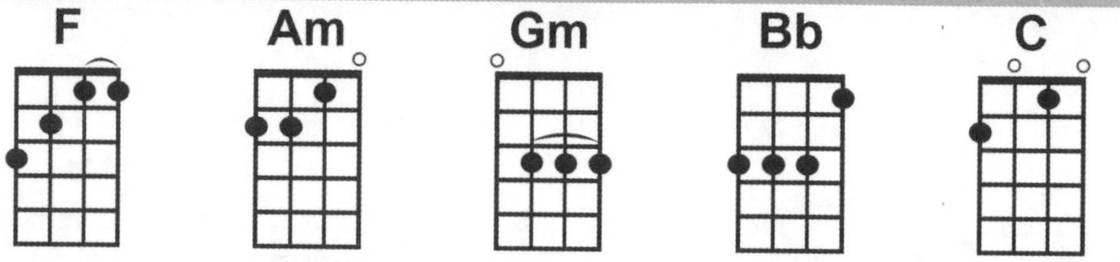
F
Am
Gm
Bb
C

Guitar

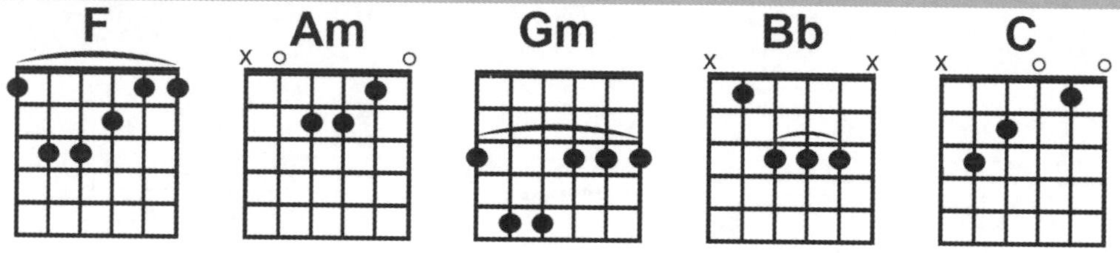
F
Am
Gm
Bb
C

Mandolin

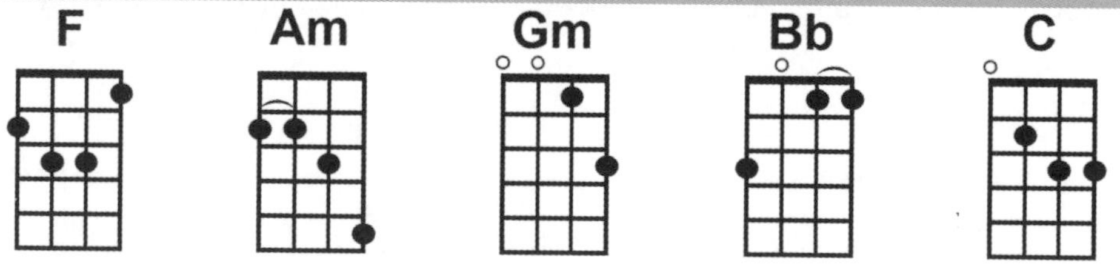
F
Am
Gm
Bb
C

Banjo

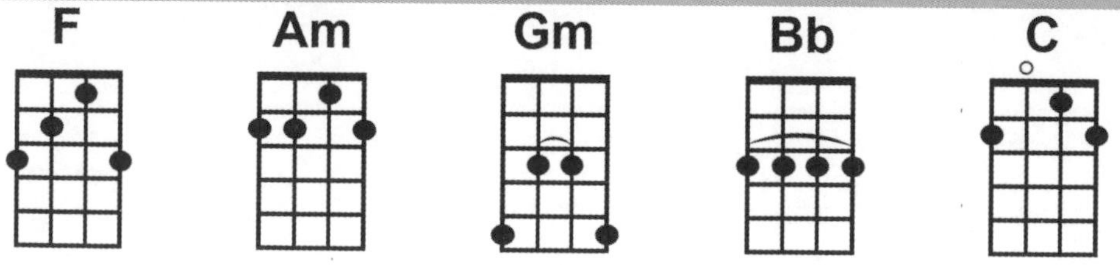
F
Am
Gm
Bb
C

Red Is the Rose

Irish Folk Song

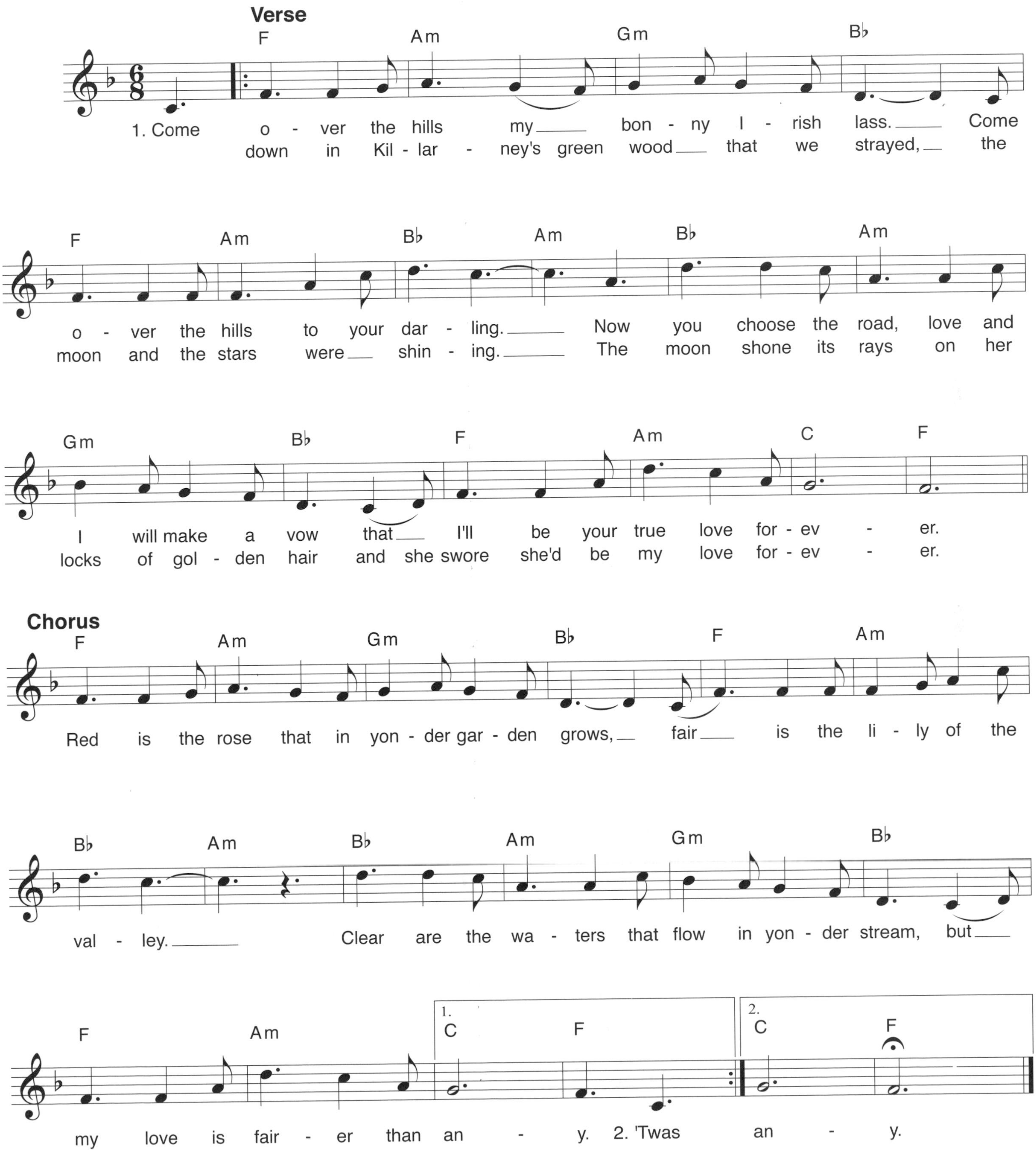
Verse
F Am Gm B♭
1. Come o - ver the hills my bon - ny I - rish lass. Come
down in Kil - lar - ney's green wood that we strayed, the
F Am B♭ Am B♭ Am
o - ver the hills to your dar - ling. Now you choose the road, love and
moon and the stars were shin - ing. The moon shone its rays on her
Gm B♭ F Am C F
I will make a vow that I'll be your true love for - ev - er.
locks of gol - den hair and she swore she'd be my love for - ev - er.
Chorus
F Am Gm B♭ F Am
Red is the rose that in yon - der gar - den grows, fair is the li - ly of the
B♭ Am B♭ Am Gm B♭
val - ley. Clear are the wa - ters that flow in yon - der stream, but
F Am
1. C F
2. C F
my love is fair - er than an - y. 2. 'Twas an - y.

Standard Ukulele

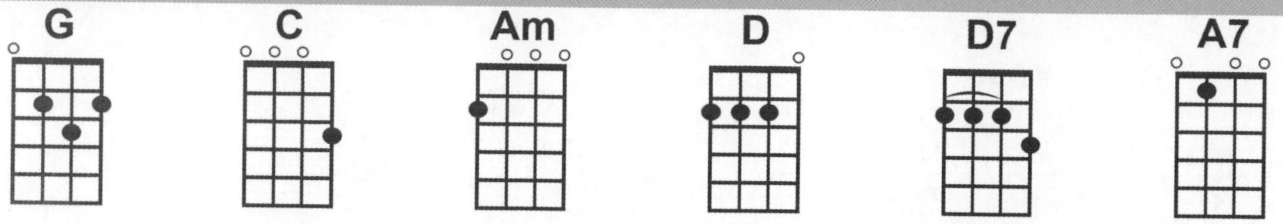
G
C
Am
D
D7
A7

Baritone Ukulele

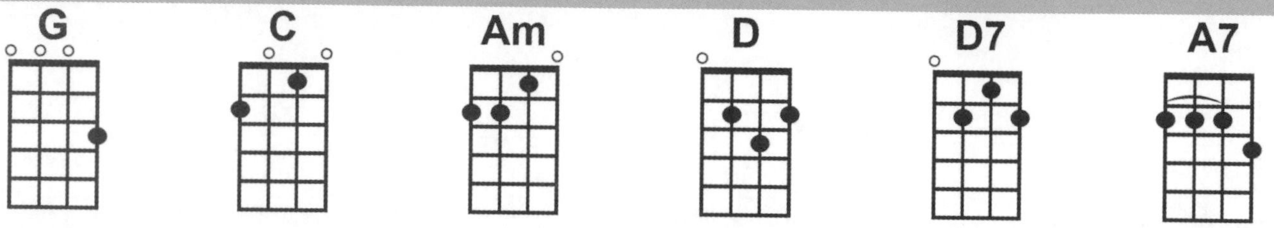
G
C
Am
D
D7
A7

Guitar

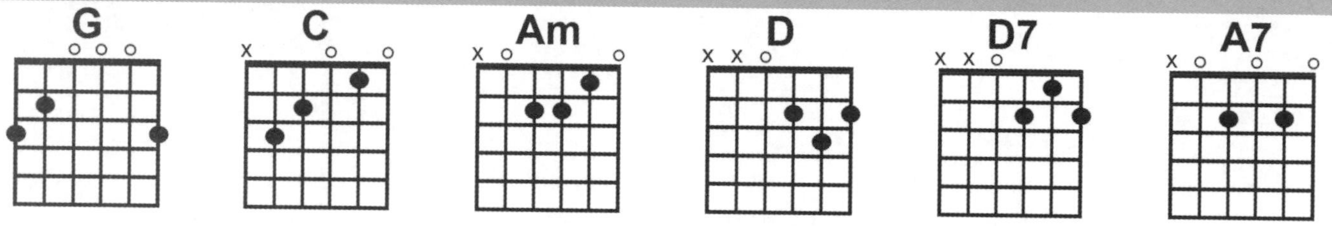
G
C
Am
D
D7
A7

Mandolin

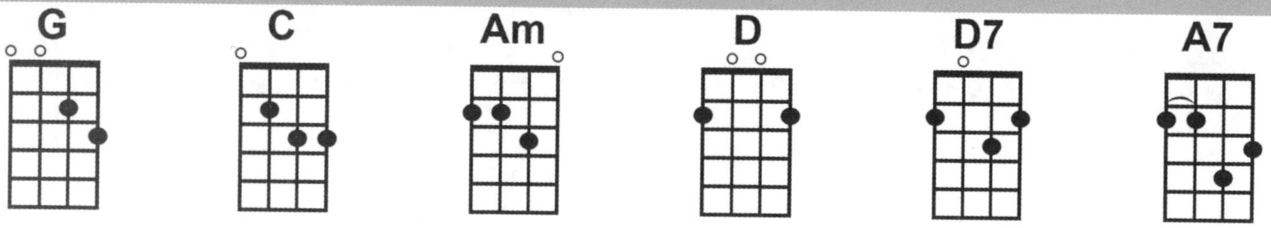
G
C
Am
D
D7
A7

Banjo

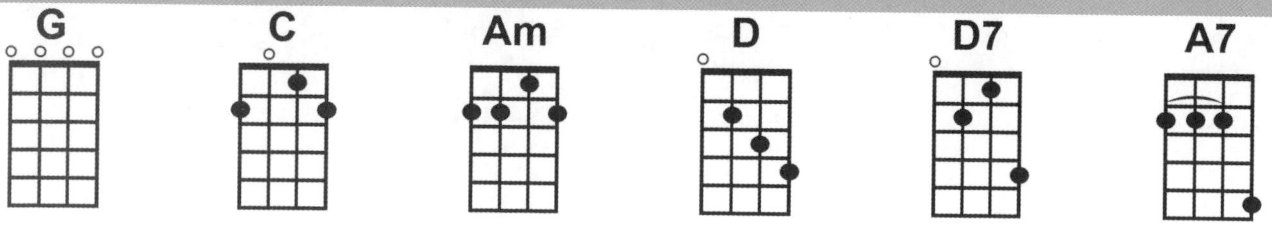
G
C
Am
D
D7
A7

Rhyfelgyrch Gwyr Harlech
(Men of Harlech)
Traditional Welsh Folk Melody
Lyrics by Ceriog

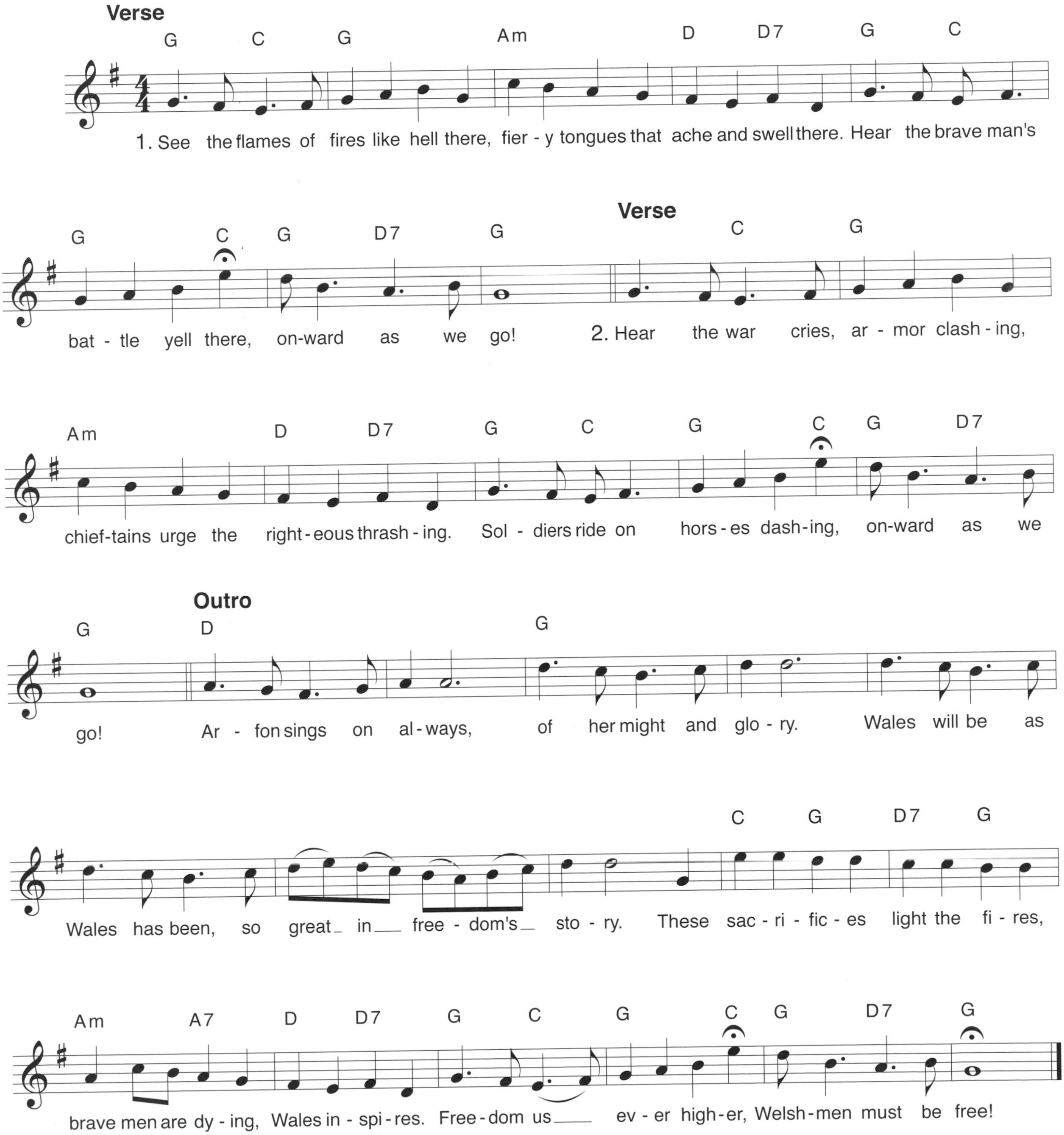
Verse
G C G Am D D7 G C
1. See the flames of fires like hell there, fier - y tongues that ache and swell there. Hear the brave man's
G C G D7 G
bat - tle yell there, on-ward as we go!
Verse
C G
2. Hear the war cries, ar - mor clash - ing,
Am D D7 G C G C G D7
chief-tains urge the right - eous thrash - ing. Sol - diers ride on hors - es dash-ing, on-ward as we
G
go!
Outro
D G
Ar - fon sings on al - ways, of her might and glo - ry. Wales will be as
C G D7 G
Wales has been, so great in free - dom's sto - ry. These sac - ri - fic - es light the fi - res,
Am A7 D D7 G C G C G D7 G
brave men are dy - ing, Wales in - spi - res. Free - dom us ev - er high - er, Welsh - men must be free!

Standard Ukulele

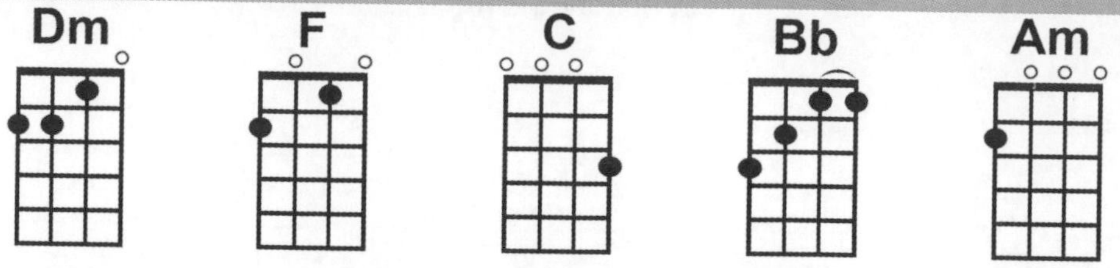
Dm
F
C
Bb
Am

Baritone Ukulele

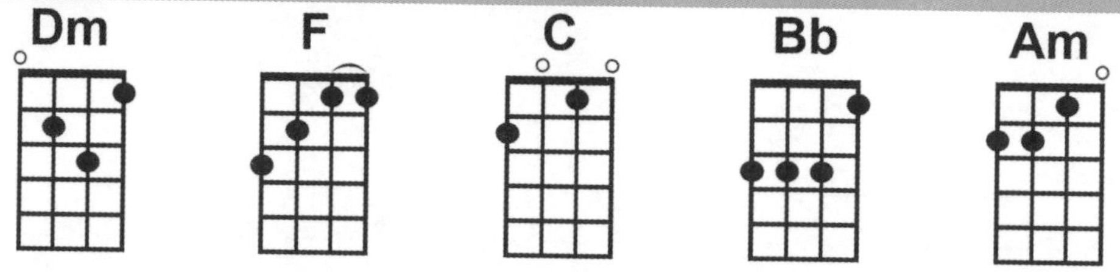
Dm
F
C
Bb
Am

Guitar

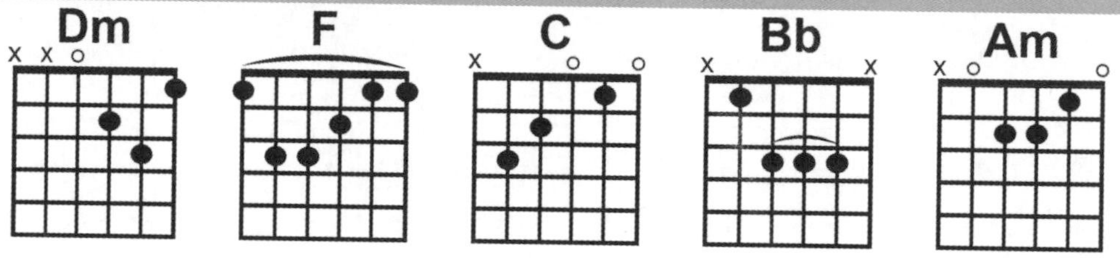
Dm
F
C
Bb
Am

Mandolin

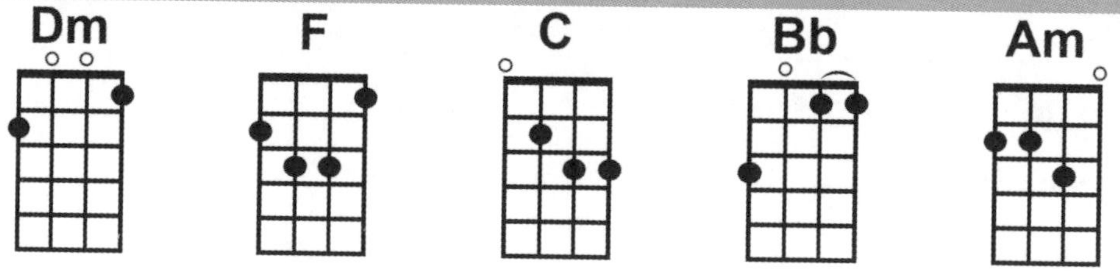
Dm
F
C
Bb
Am

Banjo

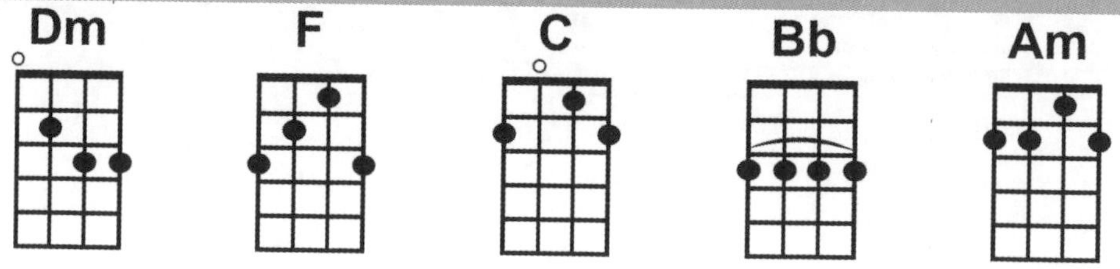
Dm
F
C
Bb
Am

The Rising of the Moon

Traditional Irish Folk Song

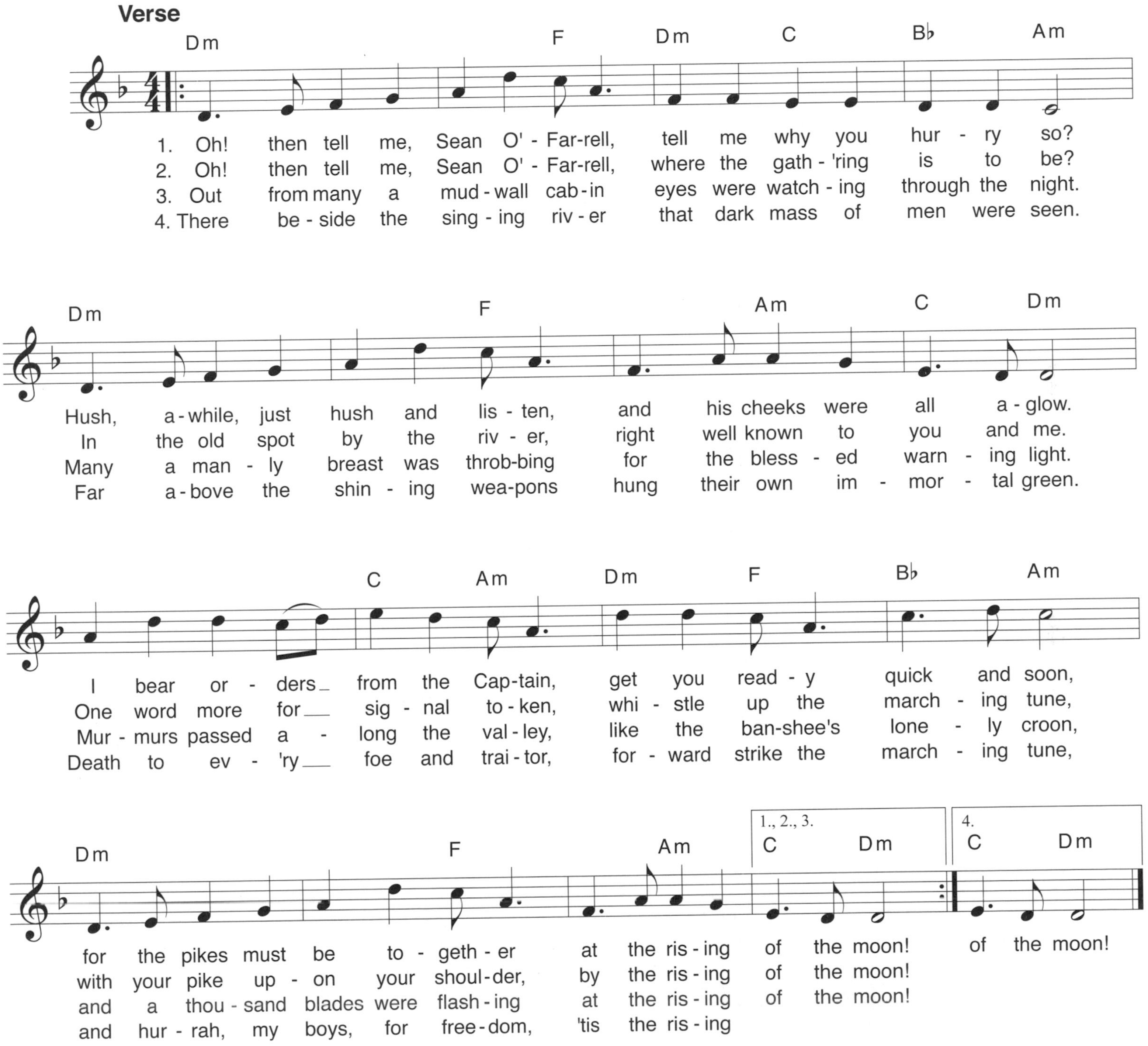
Verse
Dm F Dm C B♭ Am
1. Oh! then tell me, Sean O' - Far-rell, tell me why you hur - ry so?
2. Oh! then tell me, Sean O' - Far-rell, where the gath - 'ring is to be?
3. Out from many a mud - wall cab - in eyes were watch - ing through the night.
4. There be - side the sing - ing riv - er that dark mass of men were seen.
Dm F Am C Dm
Hush, a - while, just hush and lis - ten, and his cheeks were all a - glow.
In the old spot by the riv - er, right well known to you and me.
Many a man - ly breast was throb-bing for the bless - ed warn - ing light.
Far a - bove the shin - ing wea-pons hung their own im - mor - tal green.
C Am Dm F B♭ Am
I bear or - ders from the Cap-tain, get you read - y quick and soon,
One word more for sig - nal to - ken, whi - stle up the march - ing tune,
Mur - murs passed a - long the val - ley, like the ban-shee's lone - ly croon,
Death to ev - 'ry foe and trai - tor, for - ward strike the march - ing tune,
Dm F Am
1., 2., 3. C Dm
4. C Dm
for the pikes must be to - geth - er at the ris - ing of the moon! of the moon!
with your pike up - on your shoul-der, by the ris - ing of the moon!
and a thou - sand blades were flash - ing at the ris - ing of the moon!
and hur - rah, my boys, for free-dom, 'tis the ris - ing

Standard Ukulele

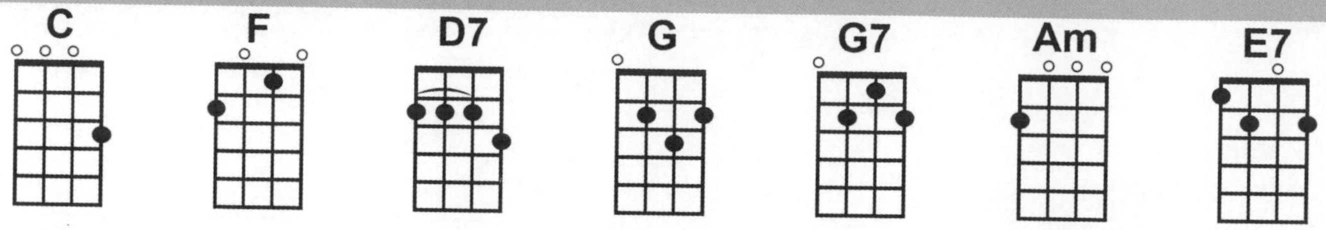
C
F
D7
G
G7
Am
E7

Baritone Ukulele

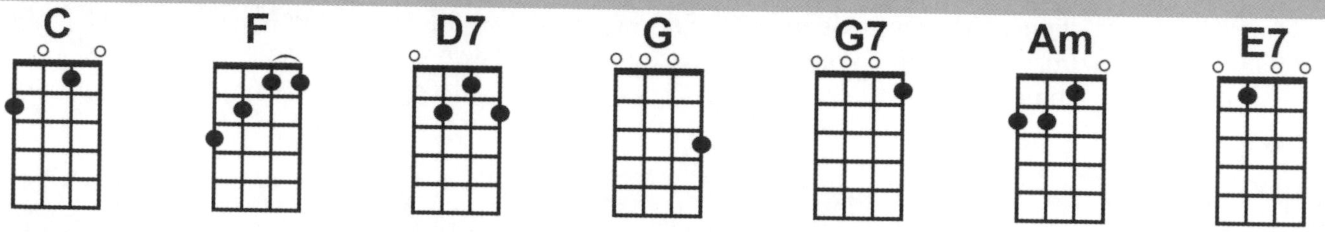
C
F
D7
G
G7
Am
E7

Guitar

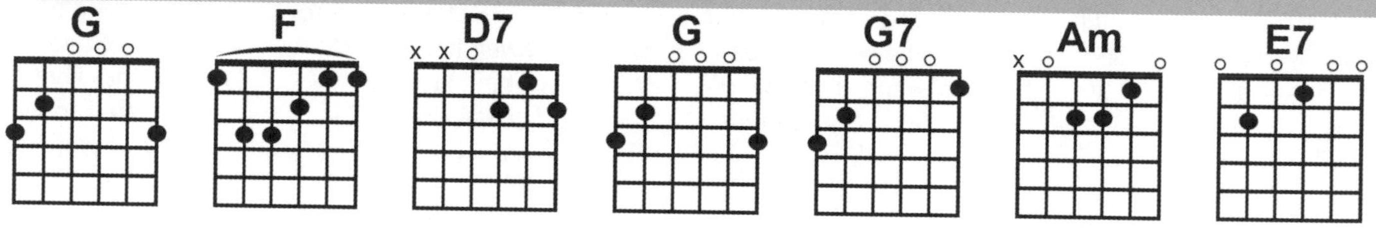
G
F
D7
G
G7
Am
E7

Mandolin

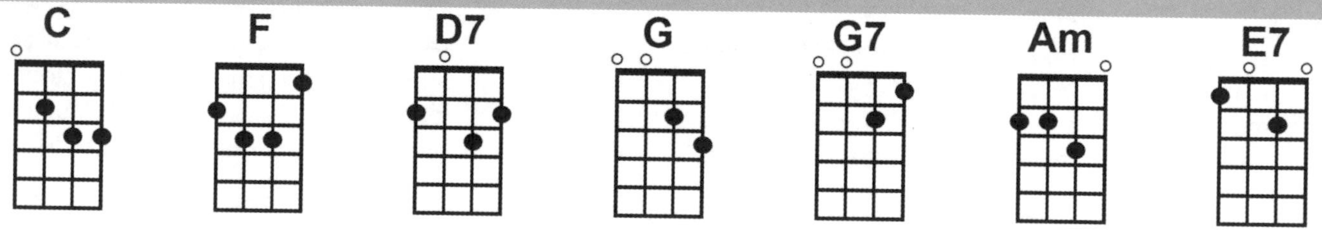
C
F
D7
G
G7
Am
E7

Banjo

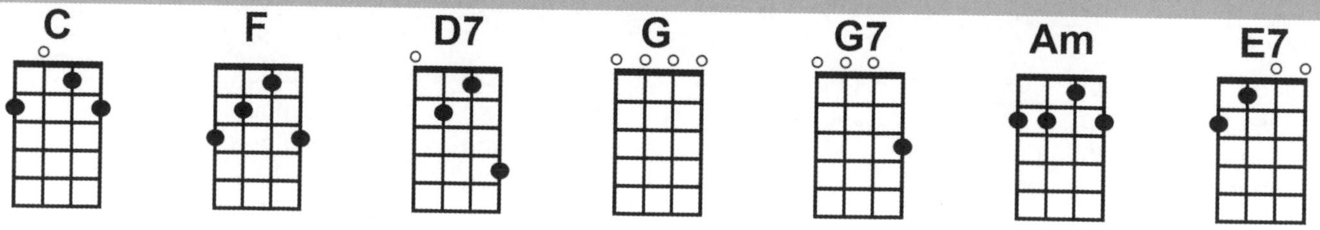
C
F
D7
G
G7
Am
E7

Rory O'Moore

Irish Folk Song

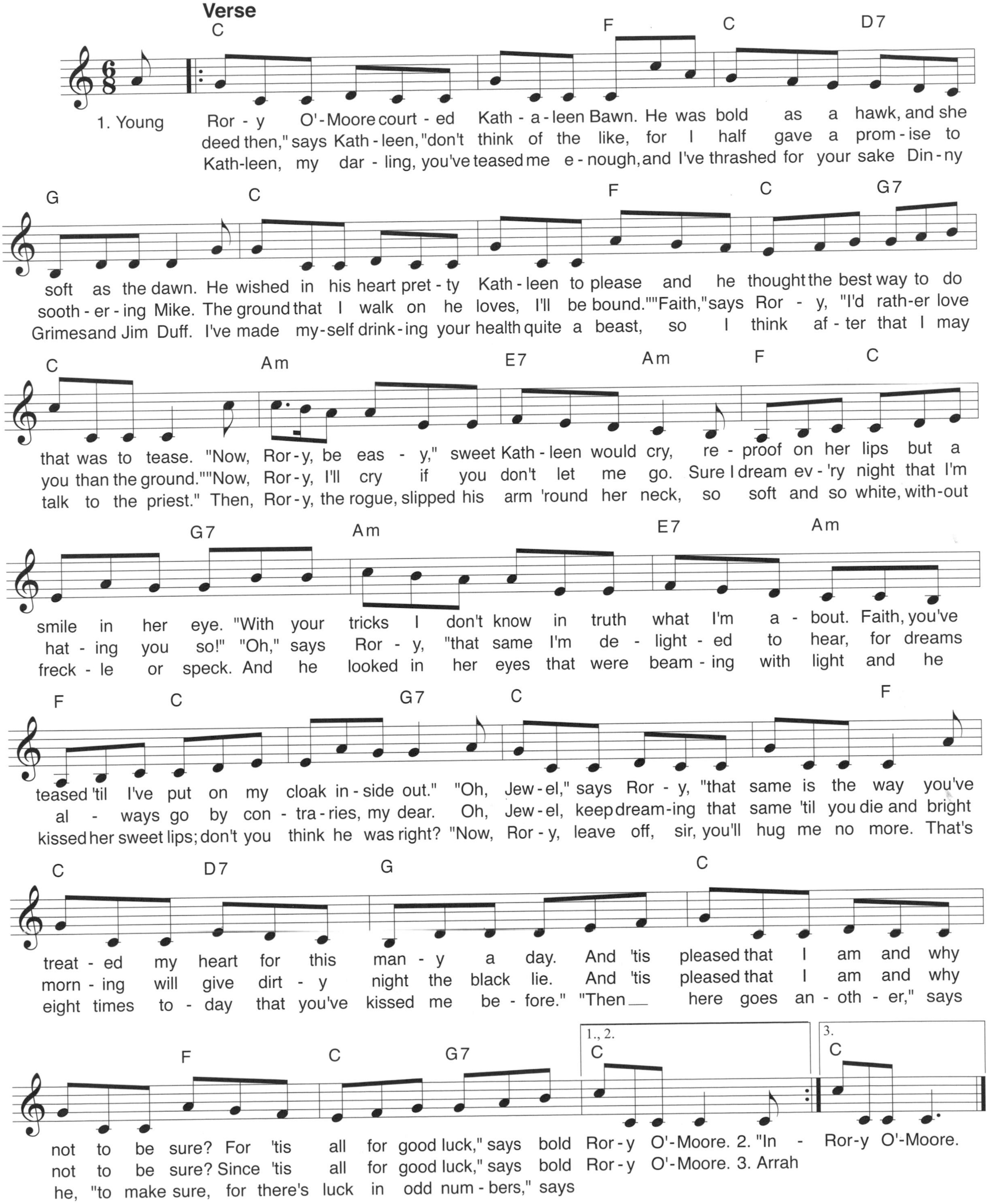
Verse
C F C D7
1. Young Ror - y O'-Moore court - ed Kath - a - leen Bawn. He was bold as a hawk, and she
deed then," says Kath - leen, "don't think of the like, for I half gave a prom - ise to
Kath-leen, my dar - ling, you've teased me e - nough, and I've thrashed for your sake Din - ny
G C F C G7
soft as the dawn. He wished in his heart pret - ty Kath - leen to please and he thought the best way to do
sooth - er - ing Mike. The ground that I walk on he loves, I'll be bound." "Faith," says Ror - y, "I'd rath - er love
Grimes and Jim Duff. I've made my - self drink - ing your health quite a beast, so I think af - ter that I may
C Am E7 Am F C
that was to tease. "Now, Ror - y, be eas - y," sweet Kath - leen would cry, re - proof on her lips but a
you than the ground." "Now, Ror - y, I'll cry if you don't let me go. Sure I dream ev - 'ry night that I'm
talk to the priest." Then, Ror - y, the rogue, slipped his arm 'round her neck, so soft and so white, with - out
G7 Am E7 Am
smile in her eye. "With your tricks I don't know in truth what I'm a - bout. Faith, you've
hat - ing you so!" "Oh," says Ror - y, "that same I'm de - light - ed to hear, for dreams
freck - le or speck. And he looked in her eyes that were beam - ing with light and he
F C G7 C F
teased 'til I've put on my cloak in - side out." "Oh, Jew - el," says Ror - y, "that same is the way you've
al - ways go by con - tra - ries, my dear. Oh, Jew - el, keep dream - ing that same 'til you die and bright
kissed her sweet lips; don't you think he was right? "Now, Ror - y, leave off, sir, you'll hug me no more. That's
C D7 G C
treat - ed my heart for this man - y a day. And 'tis pleased that I am and why
morn - ing will give dirt - y night the black lie. And 'tis pleased that I am and why
eight times to - day that you've kissed me be - fore." "Then here goes an - oth - er," says
F C G7 1., 2. C 3. C
not to be sure? For 'tis all for good luck," says bold Ror - y O'-Moore. 2. "In - Ror - y O'-Moore.
not to be sure? Since 'tis all for good luck," says bold Ror - y O'-Moore. 3. Arrah
he, "to make sure, for there's luck in odd num - bers," says

Standard Ukulele

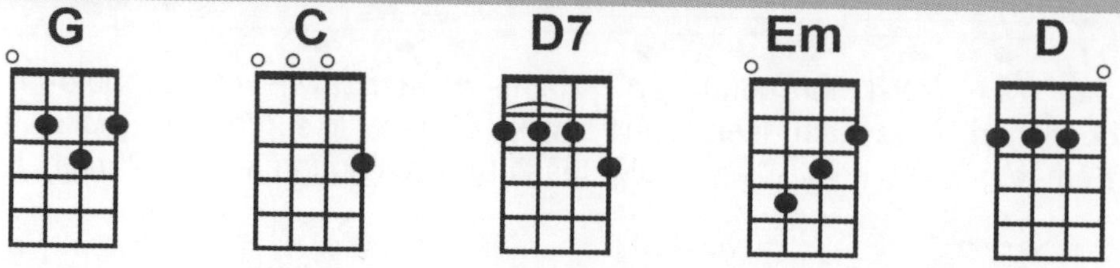
G
C
D7
Em
D

Baritone Ukulele

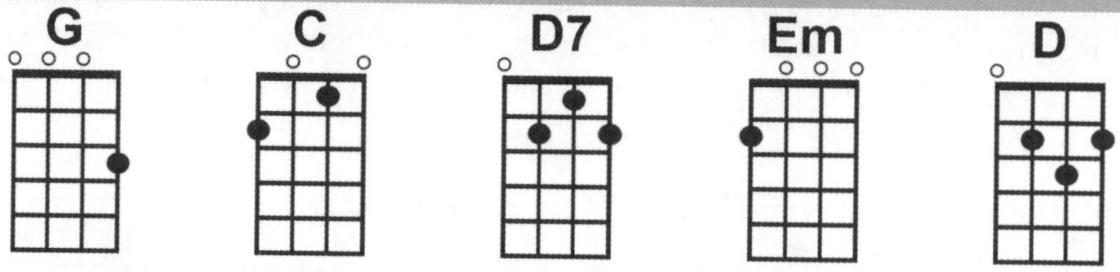
G
C
D7
Em
D

Guitar

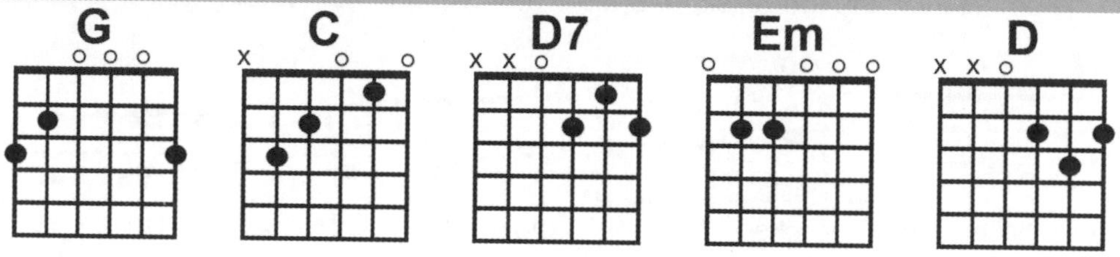
G
C
D7
Em
D

Mandolin

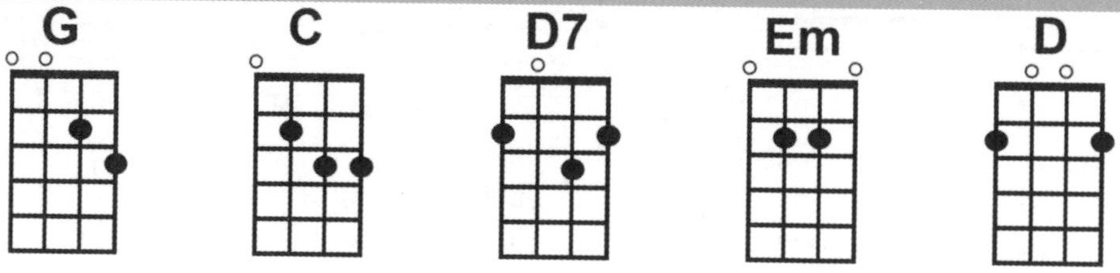
G
C
D7
Em
D

Banjo

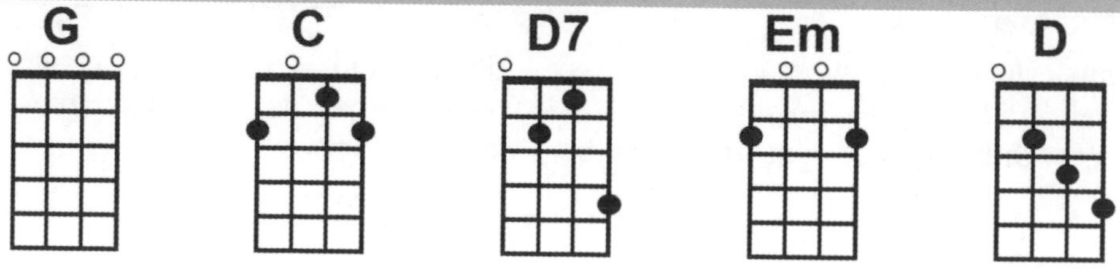
G
C
D7
Em
D

Scots Wha Hae

Scottish Folk Song
Words by Robert Burns

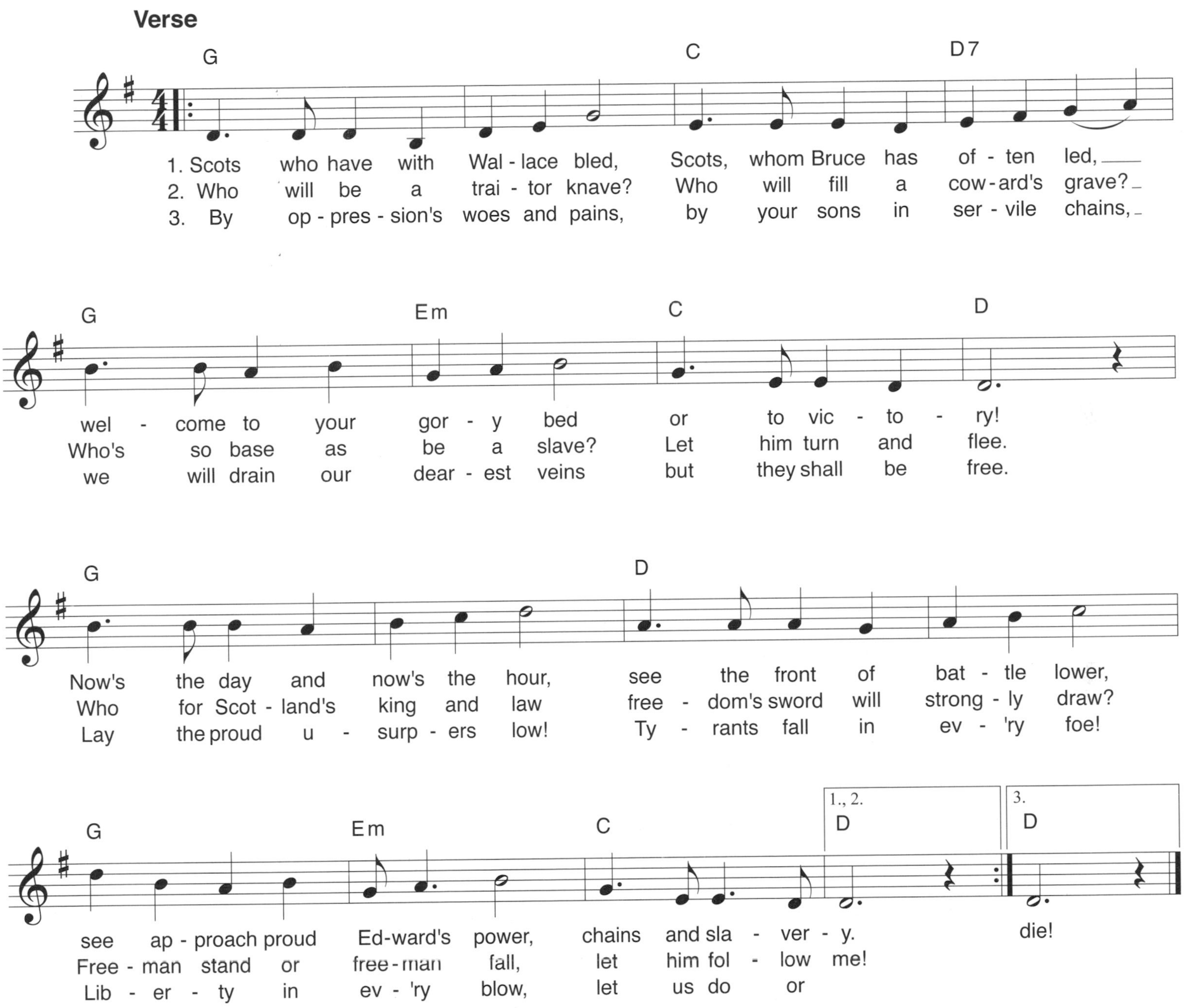
Verse
G
C
D7
1. Scots who have with Wal - lace bled, Scots, whom Bruce has of - ten led,
2. Who will be a trai - tor knave? Who will fill a cow - ard's grave?
3. By op - pres - sion's woes and pains, by your sons in ser - vile chains,
G
Em
C
D
wel - come to your gor - y bed or to vic - to - ry!
Who's so base as be a slave? Let him turn and flee.
we will drain our dear - est veins but they shall be free.
G
D
Now's the day and now's the hour, see the front of bat - tle lower,
Who for Scot - land's king and law free - dom's sword will strong - ly draw?
Lay the proud u - surp - ers low! Ty - rants fall in ev - 'ry foe!
G
Em
C
1., 2.
D
3.
D
see ap - proach proud Ed-ward's power, chains and sla - ver - y. die!
Free - man stand or free - man fall, let him fol - low me!
Lib - er - ty in ev - 'ry blow, let us do or

Standard Ukulele

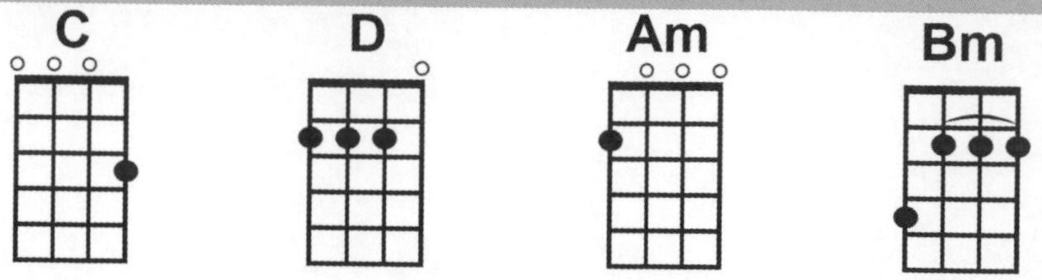
C
D
Am
Bm

Baritone Ukulele

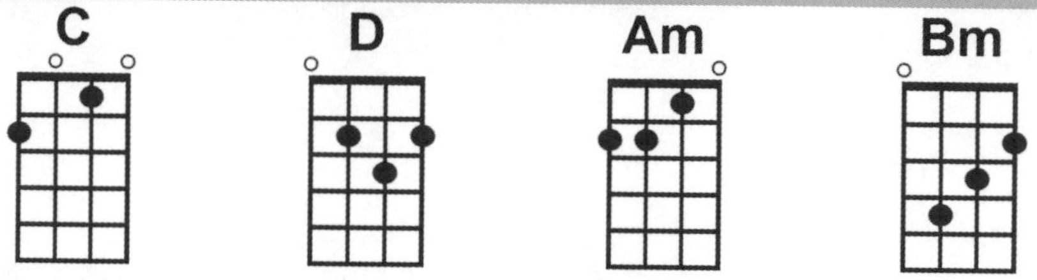
C
D
Am
Bm

Guitar

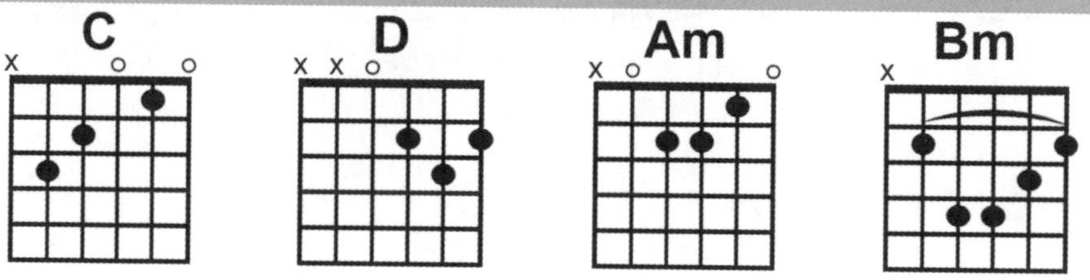
C
D
Am
Bm

Mandolin

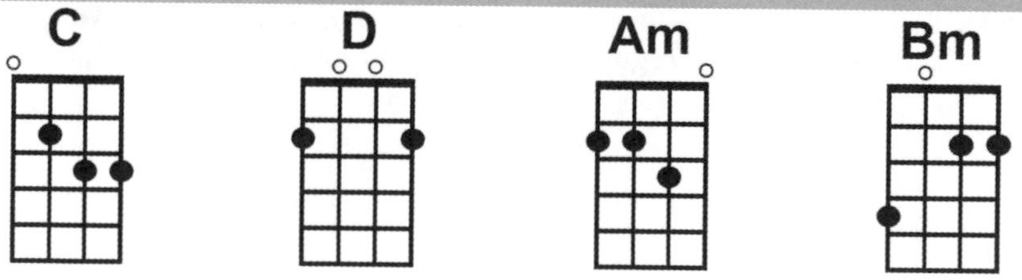
C
D
Am
Bm

Banjo

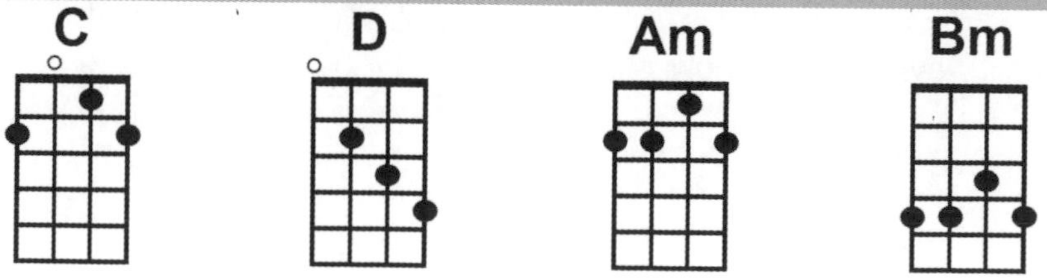
C
D
Am
Bm

She Moved Thro' the Fair
(She Moved Through the Fair)
Traditional Irish Melody

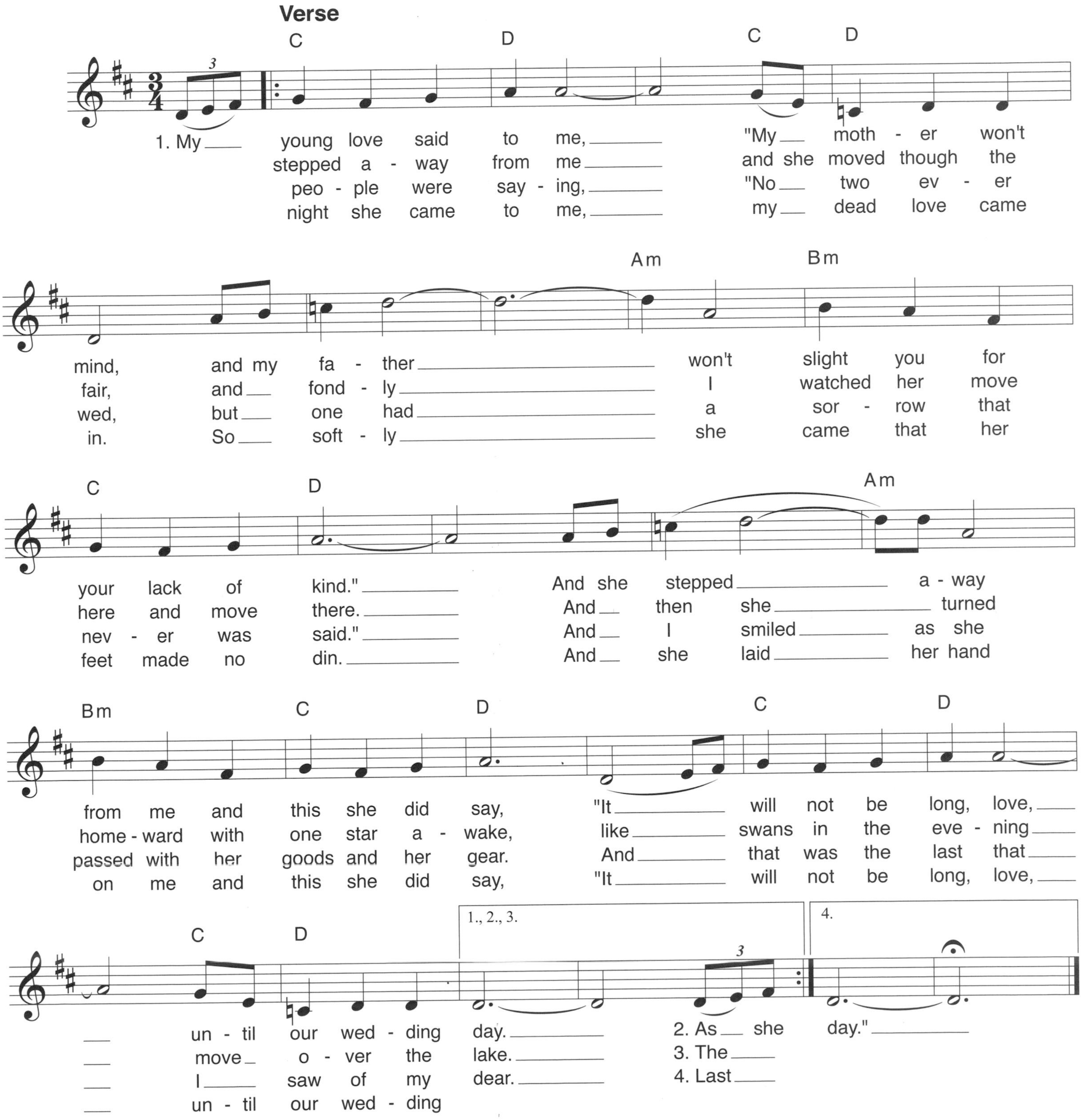
Verse
C D C D
1. My young love said to me, "My moth - er won't
stepped a - way from me and she moved though the
peo - ple were say - ing, "No two ev - er
night she came to me, my dead love came
Am Bm
mind, and my fa - ther won't slight you for
fair, and fond - ly I watched her move
wed, but one had a sor - row that
in. So soft - ly she came that her
C D Am
your lack of kind." And she stepped a - way
here and move there. And then she turned
nev - er was said." And I smiled as she
feet made no din. And she laid her hand
Bm C D C D
from me and this she did say, "It will not be long, love,
home - ward with one star a - wake, like swans in the eve - ning
passed with her goods and her gear. And that was the last that
on me and this she did say, "It will not be long, love,
C D
1., 2., 3.
4.
un - til our wed - ding day. 2. As she day."
move o - ver the lake. 3. The
I saw of my dear. 4. Last
un - til our wed - ding

Standard Ukulele

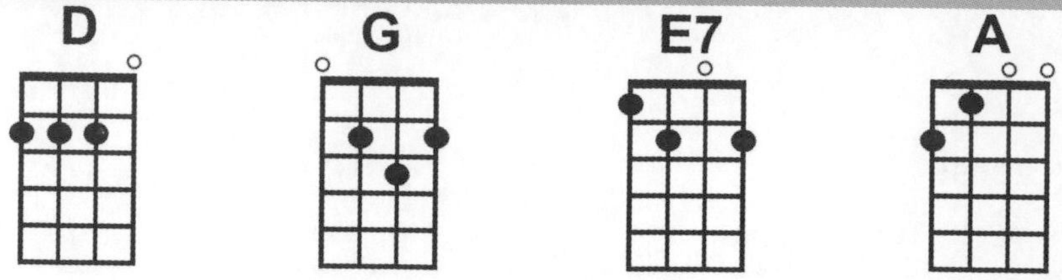

Baritone Ukulele

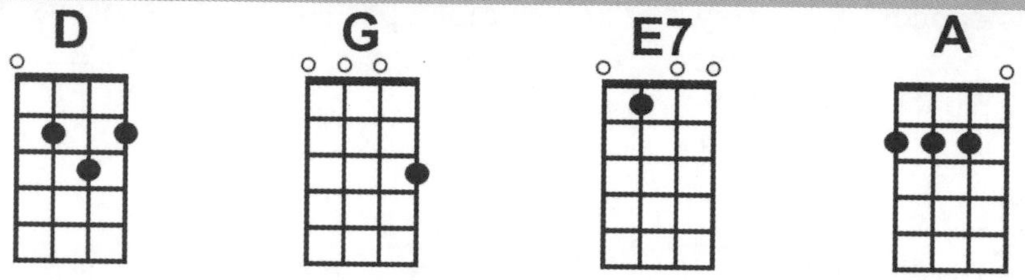

Guitar

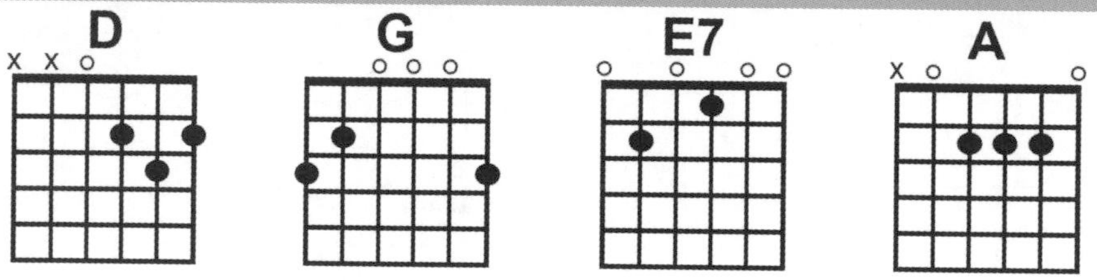

Mandolin

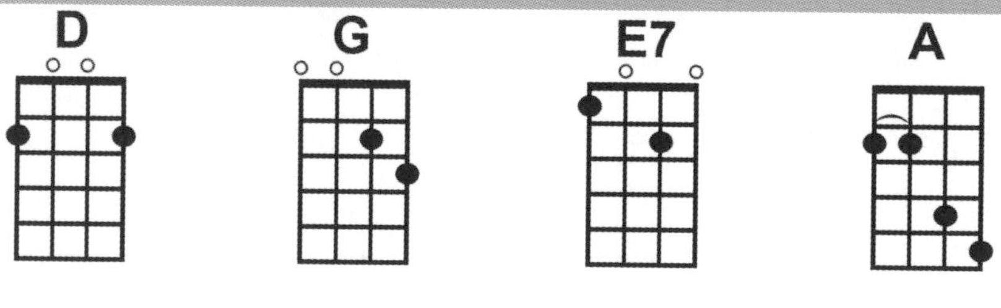

Banjo

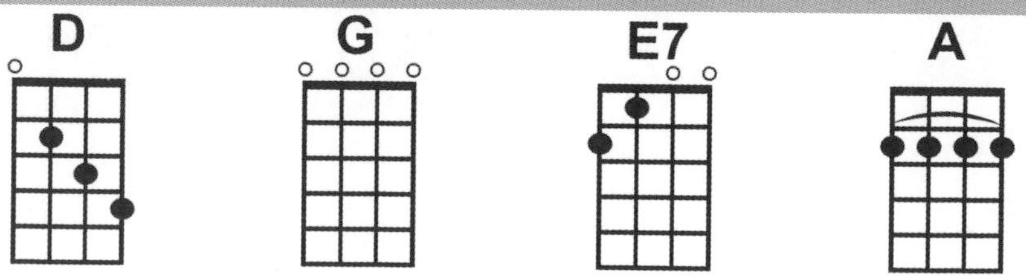

The Son of a Gambolier

Scottish Folk Song

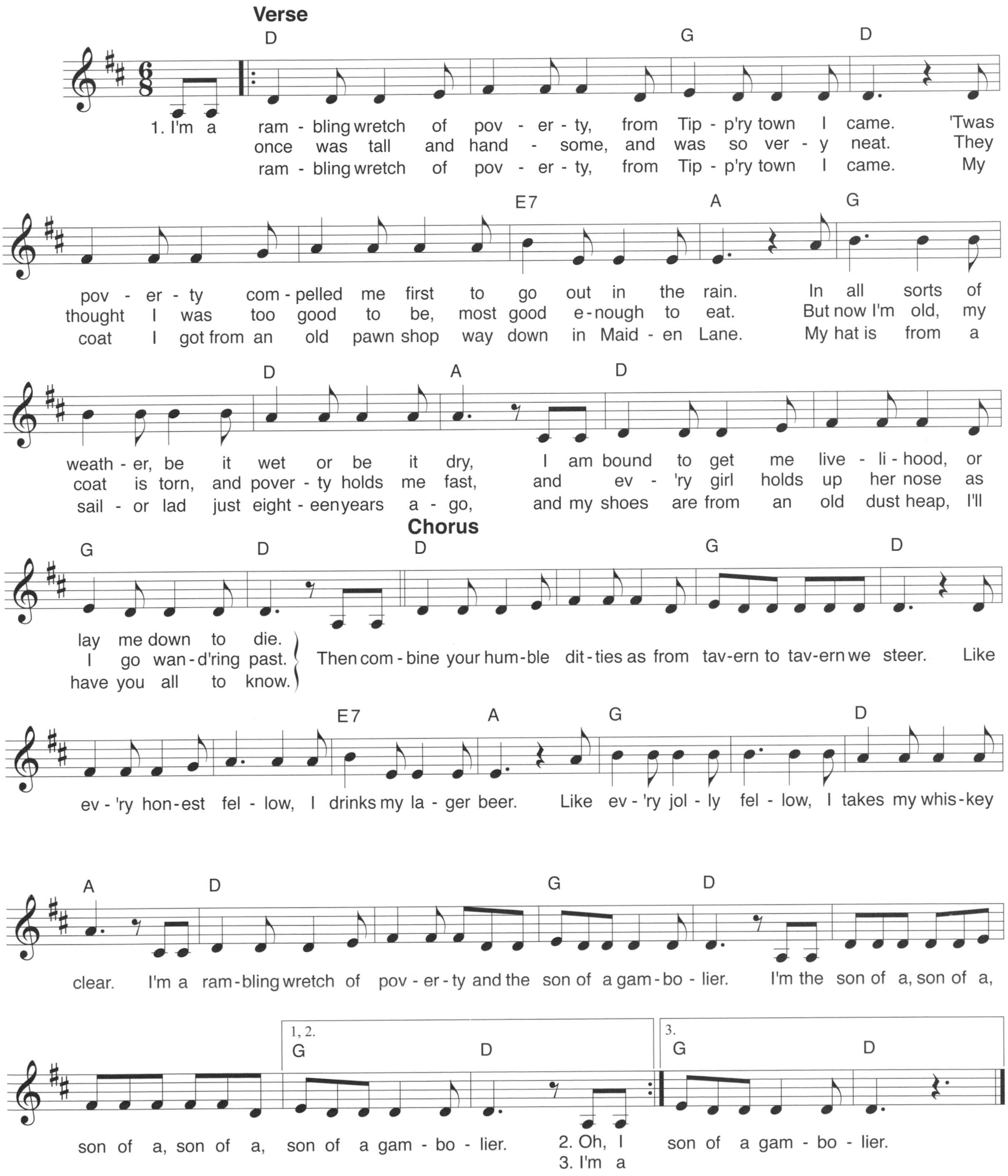
Verse
D G D
1. I'm a ram - bling wretch of pov - er - ty, from Tip - p'ry town I came. 'Twas
once was tall and hand - some, and was so ver - y neat. They
ram - bling wretch of pov - er - ty, from Tip - p'ry town I came. My
E7 A G
pov - er - ty com - pelled me first to go out in the rain. In all sorts of
thought I was too good to be, most good e - nough to eat. But now I'm old, my
coat I got from an old pawn shop way down in Maid - en Lane. My hat is from a
D A D
weath - er, be it wet or be it dry, I am bound to get me live - li - hood, or
coat is torn, and pover - ty holds me fast, and ev - 'ry girl holds up her nose as
sail - or lad just eight - een years a - go, and my shoes are from an old dust heap, I'll
Chorus
G D D G D
lay me down to die.
I go wan - d'ring past.
have you all to know.
Then com - bine your hum - ble dit - ties as from tav - ern to tav - ern we steer. Like
E7 A G D
ev - 'ry hon - est fel - low, I drinks my la - ger beer. Like ev - 'ry jol - ly fel - low, I takes my whis - key
A D G D
clear. I'm a ram - bling wretch of pov - er - ty and the son of a gam - bo - lier. I'm the son of a, son of a,
1, 2. G D 3. G D
son of a, son of a, son of a gam - bo - lier. 2. Oh, I son of a gam - bo - lier.
3. I'm a

Standard Ukulele

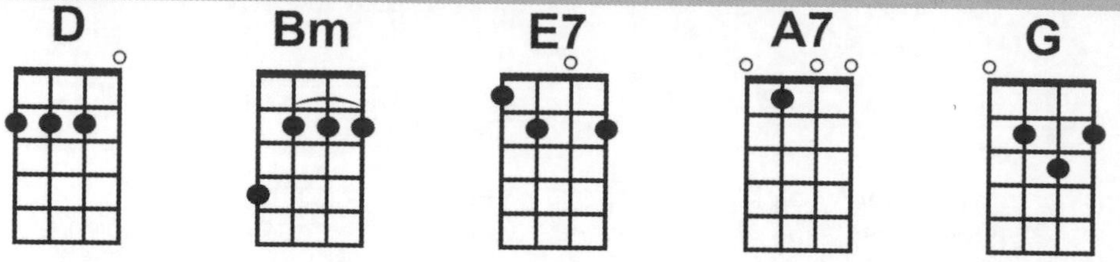
D
Bm
E7
A7
G

Baritone Ukulele

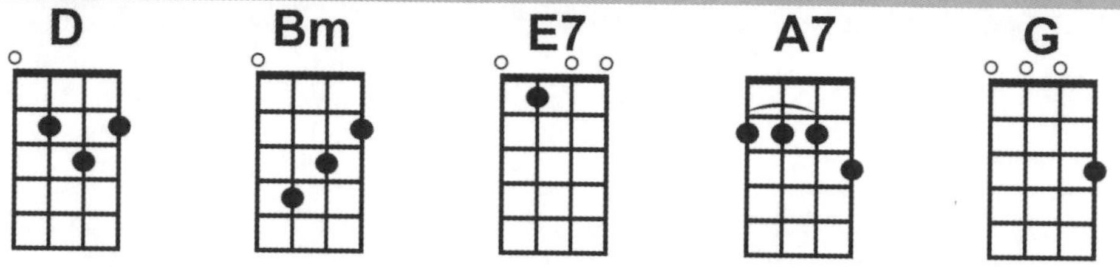
D
Bm
E7
A7
G

Guitar

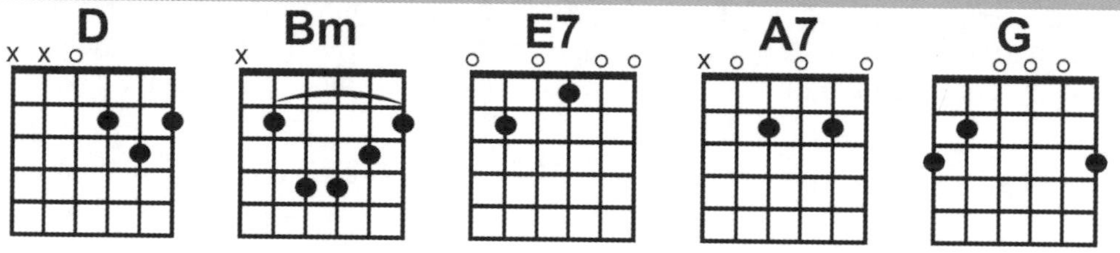
D
Bm
E7
A7
G

Mandolin

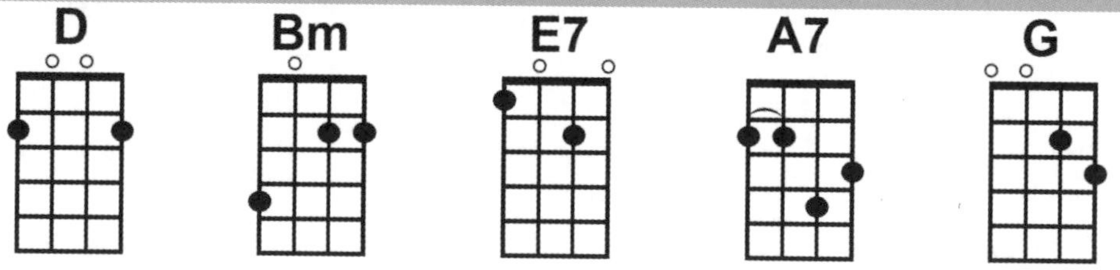
D
Bm
E7
A7
G

Banjo

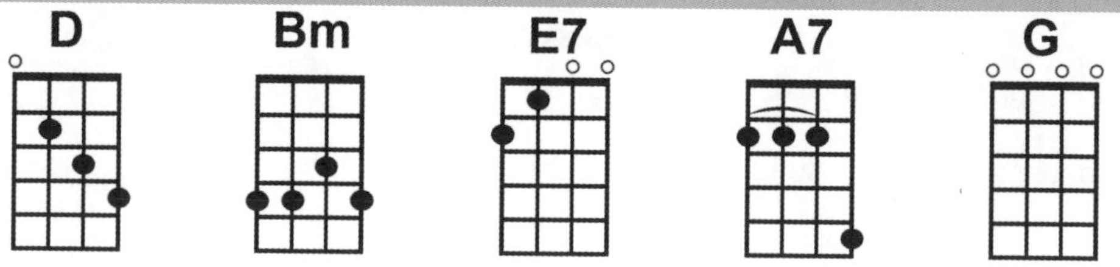
D
Bm
E7
A7
G

That's an Irish Lullaby

Irish Folk Song

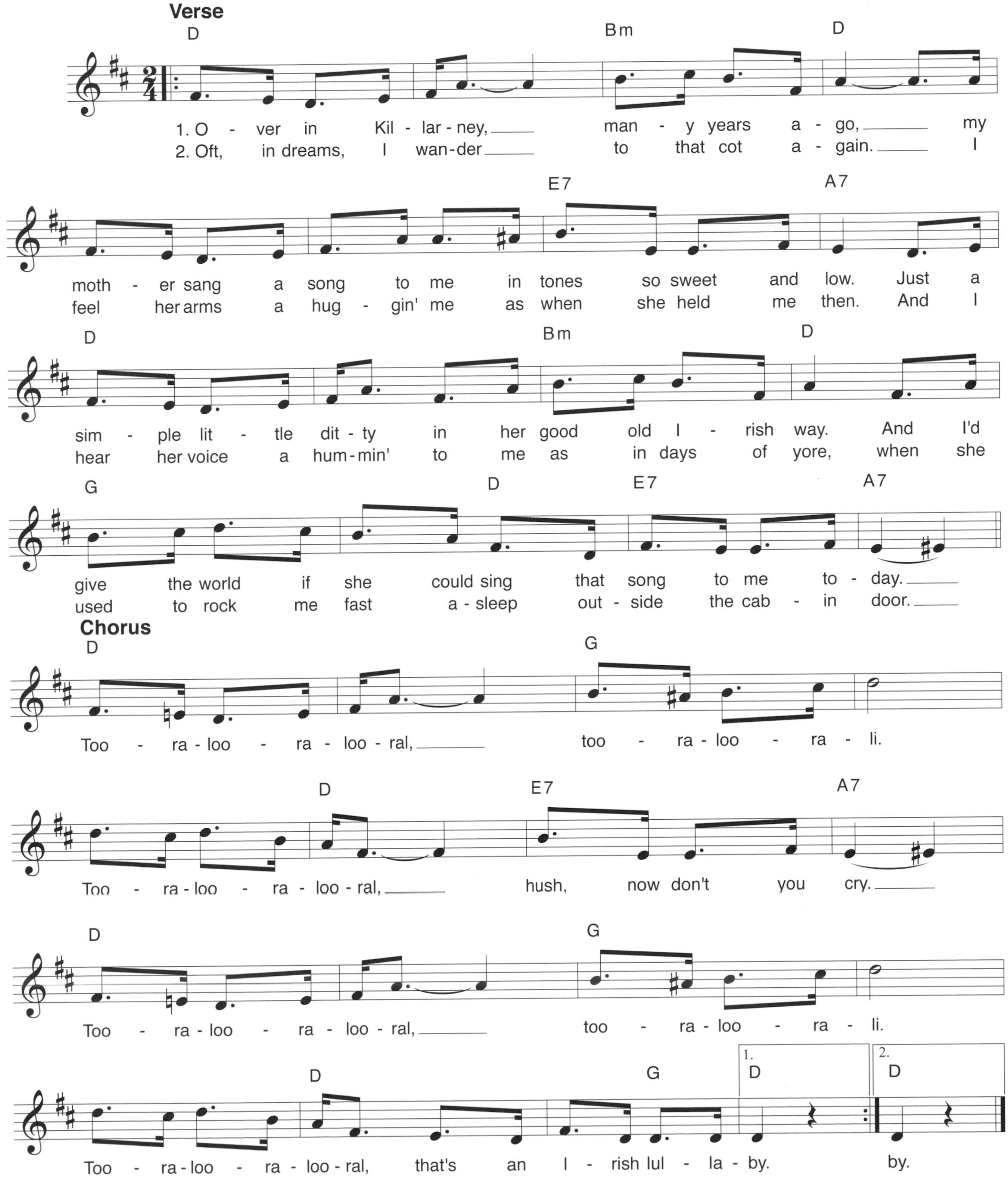
Verse
D Bm D
1. O - ver in Kil - lar - ney, man - y years a - go, my
2. Oft, in dreams, I wan - der to that cot a - gain. I
E7 A7
moth - er sang a song to me in tones so sweet and low. Just a
feel her arms a hug - gin' me as when she held me then. And I
D Bm D
sim - ple lit - tle dit - ty in her good old I - rish way. And I'd
hear her voice a hum - min' to me as in days of yore, when she
G D E7 A7
give the world if she could sing that song to me to - day.
used to rock me fast a - sleep out - side the cab - in door.
Chorus
D G
Too - ra - loo - ra - loo - ral, too - ra - loo - ra - li.
D E7 A7
Too - ra - loo - ra - loo - ral, hush, now don't you cry.
D G
Too - ra - loo - ra - loo - ral, too - ra - loo - ra - li.
D G 1. D 2. D
Too - ra - loo - ra - loo - ral, that's an I - rish lul - la - by. by.

Standard Ukulele

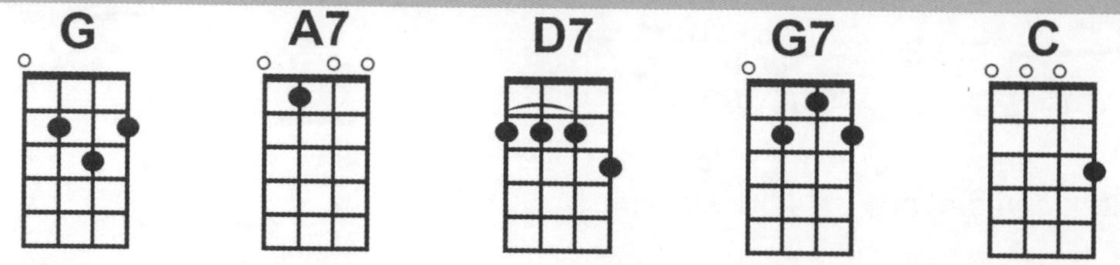

Baritone Ukulele

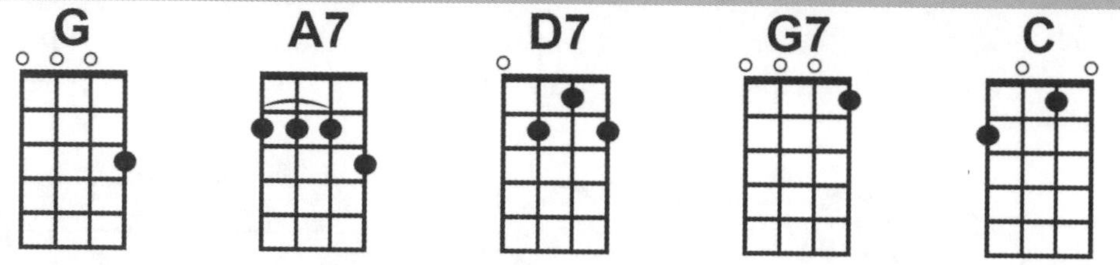

Guitar

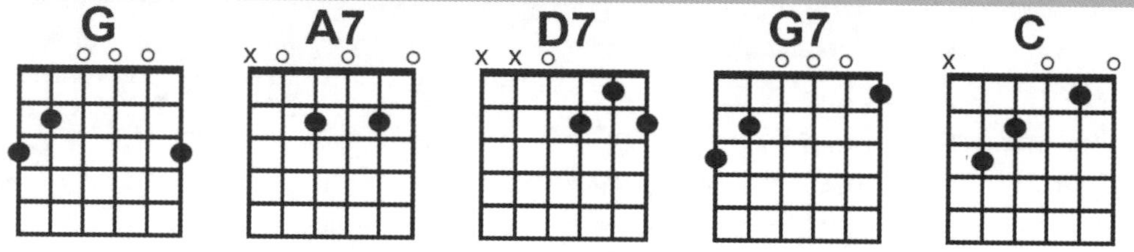

Mandolin

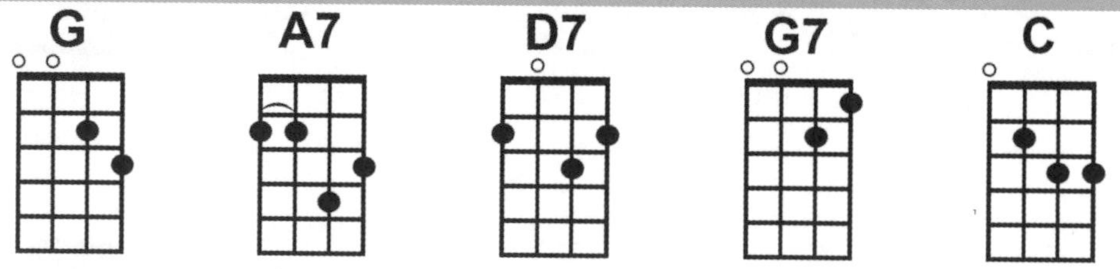

Banjo

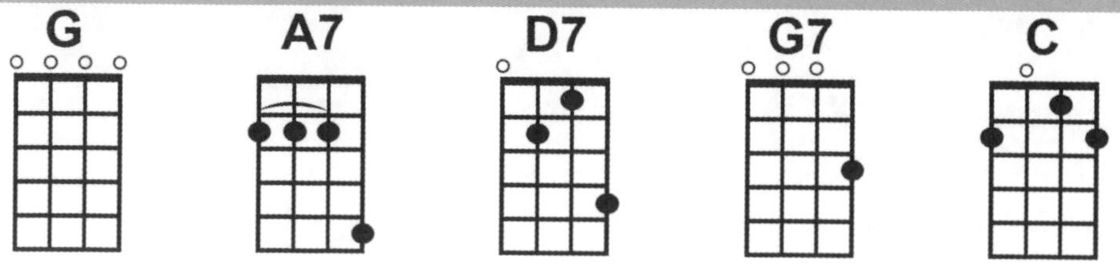

The T'read on the Tail o' Me Coat

Irish Folk Song

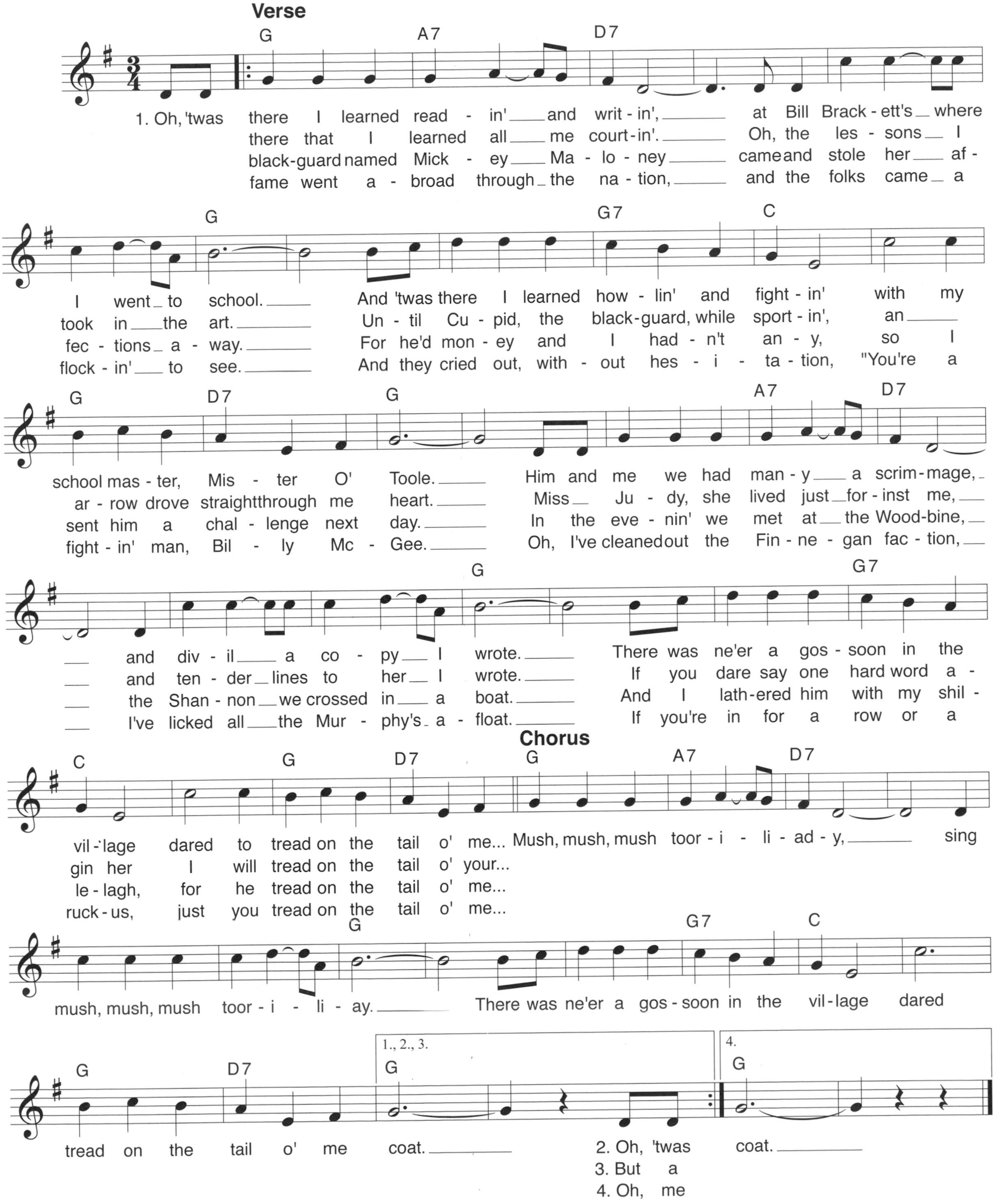

Verse
G A7 D7
1. Oh, 'twas there I learned read - in' and writ - in', at Bill Brack - ett's where
there that I learned all me court - in'. Oh, the les - sons I
black-guard named Mick - ey Ma - lo - ney came and stole her af -
fame went a - broad through the na - tion, and the folks came a
G G7 C
I went to school. And 'twas there I learned how - lin' and fight - in' with my
took in the art. Un - til Cu - pid, the black-guard, while sport - in', an
fec - tions a - way. For he'd mon - ey and I had - n't an - y, so I
flock - in' to see. And they cried out, with - out hes - i - ta - tion, "You're a
G D7 G A7 D7
school mas - ter, Mis - ter O' Toole. Him and me we had man - y a scrim - mage,
ar - row drove straight through me heart. Miss Ju - dy, she lived just for - inst me,
sent him a chal - lenge next day. In the eve - nin' we met at the Wood - bine,
fight - in' man, Bil - ly Mc - Gee. Oh, I've cleaned out the Fin - ne - gan fac - tion,
G G7
and div - il a co - py I wrote. There was ne'er a gos - soon in the
and ten - der lines to her I wrote. If you dare say one hard word a -
the Shan - non we crossed in a boat. And I lath - ered him with my shil -
I've licked all the Mur - phy's a - float. If you're in for a row or a
Chorus
C G D7 G A7 D7
vil - lage dared to tread on the tail o' me... Mush, mush, mush toor - i - li - ad - y, sing
gin her I will tread on the tail o' your...
le - lagh, for he tread on the tail o' me...
ruck - us, just you tread on the tail o' me...
G G7 C
mush, mush, mush toor - i - li - ay. There was ne'er a gos - soon in the vil - lage dared
G D7 1., 2., 3. G 4. G
tread on the tail o' me coat. 2. Oh, 'twas coat.
3. But a
4. Oh, me

Standard Ukulele

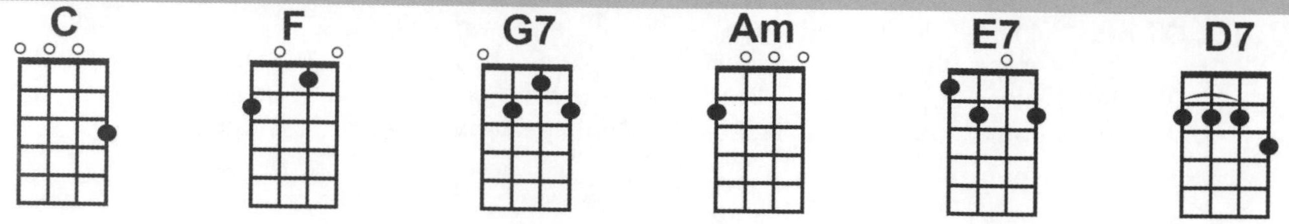
C
F
G7
Am
E7
D7

Baritone Ukulele

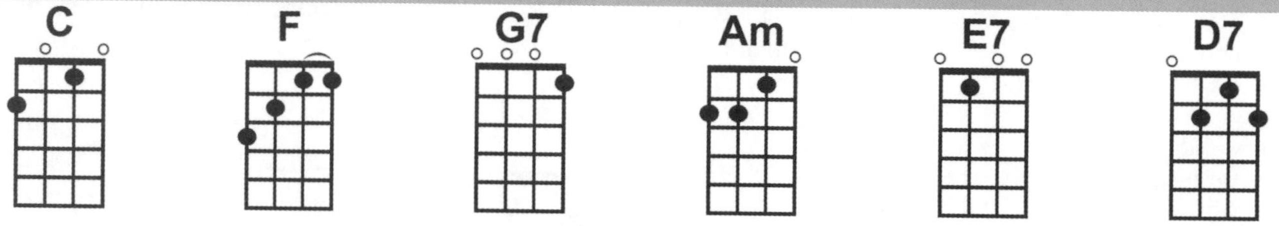
C
F
G7
Am
E7
D7

Guitar

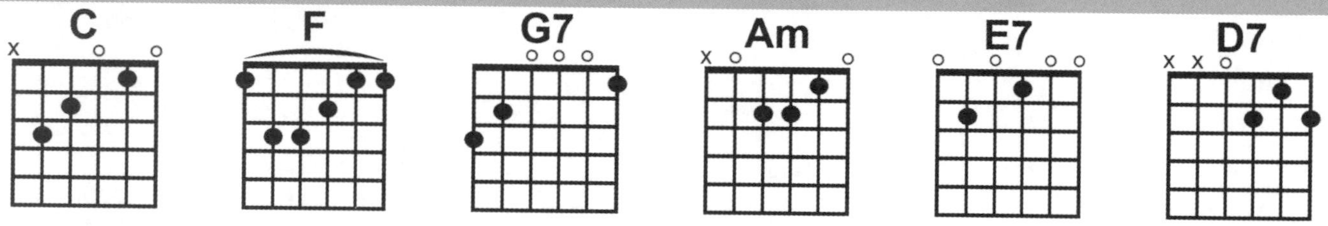
C
F
G7
Am
E7
D7

Mandolin

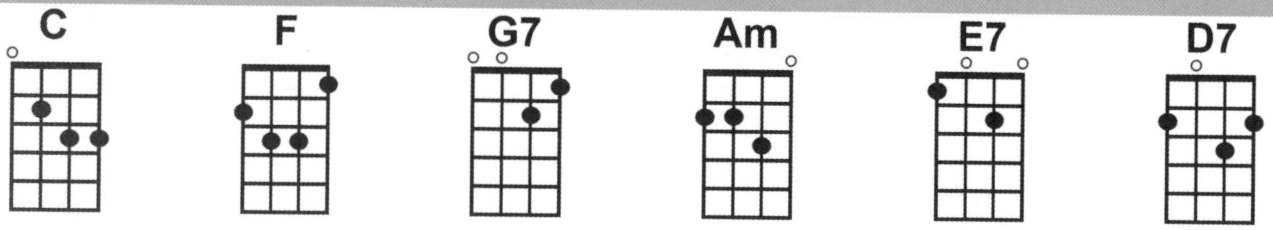
C
F
G7
Am
E7
D7

Banjo

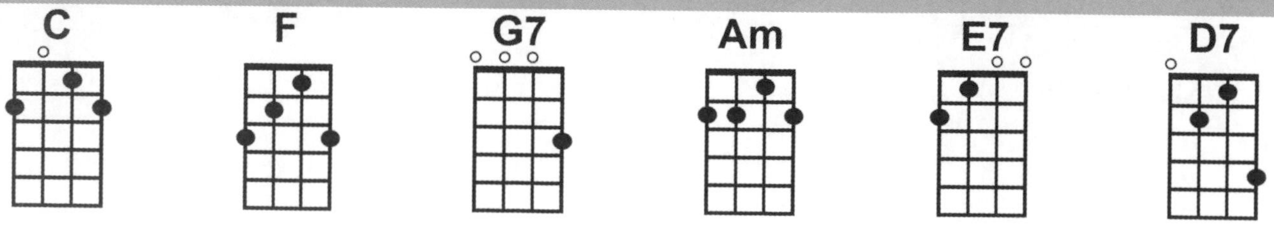
C
F
G7
Am
E7
D7

'Tis the Last Rose of Summer

Words by Thomas Moore
Music by Richard Alfred Milliken

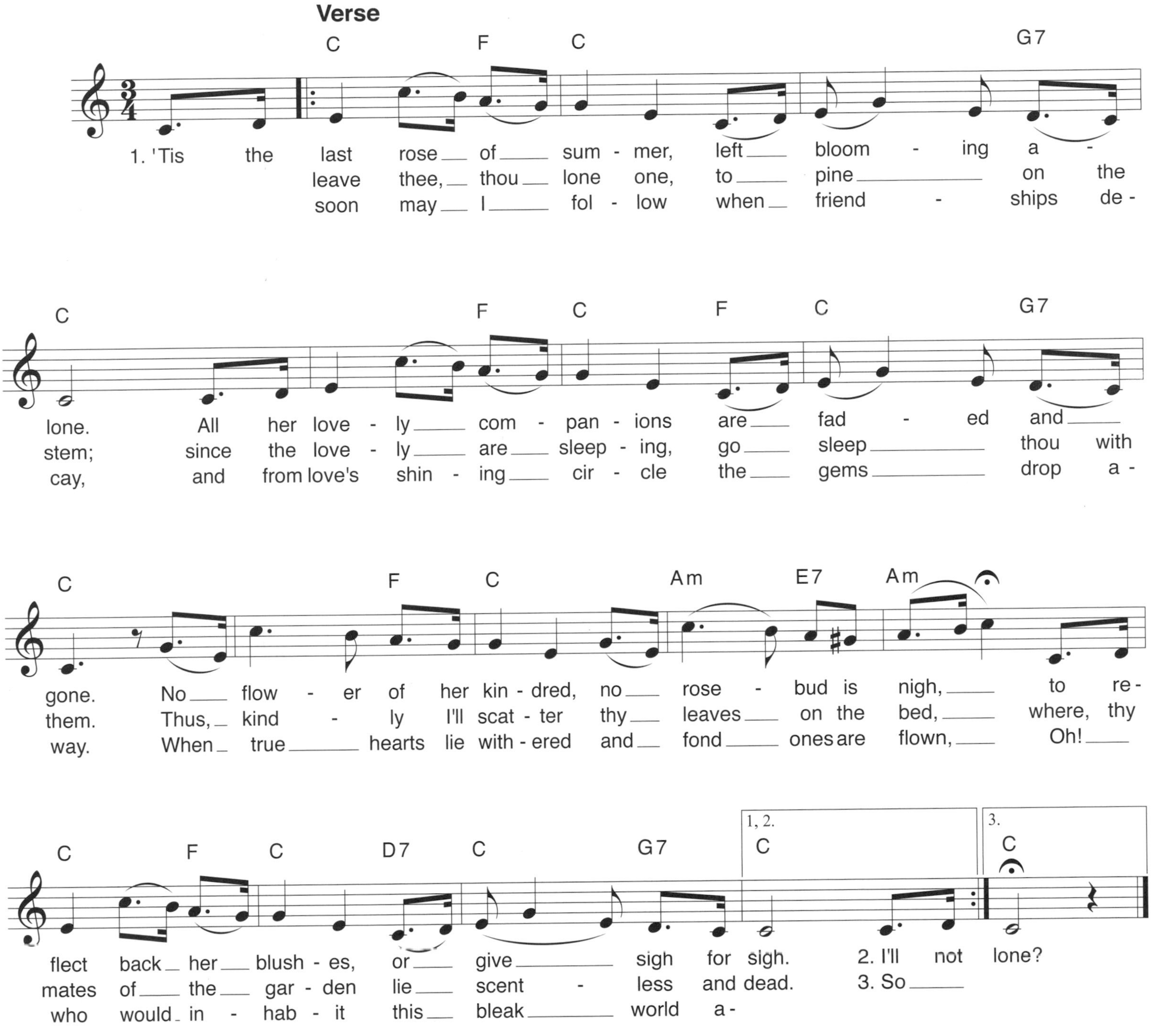
Verse
C F C G7
1. 'Tis the last rose of sum - mer, left bloom - ing a -
leave thee, thou lone one, to pine on the
soon may I fol - low when friend - ships de -
C F C F C G7
lone. All her love - ly com - pan - ions are fad - ed and
stem; since the love - ly are sleep - ing, go sleep thou with
cay, and from love's shin - ing cir - cle the gems drop a -
C F C Am E7 Am
gone. No flow - er of her kin - dred, no rose - bud is nigh, to re -
them. Thus, kind - ly I'll scat - ter thy leaves on the bed, where, thy
way. When true hearts lie with - ered and fond ones are flown, Oh!
C F C D7 C G7
1, 2.
C
3.
C
flect back her blush - es, or give sigh for sigh. 2. I'll not lone?
mates of the gar - den lie scent - less and dead. 3. So
who would in - hab - it this bleak world a -

Standard Ukulele

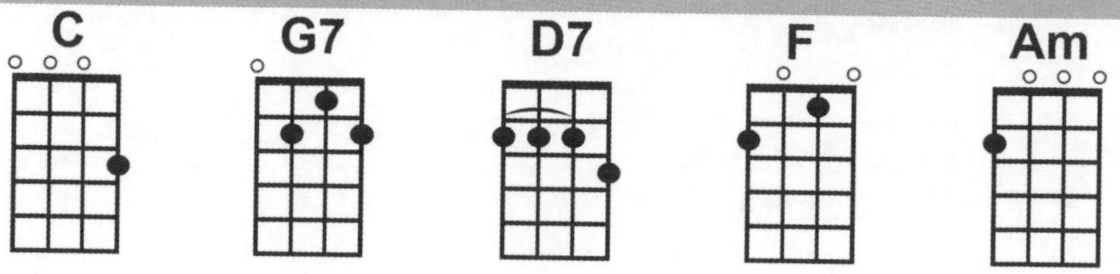
C
G7
D7
F
Am

Baritone Ukulele

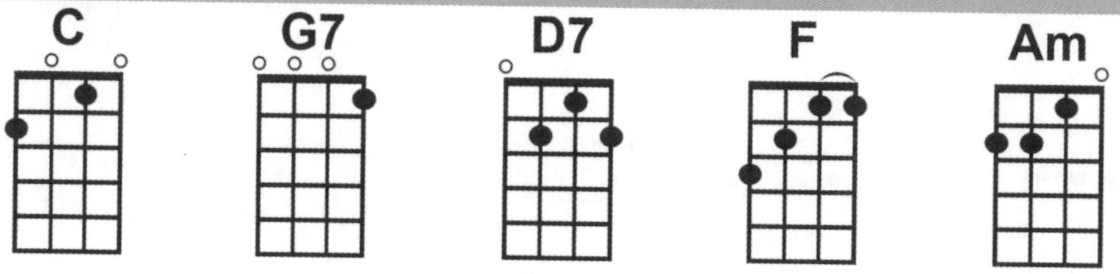
C
G7
D7
F
Am

Guitar

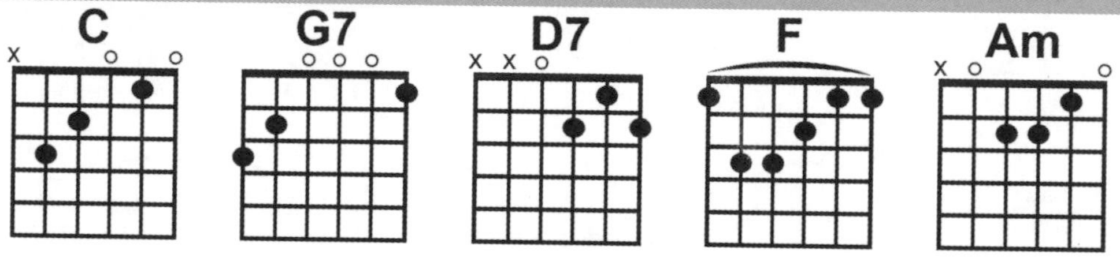
C
G7
D7
F
Am

Mandolin

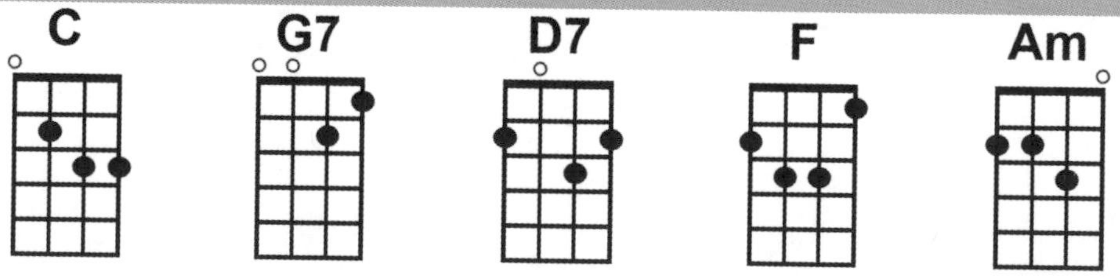
C
G7
D7
F
Am

Banjo

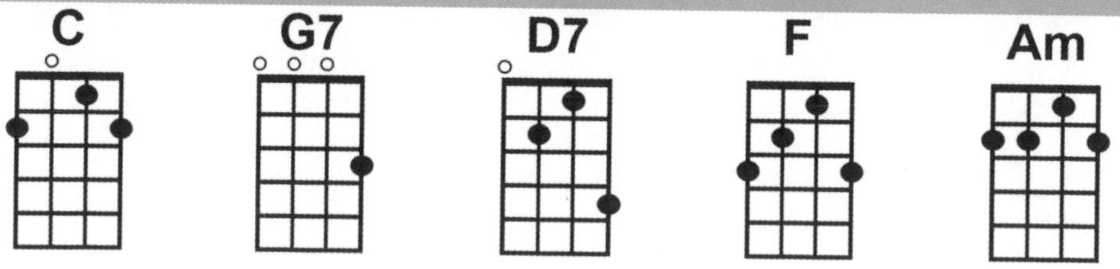
C
G7
D7
F
Am

Tourelay, Tourelay

Traditional Irish Folk Song

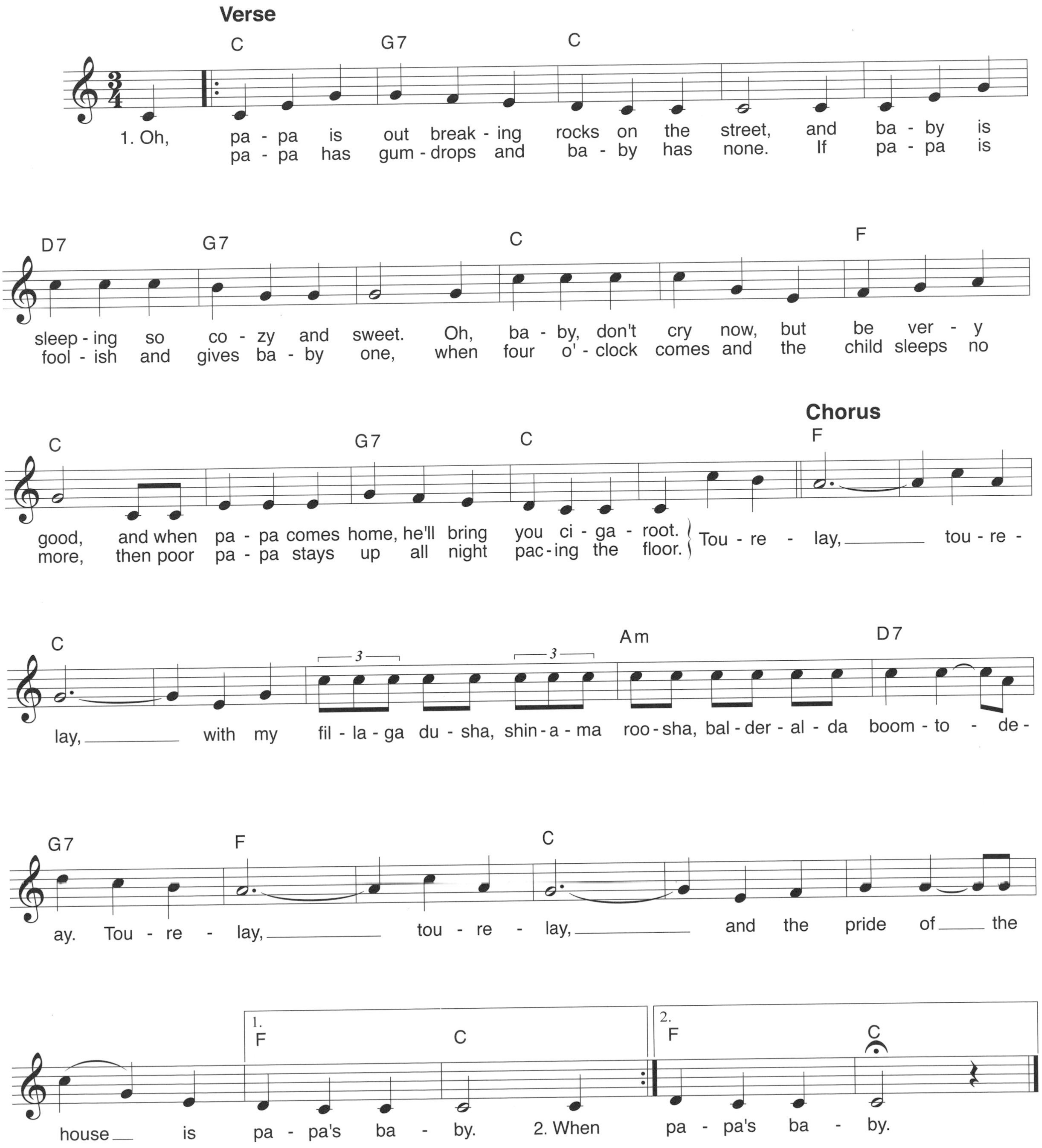
Verse
C G7 C
1. Oh, pa - pa is out break - ing rocks on the street, and ba - by is
pa - pa has gum - drops and ba - by has none. If pa - pa is
D7 G7 C F
sleep - ing so co - zy and sweet. Oh, ba - by, don't cry now, but be ver - y
fool - ish and gives ba - by one, when four o' - clock comes and the child sleeps no
C G7 C
good, and when pa - pa comes home, he'll bring you ci - ga - root.
more, then poor pa - pa stays up all night pac - ing the floor.
Chorus
F
Tou - re - lay, tou - re -
C Am D7
lay, with my fil - la - ga du - sha, shin - a - ma roo - sha, bal - der - al - da boom - to - de -
G7 F C
ay. Tou - re - lay, tou - re - lay, and the pride of the
1. F C 2. F C
house is pa - pa's ba - by. 2. When pa - pa's ba - by.

Standard Ukulele

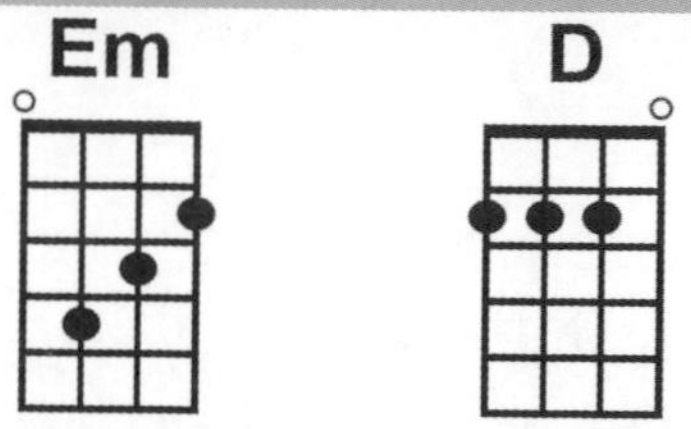

Baritone Ukulele

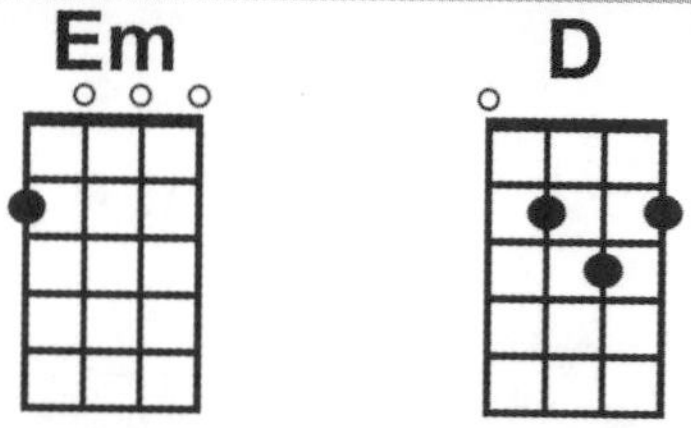

Guitar

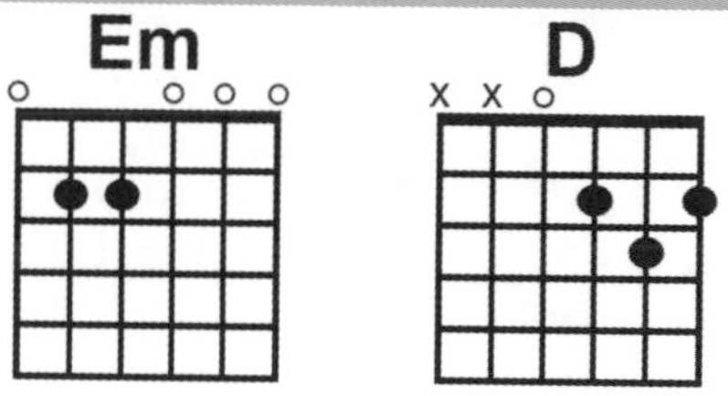

Mandolin

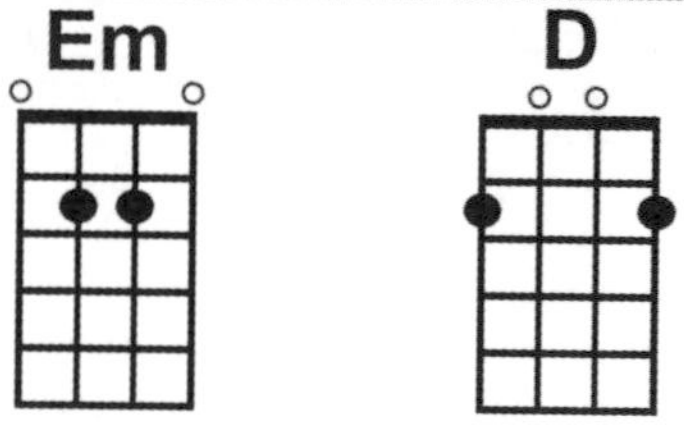

Banjo

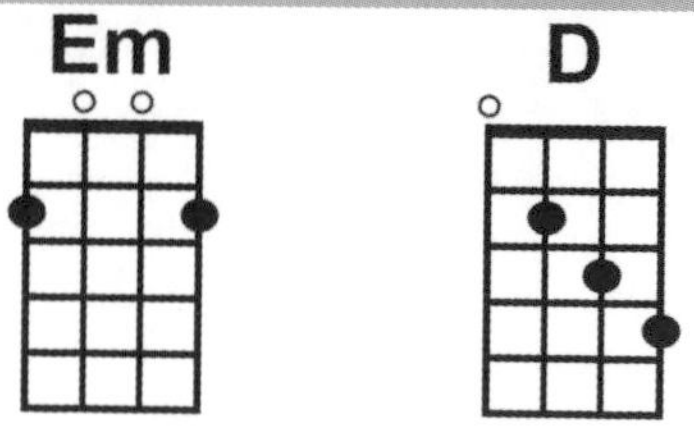

Up Among the Heather

Words by Walter Watson
Traditional Scottish Melody

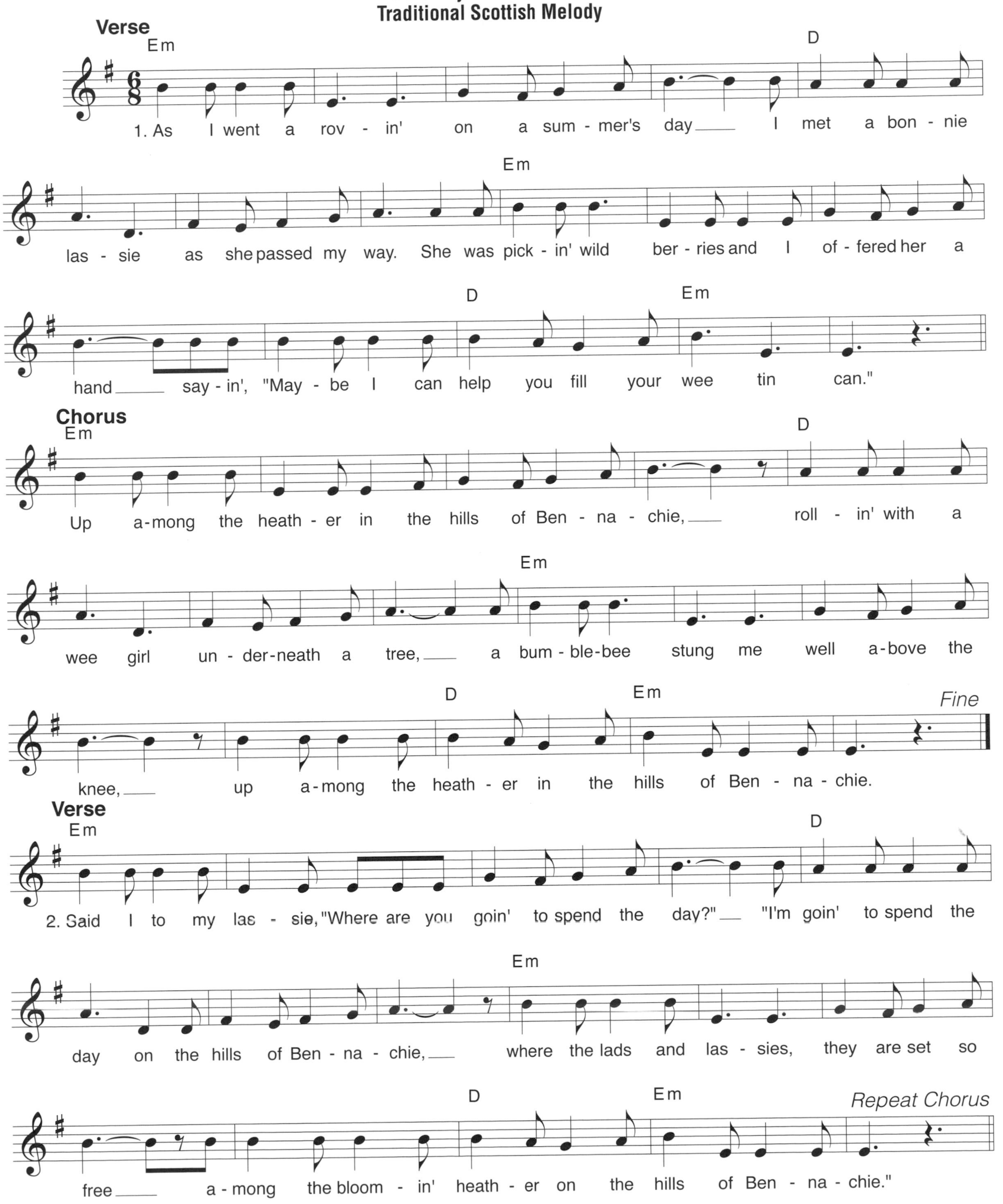
Verse
Em
D
1. As I went a rov - in' on a sum - mer's day I met a bon - nie
las - sie as she passed my way. She was pick - in' wild ber - ries and I of - fered her a
hand say - in', "May - be I can help you fill your wee tin can."
Chorus
Up a-mong the heath - er in the hills of Ben - na - chie, roll - in' with a
wee girl un - der-neath a tree, a bum - ble-bee stung me well a-bove the
knee, up a-mong the heath - er in the hills of Ben - na - chie.
Fine
Verse
2. Said I to my las - sie, "Where are you goin' to spend the day?" "I'm goin' to spend the
day on the hills of Ben - na - chie, where the lads and las - sies, they are set so
free a - mong the bloom - in' heath - er on the hills of Ben - na - chie."
Repeat Chorus

Standard Ukulele

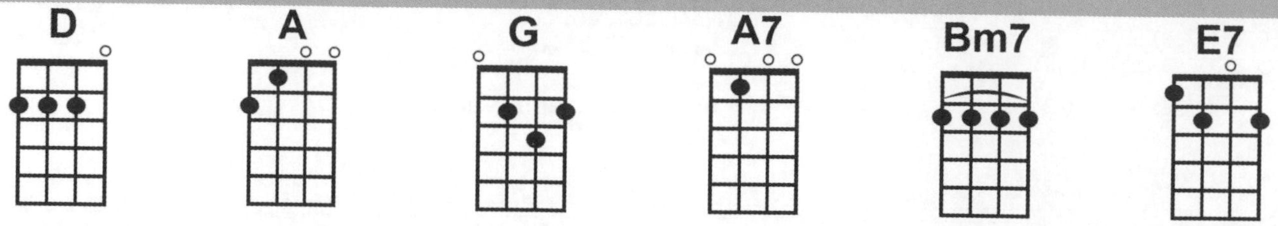
D
A
G
A7
Bm7
E7

Baritone Ukulele

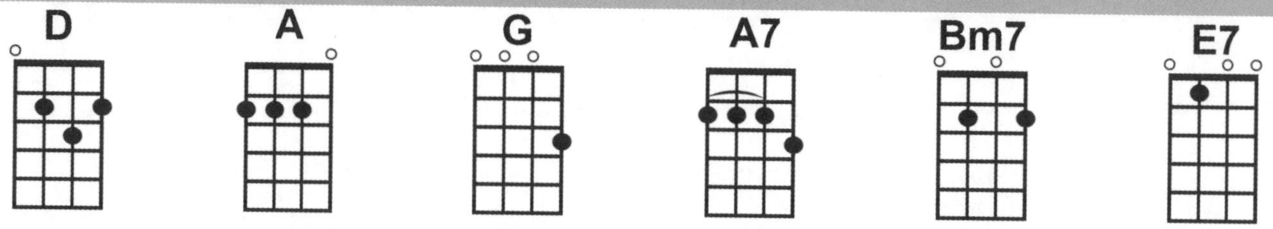
D
A
G
A7
Bm7
E7

Guitar

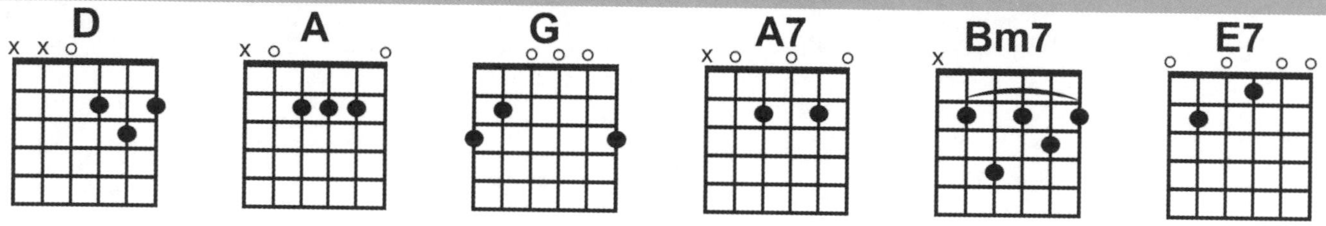
D
A
G
A7
Bm7
E7

Mandolin

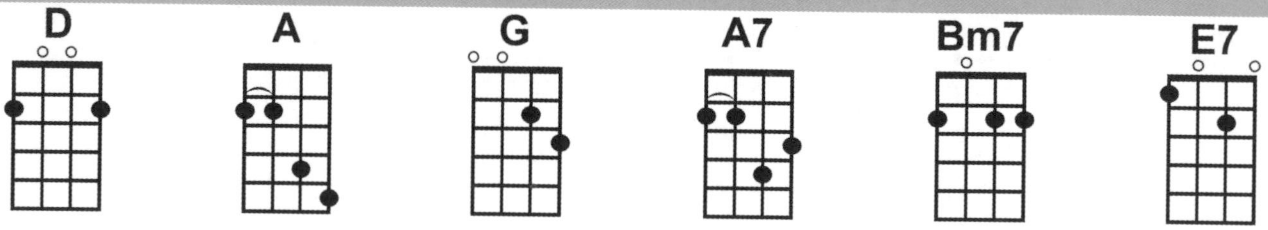
D
A
G
A7
Bm7
E7

Banjo

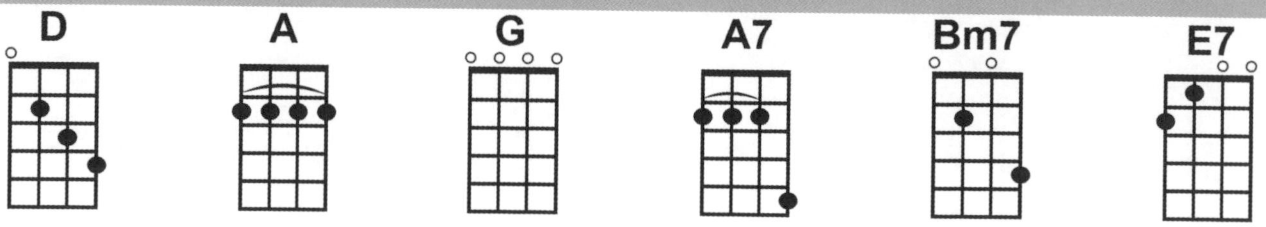
D
A
G
A7
Bm7
E7

The Wearing of the Green

Eighteenth Century Irish Folk Song

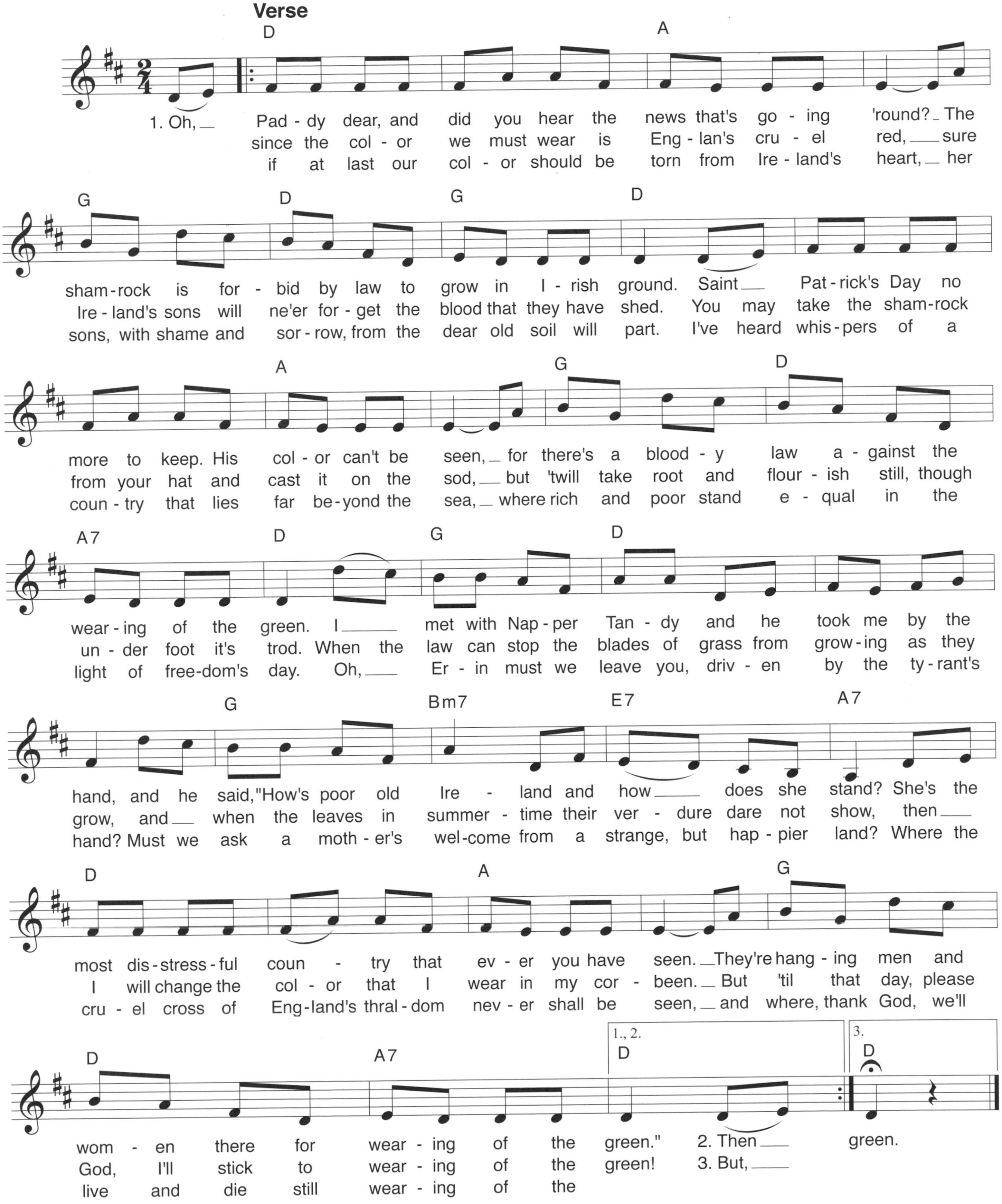
Verse
D A
1. Oh, Pad - dy dear, and did you hear the news that's go - ing 'round? The
since the col - or we must wear is Eng - lan's cru - el red, sure
if at last our col - or should be torn from Ire - land's heart, her
G D G D
sham-rock is for - bid by law to grow in I - rish ground. Saint Pat-rick's Day no
Ire - land's sons will ne'er for - get the blood that they have shed. You may take the sham-rock
sons, with shame and sor - row, from the dear old soil will part. I've heard whis-pers of a
A G D
more to keep. His col - or can't be seen, for there's a blood - y law a - gainst the
from your hat and cast it on the sod, but 'twill take root and flour - ish still, though
coun - try that lies far be-yond the sea, where rich and poor stand e - qual in the
A7 D G D
wear - ing of the green. I met with Nap - per Tan - dy and he took me by the
un - der foot it's trod. When the law can stop the blades of grass from grow-ing as they
light of free-dom's day. Oh, Er - in must we leave you, driv - en by the ty - rant's
G Bm7 E7 A7
hand, and he said,"How's poor old Ire - land and how does she stand? She's the
grow, and when the leaves in summer - time their ver - dure dare not show, then
hand? Must we ask a moth - er's wel-come from a strange, but hap - pier land? Where the
D A G
most dis-stress-ful coun - try that ev - er you have seen. They're hang - ing men and
I will change the col - or that I wear in my cor - been. But 'til that day, please
cru - el cross of Eng-land's thral - dom nev - er shall be seen, and where, thank God, we'll
D A7 1., 2. D 3. D
wom - en there for wear - ing of the green." 2. Then green.
God, I'll stick to wear - ing of the green! 3. But,
live and die still wear - ing of the

Standard Ukulele

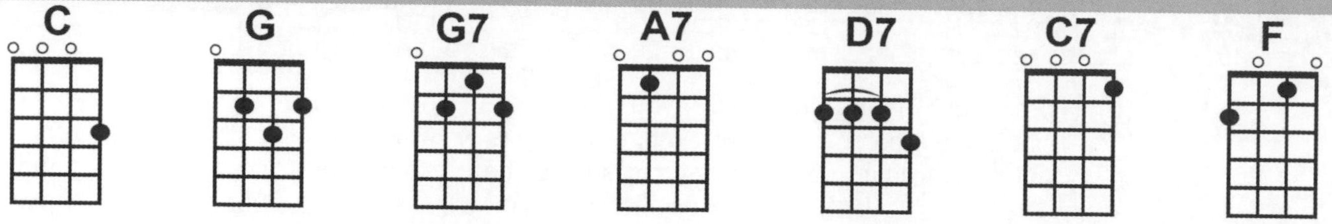
C
G
G7
A7
D7
C7
F

Baritone Ukulele

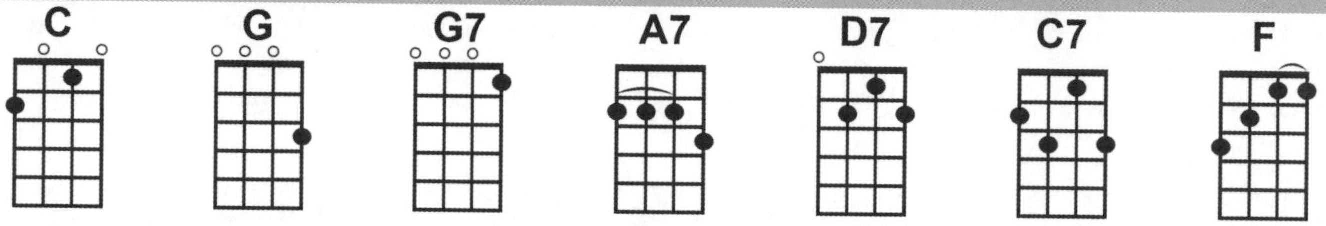
C
G
G7
A7
D7
C7
F

Guitar

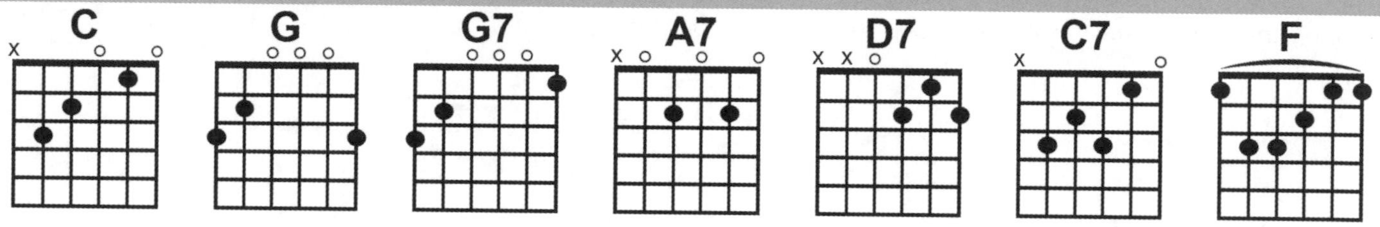
C
G
G7
A7
D7
C7
F

Mandolin

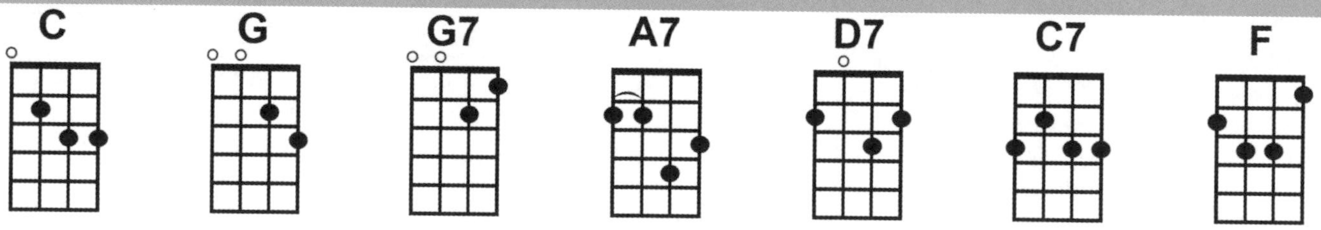
C
G
G7
A7
D7
C7
F

Banjo

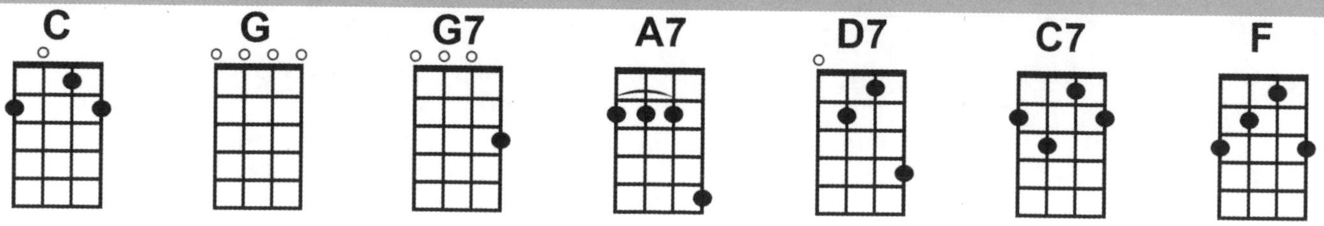
C
G
G7
A7
D7
C7
F

When Irish Eyes Are Smiling

Words by Chauncey Olcott and George Graff, Jr.
Music by Ernest R. Ball

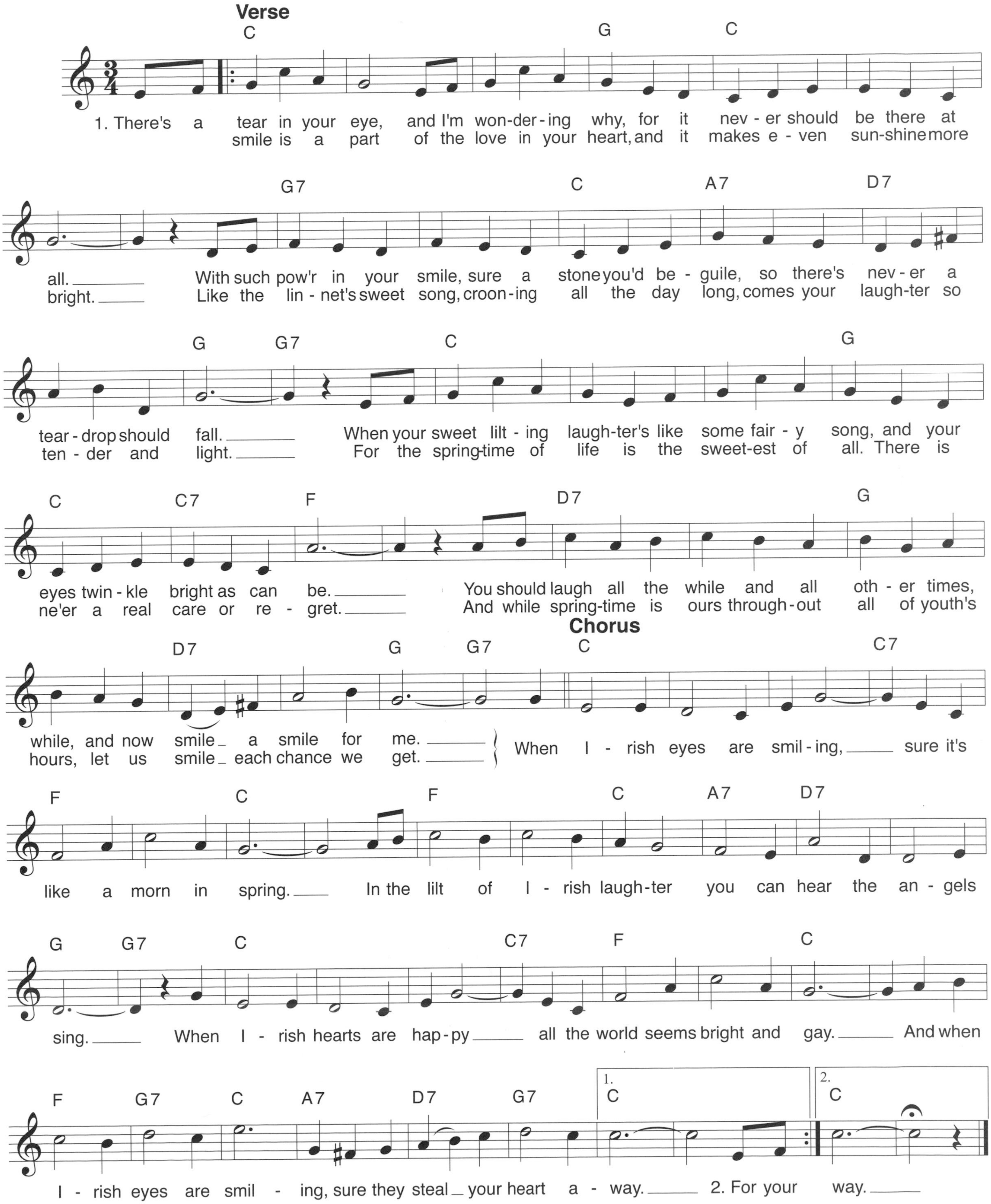
Verse
C G C
1. There's a tear in your eye, and I'm won-der-ing why, for it nev - er should be there at
smile is a part of the love in your heart, and it makes e - ven sun-shine more
G7 C A7 D7
all. With such pow'r in your smile, sure a stone you'd be - guile, so there's nev - er a
bright. Like the lin - net's sweet song, croon - ing all the day long, comes your laugh-ter so
G G7 C G
tear - drop should fall. When your sweet lilt - ing laugh-ter's like some fair - y song, and your
ten - der and light. For the spring-time of life is the sweet-est of all. There is
C C7 F D7 G
eyes twin - kle bright as can be. You should laugh all the while and all oth - er times,
ne'er a real care or re - gret. And while spring-time is ours through - out all of youth's
Chorus
D7 G G7 C C7
while, and now smile a smile for me. When I - rish eyes are smil - ing, sure it's
hours, let us smile each chance we get.
F C F C A7 D7
like a morn in spring. In the lilt of I - rish laugh-ter you can hear the an - gels
G G7 C C7 F C
sing. When I - rish hearts are hap - py all the world seems bright and gay. And when
F G7 C A7 D7 G7
1. C 2. C
I - rish eyes are smil - ing, sure they steal your heart a - way. 2. For your way.

Standard Ukulele

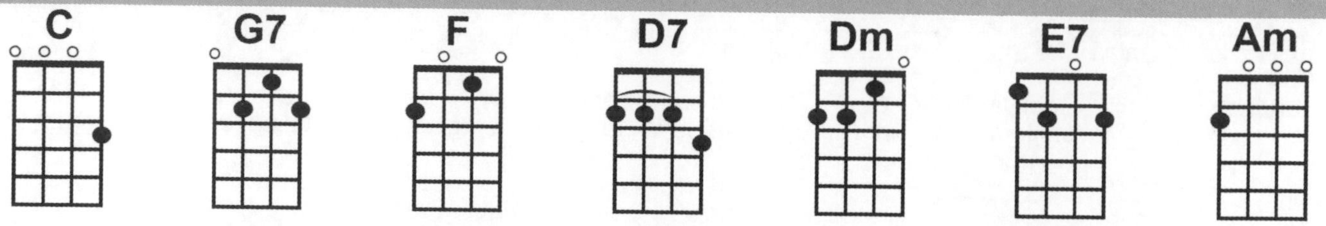
C
G7
F
D7
Dm
E7
Am

Baritone Ukulele

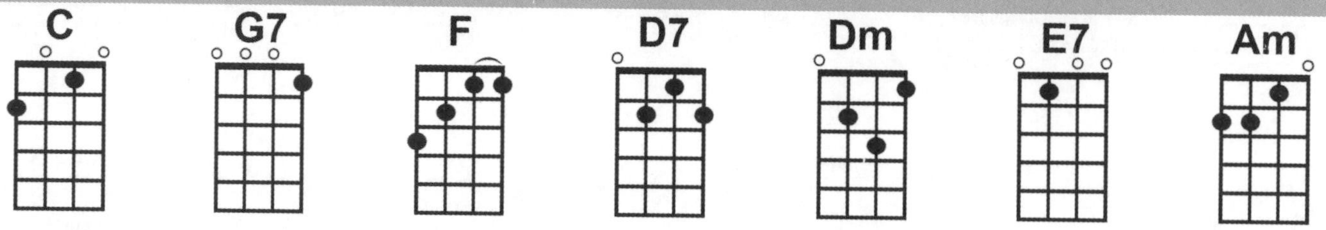
C
G7
F
D7
Dm
E7
Am

Guitar

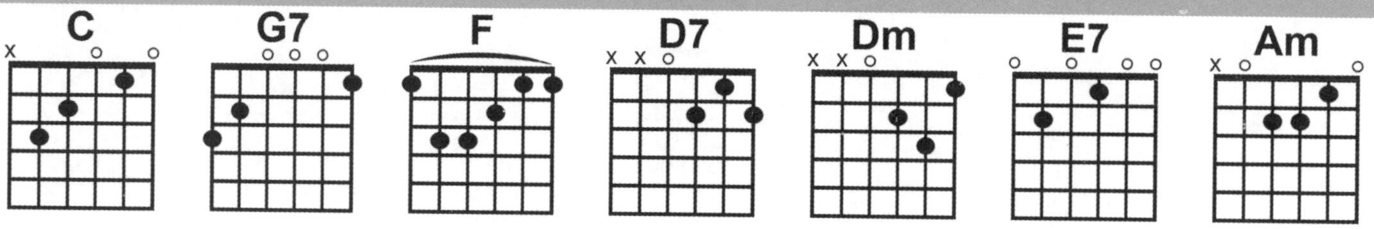
C
G7
F
D7
Dm
E7
Am

Mandolin

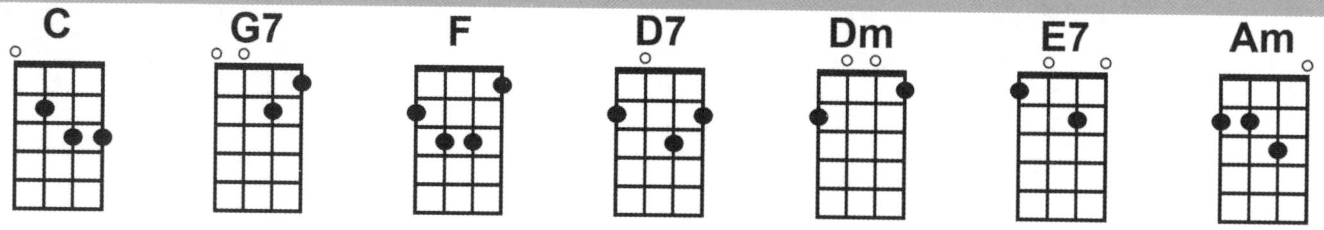
C
G7
F
D7
Dm
E7
Am

Banjo

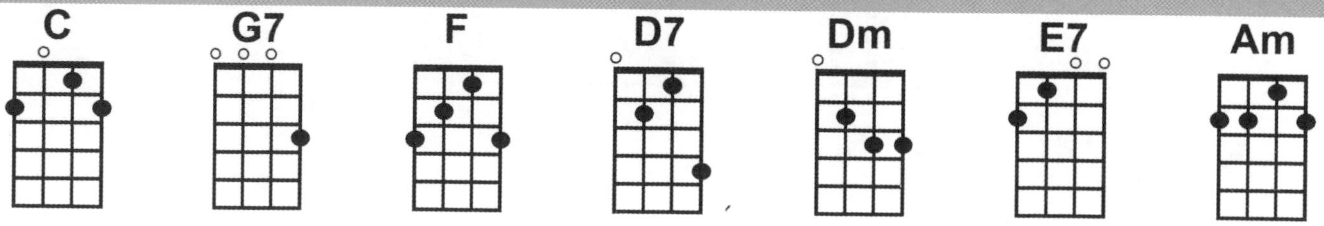
C
G7
F
D7
Dm
E7
Am

Where the River Shannon Flows

By James J. Russell

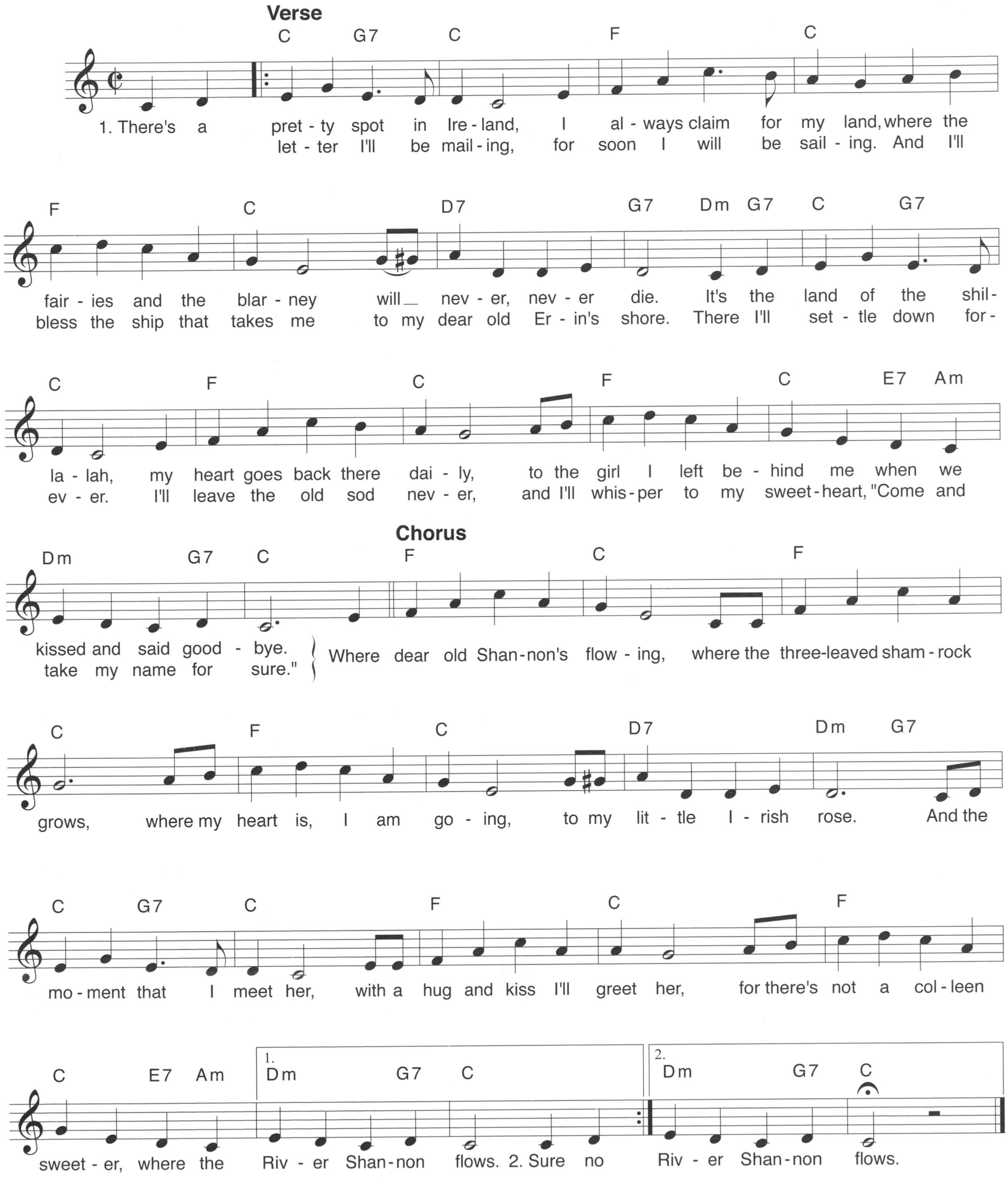
Verse
C G7 C F C
1. There's a pret - ty spot in Ire - land, I al - ways claim for my land, where the
let - ter I'll be mail - ing, for soon I will be sail - ing. And I'll
F C D7 G7 Dm G7 C G7
fair - ies and the blar - ney will never, nev - er die. It's the land of the shil -
bless the ship that takes me to my dear old Er - in's shore. There I'll set - tle down for -
C F C F C E7 Am
la - lah, my heart goes back there dai - ly, to the girl I left be - hind me when we
ev - er. I'll leave the old sod nev - er, and I'll whis - per to my sweet - heart, "Come and
Dm G7 C
kissed and said good - bye.
take my name for sure."
Chorus
F C F
Where dear old Shan - non's flow - ing, where the three-leaved sham - rock
C F C D7 Dm G7
grows, where my heart is, I am go - ing, to my lit - tle I - rish rose. And the
C G7 C F C F
mo - ment that I meet her, with a hug and kiss I'll greet her, for there's not a col - leen
C E7 Am
sweet - er, where the
1.
Dm G7 C
Riv - er Shan - non flows. 2. Sure no
2.
Dm G7 C
Riv - er Shan - non flows.

Standard Ukulele

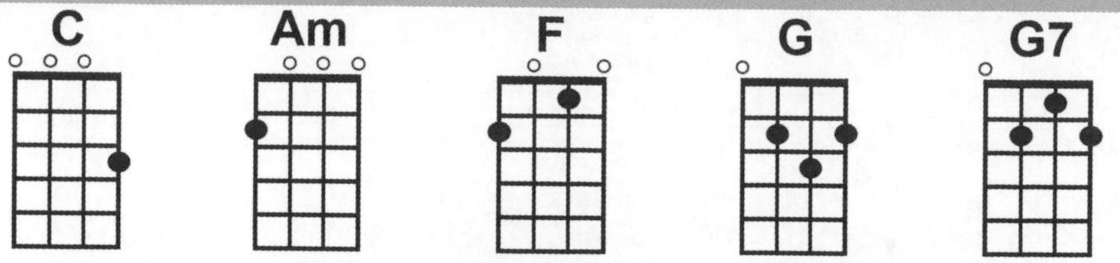
C
Am
F
G
G7

Baritone Ukulele

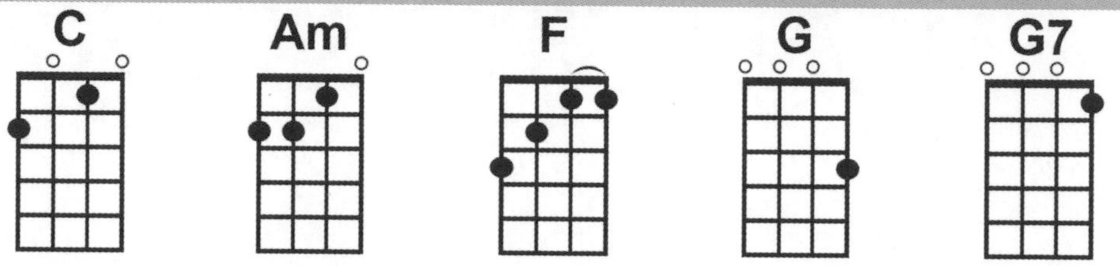
C
Am
F
G
G7

Guitar

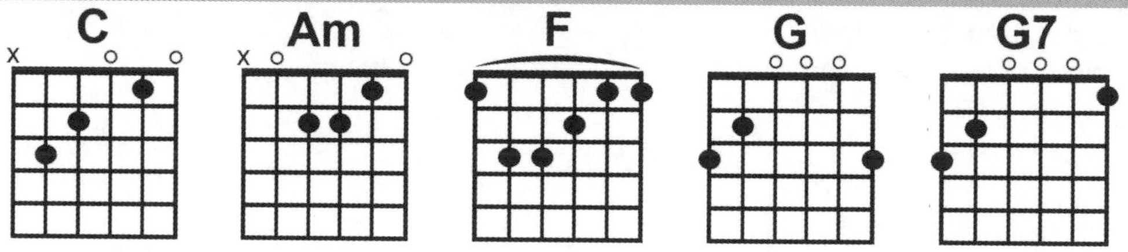
C
Am
F
G
G7

Mandolin

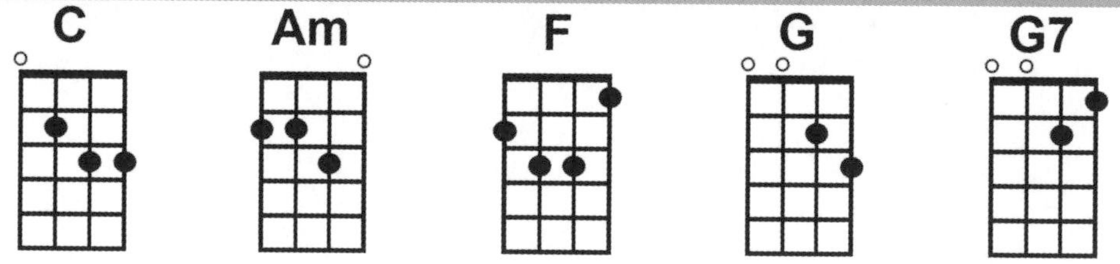
C
Am
F
G
G7

Banjo

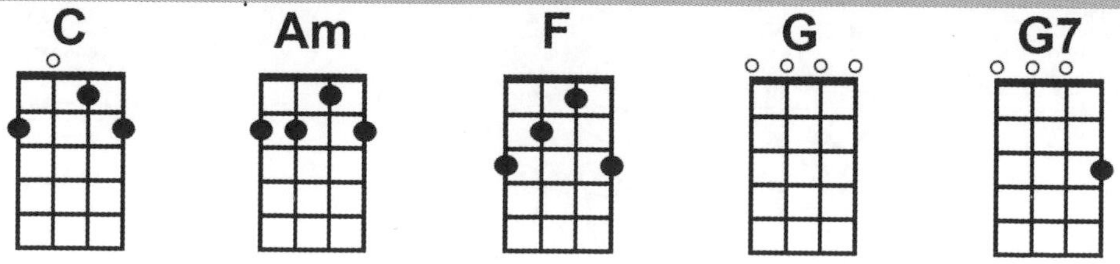
C
Am
F
G
G7

Whiskey in the Jar

Traditional Irish Folk Song

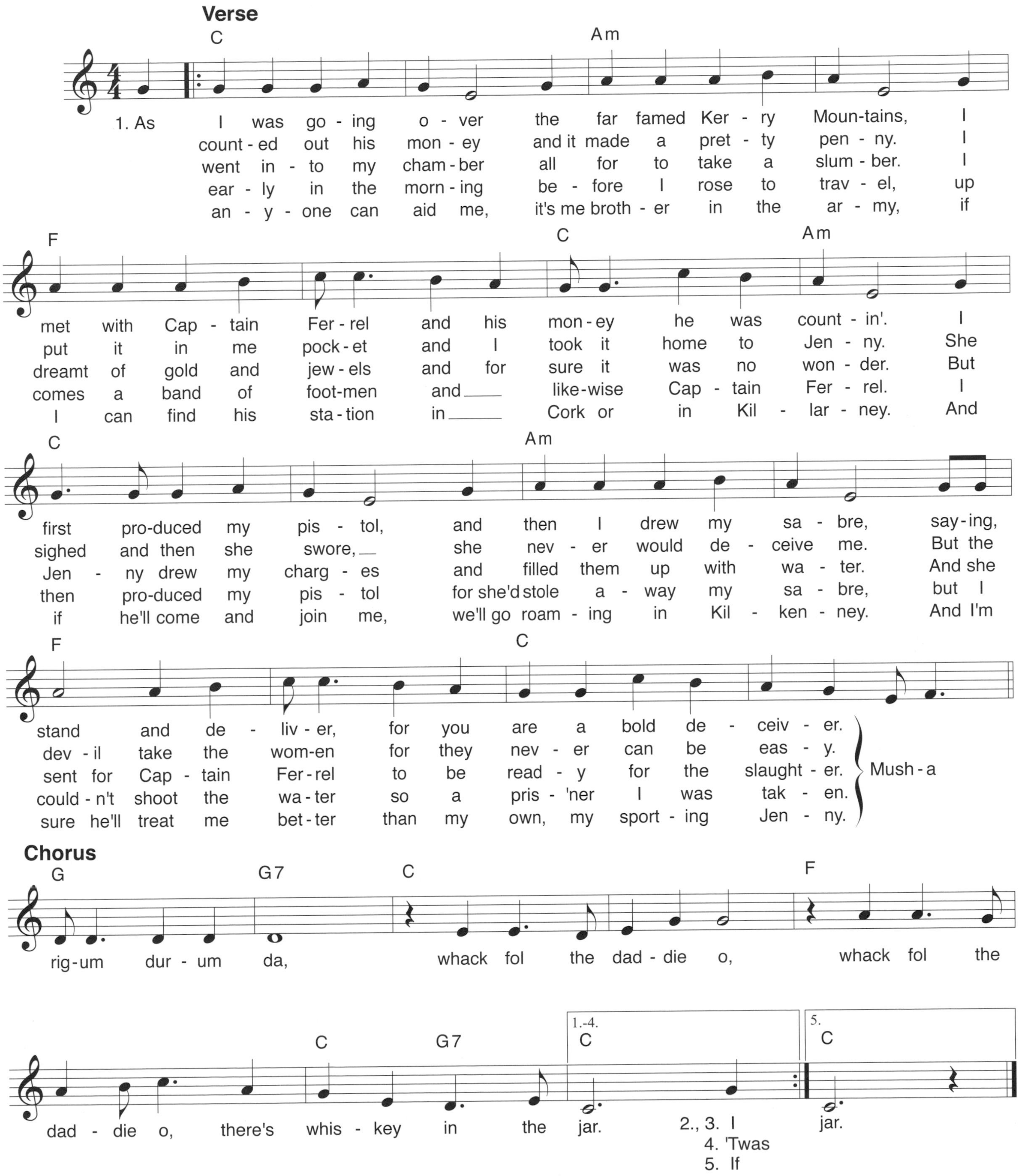
Verse
C
Am
1. As I was go - ing o - ver the far famed Ker - ry Moun-tains, I
count - ed out his mon - ey and it made a pret - ty pen - ny. I
went in - to my cham - ber all for to take a slum - ber. I
ear - ly in the morn - ing be - fore I rose to trav - el, up
an - y - one can aid me, it's me broth - er in the ar - my, if
F
C
Am
met with Cap - tain Fer - rel and his mon - ey he was count - in'. I
put it in me pock - et and I took it home to Jen - ny. She
dreamt of gold and jew - els and for sure it was no won - der. But
comes a band of foot-men and ___ like-wise Cap - tain Fer - rel. I
I can find his sta - tion in ___ Cork or in Kil - lar - ney. And
C
Am
first pro-duced my pis - tol, and then I drew my sa - bre, say-ing,
sighed and then she swore, ___ she nev - er would de - ceive me. But the
Jen - ny drew my charg - es and filled them up with wa - ter. And she
then pro-duced my pis - tol for she'd stole a - way my sa - bre, but I
if he'll come and join me, we'll go roam - ing in Kil - ken - ney. And I'm
F
C
stand and de - liv - er, for you are a bold de - ceiv - er.
dev - il take the wom-en for they nev - er can be eas - y.
sent for Cap - tain Fer - rel to be read - y for the slaught - er.
could - n't shoot the wa - ter so a pris - 'ner I was tak - en.
sure he'll treat me bet - ter than my own, my sport - ing Jen - ny.
Mush - a
Chorus
G
G7
C
F
rig-um dur - um da, whack fol the dad - die o, whack fol the
C
G7
1.-4.
C
5.
C
dad - die o, there's whis - key in the jar.
2., 3. I
4. 'Twas
5. If
jar.

Standard Ukulele

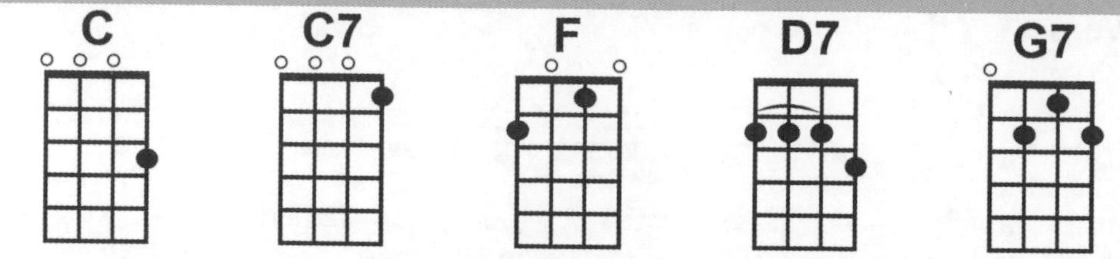
C
C7
F
D7
G7

Baritone Ukulele

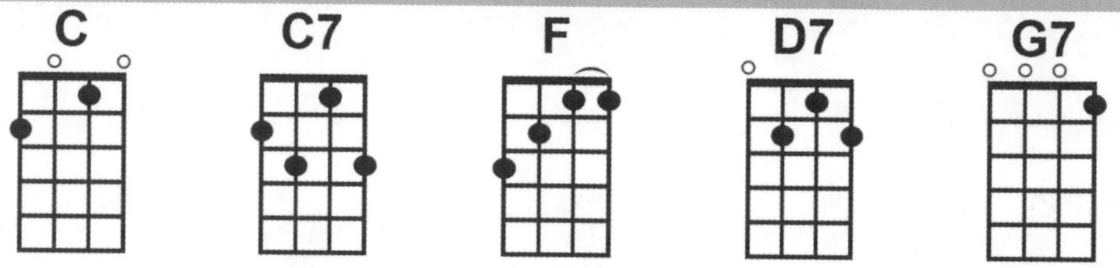
C
C7
F
D7
G7

Guitar

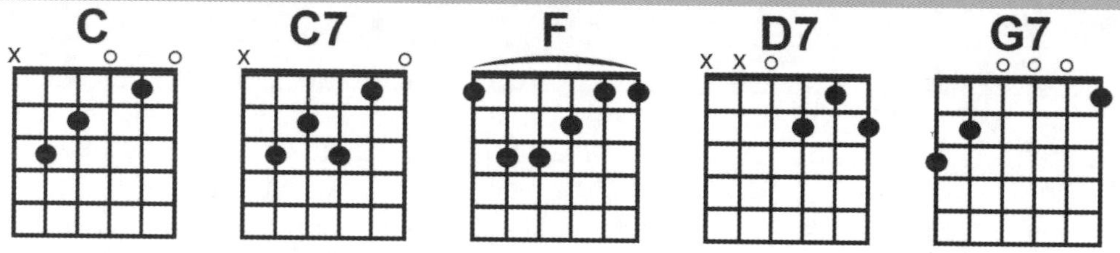
C
C7
F
D7
G7

Mandolin

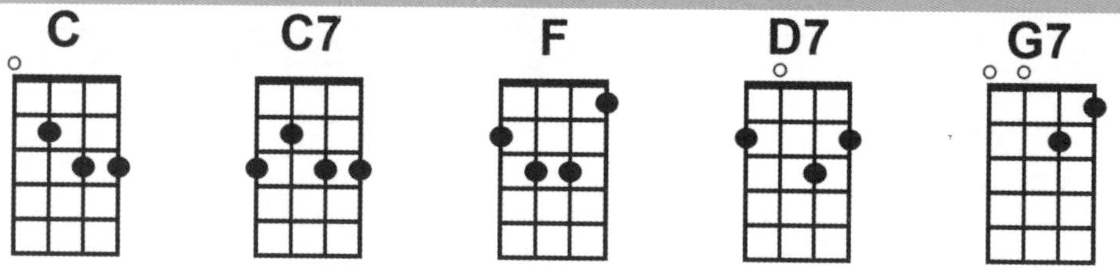
C
C7
F
D7
G7

Banjo

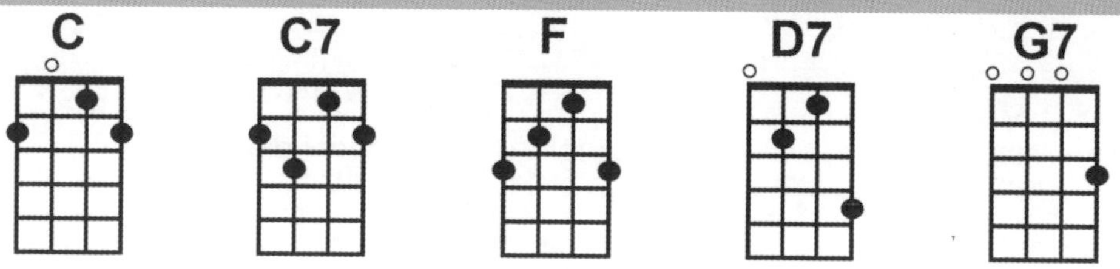
C
C7
F
D7
G7

Whiskey, You're the Devil

Traditional Irish Folk Song

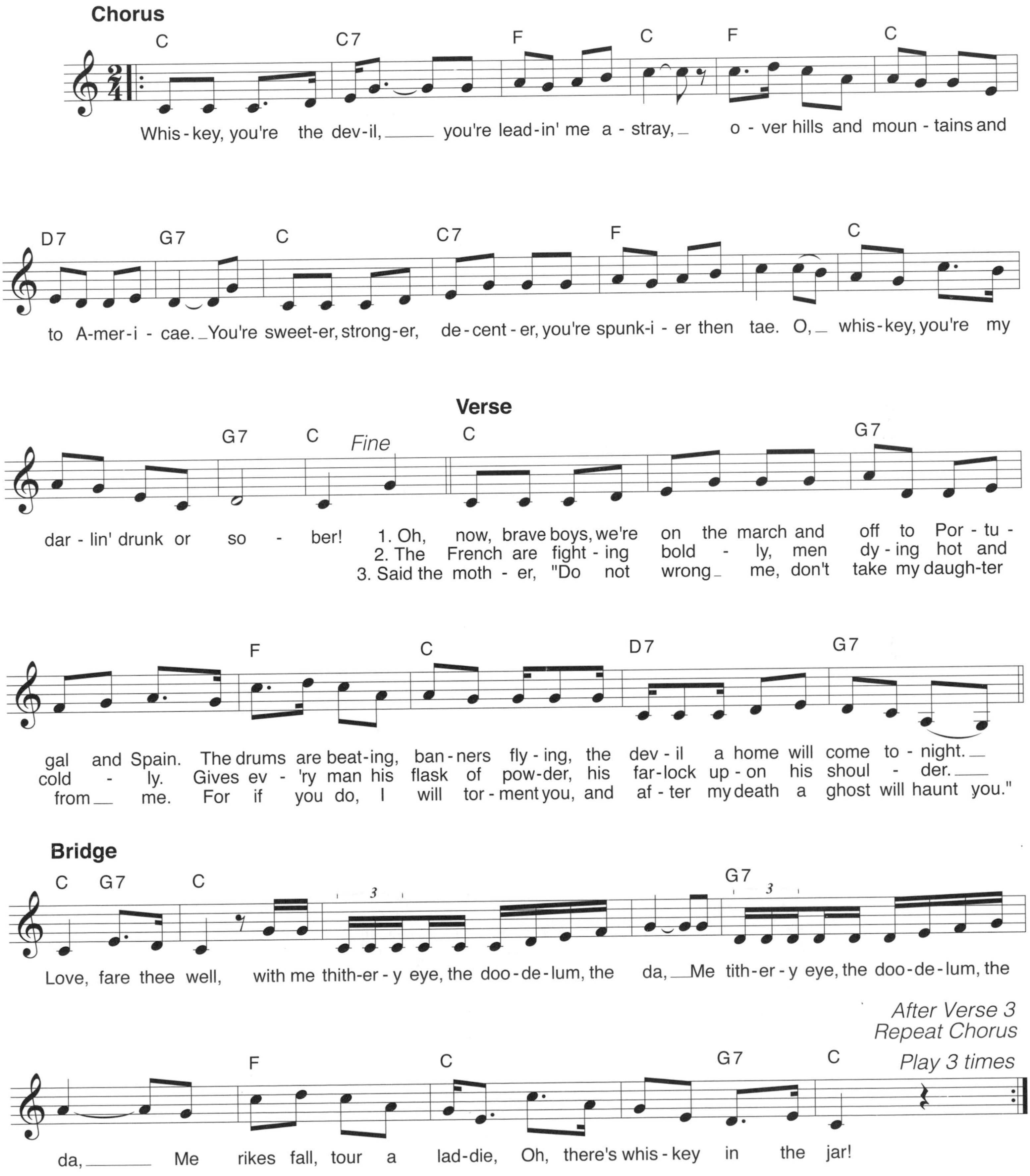
Chorus
C C7 F C F C
Whis - key, you're the dev - il, you're lead - in' me a - stray, o - ver hills and moun - tains and
D7 G7 C C7 F C
to A - mer - i - cae. You're sweet - er, strong - er, de - cent - er, you're spunk - i - er then tae. O, whis - key, you're my
Verse
G7 C Fine C G7
dar - lin' drunk or so - ber! 1. Oh, now, brave boys, we're on the march and off to Por - tu -
2. The French are fight - ing bold - ly, men dy - ing hot and
3. Said the moth - er, "Do not wrong me, don't take my daugh - ter
F C D7 G7
gal and Spain. The drums are beat - ing, ban - ners fly - ing, the dev - il a home will come to - night.
cold - ly. Gives ev - 'ry man his flask of pow - der, his far - lock up - on his shoul - der.
from me. For if you do, I will tor - ment you, and af - ter my death a ghost will haunt you."
Bridge
C G7 C G7
Love, fare thee well, with me thith - er - y eye, the doo - de - lum, the da, Me tith - er - y eye, the doo - de - lum, the
After Verse 3
Repeat Chorus
F C G7 C Play 3 times
da, Me rikes fall, tour a lad - die, Oh, there's whis - key in the jar!

Standard Ukulele

D D7 G Em A7

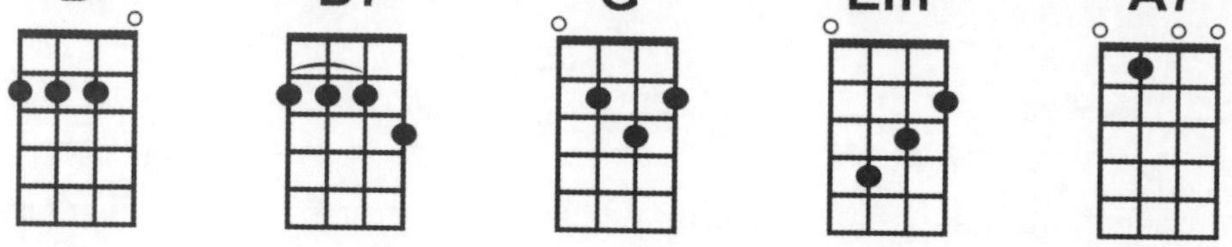

Baritone Ukulele

D D7 G Em A7

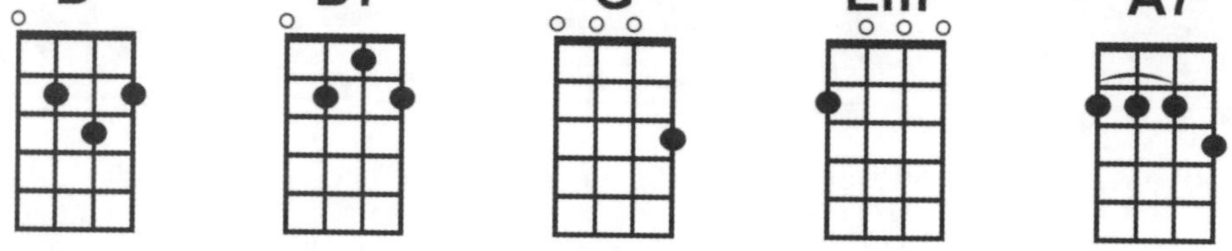

Guitar

D D7 G Em A7

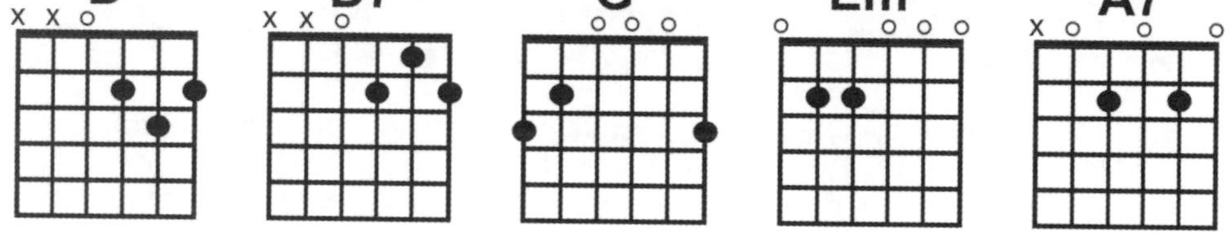

Mandolin

D D7 G Em A7

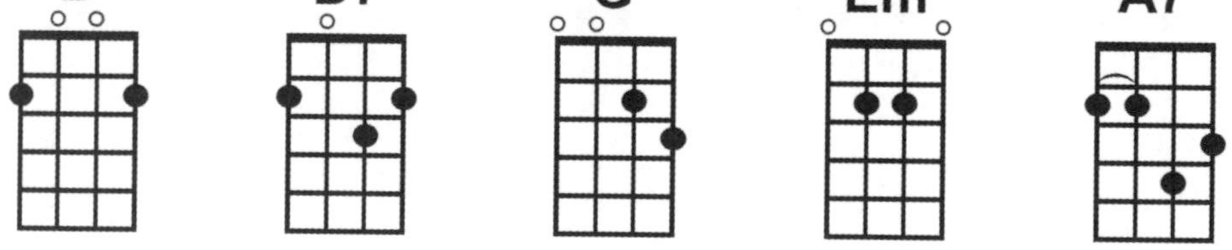

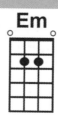

Banjo

D D7 G Em A7

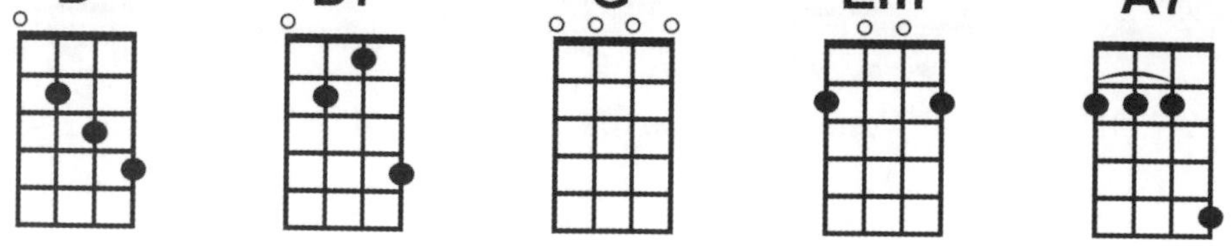

The Wild Colonial Boy

Australian Folk Song

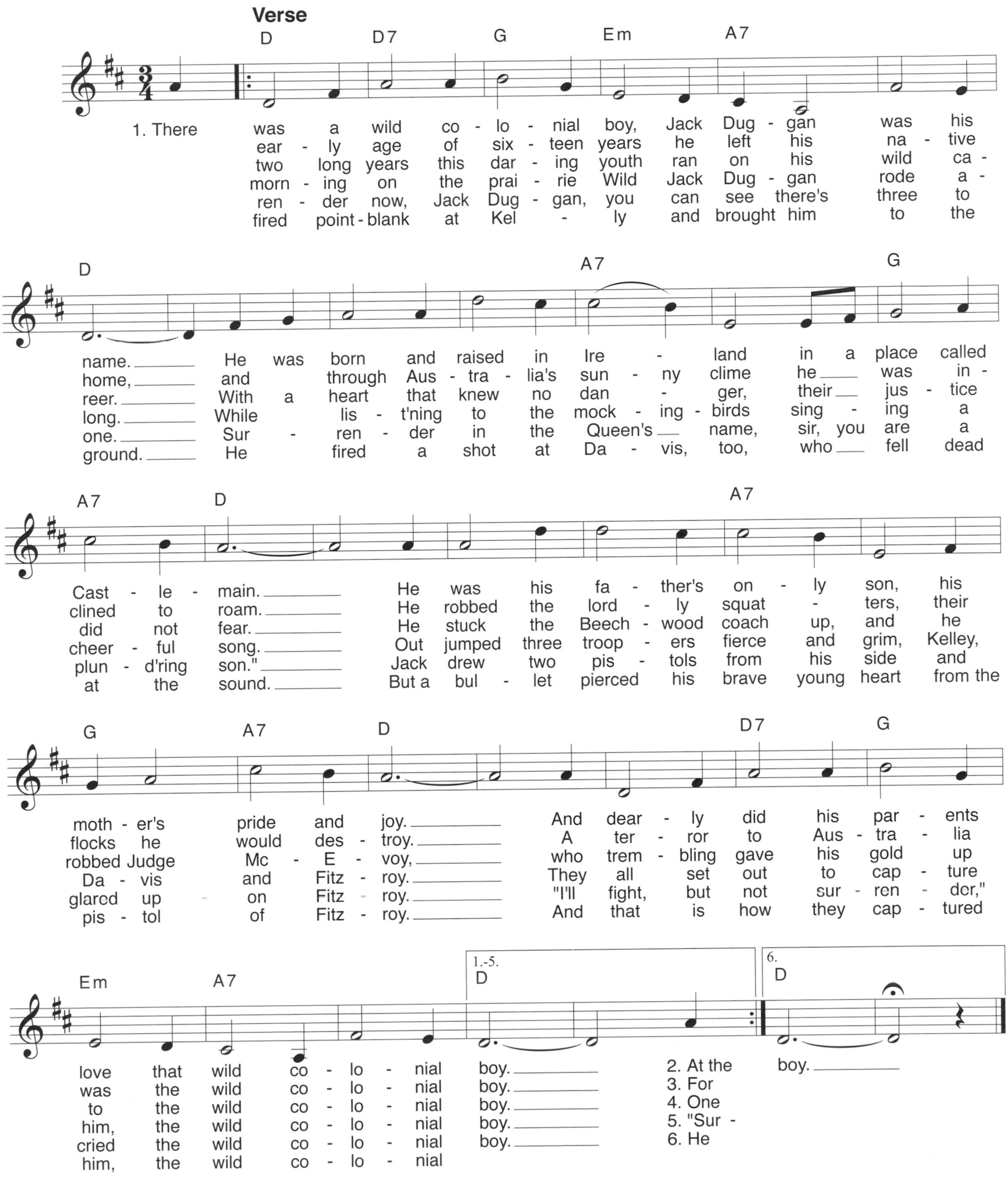
Verse
D D7 G Em A7
1. There was a wild co - lo - nial boy, Jack Dug - gan was his
ear - ly age of six - teen years he left his na - tive
two long years this dar - ing youth ran on his wild ca -
morn - ing on the prai - rie Wild Jack Dug - gan rode a -
ren - der now, Jack Dug - gan, you can see there's three to
fired point-blank at Kel - ly and brought him to the
D A7 G
name. He was born and raised in Ire - land in a place called
home, and through Aus - tra - lia's sun - ny clime he was in -
reer. With a heart that knew no dan - ger, their jus - tice
long. While lis - t'ning to the mock - ing - birds sing - ing a
one. Sur - ren - der in the Queen's name, sir, you are a
ground. He fired a shot at Da - vis, too, who fell dead
A7 D A7
Cast - le - main. He was his fa - ther's on - ly son, his
clined to roam. He robbed the lord - ly squat - ters, their
did not fear. He stuck the Beech - wood coach up, and he
cheer - ful song. Out jumped three troop - ers fierce and grim, Kelley,
plun - d'ring son." Jack drew two pis - tols from his side and
at the sound. But a bul - let pierced his brave young heart from the
G A7 D D7 G
moth - er's pride and joy. And dear - ly did his par - ents
flocks he would des - troy. A ter - ror to Aus - tra - lia
robbed Judge Mc - E - voy, who trem - bling gave his gold up
Da - vis and Fitz - roy. They all set out to cap - ture
glared up on Fitz - roy. "I'll fight, but not sur - ren - der,"
pis - tol of Fitz - roy. And that is how they cap - tured
Em A7 1.-5. D 6. D
love that wild co - lo - nial boy. 2. At the boy.
was the wild co - lo - nial boy. 3. For
to the wild co - lo - nial boy. 4. One
him, the wild co - lo - nial boy. 5. "Sur -
cried the wild co - lo - nial boy. 6. He
him, the wild co - lo - nial

Standard Ukulele

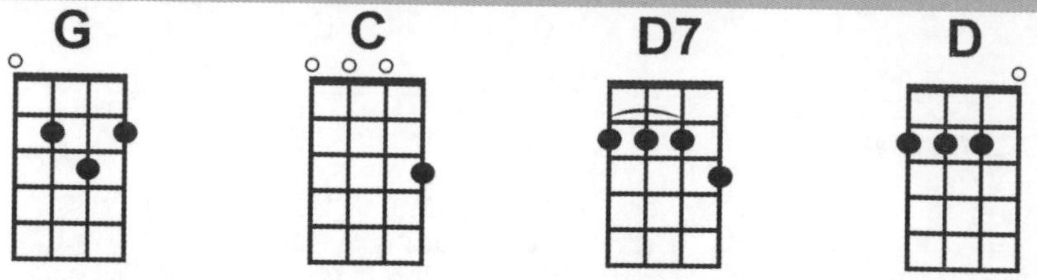

Baritone Ukulele

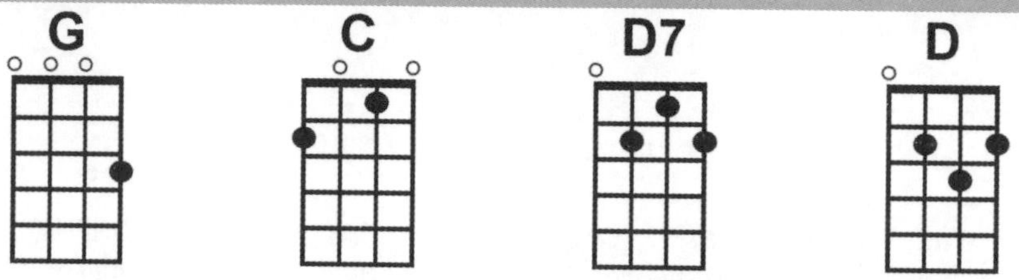

Guitar

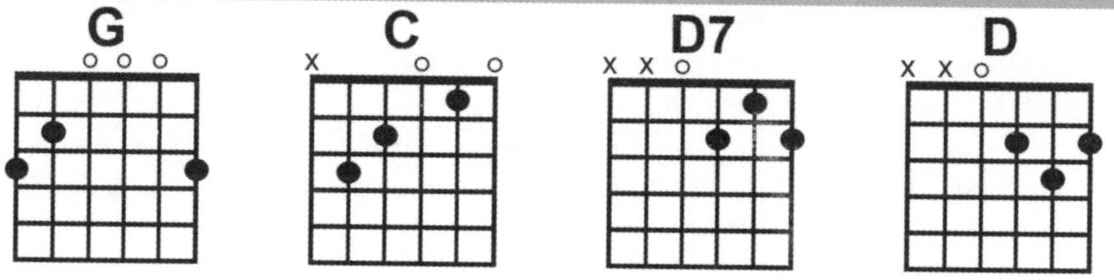

Mandolin

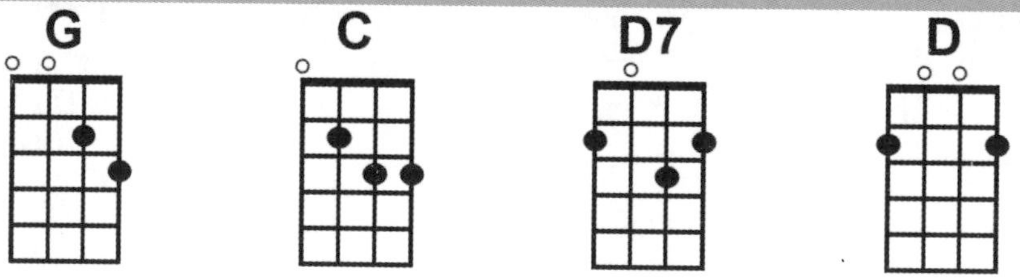

Banjo

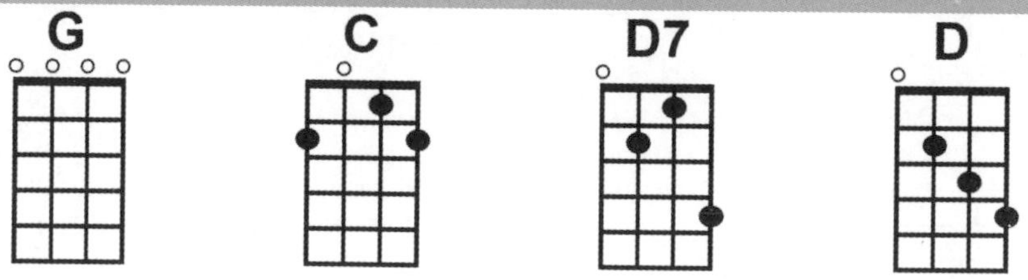

Wild Rover

Traditional Irish Folk Song

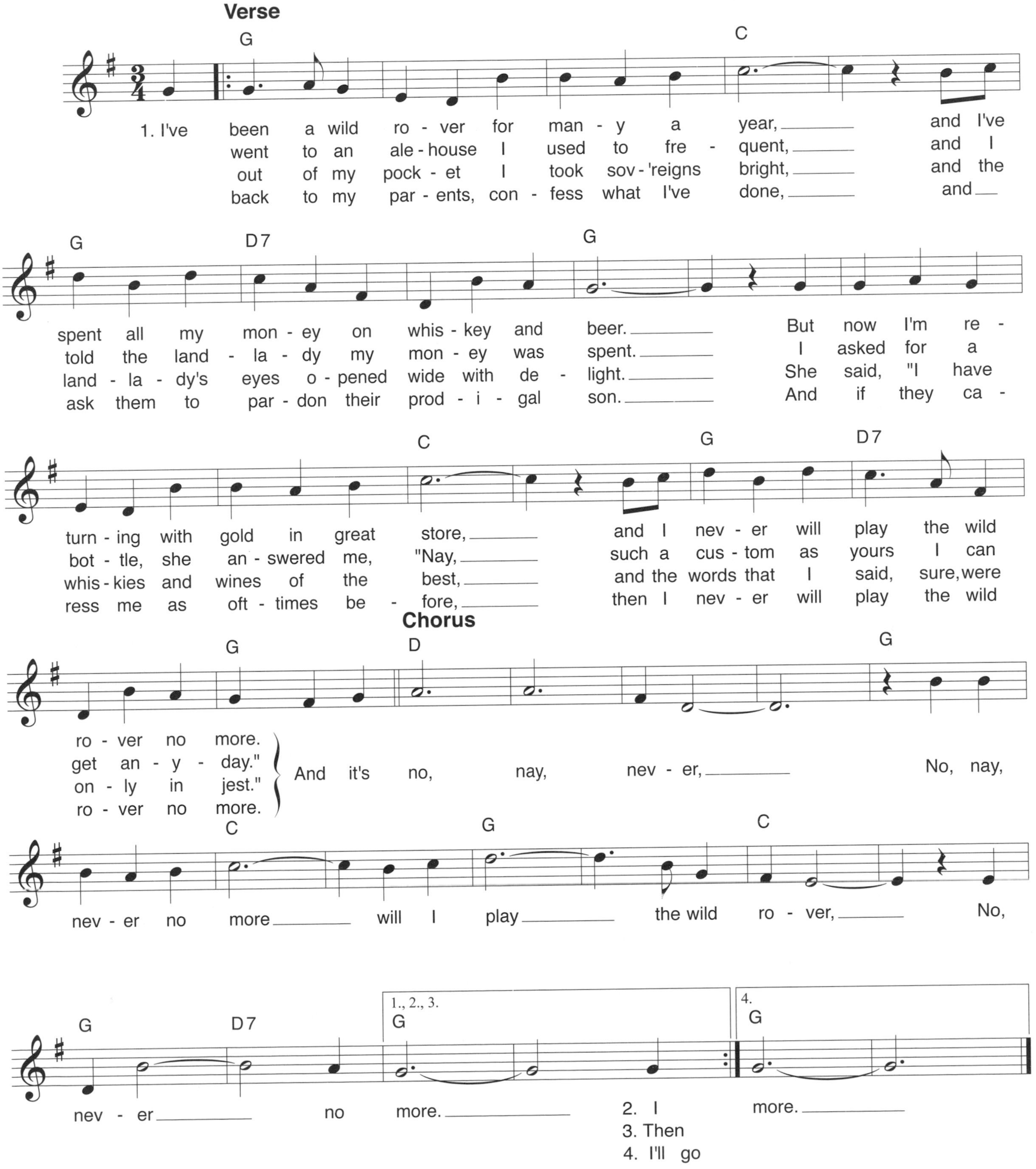
Verse
G C
1. I've been a wild ro - ver for man - y a year, and I've
went to an ale - house I used to fre - quent, and I
out of my pock - et I took sov - 'reigns bright, and the
back to my par - ents, con - fess what I've done, and
G D7 G
spent all my mon - ey on whis - key and beer. But now I'm re -
told the land - la - dy my mon - ey was spent. I asked for a
land - la - dy's eyes o - pened wide with de - light. She said, "I have
ask them to par - don their prod - i - gal son. And if they ca -
C G D7
turn - ing with gold in great store, and I nev - er will play the wild
bot - tle, she an - swered me, "Nay, such a cus - tom as yours I can
whis - kies and wines of the best, and the words that I said, sure, were
ress me as oft - times be - fore, then I nev - er will play the wild
Chorus
G D G
ro - ver no more.
get an - y - day."
on - ly in jest."
ro - ver no more.
And it's no, nay, nev - er, No, nay,
C G C
nev - er no more will I play the wild ro - ver, No,
G D7
1., 2., 3.
G
4.
G
nev - er no more.
2. I
3. Then
4. I'll go
more.

Standard Ukulele

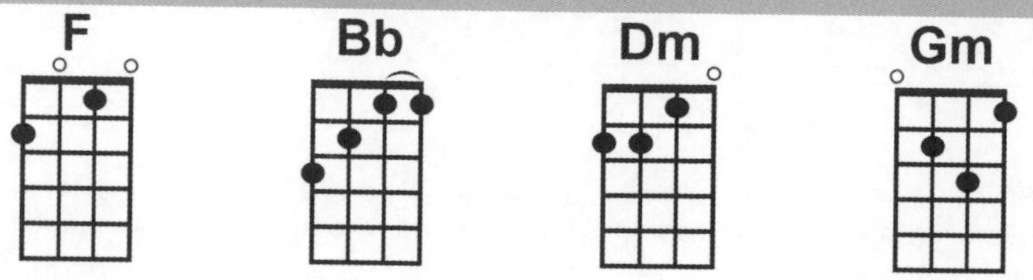

Baritone Ukulele

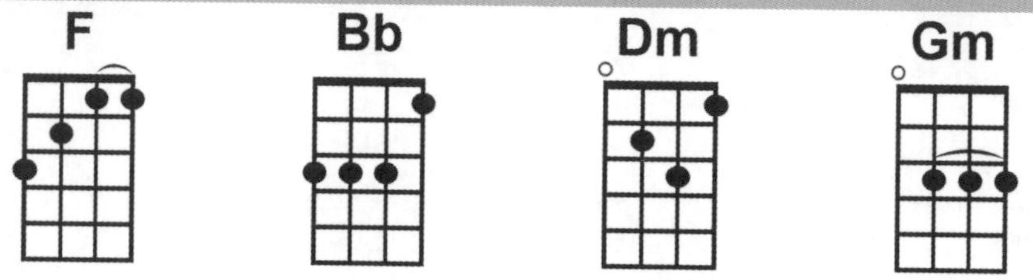

Guitar

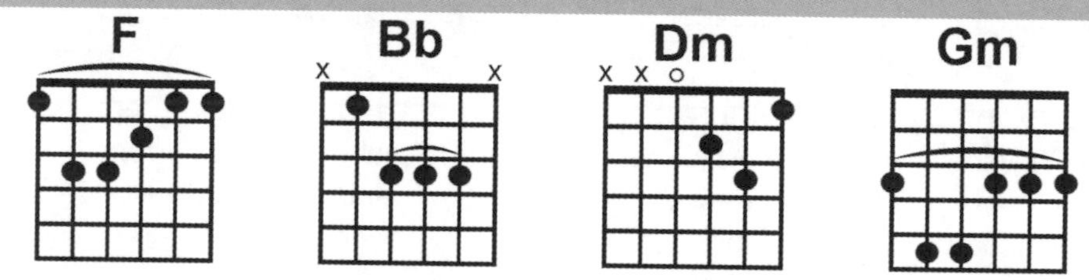

Mandolin

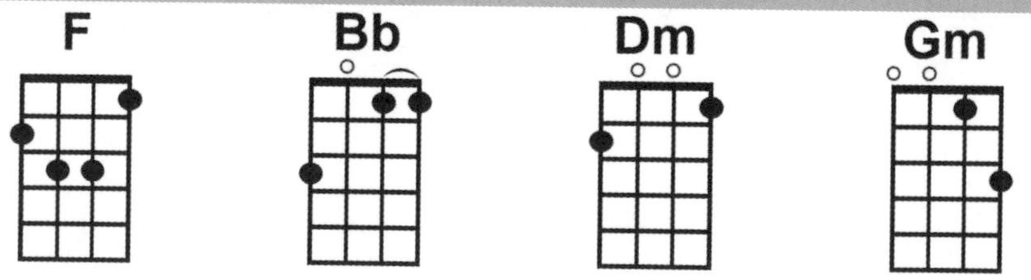

Banjo

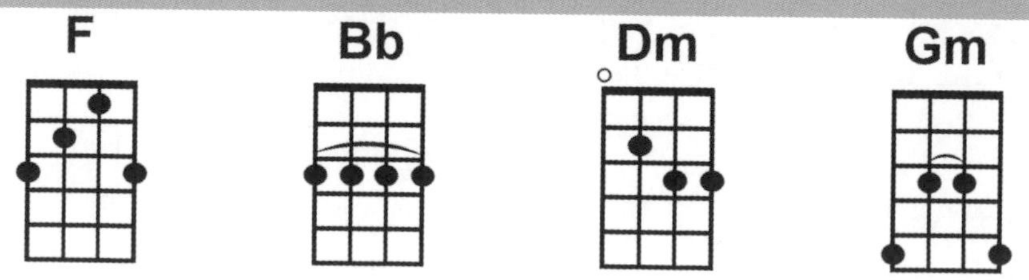

Will Ye Go, Lassie Go?

Irish Folk Song

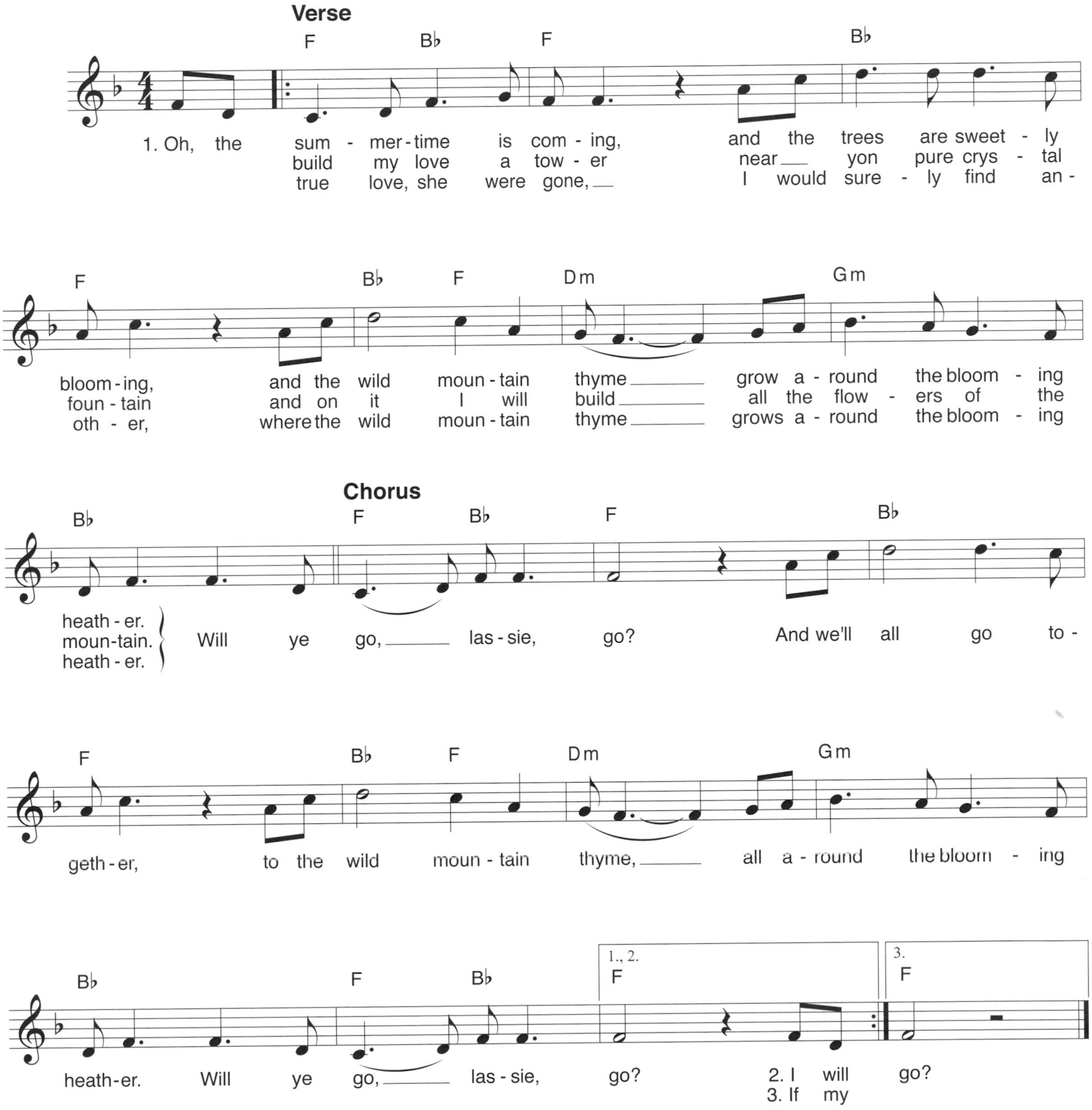
Verse
F Bb F Bb
1. Oh, the sum - mer - time is com - ing, and the trees are sweet - ly
build my love a tow - er near yon pure crys - tal
true love, she were gone, I would sure - ly find an -
F Bb F Dm Gm
bloom - ing, and the wild moun - tain thyme grow a - round the bloom - ing
foun - tain and on it I will build all the flow - ers of the
oth - er, where the wild moun - tain thyme grows a - round the bloom - ing
Chorus
Bb F Bb F Bb
heath - er.
moun - tain.
heath - er.
Will ye go, las - sie, go? And we'll all go to -
F Bb F Dm Gm
geth - er, to the wild moun - tain thyme, all a - round the bloom - ing
Bb F Bb
1., 2.
F
3.
F
heath - er. Will ye go, las - sie, go? 2. I will go?
3. If my

Standard Ukulele

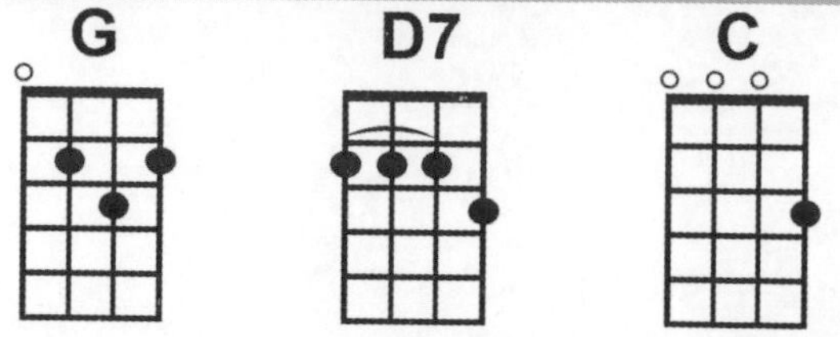

Baritone Ukulele

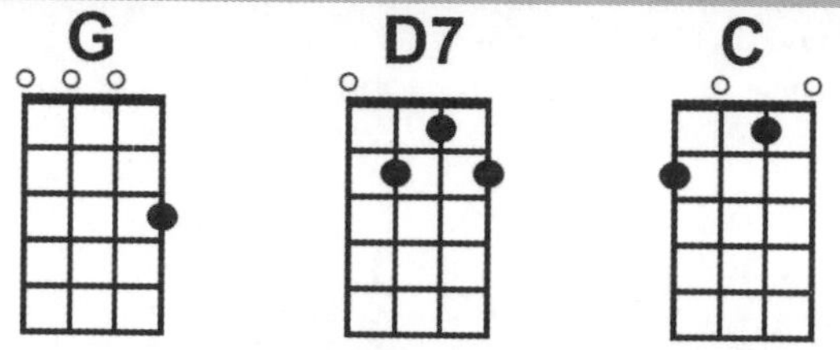

Guitar

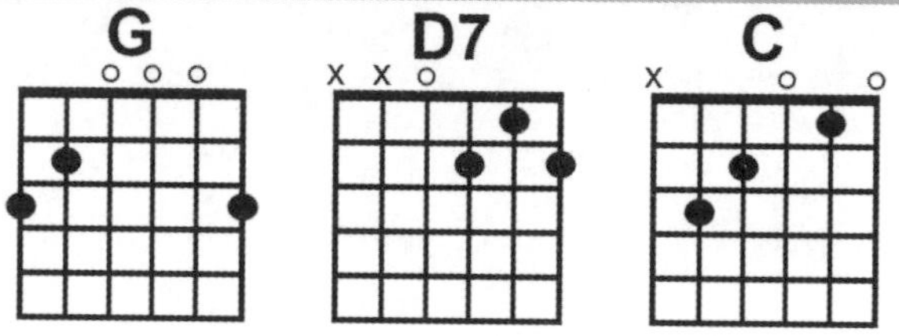

Mandolin

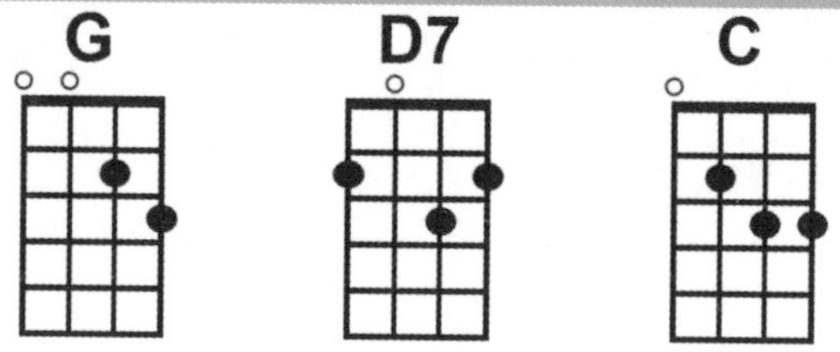

Banjo

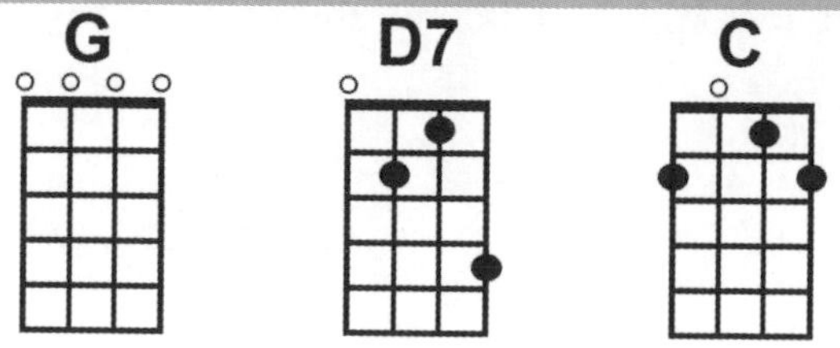

Ye Banks and Braes o' Bonnie Doon

Lyrics by Robert Burns
Melody by Charles Miller

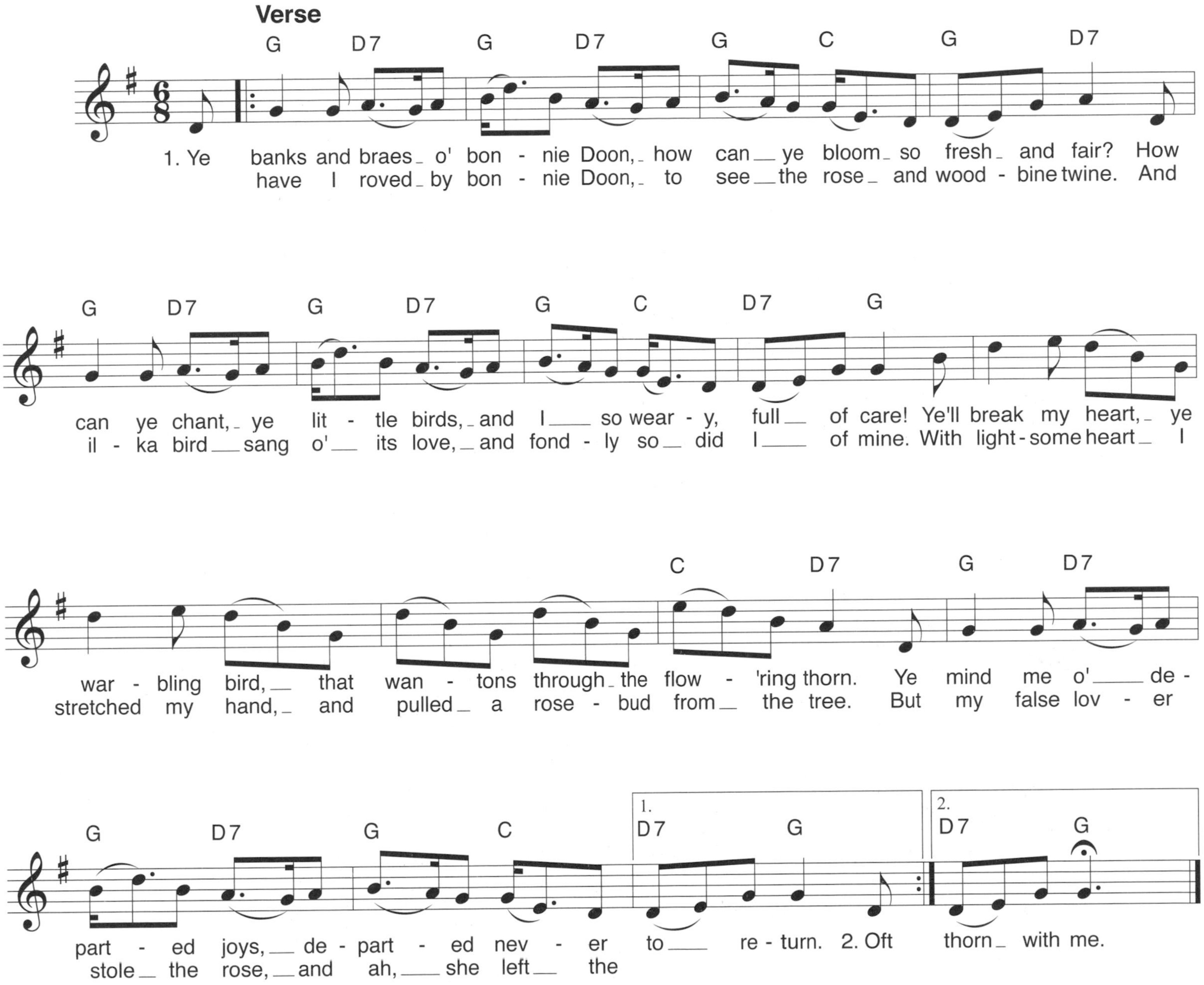
Verse
G D7 G D7 G C G D7
1. Ye banks and braes_ o' bon - nie Doon,_ how can__ ye bloom_ so fresh_ and fair? How
have I roved_ by bon - nie Doon,_ to see__ the rose_ and wood - bine twine. And
G D7 G D7 G C D7 G
can ye chant,_ ye lit - tle birds,_ and I___ so wear - y, full__ of care! Ye'll break my heart,_ ye
il - ka bird__ sang o'__ its love,_ and fond - ly so_ did I___ of mine. With light-some heart_ I
C D7 G D7
war - bling bird,__ that wan - tons through_ the flow - 'ring thorn. Ye mind me o'___ de -
stretched my hand,_ and pulled_ a rose - bud from_ the tree. But my false lov - er
G D7 G C 1. D7 G 2. D7 G
part - ed joys,__ de - part - ed nev - er to___ re - turn. 2. Oft thorn_ with me.
stole_ the rose,__ and ah,___ she left__ the

Tuning

Standard Ukulele
(Soprano, Concert, Tenor)

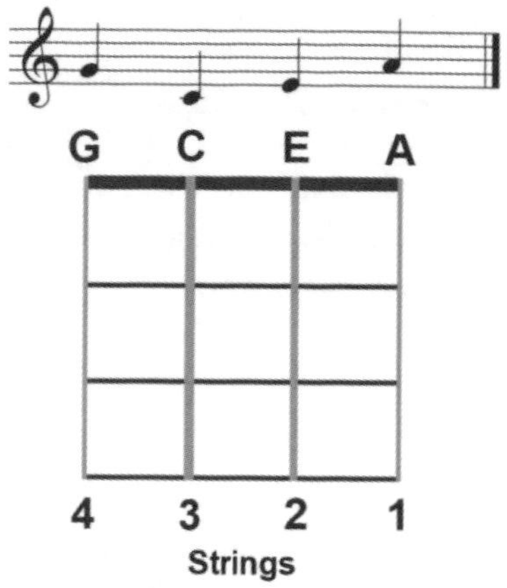
G C E A
4 3 2 1
Strings

Baritone Ukulele

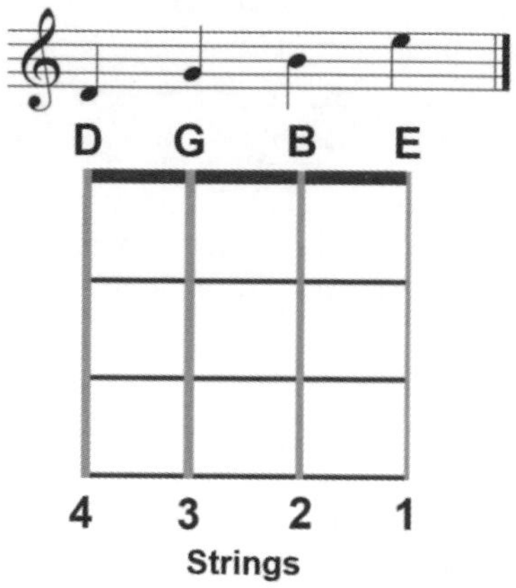
D G B E
4 3 2 1
Strings

Mandolin

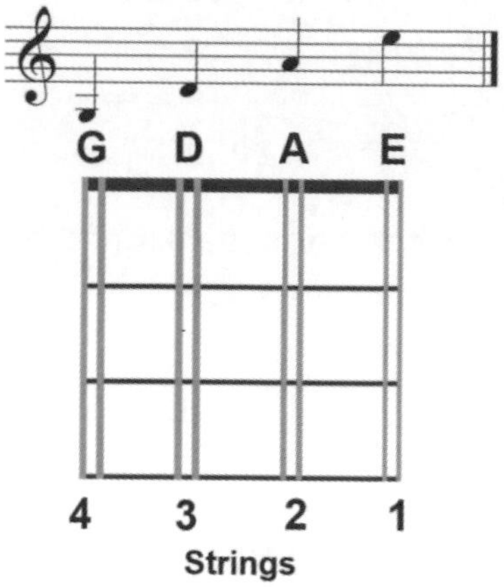
G D A E
4 3 2 1
Strings

Banjo
(Open G Tuning)

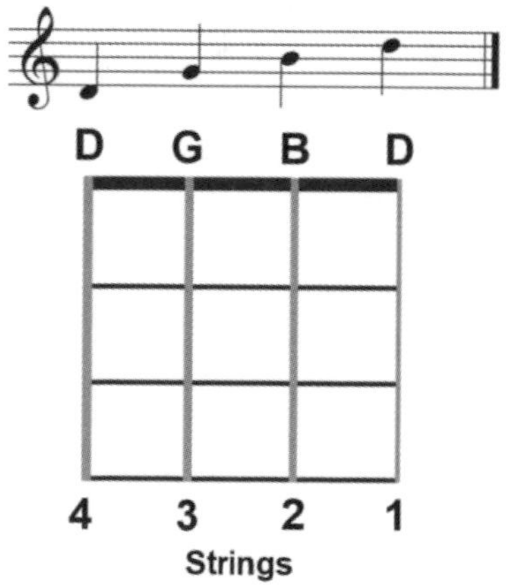
D G B D
4 3 2 1
Strings

Guitar

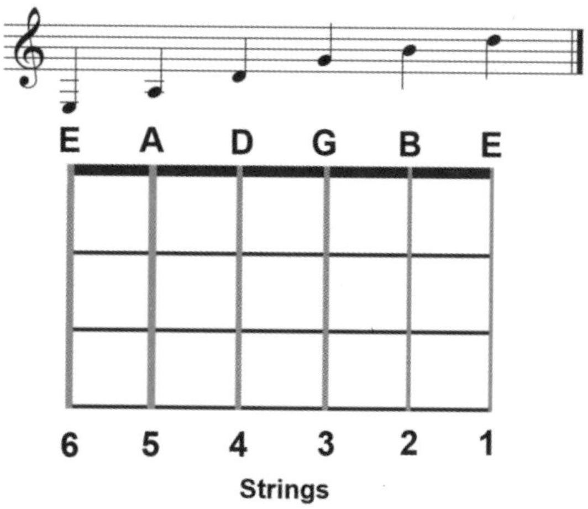
E A D G B E
6 5 4 3 2 1
Strings

All banjo chord formations illustrated in this book are based on "Open G" tuning. If an alternate tuning is used the banjo player can read the chord letters for the songs and disregard the diagrams.